KIERKEGAARD

and Radical Discipleship:

A NEW PERSPECTIVE

Until recently, most scholarship has insisted on seeing Kierkegaard as a philosopher, or a theologian, or a psychologist, or a social critic. In this book, Professor Eller argues that Kierkegaard was first and foremost a religious thinker, and that Kierkegaard himself felt his works could be best understood if they were read with this in mind.

In order to show that Kierkegaard's religious thought is essentially that of classic Protestant sectarianism, Mr. Eller has selected a typical sect—the Brethren—against which to measure Kierkegaard. After a brief discussion of the role of sects in the history of religion, Mr. Eller establishes parallels between Kierkegaard's thought and Protestant sectarianism in general. He then moves on to more detailed analysis of specific points by comparing Kierkegaard's works with the writings of the eighteenth-century Brethren. He finds that although the Dunkers, as the Brethren were often called, were by no means as sophisticated or learned as Kierkegaard, there were meaningful parallels in their writings on such topics as the importance of the individual and his relation to God, the role of reason in religion, and the problem of freedom of the will.

KIERKEGAARD
AND RADICAL DISCIPLESHIP

A NEW PERSPECTIVE

KIERKEGAARD

AND RADICAL DISCIPLESHIP

A NEW PERSPECTIVE

BY VERNARD ELLER

PRINCETON, NEW JERSEY

PRINCETON UNIVERSITY PRESS

1968

PREFACE

This book comes as the product of a rather long development. It all began, I guess, when, as a junior at La Verne College, I first discovered Kierkegaard—March 22, 1948, the check-out card in the library book says. The circumstances, I feel, were propitious for helping me become one whom S.K. hopefully might address as "my reader." I was wandering through the stacks of the college library when a bright blue volume carrying on its spine the glittering gold letters KIERKEGAARD caught my eye; it was Bretall's anthology from Princeton University Press. Curious as to who or what such a label could represent, I took down the book, flipped through its pages (starting at the back), immediately hit some of the short-and-sharp entries of the *Attack upon "Christendom,"* and was captured.

I checked out the book six times in as many months and then began buying Kierkegaard on my own. Thus I had read a good deal of S.K. before reading any books *about* him; had read S.K. before I even heard of existentialism, dialectical theology, and such; had listened to S.K. speak before I listened to anyone tell me what he said; had read deeply in the religious works before going to the pseudonymous ones—and all this I consider providential.

It was almost seven years later that, as a student at Bethany Biblical Seminary (Church of the Brethren) in Chicago, I was taking a course in the history of Christian doctrine concurrently with one in philosophical ethics. I got permission from the respective professors to submit in the two classes one double-length paper exploring the affinity between Kierkegaard and Pietism.

Each of the teachers decided to keep the copy I gave him (my only two copies). Floyd E. Mallott, the church history professor—to whom I owe much of my understanding of Brethren history—had me read part of the paper in class and encouraged me to pursue this line of investigation. Donovan Smucker, the ethics professor, wanted to submit the manuscript to *The Mennonite Quarterly Review*; but when it came time to do so, neither professor could find his copy. That primordial "J Document" was lost for several years, and only half of it has been located to this day—not that it is any great loss. But dating from that time was my determination to do a doctoral dissertation on Kierkegaard and sectarianism.

I chose my school, my field, my department—all with an eye to making this study. At the Pacific School of Religion (Berkeley, California) I did my work in historical theology under John von Rohr, a man who became mentor, friend, and colleague in an exceedingly helpful way. I also had courses— and much more than just courses—from Robert E. Fitch and Hugh Vernon White. Although Dr. White retired before my dissertation was well underway, he continued to give me help and counsel on it.

By this time (1958) I was teaching at La Verne College, but my topic, outline, and prospectus were accepted without difficulty. A grant from the Swenson Kierkegaard Fellowship Committee helped finance some of my research, and appreciated assists from my college administration kept the project moving. Things went smoothly until it came to producing a draft that would satisfy my doctoral advisors. Then, at one point, just three brief months before deadline, I seriously proposed to Dr. von Rohr that I drop the Kierkegaard half of my study and write a brief and innocuous discourse on the Brethren. He responded with a direct command, which is all that kept me at the task. The finished dissertation was accepted without dissent.

My doctorate behind me (1964), I reworked the manuscript and started the search for a publisher. It was at this point that Franklin H. Littell, authority on Protestant sectarianism and then professor of church history at Chicago Theological Seminary, read the volume and for no reason other than the benevolence of his good heart took the initiative in contacting prospects. Nevertheless, the book seemed doomed to remain forever a manuscript when the editors at Charles Scribner's Sons —for no reason other than the benevolence of their good hearts—took it upon themselves to recommend it to Princeton University Press. And at Princeton it has been the benevolent heart and kindly hands of managing editor Eve Hanle that have brought to completion this work of ten, thirteen, almost twenty years.

The greatest satisfaction to come out of this long-drawn process is the friends made along the way. To each of the persons named above I proffer heartfelt thanks—as I do to an even greater number who must go unnamed: my wife, parents, family, and friends; my colleagues of the faculty and administration here at La Verne College; my fellow scholars within the Church of the Brethren; and the librarians without whose help few books would get written and few, indeed, read. May the contribution of this book prove worthy the trust they all have put in me.

VERNARD ELLER

La Verne College
January 1967

CONTENTS

Preface

PART ONE: *THE PERSPECTIVE*

PART TWO: *THE DUNKERS AND THE DANE*

Part One

The Perspective

CHAPTER I

THE CENTRAL NERVE

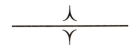

The central nerve of my work as an author
really lies in the fact that I was essentially religious
when I wrote Either/Or.[1]

Count it not presumption that this study sets itself to do for
Søren Kierkegaard what Adolf Deissmann did for the Apostle
Paul. In the following excerpt from Deissmann's classic work,
read "Kierkegaard" for "Paul" and the words retain both their
accuracy and relevancy:

"[Scholarly research] has been most strongly influenced by
interest in Paul, the theologian, and in the 'theology' of Paul.
. . . But with this doctrinaire direction the study of Paul has
gone further and further astray. It has placed one factor which
is certainly not absent from Paul, but is in no way the historically characteristic, theological reflection, in the fore-
ground, and has only too often undervalued the really characteristic traits of the man, the prophetic power of his religious
experience, and the energy of his practical religious life. . . .
Paul at his best belongs not to Theology, but to Religion. . . .

[1] *The Journals of Kierkegaard*, ed. and trans. Alexander Dru, hereafter referred to as *Dru Journals* (New York: Oxford Un. Press,
1938), 795 (1848). In Dru's and in Rohde's selections from Kierkegaard's journals the number identifies an entry rather than a page;
the date following is that of the particular entry.

The tent-maker of Tarsus ought not to be classed along with
Origen, Thomas Aquinas and Schleiermacher: his place is
rather with the herdsman of Tekoa, and with Tersteegen, the
ribbon-weaver of Mulsheim. . . . Paul is essentially first and
foremost a hero of religion. The theological element in him is
secondary. Naivete in him is stronger than reflection; mysticism stronger than dogmatism; Christ means more to him
than Christology, God more than the doctrine of God. He is
far more a man of prayer, a witness, a confessor and a prophet,
than a learned exegete and close thinking scholastic. To show
that this is so, is, I consider, the object of this sketch."[2]

And, concerning Kierkegaard, the object of this "sketch" is
not far different.

Actually, although he nowhere stated the distinction quite
as Deissmann did, S.K. wrote an entire book, plus a number
of briefer essays,[3] in the interest of subsuming his authorship
under the religious category:

"The contents of this little book affirm, then, what I truly
am as an author, that I am and was a religious author, that the
whole of my work as an author is related to Christianity, to
the problem 'of becoming a Christian.' . . . I would beg of
every one who has the cause of Christianity at heart—and I
beg the more urgently the more seriously he takes it to heart
—that he make himself acquainted with this little book, not
curiously, but devoutly, as one would read a religious work.
. . . [The reader] will totally misunderstand me, [if] he does
not understand the religious totality in my whole work as an
author. . . . What I write here is for orientation. It is a public
attestation; not a defence or an apology. . . . It goes without

[2] Adolf Deissmann, *Paul, A Study in Social and Religious History*
(first published, 1912), trans. Wm. E. Wilson (New York: Harper,
1957), pp. 5-6.
[3] In English, all of this material has been published under the
title of the book itself, *The Point of View for My Work as an Author*,
hereafter referred to as *Point of View*, trans. Walter Lowrie, newly
edited Benjamin Nelson (New York: Harper Torchbooks, 1962).

saying that I cannot explain my work as an author wholly, i.e., with the purely personal inwardness in which I possess the explanation of it. And this in part is because I cannot make public my God-relationship."[4]

Clearly, S.K. was meaning to say that his writings *cannot* properly be understood, that he desired that they *not* be read, as the work of a philosopher, a psychologist, a social critic, an aesthete, or whatever. The criteria of these disciplines are not appropriate to his orientation.

Also, it is evident that he would have included *theologian* among the things he was not. "Theological" simply will not do as a synonym for "religious" in S.K.'s context. An authorship which centered on "becoming a Christian" (as against "defining the Christian faith"), which was to be read "devoutly," and which integrally involved the author's personal God-relationship—this is not "theology" in the usual sense of the term. Rather, S.K.'s opinion of theology was expressed in such statements as:

"To me the theological world is like the road along the coast on a Sunday afternoon during the races—they storm past one another, shouting and yelling, laugh and make fools of each other, drive their horses to death, upset each other, and are run over, and when at last they arrive, covered with dust and out of breath—they look at each other—and go home.[5]

"From a Christian point of view a dogmatic system is an article of luxury; in fair weather, when one can guarantee that at least an average of the population are Christians, there might be time for such a thing—but when was that ever the case? And in stormy weather the systematic is deprecated as an evil; at such times everything theological must be edifying."[6]

As we shall discover, S.K.'s concern was over the intellec-

---

[4] *Point of View*, pp. 5-6, 9.   [5] *Dru Journals*, 16 (1835).

[6] *Kierkegaard's Diary*, ed. Peter P. Rohde, trans. Gerda M. Anderson, hereafter referred to as *Rohde Journals* (New York: Philosophi-

tualistic bias he found in theologizing; he was convinced that Christianity must be *life*-centered and so resisted passionately any tendencies that might make it *thought*-centered.[7]

However, *Point of View* notwithstanding, it must be confessed that Kierkegaard scholarship generally has proceeded to treat S.K. precisely contrary to his wishes and his own self-understanding, reading him as a philosopher, theologian, or whatever.

Recently, however, prominent scholars are showing interest in correcting the situation. For example, Perry LeFevre maintains that S.K. should be seen essentially "as a religious man struggling for his own soul" and "sympathetically understood in the context of his own pilgrim's progress."[8] Paul Holmer makes an extended plea "for a kind of understanding that fits the [Kierkegaardian] literature,"[9] and is extremely critical of a fellow scholar for expounding S.K. as though he were a theologian.[10] And Niels Thulstrup becomes quite vocal against those thinkers and schools that attempt to analyze S.K.'s ideas from perspectives that are "totally incommensurable with them."[11]

This growing trend has the effect of taking S.K. out of the mainstream of Christian philosophic-theological development but does not, to this point, suggest where he should be put.

---

cal Library, 1960), 202 (1849). The first quotation comes from a point very early in S.K.'s career, this one comparatively late.

[7] See below, pp. 131ff.

[8] Perry D. LeFevre, *The Prayers of Kierkegaard* (Chicago: Un. of Chicago Press, 1956), p. 128; cf. pp. v-vi. LeFevre's exposition of S.K. is an outstanding effort in becoming consistent with the perspective indicated.

[9] Paul L. Holmer, "On Understanding Kierkegaard," in *A Kierkegaard Critique*, hereafter referred to as *Critique*, ed. Howard A. Johnson and Niels Thulstrup (New York: Harper, 1962), p. 52.

[10] Paul L. Holmer, a review of Louis Dupre's *Kierkegaard as Theologian*, *The Journal of Religion*, XLIII (1963), 255-56.

[11] Niels Thulstrup, "The Complex of Problems Called 'Kierkegaard,'" in *Critique*, p. 295.

Does S.K. represent a "sport" in Christian thought, or is there a totally *religious* yet nontheological (antiintellectual) tradition to which he should be related? There have been forthcoming some scattered hints that may point toward an answer.

Niels Thulstrup (a Danish pastor and highly competent Kierkegaard scholar), as the alternative to his criticism noted above, proposes that "with respect to content there is in fact only one yardstick of values for Kierkegaard, namely, the authority he himself appealed to and quoted: the Bible, and in the Bible particularly the New Testament."[12]

William Barrett (a philosophy professor specializing in existentialism) anchors the line of traditional Christian philosophy-theology in what he calls "Hellenism" and the Kierkegaard-existential line in "Hebraism." He sees the latter as predominant in New Testament Christianity, as being represented to some degree in Tertullian and even more so in Augustine. However, he specifies that Augustine only opened the door but did not go inside, in that he also retained a strong orientation toward the "rationalist" strain. Barrett denies that Thomas Aquinas and the other medieval philosophers showed any significant relation to existential thought. At this point he abandons the tracing of the historical development and moves directly to the nineteenth century and Kierkegaard.[13]

L. Harold DeWolf (a professor of theology who is not particularly sympathetic to existential irrationalism) notes the presence of this strain in such contemporary theologians as Barth, Brunner, and Reinhold Niebuhr and ascribes the influence to S.K. Then, in tracing the antecedents of S.K.'s irrationalism, he starts with the New Testament, mentions Tatian, stresses Tertullian, points to aspects of irrationalism within Luther and Calvin—and thus to S.K.[14]

[12] *Ibid.*, p. 295. Cf. below, pp. 409ff.

[13] William Barrett, *Irrational Man* (Garden City: Doubleday, 1958), Pt. II, pp. 69ff.

[14] L. Harold DeWolf, *The Religious Revolt against Reason* (New York: Harper, 1949), pp. 22-54.

Three philosophy professors—William Earle, James M. Edie, and John Wild—more recently have collaborated on a work, *Christianity and Existentialism*. Although the book is a symposium, the men coordinated their ideas and thus present an integrated viewpoint. The basic frame of reference is as follows:

"What seems certain is that if we now observe the history of Christianity from the viewpoint of Kierkegaard's conception of faith *as action rather than knowledge*, we find that it is not something new but that it has been one of the two constants in Christian life from the beginning. There has always been a strain of what can be called Christian 'irrationalism' (which is not always to be understood as an 'anti-rationalism') opposed to the strain of Christian 'rationalism' in the Christian experience of the world. There have always been 'philosophers of the absurd' to challenge the Church theologians in their conception of faith as knowledge and theology as science."[15]

The authors do not proceed to trace this strain of Christian "irrationalism" consistently in any detail, but by putting scattered references together it comes to this: The line is rooted in the Bible. It achieved its clearest expression in Tertullian and the Punic fathers in contrast to the other church fathers whose faith was becoming strongly Hellenized.[16] Augustine stands in the train of these Punic fathers but also shows strong aspects of Christian rationalism as well. Thomism belongs wholly in the rationalist line, "but with Scotus, then Ockham and the Franciscan spiritualist movement, we find a gradual change of climate." This change "prepared for Luther's revolt and the new sense it gave, temporarily, to the Pauline 'primacy of faith.'" But very soon Protestantism itself became "official Churches with their own orthodox and scientific the-

[15] James M. Edie, "Faith as Existential Choice," in *Christianity and Existentialism* (Evanston: Northwestern Un. Press, 1963), p. 37.

[16] The central thrust of Edie's essay is a comparison between S.K. and Tertullian, the previous Christian thinker who, according to Edie, is most like him.

ologies." Thus, "movements of protest appear in the form of the pietist movement in Germany, the puritan revolt in England, Pascal and the Jansenist heresy in France."[17]

It is not our intent to endorse or defend any of the above analyses, particularly in their details, but to show that within the Kierkegaard scholarship of our day there is developing at least some agreement about the antecedents of S.K.'s "irrationalism" (antiintellectualism). There is also becoming apparent a second tendency, this one seemingly not related to the first and not focusing particularly on S.K.'s irrational aspect. The suggestion, first made by Emil Brunner and now gaining considerable support, is that S.K. was molded by and should be understood within the context of continental Pietism.[18] We shall relate these two developments to each other in due course.

Thus far our examination has been of tendencies which but recently have showed themselves within Kierkegaard studies. Now, however, let us put S.K. to one side for the moment and consider a completely independent and long-established school of thought within church historiography. The basic idea perhaps has never been given a more succinct and colorful statement than in the words of Leonhard Ragaz:

"[There is] one great antinomy, which runs right through the whole history of Christianity, and is indeed even older than Christianity itself. I would like to describe this contrast as that which exists between the quiescent and the progressive form of religion. In other words, it might be described as the difference between an aesthetic-ritualistic piety and an ethical-prophetic piety. Both streams may have taken their rise in the depths of the same mountain range, but they emerge from the mountains at different places, their waters are differently coloured, and they have a different taste. They arise . . . in the New Testament, but not at the same point; the one springs

---

[17] *Ibid.*, pp. 38-39.
[18] See below, pp. 35ff.

out of the thought of Paul and of John, the other out of the Synoptic Gospels."[19]

Our intention here, again, is not to commit ourselves to any of the particulars of the above analysis but only to the conception of two streams of differing color and taste. Although a great deal of scholarship has recognized, or at least hinted at the presence of, these two streams, there never has been any consensus on how to describe or even name them. In the interests of keeping the subject as open as possible, we will use a very broad terminology, calling one the Established Tradition and the other the Radical Protest.

This bipartite analysis of Christian history seems first to have been proposed during the Reformation itself, by the left-wing spiritualist historian Sebastian Franck. His *Chronica, Zeitbuch, und Geschichtbibel* (1536), included a *Ketzerchronik*, i.e. a chronicle of the so-called heretics of Christian history (up to and including the Anabaptists of his own day), intended to demonstrate that there was at least as much if not more true Christianity represented in this stream as in the Established Tradition. Franck's idea was picked up, developed, and introduced into modern historiography through the work of the Radical Pietist historian Gottfried Arnold.[20] The stated theme of his *Unparteiische Kirchen- und Ketzer-Historie* was that "those who make heretics are the heretics proper, and those who are called heretics are the real God-fearing people."[21]

---

[19] Ragaz, *Das Evangelium und der soziale Kampf der Gegenwart* (1906), quoted in Ernst Troelstch, *The Social Teaching of the Christian Churches* (1912), trans. Olive Wyon (New York: Macmillan, 1931), Vol. I, p. 434. Of course, Deissmann and others would aver that the one stream springs from a misreading of the Pauline literature rather than from the historical Paul.

[20] For an account of this Franck-Arnold background, see Troeltsch, *op.cit.*, Vol. I, p. 334, and Vol. II, pp. 946ff.

[21] Quoted in "Arnold, Gottfried," *The Mennonite Encyclopedia* (Scottdale, Pa.: Mennonite Publishing House, 1955), Vol. I, pp. 164-65.

In the late nineteenth and early twentieth centuries the treatment of this Established-Radical typology reached a climax. The crowning achievement was Troeltsch's grand design of "church" and "sect,"[22] although as the voluminous footnotes to his great book make clear, there were at the time a host of scholars engaged in this line of research—men such as Ragaz, Keller, Hegler, Ritschl, Göbel, and Weber.[23] It is significant that although these scholars were agreed that there are two streams, they were not at all in accord as to their meaning and value. Opinion ranged from that of Ludwig Keller, who was zealous to maintain that the Radical Protest represented true Christianity and the Established Tradition a monstrous perversion, through Troeltsch himself, who endeavored to give an objective assessment of both, to Albrecht Ritschl, who was certain that the Radical strain was of the devil.

From more recent times have come two major treatments which deserve notice. Monsignor Ronald Knox, in his long and detailed study of the Radical line, is inevitably of Ritschl's opinion, although obviously he does not follow him in denouncing the Protestant Radicals by use of the Ritschlian gambit that brands them as Catholics.[24]

But what may well be the most incisive analysis yet to appear is Emil Brunner's *The Christian Doctrine of the Church, Faith, and the Consummation*.[25] Brunner gives but little attention to the historical tracing of the streams, but he discloses

---

[22] One of Troeltsch's major contentions is that, if the sectarian line is to be properly understood and appreciated, the basic typology must be made tripartite and "sectarianism" distinguished from "spiritualism." His point is well taken, but it need not be taken into account at this point in our discussion.

[23] See particularly, Troeltsch, *op.cit.*, Vol. I, pp. 431ff.

[24] Ronald A. Knox, *Enthusiasm: A Chapter in the History of Religion* (New York: Oxford Un. Press, 1950).

[25] Emil Brunner, *The Christian Doctrine of the Church, Faith, and the Consummation; Dogmatics: Vol. III*, hereafter referred to as *Dogmatics III*, trans. David Cairns and T. H. L. Parker (Philadelphia: Westminster Press, 1962).

the basic ideology of the two with greater profundity than has been evident heretofore. During the Troeltschian period the focus had been preeminently *sociological*, dealing with the outward aspects of church and sect in their relation to culture. Brunner includes this interest but goes on to show that the antinomy vitally affects almost every aspect of doctrine and experience. Indeed, as regards the understanding of "faith" in the two streams, he speaks to what is essentially the same distinction that the Kierkegaard scholars have made between "theology" and "religion," "rationalism" and "irrationalism."

At this point it will be instructive to note how Troeltsch, Knox, and Brunner, respectively, trace out the Radical line. First, Troeltsch and what he calls the "sects" (as against the "churches"): He specifically identifies primitive, New Testament Christianity as of the sect type.[26] He mentions Montanism in connection with this line,[27] but does not feel that the "church" development had progressed far enough to make the distinction clear until the time of the Donatist controversy or even the Gregorian reform.[28] He recognizes that Augustine played a somewhat ambiguous role, displaying characteristics of both streams.[29] The line then runs: Waldensians, Franciscans, Wyclif and the Lollards, the Hussites. Coming to the Reformation, he notes the ambiguity in Luther (not by that token in Lutheranism) and points out how many analysts, dating as far back as Luther's Anabaptist contemporaries, had resolved this by identifying the beginnings of Luther's reform with the Radical line and his later work with the Established.[30] During the Protestant period, then, the line runs, roughly: Anabaptists, General Baptists, Pietism (which he somewhere calls "the second great expression of Protestant sectarianism"), Moravianism, Methodism.

[26] Troeltsch, *op.cit.*, Vol. I, pp. 334.   [27] *Ibid.*, Vol. I, p. 329.
[28] *Ibid.*, Vol. I, p. 333.   [29] *Ibid.*, Vol. I, pp. 158, 282.
[30] *Ibid.*, Vol. II, pp. 947-48. Troeltsch himself admits the ambiguity within Luther but is not ready to accept the distinction between an earlier and a later reformer.

Ronald Knox traces the line which he calls "enthusiasm" from the schismatics whom Paul disciplined in the church at Corinth, through Montanism (of which he says, "For us, Montanism means Tertullian"[31]), Donatism, Albigensianism, Catharism, Waldensianism, Anabaptism, Quakerism, Jansenism, Quietism, Moravianism, Methodism. His evaluation of the whole and the parts is negative.

Brunner's approach is somewhat different. He posits the New Testament Ekklesia as a norm, labels the growth of the "church" idea (the Established line) as "a disastrous misdevelopment,"[32] and then traces what he calls "delaying factors in the development of the Ekklesia into the Church, and attempts to restore the Ekklesia."[33] This line runs: Montanism, Novatianism, Donatism. Brunner recognizes the ambiguity of Augustine and even compares it with that of Luther.[34] The line continues: Cluniac and Cistercian monastic reforms, Franciscanism, Waldensianism, the Anabaptist movement, and the modern Free Churches. Luther's problem in trying to represent both streams at once is described explicitly.[35]

This review makes possible some general observations: There are many and reputable church historians who identify the parallel development of an Established Tradition and a Radical Protest running through Christian history. There is general agreement in identifying the course of the streams, even among those who differ greatly in defining and evaluating them. Also, rather clearly, the scholars who have been searching for the existential antecedents of Kierkegaard's thought have hit upon one element (i.e. antiintellectualism) belonging to the Radical Protest described in church historiography. An obvious question follows: Does the totality of S.K.'s thought and witness fit the Radical-sectarian pattern in the way that his antiintellectualism seems to do? If this is

[31] Knox, op.cit., p. 45. [32] Brunner, *Dogmatics III*, p. 58.
[33] *Ibid.*, pp. 73ff. [34] *Ibid.*, p. 31; cf. pp. 28, 131.
[35] *Ibid.*, pp. 74-76.

a possibility, the logical point of contact and comparison, in view of the fact that S.K. was a Protestant, would be with the Protestant phase of the Radical line, or what we shall call Classic Protestant Sectarianism.

The purpose of the present study is to test this possibility by endeavoring: (1) To grant S.K.'s premise that he was a totally *religious* author and conscientiously to interpret him according to his own instructions in *Point of View*. (2) To understand that this move effectually takes him out of the churchly, philosophic-theological perspective where he customarily has been considered and puts him into "a stream of a different color and taste"—a change of viewpoint which has fundamental implications regarding the understanding of S.K. And (3) to demonstrate that S.K.'s religious witness centered around a view of radical discipleship that was essentially one with that of Classic Protestant Sectarianism.

At the outset, then, to approach Kierkegaard from a religious orientation implies certain principles of interpretation: (1) As the work of a totally religious author, his writings— when taken as a whole, as an integrated and connected authorship—display a certain structure or pattern. His individual works cannot be fully understood apart from the context of this overall organization. S.K. explained what he had in mind:

"The movement described by the authorship is this: *from* the poet (from aesthetics), *from* philosophy (from speculation), *to* the indication of the most central definition of what Christianity is—FROM the *pseudonymous* "Either/Or," THROUGH "The Concluding Postscript" *with my name as editor*, TO the "Discourses at Communion on Fridays," two of which were delivered in the Church of Our Lady. This movement was accomplished or described *uno tenore*, in one breath, if I may use this expression, so that the authorship, *integrally* regarded, is religious from first to last—a thing which everyone can see if he is willing to see, and therefore ought to see.[36]

[36] "My Activity as a Writer" (1851) in *Point of View*, pp. 142-43.

"In a Christian sense simplicity is not the point of departure from which one goes on to become interesting, witty, profound, poet, philosopher, etc. No, the very contrary. *Here* is where one begins (with the interesting, etc.) and becomes simpler and simpler, attaining simplicity. . . . But since the aim of the movement is to attain simplicity, the communication must, sooner or later, end in direct communication."[37]

"Progressive revelation" is the key to Kierkegaard. To a lesser extent his authorship is a tracing of the revelation that came to him. To a much greater extent it is S.K. progressively disclosing his thought to the reader; his journals make it obvious that throughout the pseudonymous works (up to and including *Postscript*) the "edifying author" was himself far in advance of the ideas he wrote in his books, that he was deliberately holding back some vital aspects of his thought. The disclosure, then, is progressive not so much in that the course of the authorship is marked by the introduction of new and explicitly religious themes as by the fact that early themes, first presented in aesthetic or philosophic guise, are gradually revealed in their truly religious depth, grounding, and "simplicity." It is amazing how many of S.K.'s major motifs appear in one form or another in his very earliest works; and yet with none of these do we have the full picture until the concept has been followed through to its religious fulfillment in the later writings.

As S.K. insisted so strongly, the end (both *finis* and *telos*) of the entire development was the *religious*: "[What] requires no explanation at all is the last section, the purely religious work which of course establishes the point of view."[38] It follows, then, that S.K.'s later works should be made normative for understanding his earlier ones. This is not to say that a statement of late date always must take precedence over all earlier statements; it does not mean that *Attack upon "Christendom"* is necessarily S.K.'s final word. It does mean that the

---

[37] *Ibid.*, p. 144; cf. p. 97.   [38] *Point of View*, p. 42.

early, pseudonymous writings are to be read in the light of the later, religious works, that one gets a better picture of Kierkegaard and his message by standing at the close of the authorship looking backward rather than at the beginning looking forward.

(2) From this follows the rather important consideration that to expound his books in chronological order is *not* the best way to expound S.K.[39] They had to be written in the order they were, partly because S.K.'s own education was involved, partly because he was attempting a grand experiment in maieutic pedagogy. That experiment was not a complete success, as S.K. himself came to see. His laborious and repeated efforts to "explain" the authorship (as represented by the documents collected in *Point of View*) were an attempt to obviate the misunderstanding which even then he saw arising. But considering the fact that we have the entire authorship accessible to us, plus S.K.'s own explanations and warnings, it does seem rather unwise to lead people to the essential Kierkegaard by wending the tortuous length of the chronological labyrinth.

(3) Closely related to the foregoing is the caution that S.K.'s pseudonyms be given the weight and significance he intended for them. He was himself particularly concerned on this score:

"So in the pseudonymous works there is not a single word which is mine, I have no opinion about these works except as a third person, no knowledge of their meaning except as a reader, not the remotest private relation to them. . . . My wish, my prayer, is that, if it might occur to anyone to quote a particular saying from the books, he would do me the favor to cite the name of the respective pseudonymous author."[40]

[39] Howard Hong has made this point in his Foreword to Gregor Malantschuk's *Kierkegaard's Way to the Truth*, trans. Mary Michelsen (Minneapolis: Augsburg Publishing House, 1963), p. 6.

[40] "S.K.'s Personal Declaration" in *Concluding Unscientific Postscript to the Philosophical Fragments*, hereafter referred to as *Post-*

S.K. regularly followed his own precept; in the journals and elsewhere he ascribed references from the pseudonymous works to the pseudonyms themselves.

He was clear about the purpose of the pseudonyms and their relation to his nonpseudonymous works:

"But from the point of view of my whole activity as an author, integrally conceived, the aesthetic work is a deception, and herein is to be found the deeper significance of the use of pseudonyms. . . . What then does it mean, 'to deceive'? It means that one does not begin *directly* with the matter one wants to communicate, but begins by accepting the other man's illusion as good money. . . . Let us talk about aesthetics. The deception consists in the fact that one talks thus merely to get to the religious theme. But, on our assumption, the other man is under the illusion that the aesthetic is Christianity; for, he thinks, I am a Christian, and yet he is in aesthetic categories."[41]

It does not follow that S.K. personally would have rejected out of hand everything the pseudonyms said; their ideas are not so much false as they are partial and incomplete; missing is the religious source and background, the only setting in which they become an expression of S.K.'s full intention.

Regarding our use of the pseudonyms, then, two principles would seem to be in order: (a) We should honor S.K.'s request that the pseudonymous works be cited under the names of their respective authors. This certainly can do no harm, and it will alert the reader to at least the possibility that, had S.K. been speaking under his own name, he might have put the thought within a different context or expressed it somewhat differently. (b) When expounding *Kierkegaard* by using *pseudonymous* materials, we would do well to keep one eye,

---

script, by Johannes Climacus (pseud.), trans. David F. Swenson and Walter Lowrie (Princeton: Princeton Un. Press, 1941), pp. 551-52. Cf. *Dru Journals*, 1238 (1851).

[41] *Point of View*, pp. 39-41.

as it were, on the direct, religious works as a norm against which to supplement and correct the pseudonymous statements themselves. Often, of course, no modification will be called for; in some cases it definitely will.

(4) Much more than most authors, particularly in his journals, S.K. went back to discuss and comment upon his own earlier writings. Such helps, of course, should be used for all the assistance they can provide.

(5) The very nature of S.K.'s religious orientation required that his writings be unsystematic; this lack of system—which every analyst is quick to observe—was not just a personal idiosyncrasy of the author but one of his principles of conscience. Thus every attempt to expound S.K.'s thought by forcing it into a systematic mold is bound seriously to distort it. As Louis Dupre so cogently remarked:

"[S.K.'s theology] certainly is not a system, and systemization risks losing the specific character of his thought. . . . Kierkegaard would have thought it the supreme irony of his life that sooner or later his attack on the system would itself be reduced to a system. And yet, even the best known commentaries have not completely avoided this pitfall."[42]

(6) It is unfortunate, too, that biographical considerations concerning Kierkegaard the man tend to steal the center of interest from the message he wanted to communicate. It is true, of course, that S.K.'s life forms an intriguing story in its own right. It is true, also, that the life and the authorship are more closely entwined than is the case with most writers. Some knowledge of the biography is important for an understanding of the works. Nevertheless, harm is done when this biographical interest is allowed to dominate the scene or to make of S.K. more of a "bleeder in public" than he ever was. Dupre, again, put the matter well:

[42] Louis Dupre, *Kierkegaard as Theologian* (first pub. in Dutch, 1958), (New York: Sheed and Ward, 1963), p. xii.

"Kierkegaard's psychology did not create his religious philosophy, but was only the occasion, or, better, the necessary condition, for its discovery. Rather than serving as an explanation of his work, Kierkegaard's psychological constitution should be explained in the light of his writings. . . . Kierkegaard himself realized full well the peculiarity and unwholesomeness of his personality; he also knew how to distinguish it from religion."[43]

We should be reminded that S.K.'s first readers, who read his books as he intended, did not even know the identity of the author of many of the works, let alone have footnotes pointing out that such and such a passage refers to such and such a heartbreak; and the journals actually were a *private* diary. Not to discount the help that the biographical viewpoint can afford, it is yet the case that S.K. was a thinker with a message and not simply an exhibitionist exposing his own psyche. At least once in a while he should be allowed to speak his piece without having to drag his own *vita ante acta* around after him.

(7) A final principle of interpretation would apply to the study of any writer, but the wide scope of S.K.'s subject matter makes it particularly crucial in his case. Because S.K. offers so much, almost anyone can find in him what he wants. Philosophy has found the wherewithal for several types of existentialism; theology for the array of dialectical theologies; psychology for logotherapy and other "existential" schools. Literature, art, and education have found material for their purposes; and there is no knowing who will yet find what. All this is legitimate, of course, but there is also the dangerous tendency for each variety of scholar to treat S.K. as though he were essentially of the scholar's particular orientation. Distortion is the only possible result.

[43] *Ibid.*, pp. 31, 33. Howard Hong also makes this point in his Foreword to Malantschuk, *op.cit.*, p. 7.

Yet, indeed, the present case is nowise different. In the pages that follow S.K. will be portrayed as a Protestant sectary—and that by a student who is himself a church historian, minister, and teacher in the Church of the Brethren, as typical a sect as came out of the tradition. However, I am aware of my bias and so intend to protect myself by following the principles above, as well as the usual canons of research. But biased or not, the view herein presented needs to be considered along with those already in circulation.

CHAPTER II

WHERE IS TRUE CHRISTIANITY
TO BE FOUND?

Whatever of true Christianity is to be
found in the course of the centuries must be found
in the sects and their like.[1]

Into what particular church or tradition does S.K.'s religion best fit? Few questions in Kierkegaard scholarship provide quite as much employment as this; perhaps to no other has been proposed such a wide range of solutions. S.K. himself set the stage for the discussion by departing this earth at a moment when the matter of his religious affiliation was somewhat in abeyance. What follows is a survey of the options that are open and which have been argued by various scholars.

A. ATHEISTIC, OR AT LEAST SECULAR,
EXISTENTIALISM

This is a conjecture made from time to time—though always as pure conjecture. There are probably two different motives behind it: first, the too-easy assumption that S.K.'s attack

---

[1] *Søren Kierkegaards Papirer*, hereafter referred to as *Papirer*, ed. P. A. Heiberg, V. Kuhr, and E. Torsting, 2d ed., Vols. I-XI³ (in twenty parts individually bound) (Copenhagen: Gyldenalske Boghandel, Nordisk Forlag, 1909-1948), XI² A 435 (1855) [my trans.—V.E.].

on the church actually was (or would have become) an attack upon Christianity itself; and second, the subjective judgment of a thinker who finds S.K.'s "existentialism" appealing but his "Christianity" quite otherwise, who personally feels that the two elements are incompatible, and who thus assumes that eventually S.K. would have dropped his Christianity.[2]

We call this position "pure conjecture" because, in the first place, it must fly directly in the face of S.K.'s own radically Christian protestations. Second, the position is not (and indeed cannot be) supported with documentary evidence but only by the "feel" of the critic. And third, modern scholarship generally shows no inclination at all to go this direction. Although no conjecture dare be ruled out as a *possibility*, this one has little to offer as a perspective from which to view S.K.'s avowedly Christian authorship.

B. LUTHERANISM, AND THE OTHER REFORMATION "CHURCHES"

Although the question here necessarily devolves on the Danish Lutheran Church of which S.K. was a long-time communicant, this option actually represents the entire "churchly" tradition of Protestantism. No one ever has suggested that S.K. would have been any happier in another established church (i.e. Reformed or Anglican) than he was in Lutheranism. Clearly, S.K. belongs either in Lutheranism or else in an entirely different sort of tradition.

[2] Among the early Kierkegaardians who at least leaned in this direction, Walter Lowrie names Brandes, Brøchner, Höffding, and Schrempf; see Lowrie's *Kierkegaard* (first published 1938) (New York: Harper Torchbooks, 1962), Vol. I, pp. 3-6. More recently, Karl Jaspers has hinted at this view—as reported (and discounted) by Walter Kaufmann in his Introduction to S.K.'s *The Present Age and The Difference between a Genius and an Apostle* (hereafter referred to as *The Present Age*), revised trans. Alexander Dru (New York: Harper Torchbooks, 1962), pp. 11-12. Colin Wilson also has made the hint; see his *Religion and the Rebel* (Boston: Houghton Mifflin, 1957), p. 239.

Some of the facts regarding S.K.'s relation to his church should be before us as we consider this alternative: (1) S.K. was born, reared, and educated (up to the level of Master of Arts—the equivalent of our doctorate—in theology) in the Danish Lutheran Church. Although not ordained, he preached from time to time and was well acquainted with many of the clergy, including the highest officials of the church. His attendance at services was very regular.

(2) Beginning far back in his authorship, however, first in his journals and then in his published works, there appeared a stream of criticism ever growing both in quantity and in virulence. This will be traced and analyzed in a later chapter, but suffice it to say that the critique centered on the constitution of the church (particularly as regards its relation to the state and the "world"), on the government of the church (particularly as regards the nature and character of the clerical office), and on the sort of preaching that was prevalent in the church.

(3) Parallel to and a part of this critique was a growing criticism of Martin Luther. Thus S.K. was concerned not only with a "fallen" Lutheranism but traced several of the church's defects back to the Reformer himself.

(4) In 1854-1855 this critical development culminated in an open pamphleteering attack upon the church. The literature (which we read under one cover, *Attack upon "Christendom"*) was as acid as ink can get. The statement which S.K. used as his declaration of intent was published as a separate and independent document, was in formulation for over a year, and continually was quoted from and referred to in S.K.'s subsequent pamphlets. The core of it reads: "Whoever thou art, whatever in other respects thy life may be, my friend, by ceasing to take part (if ordinarily thou dost) in the public worship of God, as it now is (with the claim that it is the Christianity of the New Testament), thou has constantly one guilt the less, and that a great one: thou dost not take part

in treating God as a fool by calling that the Christianity of the New Testament which is not the Christianity of the New Testament."[3]

(5) S.K. followed his own advice; Hans Brøchner, a contemporary who was something of a friend, reported: "At the time when Søren Kierkegaard began his polemic against the Establishment, and perhaps for some time before, he had ceased to participate in church services."[4]

(6) Dupre indicates that during the final weeks of his life S.K. actually stopped churchgoers in the street in an attempt to dissuade them from the sin of worshiping in the state church.[5]

(7) While in the hospital during his final illness S.K. refused a visit from his brother Peter—not because Peter was his brother but because he was a priest[6] who had publicly taken the side of the church against S.K.[7]

(8) Also, in the hospital S.K. refused communion. The circumstances are instructive. The following conversation was recorded by Emil Boesen, S.K.'s friend from childhood, his closest confidant during the final illness, and a priest. Boesen speaks first:

[3] *Attack upon "Christendom,"* trans. Walter Lowrie (Boston: Beacon Press Paperback, 1956), pp. 57ff.

[4] "Brøchner's Recollections," in *Glimpses and Impressions of Kierkegaard*, ed. and trans. T.H. Croxall (Welwyn, Herts: J. Nesbit, 1959), p. 38.

[5] Dupre, *op.cit.*, p. 165. He does not cite the source of this information.

[6] "Priest" is the term commonly used in the Danish church for its clergymen, and thus it appears extensively in S.K.'s writings. It should not be taken as implying any sort of sacerdotal sarcasm either here or in S.K.

[7] S.K. was willing to send Peter a brotherly greeting but did not feel up to receiving him in person. Croxall, *op.cit.*, gives us a letter by the relative who carried the greeting (p. 102, 4) and a statement by Peter (p. 129) which together make it plain that both Søren and Peter realized how the matter stood.

"Do you wish to receive Holy Communion? 'Yes, but not from a parson; from a layman.' That is difficult. 'Then I shall die without it.' That is not right! 'On that point there can be no argument, I have made my choice, have chosen. The parsons are the King's officials, the King's officials have nothing to do with Christianity.' "[8]

(9) After S.K. died and was thus bereft of any means of defending himself, the church decided that decorum could best be served by "forgiving" him; that forgiveness was the last thing S.K. would have accepted from the church seems not to have come into consideration. He was buried with full ecclesiastical honors, the funeral held before a standing-room-only crowd in the cathedral church following Sunday services. Brother Peter, the priest whom S.K. had refused to see a few days earlier, delivered the message.[9]

But even in the face of this history, considerable scholarship has had the effect of joining forces with S.K.'s ecclesiastical undertakers to put him to rest in the Lutheran Church. Some do it with silence; some do it with a word; some do it with extended argument; it can be questioned whether any do it convincingly.[10] Our contention is simply that the burden of proof rests just as heavily upon those who would claim S.K. for Lutheranism as upon those who would claim him for Roman Catholicism, secularism, sectarianism, or any other

[8] Boesen's account is found in *Dru Journals*, p. 551.

[9] The primary sources describing the funeral and burial are collected in Croxall, *op.cit.*, pp. 84ff.

[10] Of course, any study of S.K.'s religion that fails to raise the question of his church affiliation as much as suggests that he remained a Lutheran. More explicit claims of varying sorts are represented by H. V. Martin, *Kierkegaard, the Melancholy Dane* (New York: Philosophical Library, 1950), p. 108; by Hermann Diem, *Kierkegaard's Dialectic of Existence*, hereafter referred to as *Dialectic*, trans. Harold Knight (Edinburgh: Oliver and Boyd, 1959), p. 157; and by Martin J. Heinecken, *The Moment Before God* (Philadelphia: Muhlenberg Press, 1956), pp. 378-79.

tradition. S.K.'s natural connections with the Lutheran Church do not answer the problem; too many objections must be taken into account.

In this regard there are two alternative interpretations which should be considered. They both have the net effect of leaving S.K. in the Lutheran fold and thus are subnumbered under the heading above:

a. The Attack as Aberration

This suggestion is that in the *Attack* of 1854-1855 S.K. had lost control of himself and thus fallen into an extremism which cannot be taken as indicative of the real Kierkegaard, i.e. the S.K. who became disaffected with the Lutheran Church was not one who seriously need concern us. It is interesting that one comes across the rebuttal to this argument much more often than the argument itself; the issue is as good as settled. David Swenson's judgment is typical: "There are students of Kierkegaard who although otherwise sympathetic, feel that this attack was the expression of something pathological in his nature. Others interpret it as the beginning of a development which would inevitably have taken place, had he lived, in the direction of a modern non-Christian liberalism, perhaps humanism; still others think he would have become a Catholic. To anyone who has read his journals, all these guesses must seem fantastic."[11]

The *Attack* is not like the peel of an orange that can be torn off and discarded in the process of getting at the Kierkegaardian fruit. Rather, S.K.'s authorship is constructed like a Spanish onion. It is obvious that the outside, yellow, 1855

---

[11] David Swenson, in the translator's Introduction to S.K.'s *Philosophical Fragments*, trans. David Swenson, 2d ed., with an introduction and commentary by Niels Thulstrup translated by Howard Hong (Princeton: Princeton Un. Press, 1962), pp. xli-xlii. Cf. Walter Lowrie, in the translator's Introduction to *Attack upon "Christendom,"* p. xiii. Cf. Diem, *Dialectic*, p. 154.

layer is of a rather different hue than the innermost, white, 1843 layer. But as easy as it is to make the distinction, just that impossible is it to say where the white ends and the yellow begins. The *Attack* is an integral part of Kierkegaard and must be treated as such—although, on the other hand, the *Attack* is not the whole of Kierkegaard (not even the whole answer regarding his religious orientation) and must not be treated as such.

b. The Attack *as Corrective*

This proposal, as the foregoing one, solves the problem by eliminating it—but without recourse to as radical a diagnosis as "aberration." It suggests that the *Attack* is to be understood as a "corrective." Now the evidence that S.K. himself so interpreted the situation—and used the very term—is unimpeachable.[12] The question, then, is: What does "corrective" connote? Is our understanding of the term the same as S.K.'s? The matter has been made extremely elusive in that it has not been discussed as a question; each scholar has taken his own reading of "corrective" and proceeded to apply it to S.K.

The general interpretation—more often implied than spoken—is that to call the *Attack* a corrective means that S.K.'s words and actions had no specific relevance except for Søren Kierkegaard, in 1855, in the nation of Denmark. He had in mind only the staging of a "demonstration" and did not expect or intend that there should result any program of actual reform.[13] Neither by directive nor by implication did S.K. mean to propose any sort of norm regarding how other people should live their Christian lives. All he said and did was so exaggerated for the sake of effect that it need not be taken too seriously—or only after having been toned down drastically. Whatever ideas in the *Attack* seem too radical can

[12] See, for example, S.K.'s statement below on p. 28.
[13] See, for example, Diem, *Dialectic,* p. 157.

be dismissed as "corrective hyperbole." Of course, no proponent of the view states the matter quite this baldly, but the point gets made one way or another.[14]

But it can be questioned whether S.K.'s understanding of "corrective" was this one. In introducing the pamphlet series which constituted the major thrust of his *Attack*, S.K. said: "Yet it is nothing ephemeral I have in mind, any more than it was anything ephemeral I had in mind before; no, it was and is something eternal: on the side of the ideal against illusions."[15] And the fact that he left the church and urged others to do so substantiates his claim to seriousness.

S.K. explained what *he* meant by "corrective": "He who must apply a 'corrective' must study accurately and profoundly the weak side of the Establishment, and then vigorously and one-sidedly present the opposite. . . . If this is true, a presumably clever pate can reprove the corrective for being one-sided. Ye gods! Nothing is easier for him who applies the corrective than to supply the other side; but then it ceases to become the corrective and becomes the established order."[16]

To call a corrective "one-sided" is quite different from calling it "exaggerated," "transitory," or "nonnormative." According to S.K.'s explanation, the statements and acts of the corrective still would stand as they are, for what they are. The most that might be done is to supplement them with some other statements, but there is no suggestion that they are to be diluted, deemphasized, or ignored.

Of course, the satire of S.K.'s *Attack* is to be read as satire, and the humor is to be laughed at (not, laughed off), but the

---

[14] In addition to Diem, see, as another example, Theodor Haecker, *Søren Kierkegaard*, trans. Alexander Dru (London: Oxford Un. Press, 1937), p. 67.

[15] *Attack upon "Christendom,"* p. 91.

[16] This journal entry has been inserted by the translator into *Attack upon "Christendom,"* p. 90.

point behind it all is to be taken just as seriously as it was intended—intended by a man who was willing to cut himself off from the fellowship of the church and, on his deathbed, decline its sacraments for the sake of making that point. The *Attack* must not be allowed to dominate our study, but it must be given its proper weight—which is to suggest that S.K.'s relationship to Lutheranism was at least questionable.

C. ROMAN CATHOLICISM

The suggestion that S.K. was essentially a Roman Catholic —at least to some degree and in some respects—is one which has had surprising persistence and strength.[17] However, it seems evident that a very real factor in this view springs not so much from evidence within S.K. himself as from a dearth of categories on the part of the analysts. In his writings S.K. was highly critical of "Protestantism"; he often used this term in his critique, and his expositors have followed his lead. Of course, the term "Protestantism" immediately suggests the dichotomy Protestantism/Catholicism; and from this it is an easy step to the assumption that "anti-Protestant" is the equivalent of "pro-Catholic." But this is an oversimplification; and the Catholic scholar Louis Dupre senses the non sequitur:

"One might be inclined to think that, after this vigorous attack on Lutheranism and even on the principle of the Reformation itself, Kierkegaard was well on the way to becoming a Catholic. . . . Indeed, the principal points on which this view is based are untenable. . . . If Kierkegaard's conception of the Church cannot be called the traditional Protestant one, it is even less Catholic. Karl Barth may be right in refusing Kier-

---

[17] An admirable summary which cites many of the scholars and their claims is Heinrich Roos, S.J., *Søren Kierkegaard and Catholicism*, trans. Richard Brackett (Westminster, Md.: Newman Press, 1954). Cf. Cornelio Fabro, C.P.S., "Faith and Reason in Kierkegaard's Dialectic," in *A Kierkegaard Critique*, particularly pp. 156-58, 190-94.

kegaard a place among the great Reformers of the nineteenth century, but this does not make him a Catholic."[18]

A close examination will show that in almost every case S.K.'s critique of Protestantism applies directly to the "churchly" tradition within Protestantism but not in the same degree, if at all, to the "sectarian" tradition. If the *tertium quid* of sectarianism be kept in the picture, and if one keeps alert to the narrower, "churchly" connotation S.K. gave to the word "Protestantism," then his pro-Catholicism simply disappears. Specific instances will come to attention throughout our study.

But when all the evidence is in it is apparent that there are no solid grounds for calling S.K. a Roman Catholic in any sense of the term; and what is more important, to view him from the Catholic perspective contributes little if anything to understanding the core of his witness and work. Dupre's conclusion—though stated in his Introduction—is:

"[I have come] to the conclusion that [S.K.'s] *Existenzdialektik* is perhaps the most consistent application of the Reformation principle that has ever been made. . . . It is precisely Kierkegaard's fidelity to his fundamentally Protestant convictions which constitutes his value for a dialogue between Catholicism and Reformation."[19]

D. SPIRITUAL ATOMISM—THE CHRISTIAN LIFE LIVED APART FROM ANY ORGANIZED CHURCH

To my knowledge no one ever has proposed this as the Kierkegaardian perspective. It should be given consideration, however, if for no other reason than that it actually was the situation in which S.K. stood at the time of his death—i.e. he was a committed, practicing Christian who, as a matter of principle, refused to participate in the life of any organized, institutional church. Nevertheless it is clear that the atomist

[18] Dupre, *op.cit.*, pp. 216, 217, 219.
[19] *Ibid.*, pp. x, xii.

position does not represent the culmination and *telos* of S.K.'s religious thought.[20]

To say this is not so much as even to imply a conjecture about what S.K. would have done regarding his church membership had he lived some years longer; that is a completely impossible and fruitless line of investigation. We are suggesting only that the tenor and weight of S.K.'s entire witness make it plain that even his leaving of the church was motivated not by the search for a *churchless Christianity* but for a truly *Christian church*.

E. CLASSIC PROTESTANT SECTARIANISM (RADICAL DISCIPLESHIP)

This, of course, is the alternative we intend to support. The present chapter is not the place to open the extensive and detailed motif comparison through which we hope to make our case, and so we now offer only a few preliminary, external, and secondary evidences to indicate that the proposal of S.K. as a sectary is not completely preposterous.

I have not found any scholar who deliberately has named sectarianism as the Kierkegaardian perspective; the best we have are oblique hints and pointers. There is, however, one notable exception to this generalization: sectarianism is mentioned explicitly by S.K. himself! The locus of the following quotation is perhaps as significant as its content. This is the next to the last thing S.K. ever wrote; it is a journal entry dated September 23, 1855; his very last entry is dated the next day; he collapsed on the street on October 2 and died November 4. Might this possibly mark S.K.'s culminating insight into the nature and orientation of his own witness?

[20] Though not addressing himself specifically to our question, it is perhaps Hermann Diem (*Dialectic*, pp. 98ff.) who has given most decisive demonstration to the fact that the existence of an organized church with its preaching, doctrine, and sacraments was an essential presupposition of S.K.'s whole dialectic.

"In the New Testament is the formula for what it is to be a Christian: to fear God more than men. Herein are all the specifically Christian collisions. As soon as one can be a Christian out of fear of men, yea, when out of fear of men one will dare even to let himself be called a Christian, then is Christianity *eo ipso* come to naught.

"One sees therefore what nonsense it is to believe that true Christianity is found in 'the church'—in comparison to which the great number Zero is a more Christian spirit than this which is: human mediocrity, brute-man's faith in . . . human numbers. No, whatever of true Christianity is to be found in the course of the centuries must be found in the sects and their like—unless the case is that thus to be a sect, or outside the church, is proof of its being true Christianity. But what is found there [i.e. in true Christianity] may be found in the sects and such, the only thing that resembles the Christianity of the New Testament, that is—a sect, which is what it is also called in the New Testament."[21]

And this was no sudden conclusion on S.K.'s part; he had expressed similar sentiments at least five years earlier, though not in quite such decisive and absolute terms:

"The 'Establishment' is on the whole a completely unchristian concept. Thus it is ridiculous to hear the Establishment brag itself up in comparison with the 'sects'—because there is infinitely more Christian truth in sectarian delusion than in the Establishment's indolence and drowsiness and inertia. And it is still more ridiculous that the Establishment appeals to the New Testament. Indeed, there Christianity itself was a 'sect' (and called such at the time) which had (and here also is its 'truth') an Awakening: this is just how legitimate it is to warn people about the sectaries. But now a sect always has the advantage over the Establishment in that it has truth's awak-

[21] *Papirer*, XI² A 435 [my trans.—V.E.]. Cf. the trans. offered by Ronald Gregor Smith in his volume of journal selections, *The Last Years*, hereafter referred to as *Smith Journals* (New York: Harper & Row, 1965).

ening, i.e. the truth which lies in an 'Awakening' even if that which the sects consider to be the truth is error and delusion."[22]

Now, of course S.K. was neither a cenobite nor a *Schwärmergeist* (as, likewise, the classic sectaries were not), but in the 1855 quotation he solidly aligned himself with sectarian nonconformity as against churchly friendship with the world and, in the 1849 statement, with sectarian "enthusiasm" as against churchly decorum. And even earlier he had made a very revealing judgment concerning one particular sect:

"The reformation abolished the monastery. Very well; I am not going to say anything more about the reformation having brought secular politics into existence. But now look at Christendom; where is there any Christianity except among the Moravians. But the Moravians are not, in a decisive sense, Christians; their lives are not in double danger. They are simply a more worldly edition of the monastery; men who look after their business, beget children etc. and then, within themselves, also busy themselves with Christianity, briefly this is the religion of hidden spirituality. But the other danger, suffering for the sake of the faith they avoid entirely, they avoid being led into the really Christian situation. There is much that is beautiful in their lives, but their peace is not really Christianity, not in the profoundest sense; it resembles the view which makes Christianity into a mild doctrine of truth."[23]

Notice that S.K.'s criticism of the Moravians is not at all that of a man of the "church" but of a brother sectary who accuses them of having deserted the cause and made their peace with the world rather than being out getting themselves burned at the stake as their forefathers did. Taken all together, these statements constitute enough evidence to merit serious investigation.

[22] *Papirer*, X[1] A 407 (1849) [my trans.—V.E.]. Cf. *Smith Journals*, XI[2] A 39 (1854) and XI[2] A 174 (1854).
[23] *Dru Journals*, 831 (1848); cf. 1234 (1851).

But although Kierkegaard scholarship has not picked up these clues, there have been some partial and even some inadvertent insights. Walter Kaufmann, completely in passing, while giving a list to show the variety of religious orientations represented by the founding fathers of existentialism, calls S.K. "a Protestant's Protestant."[24] He probably meant nothing more than that S.K. was strongly and staunchly Protestant, but the phrase makes an apt epitome of both S.K. and sectarianism. The sectaries, in many respects, do stand in precisely the same relation to mainline Protestantism as Protestantism does to Catholicism; sectarianism is the reformation of the Reformation, as it has been called.

However, it is Dupre who, via this route, has come closest to our view; all he needs is the word "sectarianism." In a statement that shows more insight into both S.K. and Protestantism than most Protestant scholars demonstrate, he says:

"[S.K.] is a person who kept protesting, who could never accept a Church which had become established, even if on the basis of protest itself. In most instances, the Protestant principle has been abandoned as soon as it has developed itself to the point of becoming a Church. Kierkegaard's intransigent Protestantism continued to protest; he protested against everything, even against the protest itself. . . . It is true that Kierkegaard placed himself beyond the pale of the Protestant *Church*. But he never abandoned the Protestant principle."[25]

"Protest" may not be the best term to characterize the basic nature either of S.K.'s religious dialectic, "the Protestant principle," or sectarianism, but given such modification, Dupre's analysis points toward what we mean in calling S.K. "a Protestant's Protestant" and also what is implied by Classic Protestant Sectarianism.

[24] Walter Kaufmann, in the editor's Introduction to *Existentialism from Dostoevsky to Sartre* (Cleveland: Meridian Books, 1956), p. 11.

[25] Dupre, *op.cit.*, pp. 221-22. Another inadvertent description of S.K.'s sectarianism is found in Fabro, *op.cit.*, in *A Kierkegaard Critique*, pp. 156-57.

A somewhat different approach to S.K.'s sectarian perspective perhaps first was suggested by Emil Brunner, although it has been picked up since by others as well. Brunner—who also calls S.K. the "greatest Christian thinker of modern times"—identifies him as one of the "two great figures of Pietism" of the nineteenth century.[26]

A recent work which becomes more explicit than anything done earlier is Joachim Seyppel's *Schwenckfeld, Knight of Faith*. The focus of Seyppel's study is Schwenckfeld rather than S.K., but in the process of comparing the two men he proposes Pietism as the link between them: "Whereas Schwenckfeld prepared Pietism, Kierkegaard was raised under its influence."[27] Seyppel then traces the historical path by which German Pietism came into Denmark and into direct contact with S.K.;[28] and he makes this very interesting reference to the thesis of E. Peterson: "It is understandable, then, to read in an article on Kierkegaard and Protestantism why some of the Dane's favorite expressions, like, for example, 'existence' and 'reality,' should be inexplicable without a reference to the ideas of Pietism."[29]

Although any direct personal influence from Schwenckfeld to S.K. would have to have been tenuous indeed, the influence from Pietism was not. In fact, S.K. himself affirmed the connection when he said: "Certainly Pietism (properly understood, not just in the sense that holds apart from dancing and externalities—no, in the sense of that which bears witness to the truth and suffers for it, that hears with understanding that a Christian is to suffer in this world and that the worldly

[26] Emil Brunner, *Truth as Encounter* (Philadelphia: Westminster Press, 1943 and 1964), pp. 112, 84; cf. pp. 42-43.

[27] Joachim H. Seyppel, *Schwenckfeld, Knight of Faith* (Pennsburg, Pa.: The Schwenckfelder Library, 1961), p. 127. Cf. Dupre, *op.cit.*, pp. xi, 171.

[28] *Ibid.*, pp. 127-29.

[29] *Ibid.*, p. 129. Seyppel cites E. Peterson, "Kierkegaard und der Protestantismus," *Wort und Wahrheit* 3, 8, pp. 579ff.

shrewdness which conforms with the world is unchristian)—
certainly it is the sole consequence of Christianity."[30] It is not
accurate directly to equate Pietism and sectarianism, although
clearly Pietism does represent a sectarian-type tendency. The
broader category of sectarianism will do S.K. more justice
than simply to call him a Pietist, but to have identified his Pietist affinities is a real gain.

But if S.K. was as typical and obvious a sectary as we have
suggested and as the remainder of this volume will be devoted
to demonstrate, how is it (the question must be asked) that
so many competent scholars have been almost unanimously
and totally blind to the fact? A number of explanations suggest themselves. In the first place, he lacked the correct external markings, he neither founded nor joined a sect—unless
his call for others to join him in leaving the church be interpreted as a tentative step in this direction.

At the same time, S.K. can be quoted strongly to the effect
that he had absolutely no desire to found a sect or new church
organization. Several factors must be taken into account,
however.

Sectarian leaders customarily express sincere reluctance and
even resistance to the idea of leaving the church and founding
a separate group. They would much prefer to reform the
church rather than separate from it. Thus we find cases—
such as the Quakers, the Wesleyans, and the early Puritans
—in which the sectaries insisted vehemently that they were
not separating from the church and in consequence of which
the church itself was forced to take as much responsibility in
cutting off the sect as the sect did in separating itself from the
church.

Perhaps the strongest consideration is the fact that S.K.'s
statements to the effect that he had no intention of founding a

[30] *Papirer* (through an error in transcription, the locus of this entry
has been lost) [my trans.—V.E.].

sect can as well be interpreted to mean that *he* had no such intention as that he was conscientiously opposed to sects as such. The truth is that any sect of which S.K. was the founder —or even a member (for one cannot conceive of S.K. as *one* of a group without his immediately becoming the *center* of the group)—would have had a very poor prognosis of success or even survival. To set up and run an actual institution requires, in addition to an ideology, some practical skills in the way of administration and organization. Of these S.K. had not a trace. Hans Brøchner, who knew him personally, said: "Kierkegaard had not a sense of actuality, if I may use the expression, which, in a given situation, could form a balance to his enormous reflective powers."[31] And S.K. was aware of the problem: ". . . I am melancholy to the point of madness, something I can conceal as long as I am independent but which makes me useless for any service where I do not determine everything myself."[32]

If a sectary, S.K. clearly was one who was constitutionally unfitted to belong to a sect. But this anomaly in no way invalidates our contention or changes the orientation of S.K.'s work. If a sectary, S.K. must be seen not as an organizer but a theoretician (if that term properly can be applied to one so opposed to "theory"). He would well qualify as "the sectaries' theologian"—except for the fact that the *sectaries'* theologian hardly qualifies as a *theologian*. Nevertheless, although this lack of external indicators does not affect the sectarian character of his thought, it has tended to block the discovery that it is sectarian—and thus the possibility has been overlooked.

Another, and perhaps more important, factor in this scholarly blindness is the fact that for most critics the very term "sectarianism" is a bad word, one they would not at all be happy to have associated with S.K. It carries connotations of

[31] Brøchner's Recollections in *Croxall Glimpses*, p. 21.
[32] *Dru Journals*, 970 (1849).

divisiveness, narrowness, and fanaticism which do not fit well with "the greatest Christian thinker of modern times." (In due course we shall see that these connotations are not properly a part of the basic concept "sect," although neither is it entirely accidental that the derogation has adhered to the term.)

Yet it is interesting to note that of the Kierkegaard scholars who approach S.K. from a religious viewpoint at all, nearly every one comes from the "churchly" (and rather high-churchly) traditions. Some of them are Roman Catholics. The Danish and German scholars are, of course, for the most part Lutheran. But even in England and in this country Kierkegaardians have tended to come predominantly from the Catholic, Lutheran, and Anglican ranks. There is an interesting exception; one of the very earliest students and translators of S.K. in America was Douglas Steere, a Quaker sectary; his presence serves simply to prove the rule. But now it is proper that the scope of scholarship be broadened and that S.K.'s thought be examined by those who look from a rather different perspective.

There is a peripheral line of evidence regarding S.K.'s sectarianism which needs to be considered at some point, and better here than elsewhere. It is not sufficient to maintain that a thinker has been understood just because his antecedents have been traced or that he dare be allowed no ideas that cannot be accounted for in his antecedents. However, there are some external findings which may serve at least to make S.K.'s sectarianism *historically* plausible.

One of S.K.'s nieces reported that both Søren's father and Emil Boesen's were members of "the Moravian brotherhood."[33] Just what this "membership" amounted to is a little difficult to ascertain, because it is quite clear that the entire family were also staunch and loyal members of the state church; but the opportunity for Moravianism to influence

[33] Henriette Lund's Recollections in *Croxall Glimpses,* p. 50.

S.K. was there in any case. Brøchner described the religion of
S.K.'s father as "pretty much that of the old pietists."[34]

A catalog of the library S.K. left behind him shows something of his interests and possible sources of influence. Both
Dru and Croxall list one group of books as the "mystics," but
whatever the heading, here is clearly a sectarian style of
thought. Dru names the authors: "Tauler, Ligouri, Sailer,
Zacharias Werner, Arndt, Thomas a Kempis, Baader, Bernard
of Clairveaux, Bonaventura, Ruysbrock, Boehme, Fenelon,
Guyon, Swedenborg, Tersteegen, Lamennais, 22 vol. of Abraham a St. Clara, etc."[35] Apart from duplications, Croxall also
lists Suso, Angelus Silesius, and (as significant as any) Gottfried Arnold.[36]

Much more valuable than these library lists are S.K.'s references to his own reading. In *Purity of Heart* he quotes from
Johann Arndt's *True Christianity*[37] (although earlier than
the Pietist movement per se, this book became a popular hand-
book of Pietist and other sectarian groups). In one of the
Edifying Discourses he calls it "an ancient, venerable, and
trustworthy book of devotions."[38] And in a reference which
the Danish editors are confident intends Arndt's book and is
a true autobiographical detail, the pseudonym Quidam wrote
in his diary: "The Bible is always lying on my table and is the
book I read most; a severe book of edification in the tradition
of the older Lutheranism is my other guide...."[39]

[34] Hans Brøchner's Recollections in *Croxall Glimpses*, p. 36.

[35] In the Introduction to *Dru Journals*, p. 1, note.

[36] In the editorial materials of S.K.'s *Johannes Climacus, or De Om-
nibus Dubitandum Est,* hereafter referred to as *Johannes Climacus,*
trans. and ed. T. H. Croxall (Stanford: Stanford Un. Press, 1958), pp.
27-28.

[37] *Purity of Heart,* trans. Douglas V. Steere (New York: Harper,
1948), p. 152.

[38] *Edifying Discourses,* trans. David F. and Lillian Marvin Swenson
(Minneapolis: Augsburg Publishing House, 1948), Vol. IV, pp. 70-71.

[39] *Stages on Life's Way,* ed. Hilarius Bookbinder (pseud.), trans.
Walter Lowrie (Princeton: Princeton Un. Press, 1940), p. 218.

In *Either/Or,* Judge William, a pseudonym, quotes Fenelon.[40] S.K. himself later said, "I have been reading Fenelon and Tersteegen. Both have made a powerful impression upon me."[41] And as the motto for a very personal little piece, "About My Work as an Author," S.K. used a verse from Tersteegen's *Der Frommen Lotterie,* another devotional of the sectaries.[42]

We have made this survey of S.K.'s religious options not so much to close some possibilities as to open one, namely, Classic Protestant Sectarianism. To that investigation we now proceed.

[40] *Either/Or,* ed. Victor Eremita (pseud.), trans. David F. and Lillian Marvin Swenson and Walter Lowrie, revised by Howard Johnson (Garden City: Doubleday Anchor, 1959), Vol. II, p. 112.

[41] *Dru Journals,* 1220, p. 443 (1851).

[42] In *Point of View,* p. 140.

CHAPTER III

CLASSIC PROTESTANT SECTARIANISM: IN WHICH A CHURCH IS NOT A "CHURCH"

Precisely to the concept "Church" is

to be traced the fundamental confusion both of

Protestantism and of Catholicism—

or is it to the concept "Christendom"?[1]

If S.K. is to be treated as a sectary, it behooves us to be very clear as to what we mean by "sectarianism." It is not our task to present a full-scale study, but we must pursue the matter far enough to make plain just what we are saying about S.K. when we mount him under the label. This clarification is all the more crucial in light of the various ways the term "sect" is used and misused among us; our concern is as much to establish what we do *not* intend by the word as what we *do*.

The "church/sect" typology is the fruit of a half-century of scholarly labors culminating in the work of Ernst Troeltsch in the opening years of the present century.[2] Although

---

[1] *Attack upon "Christendom,"* p. 34.

[2] A brief account of this entire development is given by George Huntston Williams in his Introduction to *Spiritual and Anabaptist Writers,* Vol. XXV in *The Library of Christian Classics* (Philadelphia: Westminster Press, 1957), pp. 26-27.

Troeltsch's work needs to be modified, supplemented, and reoriented at points, yet in the way of establishing terminology, defining categories, and then analyzing the historical phenomena accordingly, it has not been surpassed. Troeltsch is still indispensable for sectarian studies. Some modern scholars have ignored or belittled him to their own hurt; we shall depend heavily upon him.

The most serious weakness of Troeltsch's approach is his interpretation of ecclesiology as being essentially a *sociological* matter rather than an *ideological*, or theological, one. However, as shall become apparent, he was not nearly as guilty in this regard as are some of his successors. He was conscious of the partialness of his perspective and practically invited someone to supplement it: "This theory [the church/sect typology] is connected with a whole series of further distinctions, which belong to the subtler realm of religious psychology and to theological thought. . . . All this, however, really belongs to the history of doctrine. For our present subject it is vital to remember that the idea of the Church as an objective institution, and as a voluntary society, contains a fundamental sociological distinction."[3] Troeltsch was in no sense a socioeconomic determinist; his basic position seems to have been that ideology has sociological manifestations no less than that sociological conditions determine ideology. In fact he went out of his way to insist that the Reformation was essentially a *religious* phenomenon and not in the first place a sociological one.[4] Nevertheless, Troeltsch's work does show a sociological lopsidedness which requires supplementation if not correction.

The theological perspective which Troeltsch lacked perhaps has been supplied most adequately by Emil Brunner in Volume III of his *Dogmatics*. But if Troeltsch's weakness was that he lacked the theological acumen of a Brunner, Brunner's was that he dismissed Troeltsch too quickly: "Ernst Troeltsch,

[3] Troeltsch, *op.cit.*, Vol. II, pp. 162-63.
[4] *Ibid.*, Vol. II, pp. 465-67.

who was familiar with the sociological approach, but who, as an idealist theologian, had but little insight into the spiritual nature of the Ekklesia, quite simply reckoned the New Testament Ekklesia as belonging to the 'sect-type of Church'—a judgment in which there was doubtless some truth, but at the same time a great deal of error."[5] Brunner's work could have had enhanced precision and value had he adopted the made-to-order terminology and categories provided by Troeltsch, rounding them out with his own meanings and insights. In our presentation we shall attempt to do what Brunner failed to do; what follows is to a large extent Brunnerian content in a Troeltschian framework.

But before discussing what sectarianism is, it is of vital importance to refute a widespread misunderstanding. The Troeltschian typology was popularized and made the common background of American ecclesiological thought through the offices of a highly influential book by H. Richard Niebuhr, *The Social Sources of Denominationalism* (1929).[6] Niebuhr's thesis was then tested and proved through the brilliant sociological study made by his student and later colleague Liston Pope.[7] And since that time this view has carried the field.[8] It

[5] Brunner, *Dogmatics III,* p. 31.

[6] H. Richard Niebuhr, *The Social Sources of Denominationalism* (Meridian Books, 1957).

[7] Liston Pope, *Millhands and Preachers* (New Haven: Yale Un. Press, 1942).

[8] One need not go far to document this contention. See, for example, a book like J. Milton Yinger's *Religion, Society and the Individual— An Introduction to the Sociology of Religion* (New York: Macmillan, 1957), probably the most widely used textbook in its field. The Niebuhrian view is written into the basic assumptions of the presentation (see pp. 142ff.); and in the selection of readings, passages from Niebuhr and his followers dominate (see particularly pp. 415ff.).

This influence may be particularly strong among groups that come from a sectarian background. This certainly has been my experience both as a student and a functionary in the Church of the Brethren. The Niebuhrian typology is regarded as *the* key by which we understand ourselves. In the ethics course at seminary (taught by an instructor of Mennonite background) Niebuhr and Pope were mandatory

should be noted that Niebuhr later corrected, if not repudiated, his first position.[9] But the damage had been done; his retraction has not begun to catch up with his original proposal.

This "hypersociological" view is founded upon several principles that must be seriously challenged: (1) A theory of socioeconomic determinism is certainly skirted, or implied, if not openly maintained: "The adoption of one or the other type of constitution is itself largely due to the social condition of those who form the sect or compose the church. In Protestant history the sect has ever been the child of an outcast minority, taking its rise in the religious revolts of the poor, of those who were without effective representation in church or state and who formed conventicles of dissent in the only way open to them, on the democratic, associational pattern."[10] Niebuhr underlined this assertion by proceeding to use "the churches of the disinherited" as a synonym for "sects." But if this be the truth, then to establish S.K. as a sectary signifies nothing more meaningful than to call attention to a freak situation in which one of the "inherited" (S.K. lived on his patrimony) talked like one of the "disinherited"—thus making S.K. "the poor man's theologian."

(2) Closely related to the above is the further assertion that sects inevitably and in comparatively short time evolve back into the church type: "The sociological character of sectarian-

---

reading—plus a paper by Ernest Lefever, written as a student project for classes taught by Niebuhr and Pope, in which Brethren history is interpreted according to Niebuhrian categories.

It is standard procedure in scholarly and even popular circles among the Brethren to thank God that we have evolved out of our infantile sectarianism to the place that we now rank as a denomination, or church, along with the best of them. And the article by Val Clear, "Reflections of a Postsectarian," *The Christian Century*, LXXX (Jan. 16, 1963), 72-75, suggests that the same mentality holds in other groups as well.

[9] H. Richard Niebuhr, *The Kingdom of God in America* (New York: Harper Torchbooks, 1959), pp. ix-x; cf. pp. 1ff.

[10] Niebuhr, *The Social Sources of Denominationalism*, p. 19.

ism, however, is almost always modified in the course of time by the natural processes of birth and death, and on this change in structure changes in doctrine and ethics inevitably follow. By its very nature the sectarian type of organization is valid only for one generation. . . . Compromise begins and the ethics of the sect approach the churchly type of morals. As with ethics, so with the doctrine, so also with the administration of religion. . . . So the sect becomes a church."[11] But this point, too, would have derogatory implications if allowed to stand as part of S.K.'s sectarianism. His witness, then, would be of no particular relevance or import, not a valid type but merely a primitive and transitory stage on the way to true churchism.

(3) The basic error of the hypersociologists, the point at which they lost contact with Troeltsch, seems to be this: they committed the *quid pro quo* of assuming that what they identified as sectarianism on the twentieth century, industrial, religiously pluralistic American scene is the same phenomenon that Troeltsch identified as sectarianism on the classic, Reformation, established-religion scene of sixteenth to eighteenth century Europe. It would be foolish to try to deny the accuracy of sociological case studies like those of Pope and others; they have established at least part of the truth about how modern "sects" arise and develop. But it does not follow that everything that has ever been known as a sect reflects the same pattern.

Troeltsch suggested that in the course of their history at least some sects do tend to change their nature and lose the purity of their primitive sectarianism.[12] But he did not interpret this as a natural evolution from sect into church propelled by a socioeconomic dynamic. He made a countersuggestion—and a much more emphatic one—which the sociolo-

---

[11] *Ibid.*, pp. 19-20.

[12] For example, the English Baptists (Troeltsch, *op.cit.*, Vol. II, pp. 707-08).

gists have overlooked: "The Church-type itself, just because of this element of tension between pure Christianity and adjustment to the world which exists within it, has had a very changeful history, and is to-day becoming entirely transformed. . . . Protestantism no longer represents the pure Church-type. . . . More and more the central life of the Church-type is being permeated with the vital energies of the sect and mysticism; the whole history of Protestantism reveals this very clearly."[13] Pope's statement that "movement on the scale between sect and church is, with minor exceptions, in one direction only,"[14] is seen to hold true only within his own narrow orientation.

Troeltsch's analysis seems eminently superior to that of the hypersociologists: the ecclesiological changes so readily apparent in Protestant history are not indicative of any dynamic principle within the typology itself but rather a breakdown and realignment of the whole typology in the face of a drastically changed world. This is not to say that churchly *tendencies* and sectarian *tendencies* are no longer operative or distinguishable; it is to say that the Troeltschian typology cannot be applied as clearly and cleanly to the contemporary scene as Troeltsch did it to the post-Reformation period.

Indeed, Troeltsch himself prohibited the transferral of his typology to the modern period. He concluded his long and masterful opus by saying:

"Our inquiry is over. It was possible to treat it exhaustively as far as the eighteenth century. . . . With the nineteenth century Church History entered upon a new phase of existence. As a result of the dissolution of the unity of civilization controlled by a State Church, combined with the development of the independence of modern thought, it has since then no longer possessed a fixed and objective ideal of unity. The result has been that the social philosophy of the Christian com-

[13] *Ibid.*, Vol. II, pp. 1007-09.
[14] Pope, *op.cit.*, p. 120.

munity has also suffered an undeniable disintegration, through its dependence upon continually changing conditions. . . . Under these circumstances it is impossible to give a description of the present situation, and to deduce from it principles for the future."[15]

And recent studies in the Radical Reformation strongly support Troeltsch's contention that uncritical shuffling between classic and modern sectarianism is out of order.[16]

Ours, then, is a plea for the right to use Troeltsch's concept of "sect" free from all implications that the hypersociological school has read back into it, a plea to disassociate "sect" from the image of store-front, fundamentalist, shouting churches of the poor white trash; for if this be sectarianism then there is no need to say anything more about S.K. being part of it.

We have used the term "Classic Protestant Sectarianism." The intention is specifically to distinguish "classic" (Troeltschian) sectarianism from "modern" (hypersociological) sectarianism. The word "Protestant," in turn, serves two purposes. First, it distinguishes the sectarianism in which we are interested from that of the Roman Catholic tradition. Scholars are agreed in tracing a sectarian strain through medieval Catholicism, leading up to and apparently affecting rather directly the radical wing of the Reformation. Without denying any of the real relationships and affinities between the Protestant and Catholic strains, it is apparent that they are enough different in character and milieu that they can and should be differentiated. And if S.K. was a sectary at all, surely he was one of the Protestant sort.

---

[15] Troeltsch, *op.cit.*, Vol. II, pp. 991-92.

[16] See particularly Claus-Peter Clasen, "The Sociology of Swabian Anabaptism," *Church History*, XXXII (1963), 150ff. Works such as Roland H. Bainton, *The Age of the Reformation* (Princeton: Van Nostrand, 1956) and Franklin Hamlin Littell, *The Origins of Sectarian Protestantism* (New York: Macmillan [1952] 1964), and George Huntston Williams, *op.cit.* and *The Radical Reformation* (Philadelphia: Westminster Press, 1962), are also to the point.

But in the second place, and perhaps more importantly, we use "Protestant" to mean "orthodox," or more precisely, "not heterodox." Of course in one sense the very fact that a sect is a sect indicates that it has slipped out of closely defined, churchly orthodoxy—ecclesiologically, if in no other way. We then are using orthodox in a rather broad sense, to include, say, any group that could have qualified according to the admission requirements of the present World and National Councils of Churches. Thus the word "Protestant" excludes the esoteric cults and the free-thinking, peripherally Christian societies which so frequently are classed together with the sects. Troeltsch took considerable pains to set up his typology precisely so that the sects could and would be distinguished from these other groups. We propose, then, to compare S.K. with Classic Protestant Sectarianism and nothing else.

So much for what we do not mean by "sectarianism"; we proceed to our proper work of explaining what we do mean. In what follows the spectrum analogy is my own contribution; the terminology and categories are drawn from Troeltsch; the description and analysis of those categories depend heavily upon Brunner.

The analogy which accounts for the accompanying chart is taken from the field of physics. It is a spectrum analysis of visible light. The background of the diagram is a continuous field of color, i.e. white light separated into all its constituent, monochromatic wavelengths. A number of implications from this spectrum are crucial to the analogy. The chart bears the names of what physicists call the seven primary, or rainbow, colors. Actually, however, there is nothing *primary* about them; they happen merely to be hues that are conspicuous to the human eye; they are not even arranged symmetrically on the spectrum.

Any given point on the scale is simply and only a specific wavelength of light; it is in no way dependent upon any other wavelength for its existence or definition. There is here no

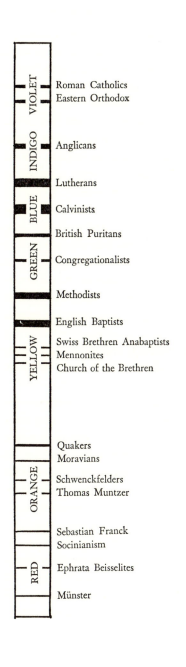

VIOLET — Roman Catholics / Eastern Orthodox

INDIGO — Anglicans

Lutherans

BLUE — Calvinists

British Puritans

GREEN — Congregationalists

Methodists

English Baptists

YELLOW — Swiss Brethren Anabaptists / Mennonites / Church of the Brethren

Quakers / Moravians

ORANGE — Schwenckfelders / Thomas Muntzer

Sebastian Franck / Socinianism

RED — Ephrata Beisselites

Münster

theory of color mixing; green is no more a mixture of yellow and blue than blue is a mixture of indigo and green. Greenish-yellow is just greenish-yellow, not some of green and some of yellow; it is only the limitation of our terminology that forces us to use a hybrid term; but the greenish-yellow is no less "pure" a color than is bright yellow itself. Likewise on the ecclesiological spectrum, no one type is any more "primary," any "truer," any "purer" than any other; the fact that a given church happens to fall directly on a primary color implies no value judgment one way or another.

Further, there is here absolutely no implication of movement or polar attraction. To move left from blue center is not to say that one *must* drift on into green (or vice versa); any point is as legitimate a stopping point as any other. Sooner or later, of course, value judgments will come into any discussion of ecclesiology, but the spectrum itself is purely descriptive; the chart has no way of defining what is a "good" spot for a church to fall.

Theoretically there is one wavelength that is yellower than those on either side of it, but as a matter of fact this can be only an arbitrary decision of the human eye. Yellow, then, must be considered as a *range* of wavelengths—but a range, note well, the outer boundaries of which simply cannot be defined, located, or demarcated. This does not mean that yellow is in any way a vague concept or that no real distinctions can be made between yellow and green. It does mean that yellow can be defined, discussed, and understood only by looking at the bright center, not by trying to determine how far it extends in either direction. Ask not, therefore, whether Methodism (for example) is in the yellow or in the green; it *is* more yellow than Congregationalism but more green than the Baptists.

Against the colorful background of the continuous spectrum appear dark, absorption markings known as Fraunhofer lines. These come about when a given substance betrays its presence and identifies itself by "blotting-up" the particular wavelengths of light that come at its characteristic spot on the spectrum. We propose to do for ecclesiology what Fraunhofer first did for sunlight by analyzing the spectrum and identifying certain of the lines.

Note that this spectrum and these lines hold only for the classic period, Europe of the sixteenth, seventeenth, and eighteenth centuries. We have heeded Troeltsch's warning that in the modern period the pattern has been so broken up that it is problematical whether the same techniques of analysis will apply. To put modern churches onto this same graph sooner or later would result in distortion—although, obviously, many of the ecclesiological principles explained by the chart still are in operation on the present-day scene. By the same token the line that does appear refers to the group as it existed during its primitive, classic phase; whether each or any of these is still operating on the same wavelength we will not venture to judge. Also, we have not attempted to include every group that could be spotted here; the proliferation (particularly toward the red end of the spectrum) is endless. Fraunhofer originally identified 754 lines out of the now more than 25,000 which have been discovered; our proportion is equally modest.

This spectrum enables us to arrive at rather precise definitions of some terms that commonly appear in ecclesiological analysis. In a number of cases we still will need to allow one word to carry several different meanings (because human language simply does not conform to discrete laws), but communication can be vastly improved nonetheless. In each case the definitions are listed in order from the broadest to the narrowest.

A. *Church*: (1) The spectrum as a whole, i.e. the ecumenical body of Christ.

(2) Any given line on the spectrum, i.e. *a* church, or *the* churches.

(3) Any line except those of the orange-red end of the spec-

trum, i.e. an organized, "orthodox" group as opposed to a "spiritual religion" or a "cult" (again, the admission requirements of the Councils of Churches might be taken as a rough measure).

(4) A line of the violet-indigo-blue-to-green end of the spectrum, i.e. an example of the Troeltschian "church"-type.

In most instances the context in which "church" is used will indicate the intended meaning; however, confusion is a real possibility when we realize that the first three definitions include the sects while the fourth specifically excludes them. Whenever, in the pages that follow, misunderstanding seems possible, we will use quotation marks to denote "church" in sense 4.

B. *Protestantism*: (1) Anything other than Roman Catholicism. Anglicans, Southern Baptists (despite their protests), and even the Eastern Orthodox churches tend to get pulled into this category.

(2) The indigo-blue-green-yellow-to-orange sector of the spectrum, i.e. all those groups whose heritage and theology trace back to the Reformation.

(3) The indigo-blue-to-green portion of the spectrum, i.e. the Reformation "churches" (Lutheran, Reformed, and Anglican).

Kierkegaard very often assumed a 3 usage, i.e. he spoke critically of "Protestantism," but in a way which, although applying directly to the Reformation "churches," could have little if any reference to the Reformation sects.

It is here appropriate to consider a crucial question: Were the sects truly Protestant or were they not? The only accurate solution is to have it both ways. This Troeltsch did very explicitly:

"[Anabaptist sectarianism] attacked the new theological dogmatism, the compulsory State Church, and the tendency to secularization [of the Reformation "churches"]. . . . The Anabaptists deliberately opposed the results of this compromise, and in so doing they opposed the whole idea of the Church, and of an ecclesiastical civilization. This violent opposition, however, proves that in reality it had been caused by the Reformation itself. . . .

"In the Baptist [read Anabaptist] movement we are dealing with a by-product of the Reformation, which is closely connected with the Scriptural purism and moral earnestness of the Reformation, but whose deep inward opposition to the ecclesiastical idea of the Reformers is also quite evident. . . . At bottom, therefore, the whole movement belonged to the Reformation. It was caused by the Reformation; it appealed to its principles and ideals, and it remained in closest touch with it. . . .

"In the last resort, however, the sect is a phenomenon which differs equally from the ecclesiastical spirit of Protestantism and of Catholicism. It is an independent branch of Christian thought; it is the complement of the Church-type, and it is based upon certain elements in the New Testament ideal."[17]

Insofar as they sought to reform the Reformation by appealing to Reformation principles and ideology, the sectaries surely admit the nomenclature "Protestant"—or even "Protestants' Protestants." But insofar as they drastically were opposed to the way the Protestant "churches" were taking, just as surely they must be differentiated from Protestantism. The only thing to do is to leave the word "Protestant" open so that the sects can be considered as both in and out.

C. *Sect*: (1) In an entirely neutral sense, synonymous with *Church* 2, i.e. referring to any line of the spectrum. This usage is somewhat antiquated though still found in legal documents.

(2) In an anything but neutral sense, referring to any position on the spectrum other than one's own, in short, a subtle way of impugning another church's pedigree. In this regard it is interesting to find in the literature of the sects depreciating references to the "churches" as being "sects"; sects as well as

17 Troeltsch, *op.cit.*, Vol. II, pp. 698, 699, 701.

churches found it in order to deplore the others' "sectarianism." It is in this sense that "sect" carries connotations of narrow-mindedness and fanaticism. But that the word connotes such derogation is no accident; "sect" was designed specifically as a swear word for bludgeoning one's ecclesiological enemies. It is undoubtedly in the effort to avoid this stigma that there has been some tendency of late to substitute the word "free church" for "sect." This, however, seems an unwise move, because, as we shall see, the term "free church" needs to be reserved for a slightly different concept. The better alternative is simply to live down, rise above, and transform the ugly word "sect"—just as has had to be done with "Yankee," "Protestant," and even "Christian."

(3) The green-yellow-orange-red end of the spectrum, i.e. anything other than a "church." This usage groups together too wide a range of ecclesiology to be meaningful—although it did come in handy when, for instance, a Lutheran wanted to imply that a Mennonite is no different than a Münsterite. But we see here a tendency that seems to affect ecclesiologists generally: they are able to make and maintain the finest distinctions in that area of the spectrum where they happen to live; but once they get a few shades beyond, they start expanding their categories in fine style. Troeltsch fought valiantly to prevent this from happening to "sect" when he spelled out a very clear distinction between "yellow" and "red";[18] would that it had been kept as clear since.

(4) The green-yellow-to-orange middle of the spectrum. This is a broad, generic usage of "sectarianism," but, we maintain, a proper one.

(5) The yellow range of the spectrum. This is the more specific and technical but equally proper use of the term.

In the pages that follow we will *not* use "sect" in sense 1; we expressly deny senses 2 and 3; we may use 4 at times; but

[18] Troeltsch, *op.cit.*, Vol. II, pp. 742ff.

for the most part we intend the closer distinction of 5. For instance, as regards S.K., our thesis is not merely that he shows certain 4-type sectarian tendencies but that his own Fraunhofer line would fall in the bright yellow of 5.

D. *Free Church*: (1) Synonymous with *Sect* 4. As we have noted, there is some tendency to use this as a nice word—or at least a later terminology—for "sect." Troeltsch used the term "free church," but in another sense.

(2) The green range of the spectrum. Troeltsch's usage would indicate that "free church" is primarily of British origin, referring to those British churches which were different from "churches" in that they had adopted the principle of voluntary membership but which also were different from the sects in that they still retained such churchly marks as infant baptism, creeds and confessions, a strong clerical caste (or episcopacy), etc.[19]

We will follow Troeltsch and avoid usage 1; thus is made possible a real and significant distinction which otherwise would be lost.

E. *Spiritual religion*: The red-to-orange end of the spectrum. The word "spiritual" suggests that direct inspiration here begins to dominate over the objective biblical and historical controls that have given the church its form and structure up to this point.

Troeltsch used the terms "mysticism" and "spiritual religion" interchangeably, although it can be questioned whether "mysticism" is an ecclesiologically useful term at all. In fact, the word means so many things to so many people that we would prefer to avoid it altogether.

Frankly, our typology encounters difficulty at the red end, not because the pattern fails, but because spiritual religion can take either of two different lines of development. Both strains clearly classify as spiritual religion, but they are distinct

[19] Troeltsch, *op.cit.*, Vol. II, pp. 656ff.

enough to require separate terms in identifying them. Spiritual religion, then, shows itself either as "atomism" or as "cult."

F. *Atomism*: The phenomenon of the red end of the spectrum in which the concept "church" is dissolved into an ultra-individualistic, totally unstructured independency.

G. *Cult*: The other phenomenon of the red end, in which the group is structured and organized—as opposed to atomism—but over an esoteric, directly revealed pattern, i.e. depending upon a special, private revelation (and we would include throwbacks to Old Testament modes) rather than upon the New Testament norm.

In all of the foregoing we have attempted to follow Troeltsch as closely as possible. He did not propose a spectrum, but the terminology is his, and our "colorful" definitions are intended to conform with his usage. The one exception regards the bipartite division of spiritual religion; Troeltsch simply left out of account those groups which we have denominated cults. It is important that they be included in the picture, if for no other reason than that they do not unconsciously get slipped in with the yellow sects, where they do *not* belong. Rather, they seem clearly to qualify under spiritual religion, as we have proposed.

There is one other basic term which can and should be related to the spectrum. We are still following Troeltsch in suggesting that *Pietism* cannot be located at a point or even on a range of the spectrum. It is a broad, unfocused movement of sectarian tendency and emphasizing many sectarian motifs, but ecclesiologically it has manifested itself in different ways at different points of the spectrum. For example, the main thrust of German Pietism under the aegis of Spener and Francke deeply influenced the life of the Lutheran Church but without changing its "blue" status. Even so, Pietist influences did loom large in accounting for the green of Methodism, the yellow of the Church of the Brethren, the orange of

Moravianism, the atomist red of men like Tersteegen and
Ernst Christoph Hochmann, and the cultic red of groups like
the Ronsdorfers and Buttlarites.

When written with the small "p," we intend pietism as referring to this sort of tendency whenever, wherever, and on
whatever part of the scale it appears. Capital "P" Pietism refers to the identifiable historical movement originating within
the Lutheran Church of the seventeenth and eighteenth centuries, organized around Spener and Francke. Radical Pietism refers to the left wing of this movement, which manifested itself in the red-to-orange end of the spectrum.

At this point we turn to Brunner for help in analyzing the
ideological content of our spectrum. It is not easy to fit Brunner's discussion of ecclesiology into this Troeltschian framework, for Brunner chose to ignore his predecessor and operate
within an entirely different scheme of thought. However, it
is our assumption that the concepts of the two men are compatible, and the following represents a rigorous effort to correlate them.

What has been said heretofore would indicate that "sectarianism" is predominantly, if not exclusively, an *ecclesiological* concept, i.e. one referring to a doctrine of the nature
and form of the church. This is a misimpression we shall be at
some pains to correct; sectarianism is a *religious perspective*
which includes a whole catena of beliefs. A particular value
of Brunner's presentation is its demonstration of how ecclesiology depends upon and immediately involves a wide range
of interests. He quotes with approval the formula "ecclesiology
is Christology and Christology ecclesiology";[20] and it would
be just as accurate, in addition to "Christology," to read
"pneumatology," "pistology," and even "sociology."

However, many scholars seem to have a penchant for grasping *one* of these doctrinal strands, making it the key, and rel-
egating the others to subsidiary status. But this is as futile an

[20] Brunner, *Dogmatics III*, p. 40.

exercise as, say, trying to identify *the* central principle of Reformation thought: is it the sovereignty of God (theonomy), the authority of scripture, justification by faith alone, or a felt existential need for salvation? Obviously one can start with any of these and immediately proceed to any and all of the others; all were integrally involved in the Protestant development; and there is nothing to be gained by trying to give one preeminence over the rest. Just so with sectarianism; we are dealing with a core of principles, not a core principle.

Thus we have chosen ecclesiology as the principle for the *constructing* of our spectrum, not by way of implying that a sectary chooses to become such on the basis of a conviction about the nature and form of the church (this may or may not be the case), but because, in ecclesiology, doctrine must manifest itself in concrete ways that can be plotted and dissected much more precisely than would be the case with Christology, pneumatology, or whatever. We will see, however, that the spectrum now can be *interpreted* according to these other principles as well as by the outward form of church organization. Henceforth, then, we intend "sectarianism" to imply a total religious perspective and not simply a doctrine of the church.

Ecclesiology: Approached from this point of view, the spectrum represents something like the following. In the violet range the church is understood as: a (1) hierarchically authoritative (priestly dominated), (2) formally constituted (the entire life and organization of the church is closely prescribed by church law), (3) territorially comprehensive (the church is coincident with the community and the citizenry belongs to the church as a matter of course) (4) institution (in contrast to a fellowship, or *Gemeinde*) transmitting (5) an objective deposit of grace through (6) *ex opere operato* sacraments administered by (7) a sacrosanct priesthood.

In the blue sector, (1) hierarchical control is greatly weakened but there is still a strong clergy/laity distinction. (2) The life of the church is still rather highly prescribed though perhaps less so than in the violet. (3) There is no change as to territorial comprehension. (4) The church is still essentially an institution. (5) There has been a radical shift at this point, for the "objective deposit" is now understood as (6) "the Word of God," a much more personal and subjective entity than the sacraments. However, this "Word" is still highly objectivized through the emphasis upon its dogmatic definition in creed, confession, and symbol. It must therefore be administered by (7) an academically, theologically qualified clergy.

In the green, there is a general "loosening-up" in all categories, but the drastic change comes in (3) territorial comprehension, because the church now is disestablished and membership is voluntary. (5, 6) Religious experience, as opposed to dogmatic definition, is growing in prominence, but there is still (4) a rather strong institutional bent seen in the retention of such churchly accouterments as infant baptism, creeds, clerical authority, vestments, etc.

In the yellow of sectarianism, (1) the government of the church is completely democratic and nonauthoritarian, strongly congregational in its orientation. The clergy/laity distinction has become a purely functional one, without any sacerdotal implications whatsoever, although the group is still highly enough structured as to require "offices." (2) Worship and church life have become quite free and informal; vestments, liturgy, the church year, orders of worship—all have been sloughed away. The sacraments have been retained as acts of obedience to New Testament commands, but they are called "ordinances" expressly to avoid the churchly implications of "sacrament." (3) Membership is now emphatically voluntary, and infant baptism has been rejected in becoming consistent with that emphasis. Further, any sort of territorial consciousness has been completely transcended; wherever two or three members happen to be, there is their church; political boundaries are beneath their notice. (4) The church is now essentially a *Gemeinde* rather than an institution. (5, 6) The Word of God still stands as a powerfully objective norm, but the dogmatic understanding of that Word has been radically deemphasized; any sort of creedal definition has been expressly rejected, and systematic theology has lost its appeal. The Word of God now must involve the inner movings and leadings of the Spirit—in conjunction with the objective authority of its written letter.[21] (7) The written Word is interpreted and the living Word experienced directly—though by the *Gemeinde* rather than by individuals in isolation—so there is no need for the mediatorial role of a clergy.

In the orange sector the church begins to lose all structure. (1) There is now no clergy, even in the functional sense. (2) Outward organization is at a minimum, and the sacraments are not observed even as ordinances. (5, 6) The Bible begins to lose its role as either a pattern of organization or a definition of faith. The subjective action of the Spirit is moving into domination.

In the red sector, under the alternative of *Atomism*, the concept of the church as a structured fellowship is gone, and there are left only individual Christians, each under the direct operation of the Spirit within him. Under the alternative of *Cult*, organization and even institutionalism again appear, but the New Testament revelation is no longer normative; that objective standard now has been replaced by another, namely esoteric, private, extrabiblical inspiration.

Enthusiasm: This word customarily has been used in a highly prejudicial sense, but if understood etymologically as the immediate action of God within the heart, it becomes the

---

[21] Notice in this regard that any sort of biblicism or moralistic legalism, although an error into which sects as well as churches often have fallen, is not an inherent aspect of sectarianism but actually an anti-sectarian trend in the direction of objectivization rather than greater freedom of the Spirit.

accurate designation for one of the core principles of sectarianism (not as entirely different from or independent of ecclesiology but as a closely related aspect of the total religious perspective). Brunner makes the connection explicit when he gives over the first chapter of his ecclesiology to a discussion of the work of the Holy Spirit.

Our spectrum can be read as gradations of enthusiasm, though in such case it will not allow as many and as fine distinctions as when we read it ecclesiologically. Now the chart is essentially bipolar. At the violet end, the revelation of God is understood predominantly (if not exclusively) in *objective* terms by way of sacraments, the scriptural word, creeds, dogmatics, institutions. At the red end, God's revelation is understood predominantly (if not exclusively) as *subjective*, as the immediate, inner working of the Spirit. Sectarianism falls midway between these two poles and is seen to be an attempt at retaining the authority of the normative, objective biblical revelation while yet giving due place to the enthusiastic role of the Holy Spirit.

In this regard we note the appearance of a pattern which will recur time and again and which thus becomes part of the basic dynamic of sectarianism. The sectary, in virtue of his place on the spectrum, is by nature a dialectician (though for the most part subconsciously so) striving to maintain a balance between two complementary principles. Thus it is perhaps not entirely by accident that S.K., the sharpest dialectician of all time, also should show up in the yellow center.

Faith: As Brunner's book moves from pneumatology into ecclesiology, so does it move from ecclesiology into pistology. Our spectrum can be interpreted according to the nature of faith. At the violet end, faith is correct beliefs: "Faith was misunderstood as affirmation of doctrine or facts. In this manner correct doctrine became the object of faith. . . . At the same time as the priestly sacramental institution there came into

61

being 'orthodoxy,' the belief in true doctrine, and the guarantee of this belief by Church creed or dogma."[22] At the red end, which is only implied in Brunner, faith is *life*, the pious life of love: "It doesn't matter what you believe, your manner of living is what counts." The middle way of dialectical balance is ascribed by Brunner to the New Testament church, but it is also a characteristic of sectarianism: "Thus the Ekklesia has to bear a double witness to Christ, through the *Word* that tells of what He has bestowed upon it, and through the witness of its *life*, through its being, which points to Him as its vital source. These two testimonies of the Ekklesia through Word and life corroborate each other, and neither is fully effective without the other. . . . True faith is indivisibly both, faith in Christ and existence in Christ."[23]

Individualism: Here again the spectrum consists of gradations between two poles. The violet extreme understands the church to be a *collective*. Brunner puts the matter most succinctly: "The interpretation of *communio sanctorum* in the neuter sense is the source of spiritual collectivism, which confuses the nature of fellowship with the nature of participation in a thing. The thought of a *sanctum* in which individuals participate has no place in the New Testament. For "that" in which the individuals participate is precisely not a thing, but a Person—the Christ. *Participatio* in something creates a collective; fellowship with the Christ creates fellowship with one another."[24] The red extreme of atomism (which, again, is not in Brunner's picture) rejects sociality, sees the church—if church it may be called—as ultraindividualistic, every man for himself. Sectarianism is the dialectical attempt to recognize both the corporate and the individual aspects of Christianity through "fellowship" (*Gemeinschaft*).

The Work of Christ: Although this principle may not operate on the spectrum quite as neatly as some of the others,

[22] Brunner, *Dogmatics III*, p. 135; cf. pp. 134ff.
[23] *Ibid.*, pp. 134-36.　　　　[24] *Ibid.*, p. 27.

it does seem to have a valid application. At the violet end, the work of Christ is seen predominantly (if not exclusively) as atonement and justification—thus the emphasis is on "the Christ of faith." At the red end, particularly among some of the atomists (and admittedly it is here that the pattern might be a little difficult to demonstrate), the work of Christ is seen predominantly, if not exclusively, as that of teacher and model —thus the emphasis is on "the historical Jesus." In the yellow center (and here the pattern is again very clear) there is once more the attempt to give dialectical recognition to both emphases; the sects give much more attention to discipleship (*Nachfolge*) than do the churches, while striving nonetheless to retain a strong concept of Christ as divine Savior.

Relation to the World: This is a very real aspect of sectarianism which, unfortunately, has been emphasized out of all proportion. Even Troeltsch tended to make it central; the "hypersociological school" would make it all-controlling. However, we can recognize the truth in the position without following the sociologists all the way. In particular, we maintain that *for the most part* (and especially so during the classic period) the sectarianism of a person's faith determined his relationship to the world rather than his status in the world determining the sectarianism of his faith.

This reading of the spectrum has some resemblance to H. Richard Niebuhr's famous "Christ . . . Culture" typology[25] and perhaps can be correlated with it to a certain extent. However, our interest goes only far enough to cast some light on the nature of sectarianism; we will not attempt a detailed analysis of all the various options of Christian social ethics.

At the violet pole stands "the Church *of* (ideally, *in control of*) the World"; at the red pole stands "the Church *outside of* the World," disdainful of and inimical toward all worldly values and influences. At the yellow center stands the sect, "the Church *in tension with* the World," striving to be *in* the world

[25] See Niebuhr's *Christ and Culture* (New York: Harper, 1951).

in a real and influential sense while not being *of* the world. Again, the dialectical balance is a fine one; and in this case historical reality tended to confuse the matter, because the classical sects also were *kicked out* of the world. Thus it is not easy to discern to what extent the sectary's actual relationship to the world manifested his ideology or his misfortune; to achieve a balance between *in* the world but *not of* the world is particularly difficult when one is not wanted in the world.

There probably are other doctrines and principles that could be read into—or explicated out of—the spectrum. The goal we have had in mind is not a definitive presentation but merely the clarification of what we intend by "sectarianism," the sort of sectarianism with which we propose that Søren Kierkegaard be affiliated.

However, as we stand poised to begin in earnest the demonstration of S.K.'s sectarianism we are faced with a major procedural problem: What is the body of sectarian literature to which the Kierkegaardian literature should be compared? From what writings are we to draw the motifs, markings, and clues of sectarianism for which we hope to find counterparts in the works of S.K.? We could let any and all writers of such bent speak for this view of radical discipleship. This at once would make our project easy—and valueless—for we could then compare S.K. with John Wesley at one point, with George Fox at another, with Menno Simons at another, roaming the field at will. And of course somewhere among such a host of writers one could find a quotation that would parallel almost anything ever written by S.K.—or anyone else for that matter. Certainly our demonstration would be much more possible and convincing if we were to pick just one, typical sect as a "control" and then make the comparison straight across. If S.K.'s ideology shows any marked resemblance to that of one such sect, then surely it may be assumed that S.K.'s religious orientation is essentially akin to that of classic, Protestant sectarianism.

The group we have selected to serve as this "control" is the eighteenth century Brethren (forerunner of the modern Church of the Brethren and related bodies). In the first place, it is inconceivable that anyone might argue that this was not a typical sect; it has all the hallmarks. In the second place, this does make a direct comparison quite possible; the collection of eighteenth century Brethren writings actually is much smaller than the collected writings of S.K. There is no problem in ascertaining what the Brethren believed and stood for; their writings display little or no variation of opinion among themselves; they represent more of a fixed quantity than does the single author Kierkegaard. And furthermore, our case can be made by using the Brethren; there is no need to go beyond their writings in order to get a fully rounded picture either of sectarianism or of S.K.'s relationship to it.

It must be made emphatic at the outset that no claim is either intended or implied regarding any sort of special connection or affinity between S.K. and the Brethren per se. Indeed, we are not even suggesting that S.K. would have joined the Brethren (or any other sect) had the opportunity presented itself; there are a whole gamut of personal factors that make such a matter totally unpredictable. However, the Brethren can be used—and here are to be used—simply as an example of a broad religious perspective for which, we are convinced, S.K. does show a real and basic propensity.

CHAPTER IV

A SECT CALLED THE DUNKERS

Franklin . . . mentions a sect,

the Dunkers,

who would not compose a written creed. . . .[1]

If we are to use the Brethren as the control of our comparison, it would be well to know something about the sect.[2] What

[1] *Papirer*, X^4 A 73 (1851) [my trans.—V.E.].

[2] The definitive history of the church's origin and earliest, European phase (to c. 1730) is Donald F. Durnbaugh's *Brethren Beginnings: The Origins of the Church of the Brethren in Early Eighteenth-Century Europe*, hereafter referred to as *Beginnings* (unpublished Ph.D. dissertation, Un. of Pennsylvania, 1960). Much of the same information, though in a quite different format, has been published by Durnbaugh in *European Origins of the Brethren*, hereafter referred to as *Origins* (Elgin, Ill.: Brethren Press, 1958); this is a source book reproducing many of the primary documents from which Durnbaugh wrote his dissertation.

There is no such adequate source covering the American phase of Brethren history through the eighteenth century. The greatest amount of factual material is preserved in the first and thus "classic" Brethren history, namely, Martin Grove Brumbaugh's *A History of the German Baptist Brethren in Europe and America* (Mt. Morris, Ill.: Brethren Publishing House, 1899). Brumbaugh had access to more primary source material than ever has been available since, and to this degree his work is irreplaceable—though Durnbaugh must take precedence in every respect as regards the European period. However, Brumbaugh's

follows, then, is a brief account of Brethren beginnings and history through the eighteenth century, designed to establish the acquaintance and introduce the men whose writings will be quoted in the study proper. As a convenience to the reader, each author's name is italicized as it appears for the first time.

The "pure" initial phase of Brethren sectarianism extended through two generations of leadership during most of the eighteenth century. It is with Brethren thought of this period —and only this period—that we propose to compare the thought of Kierkegaard. In one respect our control group does not conform to the standards of Classic Protestant Sectarianism upon which we insisted so strongly in the previous chapter; for the greater part of the century the sect was located in pluralistic America rather than state-church Europe. This forms no obstacle, however, for the group spent its formative years in the state-church environment and even in America lived in sufficient cultural and linguistic isolation to be constitutionally unaffected at least for the period of our study. The eighteenth century Brethren are as typically sectarian as any example that could be found.

The founding fathers did not choose to give the sect a name but let people refer to it as they would; thus, particularly in the earliest sources, quite a variety of nomenclature is

---

book is not the best sort of history writing: it is not well organized; it is very inadequately documented; it abounds in factual errors and unwarranted conclusions. But although it must be used with caution, nothing has appeared to succeed it.

Floyd E. Mallott's *Studies in Brethren History* (Elgin, Ill.: Brethren Publishing House, 1954) is a more recent and more scholarly treatment, but because it covers almost 250 years of history in comparatively brief compass, it cannot afford nearly as much information regarding the eighteenth century as does Brumbaugh.

A most valuable resource for the study of Brethren history is the bibliography compiled by Donald Durnbaugh and Lawrence Shultz, an attempt to construct an exhaustive listing of books and pamphlets written by Brethren authors from the origin of the church until 1963. It is found in *Brethren Life and Thought*, IX, 1-2 (combined) and XI, 2.

found.[3] In America, when a legal name became a necessity, German Baptist Brethren eventually was settled upon. The Church of the Brethren, the name of the main wing of the denomination today, is of twentieth century origin. However, the label by which the group was most widely known until quite recent times is "the Dunkers," a fun-poking Anglicizing of the German word "to dip," referring, of course, to the practice of baptism by immersion. We customarily will use the "timeless" designation, the Brethren, although Dunkers also is an acceptable usage that no longer carries offensive connotations.

Alexander Mack (1679–1735) clearly was the leader of the original group of Brethren and thus, in a real sense, the founder of the church. In another sense, however, he lacked many of the marks that usually go with founders. At no time has there been any inclination for the church to bear his name either officially or popularly. His writings have never become symbolical or even authoritative. There is no evidence that his theological views dominated the group. And though he certainly was a respected and beloved leader, there is nothing to suggest that he "controlled" the church or that it felt particularly beholden to him.

Nevertheless, Mack's personal history is of significance, simply because it is so representative of the religious development of the founding Brethren as a group.[4] He was born July 27, 1679, in Schriesheim, a village of the Rhenish Palatinate, some five miles north of the university town of Heidelberg. He was reared in the German Reformed Church, as were most of the early Brethren. His father was a prosperous millowner (whose mill Alexander later inherited) who had been at times mayor

[3] See Durnbaugh, *Origins*, p. 14, and *Beginnings*, p. 1.
[4] The best account of Mack's background is the sketch by Hermann Brunn, "Alexander Mack, The Founder, 1679-1735," in *Schwarzenau, Yesterday and Today*, ed. Lawrence W. Shultz (published by the editor, 1954), pp. 37ff.

and a member of both the town and church councils. Alexander had uncles connected with the city and university administrations in Heidelberg; his father-in-law operated the village guesthouse; and his wife's grandfather had been a mayor of Heidelberg. Most of the early Brethren were of the propertied "burger" class rather than the peasantry; this sect was *not* "a church of the disinherited."

Growing up in Germany contemporaneously with Alexander Mack was the Pietist movement, centering in the Lutheran church of Spener and Francke but actually sweeping the entire religious scene.[5] Out of Pietism proper developed a left wing, Radical Pietism.[6] Whereas Pietism proper remained within the context of the state churches, the Radical Pietists left the church. Many went the way of "atomism";[7] some formed "cults."

Radical Pietism—which, of course, was illegal in the state-church situation—"infiltrated" the Palatinate during the opening years of the eighteenth century, and the young Alexander Mack was one of those it captured. The particular separatist leader who influenced Mack and became his tutor was Ernst

[5] A brief account of the Pietist movement is given in Durnbaugh, *Origins*, pp. 32-34, and *Beginnings*, pp. 1-4, but the best full-length treatment is Dale W. Brown's *The Problem of Subjectivism in Pietism* (unpublished Ph.D. dissertation, Northwestern Un., 1962). Brown provides a thoroughgoing description of Pietism in the process of analyzing the problem of its subjectivism.

[6] Durnbaugh's *Origins* also includes a brief account of Radical Pietism, pp. 35-36; *Beginnings* gives a longer sketch, pp. 4ff.; but the full-length treatment that establishes the concept and gives it definitive analysis is C. David Ensign's *Radical German Pietism (c. 1675-c. 1760)* (unpublished Ph.D. dissertation, Boston Un., 1955).

[7] In the German-Pietist-Brethren milieu, "separatism" is the term used for a personal Christianity practiced apart from any organized church. We avoided the term in previous chapters and coined the phrase "spiritual atomism" because, of course, in British usage "separatism" identifies an entirely different phenomenon. However, in discussing the Brethren we will revert to the term "separatism," which is the proper one in this context.

Christoph Hochmann von Hochenau (1670–1721), one of the more sane and level-headed of the Radicals.[8] When Mack's new affiliation became known it meant a break with his home, his church, his community—and the loss of his patrimony. In 1706 Mack and his young family fled Schriesheim as religious refugees, finally settling in Wittgenstein in the little village of Schwarzenau, a place where separatists were tolerated, where Hochmann had established something of a headquarters, and where others of his "disinherited" followers were tending to congregate. It was out of this group that the Brethren were to be organized.

At Schwarzenau, Mack and a handful of others soon became deeply dissatisfied with the lack of order and discipline that "spiritual religion" entailed, particularly the wild excesses of some of the cults in the area; they became convinced that the New Testament prescribed at least some rudiments of outward organization. It is clear that at least part of the influence pushing the Brethren-to-be in this direction was that of Reformation Anabaptism, mediated through the Mennonites who were active (or at least extant; their faith was much deteriorated from what it had been in the sixteenth century) within the realm of Mack's contacts. This growing interest in order and outward obedience tended to focus upon baptism as the symbol of disciplined, corporate Christian life and witness within a *Gemeinde*.

Thus, in 1708, in the River Eder at Schwarzenau, eight persons (three couples and two single men) were baptized by trine immersion.[9] This act marked the founding of the sect and a clean, decisive break with separatistic Radical Pietism.

[8] A brief account of Hochmann appears in Durnbaugh's *Beginnings,* pp. 10-12; the definitive biography is Heinz Renkewitz's *Hochmann von Hochenau* (Breslau, 1935).

[9] Lots were cast to determine who should baptize Mack, who then proceeded to baptize the other seven. But the name of that first baptizer and the exact date of the baptism purposely were suppressed in order to forestall any later inclinations toward "founder worship."

Thus in two deliberate and well-demarcated moves—the first, their earlier, individual leave-takings from the established church; the second, their act of baptism—the Brethren had distinguished themselves from churchism on the right and from spiritual religion on the left and had taken their stand in sectarianism.

In the process of comparing S.K. and the Brethren we will, of course, be examining and documenting the entire gamut of Brethren belief and practice. However, it would seem helpful in this introduction to include at least a brief summary of Brethren thought as a background against which to understand the chapters that follow.

Clearly the two major streams of historical influence that molded original Brethrenism were: (1) Radical Pietism, particularly of Hochmann's variety, and (2) Anabaptism, mediated by contemporary Mennonites and the literature they possessed.[10] We must not overlook the very real though more indirect influences of the Calvinism in which most of the early Brethren had been reared and of the "churchly" Pietism that formed the background of the more radical strain; but these are secondary.

Yet Radical Pietism and Anabaptism are not simply two ingredients of a blend (in which case the analytical problem would be to determine the proportions of each); rather, they are the two poles of the dialectical tension out of which Brethrenism was created and within which its existence had to be maintained.

[10] Donald Durnbaugh has done a consummate job of tracing the historical role of these two factors, summarizing earlier discussion of their relationship and presenting his own analysis, in a two-part article, "The Genius of the Brethren," *Brethren Life and Thought*, IV, 1-2 (1959), 4ff. in both issues. Though I have no quarrel with his evidence and its treatment, I do feel the need of modifying the entire framework in which the discussion has taken place. My position has been presented in detail in my article, "On Epitomizing the Brethren," *Brethren Life and Thought*, VI, 4 (1961), 47ff. Much of what follows is quoted from that piece.

This dialectic can be charted and made graphic with the aid of a drawing, namely the personal emblem, or seal, of Alexander Mack, Jr., which in recent years has been popularized as something of a symbol for the church as a whole. Around this emblem we have constructed the accompanying chart.[11] It is divided into three columns: a Brethren column sandwiched between the Anabaptist column and the Radical Pietist. Prominent in the Brethren column is the Mack seal, which is composed of three elements. The first, a cross, can represent the ecumenical Christian background which is held in common by the Brethren, Anabaptists, Radical Pietists, and indeed all the groups that make up the ecclesiological spectrum. In our effort to portray what is distinctive about Brethrenism (and sectarianism) it would be unfortunate were we to lose sight of its basic orientation toward the faith that is common to all Christians. Similarly, this cross could be taken as emblematic of the solid Protestant orthodoxy which the founding Brethren had inherited. All of the first generation were reared and educated in the state churches, and their defection from these did in no way mark a renunciation of all they had received there.

The other two elements of the seal, the heart and the fruit, can be used to symbolize the distinctive emphases of Radical Pietism and Anabaptism respectively. The heart is most appropriate as a visual sign for the Radical Pietist ideology. Similarly, its motto could have been *"Love* Jesus"; its goal, the line from a hymn of English Pietism: "O, for *a closer walk* with God." The focus of faith is *inner* experience. The quota-

[11] The quotation from Menno Simons is found in his "Foundation of Christian Doctrine [1539]," in *The Complete Writings of Menno Simons*, trans. Leonard Verduin (Scottdale, Pa.: Herald Press, 1956), p. 111. The quotation by Mack Senior comes from his "Rights and Ordinances [1715]," in Durnbaugh, *Origins*, pp. 384-85. The quotation by Hochmann is from his "Letter to Count von Solms [1708]," in Durnbaugh, *Origins*, p. 126. The quotation by Mack Junior is from his "Foreword to 'Rights and Ordinances' [1774]," in Durnbaugh, *Origins*, p. 120.

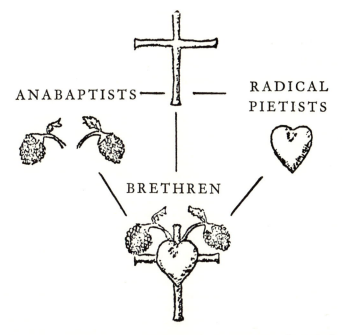

tion from Mack's mentor, the Radical Pietist leader Hochmann, is an eloquent summary of the position which, above
all, stressed the *affective* aspects of the Christian life.

On the opposite side of the chart, the fruit of the vine (John
15:1–11) is a visual symbol of Anabaptism. The motto is:
"*Obey* Jesus." The goal is restitution of the primitive Christian
life and church order, the Ekklesia. And the focus of the ideology is upon outward obedience, or fruitbearing. Notice how
the quotation from Menno revolves around "commandments,"
"a pious, penitent life as the scriptures teach," "power and
works," and "fruit"—the *effective* aspects of the Christian life.

The Brethren symbol includes both the heart and the fruit.
Take away either of these components and it is no longer
Brethrenism that is symbolized. Let either gain the ascendancy
and the picture of Brethrenism is correspondingly distorted.

ANABAPTISTS BRETHREN RADICAL PIETISTS

Obey Jesus

Restitution of the early Christian life and church order

outward obedience

What does it profit to speak much of Christ and his word, if we do not believe him, and refuse to obey his commandments? Again I say, awake and tear the accursed unbelief with its unrighteousness from your hearts, and commence a pious, penitent life as the Scriptures teach. . . . We are referring to a penitence possessed of power and works, such as John the Baptist taught saying: Bear fruit that befits repentance.

(*Menno Simons*)

That which the Holy Spirit ordained for the faithful was written outwardly. All believers are united in it, for the Holy Spirit teaches them inwardly just as the Scriptures teach them outwardly. . . . Therefore, when a believing person whose inner ears are opened reads the Holy Scriptures outwardly, he will hear as the Lord Jesus intends his teaching to be understood. He hears that which the apostles want to express in their writings. He will also be impelled, through his inner hearing, to true obedience which makes him obey even in outward matters. Outwardly, he reads the Scriptures in faith and hears the inner word of life which gives him strength and power to follow Jesus.

(*Alexander Mack*)

Love Jesus

"O, for *a closer walk* with God"

inner experience

To sum up, my feeling is briefly aimed therein that one must seek Jesus in one's heart as the only true foundation of salvation and the heart must be completely purified through the true living faith in Jesus. In case it is wished to perform in true singleness of heart also those outward actions which the first Christians did in addition to these inner unmovable bases, I cannot consider this a mortal sin, if one only remains in impartial love toward those who cannot feel in their minds this necessity for these outward acts. The freedom of Christ suffers neither force nor laws.

(*E. C. Hochmann*)

Some *felt powerfully drawn* to seek again *the footsteps* of the first Christians. They *passionately yearned* to avail themselves in faith of the *ordained testimonies of Jesus Christ* according to their right value. At the same time, it was emphatically *opened to them in their hearts* how necessary is *obedience in faith* if a soul wishes to be saved.

(*the origin of the Church of the Brethren as described by Alexander Mack, Jr.*)

Notice in the quotation from Mack's *Rights and Ordinances* how inner experience and outward obedience appear together. The two are not synthesized, nor is the combination an eclectic one; they are held in creative tension. And as shall appear subsequently, it is nothing short of amazing how often and in regard to how many different doctrines and practices eighteenth century Brethren writers followed this pattern, playing off inner experience against outward obedience and then outward obedience against inner experience.

Notice, also, the more subtle expression of the dialectic as it appears at the bottom of the chart in the younger Mack's description of how the church was founded, the earliest such written account. "Felt powerfully drawn," "passionately yearned," and "opened to them in their hearts" are all Radical Pietist phrases describing inner experience. And yet without exception these phrases are coupled to an Anabaptist emphasis on outward obedience: "the footsteps of the first Christians," "ordained testimonies of Jesus Christ," "obedience in faith."

When this dialectic operated as it should, the two emphases checked and balanced each other. When the Radical Pietist tendency would slide off into subjectivism, private inspiration, mysticism, enthusiasm, or vaporous spiritualism, it was pulled up short by the demand for concrete, outward obedience to an objective scriptural norm. Conversely, when the Anabaptist tendency would slide off into formalism, legalism, biblical literalism, or works-righteousness, it was checked by the reminder that faith is essentially a work of God in the heart of the individual believer, an intensely personal relationship rather than a legal one. Thus, within Brethrenism, Anabaptist influences *disciplined* Pietism at the same time that Pietist influences *inspired* Anabaptism.[12]

[12] Although the above analysis gets at the heart of Brethren ideology, it must be admitted that the historical process itself was not quite as symmetrical as the chart would indicate. Several factors served to complicate the picture. In the first place, Radical Pietism was much more

75

An understanding of this dialectic also makes it rather easy to explain what happened to the Brethren in the early nineteenth century when they exchanged their pure, primitive sectarianism for something less attractive. It is not easy to live in a dialectic relationship where nothing is fastened down once for all, not easy to *keep* one's balance in a dynamic situation which means that one continually must be *regaining* one's balance, not easy to swim and keep swimming in seventy thousand fathoms of water (as S.K. would put it).

After a hundred years the Brethren got tired. Their recourse was not to abandon their previous beliefs and practices but to try to stabilize the situation which hitherto had been dialectical. Legalistic biblicism and microscopically detailed legislation by the Annual Meeting were used to guy into place the inherited ideology. But although this did have the effect of preserving the inheritance, it killed it in the process. Once the dialectic movement was halted, all the earlier dynamic of the faith was gone as well.

This phase could not last long among the Brethren, how-

---

extreme and unbalanced in its emphasis than Anabaptism was in its— although the zeal and evangelistic fervor that Pietism stressed were precisely what the Brethren found lacking in the Mennonites of their day. On this point we need to be aware of the distinction which Mack himself made, namely that between the idealism of the older Anabaptist writers whose works he consulted and the "deteriorated" faith of the Mennonites with whom he came in contact (see Mack's "Basic Questions," in Durnbaugh, *Origins*, pp. 340, 342-43). The latter were as much in need of some Pietist "life" as the Radical Pietists were of some Anabaptist "backbone."

Another factor ruining the symmetry is that because the Brethren came into being as a break-out from Radical Pietism rather than Anabaptism, they continually had to answer charges from their former colleagues of the Pietist quarter. Almost all of eighteenth century Brethren doctrinal writings arose out of this situation and represent the pull away from Radical Pietism toward Anabaptism. The pull in the other direction, away from Anabaptism toward Radical Pietism, does not find similar expression in Brethren writings, although historically it seems to have been very real in its operation (see Durnbaugh, "The Genius of the Brethren," Pt. I, pp. 20-24).

ever; it was too contradictory to their original genius. By the middle of the century the tight, legalistic authoritarianism showed signs of collapse, and the next seventy-five years witnessed a great transformation in the direction of freedom and openness. But the modern Church of the Brethren that was born out of that reaction hardly was a resurgence of eighteenth century sectarianism. Although certain emphases and characteristics have persisted, today's church has taken its place as a common and respected member of the American "denominational" milieu, i.e. neither church nor sect in the classic sense.

At this point we resume our survey of the eighteenth century history.

Following the Schwarzenau baptism of 1708 the church proceeded to expand and grow at several points in western Germany—invariably at places where Radical Pietism already had been active. By and large the Brethren recruited their membership out of separatist ranks rather than directly out of the churches. But as the sect grew, so grew opposition from the radicals to the left and persecution from both church and state on the right. In 1719, motivated by a desire both for religious freedom and economic betterment, a group of about twenty Brethren families, under the leadership of *Peter Becker* (1687–1758), migrated from Krefeld to Pennsylvania. They settled in and around Germantown, a suburb of Philadelphia which earlier had been settled by Mennonite emigrants from Krefeld.

The next year, 1720, the bulk of the Schwarzenau group, some forty families, under the leadership of Alexander Mack, emigrated to Surhuisterveen in Holland, another Mennonite settlement. They stayed until 1729 before moving once more to join their brethren in Pennsylvania. The emigration of a few individual families continued for several more years, and by the 1730's the church was transplanted to the New World, the European remnant being left to die out very shortly.

The Brethren always have been better at doing than at

writing, but the literature necessary for an ideological study is particularly scant for the European period. The writings of Alexander Mack consists of two brief but crucial apologetic tracts directed against the separatists (1713 and 1715), a few hymns, letters, and notes. Mack died in 1735, after only six years in the New World, and there is virtually no material from this part of his career. Otherwise from Europe there come only a few hymns and letters, and a lengthy history of the imprisonment of the so-called Solingen Brethren, six members from Solingen who were cruelly incarcerated for almost four years as a consequence of having submitted to rebaptism. These are the literary remains of the European phase of Brethren origins.[13]

In America, after the first party of Brethren arrived with Peter Becker in 1719, there was a quiescent period of some four years while the immigrants were getting themselves located and established. Then in 1723–1724 came an awakening that initiated the spread of the church from the mother congregation at Germantown through the hinterlands of the Pennsylvania-German country. By the end of the century there were congregations (almost exclusively rural) through much of Pennsylvania (one in New Jersey) and south into Maryland, Virginia, and what is now West Virginia.

When Mack arrived in 1729, he took over the leadership of the church from Peter Becker, although Becker remained active and succeeded Mack again upon his death in 1735. However, in the very spread of the church had been planted the seeds of trouble, namely the Ephrata movement. *Conrad Beissel* (1690-1768) was a vagrant soul who during his youth in Germany had dallied with several of the Radical Pietist groups and who, throughout his career, painted a very representative picture of the more esoteric type of "spiritual religion" both separatist and cultic. Upon arriving in America

---

[13] All these materials appear in English translation in Durnbaugh's *Origins*.

he spent a year in Germantown as an apprentice in Peter Becker's weaving shop. He then went out into the Conestoga country to live as a hermit. It was there that Becker and the other Germantown Brethren met him while on their missionary journey of 1724. They made enough converts in the area to warrant the organization of a separate congregation. Beissel—who earlier had tried baptizing himself in private—surprisingly submitted himself to the Brethren for baptism and was chosen as minister of the group.

Within four short years Beissel had split his congregation, and in 1728 he underwent and performed upon his followers an "*un*baptizing immersion" through which the Brethren were "given back" their baptism. Another four years saw the Beisselites founding the famous Ephrata community, a Protestant (or at least non-Catholic) monastery in which the seventh day was observed, celibacy enforced, habits worn, visions and ecstacy enjoyed, and Father Friedsam (he whom the Brethren had lately trusted as Brother Conrad) as much as worshiped.

During the late 1730's (after Mack's death) a "spiritual awakening" hit the Brethren full force, and Beissel reaped the harvest. A number of prominent Brethren went to Ephrata, and some leading families were split as wives or children went on their own. Two of Alexander Mack's sons went; one, we shall see, returned.

Of course, the Ephrata community should not be understood as a branch of the Brethren, nor should the two groups be confused, as often has happened. The Beisselites must be considered as a defection, their true significance being as a symbol of the tension and attraction that Radical Pietism still held for the Brethren who had broken out of it a generation before. When, in the pages that follow, we are developing the Brethren ideology we will *not* cite the writings of Beisselites or of those who were on the way to becoming such.

The "first generation" authors, then, include: Alexander

Mack, whose works we have already described; and Peter Becker, who has left us only a hymn or two.[14] *John Naas* (1670–1741), a prominent leader in Germany who did not come to America until 1733 and then settled in New Jersey and organized the congregation there, has also given us a few hymns plus an interesting account of his transatlantic crossing.

Michael Frantz (1687–1748) was of the first-generation age group and European-born although an American convert. After Beissel wrecked the Conestoga congregation, the care of the remnant reverted to the nonresident Peter Becker. On a visit in 1734 he baptized Frantz and put him in charge of the congregation—on a trial basis. Becker had learned caution about giving the Conestogans into the hands of a new convert; Frantz was advanced to full authority the next year. Frantz's first act in 1734 was to lay a fence rail on the floor of the barn in which the group met, invite those who accepted his leadership to stand on the right side of it with him and those who chose Beissel's leadership to stand on the left. He had a very successful ministry until his death in 1748. In 1770, the Sauer Press published a collection of his works, both poetry and prose, which is one of the very valuable sources of eighteenth century Brethren thought.

One name that most Brethren histories would include among the first-generation authors is here conspicuous by its absence; this is *Christopher Sauer* (1695–1758),[15] founder of the famous printing establishment of Germantown, at least for a time the largest in America. Sauer may well have been the most influential German-American of the colonial period.

[14] The eighteenth century Brethren had quite a penchant for hymn- and poem-writing (usually stanza upon stanza upon stanza). Almost without exception, the men who wrote anything also wrote poetry; and in several cases poetry is all they have left us. Undoubtedly this trend reflects the devotional tradition of Pietism.

[15] The name was also spelled Saur and Sower.

The periodicals, pamphlets, and books from his press were certainly the major information media and opinion molders of the entire Pennsylvania-German community. As a contemporary and competitor of Ben Franklin, Sauer was also in many respects his counterpart among the Germans. And although it has been recognized that there were problems, historians have assumed that Sauer was a Dunker. There is not the slightest doubt but that he was intimately connected with the Brethren. Himself a separatist, he knew them in Schwarzenau and in fact bought Mack's house when the Brethren went to Holland. In this country Sauer lived among the Brethren, attended their services, built his Germantown home so that it could be used as a Brethren meetinghouse, allowed, if not encouraged, his son to join the church when he was sixteen, the normal age for baptism. Nevertheless, recent scholarship has made it very problematical that Sauer himself ever submitted to baptism and thus attained full church membership; as much as can be said about him with certainty is that he was a Pietist separatist with some strong affinities (but also some separatistic criticisms) for the Brethren.[16]

Although no great risk would be run in using Sauer's works as a source of eighteenth century Brethren thought, and although these comparatively voluminous materials could prove quite useful, we have chosen the path of scholarly caution; Christopher Sauer will not be cited in the pages that follow.

In 1742 was held the sect's first Annual Meeting, a gathering which since has taken place virtually without interruption down to the present day. It was called to formulate the church's response to the "ecumenical movement" of Count Zinzendorf; the Brethren had cooperated in Zinzendorf's synods until they came to suspect that the Count's intention

[16] See Donald Durnbaugh, "Christopher Sauer: Germantown Printer," *The Gospel Messenger* (May 24, 1958), p. 10.

was to capture all the Pennsylvania-German sectaries for Moravianism.

During the eighteenth century the Annual Meeting was not constituted by formal representation from the congregations but simply by whatever Brethren—particularly ministers—could be in attendance. The ministry itself was not a very formal office. In the earliest period the leaders would admit no title but "teacher" (*Lehrer*); they were at pains to avoid anything smacking of churchly ecclesiasticism. In time a three-degree ministry was developed: (1) deacons, who were hardly clerical figures at all, their responsibility being to care for the poor, visit the afflicted, etc.; (2) exhorters, i.e. preachers; and (3) elders (bishops), who carried the charge of a given congregation. All of these were called *by* the congregation, *out of* the congregation, *at the discretion* of the congregation; none were salaried, none were formally educated, none were sacerdotally set apart.

And the Annual Meeting simply gave structure to the form of government that had been implicit from the beginning. Each congregation had great freedom in managing its own affairs, but the brotherhood—as a brotherhood, not as an overhead governing body—was the constituent entity of the church. Thus the congregations, as well as the individual members, were of a "family," which family stood by to act when help was called for (and that either "asked for" or "obviously necessary"). The minutes of the Annual Meetings will prove very valuable for our purposes, the only difficulty being that they are rather incomplete through the eighteenth century and almost nonexistent before the Revolutionary War.

As much of the history of the latter half of the century as we need consider will be forthcoming as we introduce the men whose writings form our source material. The first of the "second generation" authors was *John Price* (c. 1702-c. 1724), himself a minister and the son of a minister who was a member of Peter Becker's original immigrant party.[17] A brief collection of Price's hymns was published in 1753.

The two towering figures of the second generation are *Alexander Mack, Jr.* (1712–1803), and *Christopher Sauer, Jr.* (1721–1784). Mack Junior was the older of the two and *the* Brethren writer of the eighteenth century. Born in Schwarzenau, baptized in Holland, "prodigalized" at Ephrata, shortly before 1748 he rejected Beissel and returned to Germantown. There in 1748 he and Sauer Junior were given joint oversight of the congregation, in which they proceeded to labor as "brothers" beyond the call of even Brethren duty. Mack's steady and loving hand guided the church until his death in 1803, during which half-century it also produced several important tracts, a considerable amount of poetry,[18] and an astonishing amount of correspondence—all of which will be used extensively in the pages that follow.

One of Mack Junior's letters constitutes an invitation for a second attempt at epitomizing the Brethren, this time not in terms of their historical genesis but in search of the core principles that establish Brethrenism as an identifiable ideology. We are suggesting that this core is epistemology, the manner in which the Brethren went about attaining religious truth. Mack's letter is not a disquisition on epistemology—that would be the farthest thing from the Brethren mentality—but a concrete demonstration of the epistemology in action.

We present excerpts from the letter, interspersing within them a running commentary; our analysis and conclusions

[17] Young John was a sickly youth (he died at twenty-two years), and the story goes that his father urged him to marry early in an attempt to perpetuate the family. The advice was taken, and John married an Indian girl who had been left behind with the Prices when her people had been forced west. The plan was a success—I am a descendant of that union.

[18] Mack's poetry has been collected and translated by Samuel B. Heckman in *The Religious Poetry of Alexander Mack, Jr.* (Elgin, Ill.: Brethren Publishing House, 1912).

then follow. The document, an open letter to the brotherhood, first was printed as an appendix to the 1799 edition of his father's *Rights and Ordinances* published by Samuel Sauer.[19] Whether this was a way of preserving what actually was an earlier letter, we do not know.

"Inasmuch as we have understood that some brethren have difficulties with regard to feetwashing [Since its inception the church had interpreted John 13:1-17 as a positive command and had practiced feetwashing as a part of its agape meal and communion service.], which Jesus has commanded to his disciples as if it had been performed between the supper and the breaking of bread. And because they think it not rightly done if the feet are washed before the meal, we felt moved in sincere love to give the reasons why we wash feet before the meal. At the same time, we would say that it is our belief and view that if a brother or any other person can in love and moderation instruct us according to the word of the Lord more fully and otherwise than is here pointed out, we would be ready to accept it not only in this point of feetwashing but in other matters as well. And we would not at all rest upon long usage but would let the word of the Lord be our only rule and guide.

[There follows a detailed analysis of the pertinent biblical materials. Major attention is given to John 13:2, the words to the effect that "after supper" Jesus washed the feet of his disciples. The conclusion is that in the original Greek the phrase translated "after supper" actually meant "after the supper was ready."]

"Now these other evangelists say nothing at all about feetwashing, and on the other hand, John writes nothing about the institution of breaking bread. Therefore, scripture must be

[19] Here reproduced is the Kurtz-Quinter translation from a parallel-text edition of 1860, the English half of which was reprinted subsequently in Ashland, Ohio, 1939.

understood and looked upon with a spiritual eye of love and calmness....

"Such [i.e. dogmatism and disputation] ought not to be the manner and mind of the true lovers of wisdom. But true wisdom and her lovers must be minded as James teaches and says, 'But the wisdom from above is in the first place pure; and then peace-loving, considerate, and open to reason (James 3:17).'

"But commonly it is the case that when a person receives some knowledge in selfishness and maintains it in self-assertiveness, he is not willing to be instructed. He will dispute in his own wisdom about the shell and drop the kernel. Therefore, dear brethren, let us all be wise; and especially concerning the feetwashing let us be careful how we are to conduct ourselves, in love, peace, and humility submitting to one another.

"For Christ indeed has given no particular command about the time at which it should be performed, whether before or after the meal. But he has commanded that it should be done —and also that we should love one another. Christ has not said that his disciples should be known by their washing of feet or their breaking of bread, but he did say, 'Love one another; as I have loved you, so you are to love one another. If there is this love among you, then all will know that you are my disciples.'...

"Therefore, it is of the utmost necessity to maintain love and peace and to determine to pray to our dear Lord for still more wisdom. For I can say in truth and from experience that in the church's beginning we washed one another's feet *after* the meal and *after* the breaking of bread—yet accompanied by a blessing and an awakening of love. Afterward, we came to a better understanding and washed feet *after* the meal but *before* the breaking of bread—also with a blessing. Then, when Reitz published an edition of the New Testament in the original Greek and a brother came among us who understood that language, he pointed out to us how Jesus properly washed feet before the meal, and we in single-heartedness have done it ever since and on each occasion *before* the meal. . . . [How many times have churches deliberately revised their "liturgical practice" on the basis of new light that has come through biblical scholarship?]

"Yet I say this, if I should come into a congregation that was holding a love feast, and if the leaders of that congregation did not yet understand it otherwise but that the feetwashing should come *after* the meal, I would participate with them in great simplicity and love. Even so, I would lay my views before them according to the scriptures and wait in love and have patience with them until they could see it so likewise. [A dialectic is in operation here: The preservation of *Gemeinschaft* is of supreme value; however, uniformity, or unanimity, in the truth is also of high value. The pressure toward unanimity dare not be allowed to destroy *Gemeinschaft*, but neither dare the joys of *Gemeinschaft* be allowed to stifle the search for concord. And it is Mack's faith that if this dialectical balance be patiently maintained, eventually the Spirit can and will bring about unanimity—while in the process enhancing rather than destroying *Gemeinschaft*.]

"Therefore, the scriptures call for spiritual eyes, mind, and understanding. Otherwise, through literalistic interpretation, if a person without true illumination were to try to hold fast to the letter in one place, he would have to disregard and act contrary to it in another place, and thus we would have nothing but trouble and division. [The very nature of the scriptures makes biblicism impractical; thus, literalism is as impossible as it is illegitimate, an obstruction to the *Gemeinschaft*-creating work of the Holy Spirit.]

"Therefore, dear brethren, let us watch and be careful. And above all, preserve *love*, for then we will preserve *light*. [This sentence could well be taken as the motto of eighteenth century Brethrenism; the preservation of *Gemeinschaft* is the precondition for the reception and preservation of religious truth.] For the Spirit of Truth testifies in 1 John 2:10, 'Only the man who loves his brother dwells in light: there is nothing to make him stumble.' Then our good God, who is love purely and impartially, can and will add by degrees whatever may be lacking in this or that knowledge of truth. [Much more important than *having* the truth is being in position to *receive* the truth; thus the life of the church always must be open-ended toward God.]

"I now conclude, again begging all my brethren to read and consider this in love and with a calm spirit. Thus I am your weak brother,

"ALEXANDER MACK, JR."[20]

The epistemology derived from this letter can be described in eleven basic principles. Most of these are documented by the letter itself; any that are not will become documented in the course of succeeding chapters.

(1) The ultimate source and standard of all Christian truth is the mind of Christ; he is the supreme revelation and indeed the very presence of God himself.

(2) The mind of Christ is given its authoritative definition and proclamation through the pages of the New Testament.

(3) The only reliable interpreter of the New Testament is the Holy Spirit, the same Spirit that inspired its writing in the first place.

(4) The best qualified receptor for Spirit-revealed truth is the Christian *Gemeinde*.

(5) Such a *Gemeinde* must receive truth as a gift of God's grace rather than possess it in pride as something of its own achievement. The desire to push through to and grasp the truth too quickly destroys *Gemeinschaft* and thus cuts the group off from the source of truth.

[20] At points I have amended the translation and added italics.

87

(6) Such a *Gemeinde*, convinced that truth is a growing, living, personal thing and that no group ever has the "last word," must always be open and eager for new leading rather than complacent in knowledge already attained.

(7) Such a *Gemeinde* must come to the scriptures having previously made the commitment to obey and follow as literally and completely as possible whatever leading may be discovered therein.

(8) Such a *Gemeinde*, above all, must preserve the love for one another without which any religious insight, no matter how correct it may be technically, loses its truth.

(9) Such a *Gemeinde* will respect and maintain brotherhood with all sincere seekers of the truth, although at the same time they will see it as their Christian duty to point out what they feel to be the errors in the other's thinking.

(10) Such a *Gemeinde* will welcome all the help that scholarship and research can bring to the study of scripture, even though scholarship alone will not be recognized as the final authority.

(11) Such a *Gemeinde* will renounce all methods of literalistic, mechanical, dead-letter interpretation which overlook the dynamic, two-way aspect of revelation.

At this point we pick up and continue our historical survey with Mack Junior's closest friend and colleague. Sauer Junior (whose mother spent fourteen years at Ephrata) followed his father in the printing trade, operating the bindery and overseeing the production of *English* publications[21] until Sauer Senior's death in 1758, at which time he took over the entire establishment. His proprietorship was just as outstanding and influential as his father's had been. Although it is not easy to identify the materials Sauer *wrote* from within those he *pub-*

[21] Though presumably most of the Brethren did learn at least some English in America, almost without exception the documents we shall use originally were in German. Particularly the outlying rural congregations maintained a virtually unmitigated German culture and milieu until well into the nineteenth century.

lished, we do have some articles, poetry, and correspondence from his pen.

Sauer's experience during the Revolution is the most noteworthy instance of persecution against the Brethren but at the same time is representative of the pressures encountered by the church as a whole. The Brethren found themselves out of step with the Revolution on at least three counts. In the first place, and primarily, their nonresistant convictions prohibited them from joining the army or voluntarily participating in the war effort. In the second place, their objection to the swearing of oaths hampered them in declaring allegiance to the new government. In the third place, a condition for their having entered the country originally was a pledge of fealty to the British crown, and the Brethren were not ones easily to renounce their solemn word. Sauer labored under the additional handicap that his sons were active loyalists.

In 1778 Continental soldiers roused Sauer from his bed in the middle of the night, stripped him, mistreated him, and drove him on a forced march to a military prison where he spent almost a month before General Muhlenberg interceded with General Washington and obtained his release. Yet later the government, without granting him so much as a hearing, proceeded to confiscate and sell all of his property and effects and to defame him as a traitor. Sauer, a broken man, lived for a time on charity and died in 1784 poverty-stricken. It is understandable that in some respects the Revolutionary War marked the beginning of a Brethren "flight to the wilderness."

We have yet to meet two authors whose work came just at the close of the century, *Jacob Stoll* (1731–1822) and *Christian Longenecker* (1731–1808). The two, both born the same year, both second-generation Brethren, grew up together in the Conestoga congregation, the church of Beissel and Frantz (though they proved to be heirs of Frantz rather than Beissel). Conestoga was the center from which the brotherhood grew; Germantown more a center of leadership. Both Stoll and

Longenecker were called to the ministry. In 1772 the old congregation was divided into three new ones; Stoll lived in what
continued to be Conestoga territory and in time became elder
of that congregation; Longenecker lived in the White Oak territory and became elder of that congregation.

In 1806 Stoll published a sizable volume of poetry—probably
the best of the period. Longenecker became involved in an unfortunate church fight and was disciplined by Annual Meeting on several occasions. He retained his office, however; and
the fact that the quarrel was not doctrinal in character means
that the theological tract he published in 1806 still can be
used as an accurate reflection of eighteenth century Brethren
thought.

As a final attempt at epitomizing the Brethren we record
the account made by one who observed them firsthand. The
following is by Morgan Edwards, the great colonial Baptist
historian. He begins the description by noting a difficulty that
must plague all such efforts:

"It is very hard to give a true account of the principles of
these Tunkers as they have not published any system or
creed. . . .

"They are *general baptists* in the sense which that phrase
bears in Great Britain; but not Arians nor Socinians, as most
of their brethren in Holland are. General redemption they certainly hold; and, withal, general salvation; which tenets
though wrong are consistent.

"They use great plainness of language and dress, like the
Quakers; and like them will never swear nor fight. They will
not go to law; nor take interest for the money they lend. They
commonly wear their beards; and keep the first day Sabbath,
except one congregation [Edwards, as so many others, did not
distinguish Ephrata]. They have the Lord's Supper with its
ancient attendants of *love feast, washing feet, kiss of charity,*
and *righthand of fellowship.* They anoint the sick with oil for
recovery, and use the *trine immersion,* with laying on of

A SECT CALLED THE DUNKERS

hands and prayer, even while the person baptized is in the
water; which may easily be done as the party kneels down to
be baptized, and continues in that position till both prayer and
imposition of hands be performed. . . . Every brother is allowed
to stand up in the congregation to speak in a way of exhortation and expounding, and when by that means they find a
man eminent for *knowledge* and *aptness* to teach, they choose
him to be a minister, and ordain him with imposition of
hands, attending with fasting and prayer, and giving the right
hand of fellowship. They also have *deacons*; and ancient
widows for *deaconesses*; and *exhorters*, who are licensed to use
their gifts statedly.

"They pay not their ministers unless it be in the way of presents; though they admit their right to pay; neither do the ministers assert the right; esteeming it *more blessed to give than
to receive*. Their acquaintance with the Bible is admirable. In
a word they are meek and pious Christians; and have justly
acquired the character of the *Harmless Tunkers*.[22]

This much background, we trust, has given the reader not
only "a knowledge of the Brethren" but also something of "a
feel for sectarianism as a whole." But as we come now to compare the religious thought of Søren Kierkegaard with that of
these Brethren sectaries the first impression must be that it
simply cannot be done; they lived in different worlds. But a
closer and more thoughtful analysis will indicate that their so
very apparent differences are not really fundamental, that beneath these conspicuous but deceptive divergencies there is a
hard core of essential agreement.

The least disturbing of the distances between them is the
ocean of water that separates the Old World from the New
and the century of time that separates the Dunkers from the
Dane. This difference in space and time and the consequent

---

[22] Morgan Edwards, *Materials toward a History of the American
Baptists* (Philadelphia, 1770), Vol. I, Pt. 4, p. 66. This passage is quoted
in Brumbaugh, *op.cit.*, pp. 525-27.

difference of historical environment have their effects, to be sure, but they form no unbridgeable chasm. The greater gap comes in their qualities of mind and thought. By natural endowment S.K. was an authentic genius, one of the world's truly great intellects; none of the Brethren could begin to approach him in this regard. The breadth of S.K.'s interests, the number of fields in which he could and did operate with sheer brilliance, is astounding. An entire century of Brethren thought covers but one small segment of that about which the one man S.K. wrote definitively during a ten-year career. S.K. was a scholar and student, eminently educated, with a world of knowledge at his fingertips. Not a single Dunker so much as attended college. S.K. was highly cultured, a connoisseur and one who could display immense sophistication in the arts, in philosophy, in "gracious living." This was a world the Brethren knew not of—and what little they did know of it, they cared not for.

None of this is to imply that the Brethren were illiterate peasants; that suggestion is far from the truth. Although not strong in formal education, they were intelligent, interested laymen. If Christopher Sauer, Jr., read but a fraction of the material he published, he was very well read for his day and age. Alexander Mack, Jr., in wrestling with exegetical problems of biblical interpretation, mentioned that he had compared the translation in four different languages, talked with a person who could read Greek, and consulted various authorities.[23] Most of the Brethren writings reflect at least some awareness of the broader world of learning and events. Nonetheless, the educational-cultural distance between the Brethren (and for that matter, most sectaries) and S.K. was immense. It might be pointed out that not all men of the "church" are of S.K.'s class either, but in any case it is true

[23] Alexander Mack, Jr., *Apology* (Ephrata, Pa.: 1788) typescript trans. by N. P. Springer (Mennonite Historical Library, Goshen, Ind.), p. 3; and Mack's "Open Letter on Feetwashing," see above, pp. 85-86.

that the churches have put more of a premium on these qualities than the sectaries ever did.

But how little this immense distance actually amounts to
becomes apparent once we discover the evaluation in which
S.K. held his own gifts and advantages. We shall have occasion in a later chapter to give detailed attention to S.K.'s
thought regarding the Christian and "the world"; here we
need note only that in Christian history but few men of S.K.'s
caliber have been able to match him in the degree to which
he realized the Pauline precept of "counting all things as loss
for the sake of knowing Christ Jesus my Lord." S.K. knew
and taught that the movement into Christianity is *away from*
the interesting, the sophisticated, the multifarious, *toward* the
attainment of greater and greater simplicity.[24] S.K. was a
scintillating aesthete, but his aesthetic powers were dedicated
to the dethronement of aesthetics. S.K. was a brilliant philosopher, but his philosophic powers were dedicated to the dethronement of philosophy. S.K. was a great thinker, but his
rational powers were dedicated to the dethronement of reason.
S.K., in very truth, used his gifts against themselves in the interests of attaining Christian simplicity.

And S.K. knew and taught, early and late, that his endow-
ments were worth nothing, that people like the meek, pious,
harmless Dunkers might have the same simplicity he had had
to *attain* and might have it without tracing the tortuous Kierkegaardian path through aesthetics or philosophy. Early, in
his very first Edifying Discourse (1843), he said:

"And yet every man can say it [i.e. "I went to God; He became my schoolmaster."], dares to say it, can say it in truth,
and if he does not say it in truth, then it is not because the
thought is not true, but because he distorts it. Every man dares
say it. Whether his forehead was flattened almost like a beast's
or arched more proudly than the heavens; [etc.]—it has nothing to do with the matter, my hearer, absolutely nothing.

---

[24] See his words quoted above, pp. 14-15.

Every man dares say it when he has faith; for this is precisely the glory of faith."[25]

And late, toward the close of his authorship, he said:

"I cannot abandon the thought that every man, absolutely every man, however simple he is, however much he may suffer, can nevertheless grasp the highest, namely religion, I cannot forget that. If that is not so, then Christianity is really nonsense. To me it is frightful to see the thoughtlessness with which philosophers and the like make use of the difference-categories such as genius, talent, etc., in religion. They do not suspect that in that case religion is finished and done with. I have only one consolation, the blessed consolation of knowing something which can bring comfort, and blessedly comfort every man, absolutely every man. Take away this comfort and I can't be bothered to live."[26]

But he went even farther. Not only is this simplicity no handicap to the Christian life; it is a positive advantage.

"Every man has a basic primitive disposition (for primitiveness is the possibility of 'spirit'). God knows this best, for it is he who has created it. All earthly, temporal, worldly cleverness tends to destroy its own primitiveness. Christianity aims at following it. Destroy your own primitiveness, and in all probability you will get through the world well, perhaps even be a success—but eternity will denounce you. Follow your primitiveness, and you will fail in the temporal world; but eternity will accept you."[27]

Some people may be offended to have S.K. compared to the Brethren sectaries; S.K. himself would not be.

There are other significant contrasts between S.K. and the Brethren that are of an entirely different character. If a sectary, S.K. appears at a different point on the "sectarian cycle" than

[25] "Faith's Expectation" (Discourse I) in *Edifying Discourses*, Vol. I, p. 13.

[26] *Dru Journals*, 1031 (1850).

[27] *Smith Journals*, XI[1] A 385 (1854).

do the Brethren. The main thrust of S.K.'s polemic is directed, of course, against the church; his role is that of critic, discovering and disclosing the flaws of Christendom. Surprisingly, there is but very little of comparable material in the Brethren literature—and obviously not because the Brethren were any happier with churchly ways than was S.K. But the Brethren had fought that battle long past, long even before they became Brethren and started to create a literature. By the time we locate them, they had, as it were, shaken the dust of the church from their feet—nothing was to be gained (or even hoped for) by fulminating against it.

Conversely, a major interest of the Brethren writers does not appear the same way in S.K. They, bearing responsibility for the operation and continuance of an actual organization, of necessity had to give attention to such practical matters as mode of baptism and communion, church organization and government, the ministry, discipline. But for S.K. these things were not central, nor should they have been; his approach was proper for his situation, that of the Brethren for theirs. But although the contrast is a real and noticeable one, it marks only a difference in phase of the same sectarian development and not a difference in basic religious orientation.

A similar point of contrast lies in the fact that S.K.'s polemic was directed against the church on the right, and thus its thrust was in the direction of less rigidity, less structure, less conformity, less overhead. The polemic of the Brethren, on the other hand, was directed primarily against the separatists on their left, thus pulling in the direction of greater form, greater order, greater discipline. But again the contrast is not really basic; the same dialectic is operative in both cases, and although working in from opposite directions, S.K. and the Brethren meet at a common center.

So much for the divergencies that are more visible than real. We must say a word about the sort of *affinities* for which we are to look. S.K. and the Brethren had in common a great body of beliefs that represent nothing more or less than their mutual Protestant-Christian heritage; their churchly opponents as well would hold all these in common with them. Thus one could demonstrate, say, that both S.K. and the Brethren believed in the existence of God, the deity of Christ, the reality of the atonement, etc.—but there would be no point in doing so. We shall simply assume what is clearly the case, that both S.K. and the Brethren were, in their basic doctrinal orientation, orthodox, evangelical Protestants—unless there appears evidence to indicate otherwise.

Thus although this doctrinal orthodoxy is the necessary background against which our study takes place, we are interested primarily in those affinities in which the Dunkers and the Dane agreed *against* "churchly" thought, or where they *emphasized* points to which the churches customarily gave but passing attention. Affinities of this sort are the ones that will establish S.K.'s sectarian perspective. And we should be reminded again that the use of the Brethren in this comparison is *not* to demonstrate any sort of special relationship between them and S.K.; our interest, rather, is in relating S.K. to the sectarian tradition as a whole, of which the Brethren have been selected merely as an arbitrary representative.

But as we contemplate our motif comparison we face an insoluble problem; whatever we do will be wrong, will be, in effect, to say something false about the parties we are comparing. For we are forced to make a list of their beliefs, and for sheer convenience of treatment the list must follow at least some sort of logical order and organization. But to do this inevitably is to impose a pattern, a system, a "theological" perspective which is not true to the sources. Both S.K. and the Brethren deliberately refrained from compiling anything like a summary or prospectus of their faith, anything remotely resembling a dogmatic definition or creed. Any such would have been false to their sectarian understanding of faith as free, existential encounter between living men and a living God. Sectarian literature properly is written as "occasional literature," as specific insights into specific concerns in specific situations. But "the faith once delivered . . ."? Of course! But just as surely the faith which must be delivered anew to Søren Kierkegaard, to Alexander Mack, and to you! And any attempt to give such faith a comprehensive definition, a completed form, is not a true work of faith.

This is not at all to suggest, however, that sectarian faith is without positive and enduring content, or that it is entirely random, lacking all consistency and structure. The thought of both S.K. and the Brethren does display quite distinctive and identifiable pattern, but it is *free* rather than *fixed* pattern. It can be likened to a Chinese-checker board (a geometrical network of points, each of which is connected to its neighbor through the interstices) or to a familiar style of octagonal tile flooring. Pattern enough is here, but the pattern can be read in any number of ways. One can take a particular point as a center and see a circumference of other points radiating from it, although he must realize that it would be just as accurate to take one of the circumferential points as the center with what had been the center now on the circumference. The possibilities are endless. This is *free pattern*, incorporating that which is regular and stable but defying fixed interpretation or description.

With a Chinese-checker board no problem exists; the whole is presented simultaneously, and the viewer is free to discover patterns to his heart's content. But our comparison can be constructed only paragraph by successive paragraph; we necessarily must commit ourselves to one fixed pattern and thus inevitably suggest that this is the way it was with S.K. The only help is constantly to keep in mind that the thought of both the Dunkers and the Dane was much more spontaneous, adaptable, and alive than our dissection of it can indicate.

97

We stand, then, ready to begin the comparison of motifs—
and in fact (all unbeknown to ourselves) already have made
that beginning, for the lack of fixed system in S.K.'s thought
properly can be understood as our first major correlation between the religious perspective of Kierkegaard and that of the
Brethren sectaries.

Part Two
The Dunkers and the Dane

CHAPTER V

THE DECISIVE CHRISTIAN CATEGORY

*"The individual"—that is the
decisive Christian category, and it will be decisive
for the future of Christianity.*[1]

*"Den Enkelte" ("the individual"—in contrast
to "the public") [is] a thought in which is contained
an entire philosophy of life and of the world.*[2]

*This category is the point at which and
across which God can come to seize hold of the race.
To remove that point is to dethrone God.*[3]

Kierkegaard claimed "the individual" as "his category,"[4] and there is nowhere else to begin a presentation of his thought. This is not to suggest that S.K.'s procedure was that of a systematic philosopher and this the fundamental presupposition

---

[1] The second of "Two Notes on 'the Individual'" in *Point of View*, pp. 133-34.

[2] *Point of View*, p. 21.

[3] *Papirer*, X[1] A 218 (1849), quoted in Dupre, *op.cit.*, p. 36.

[4] *Point of View*, p. 21.

which *must* come first. It is to say, rather, that this is where
S.K. chose to start and that we can best understand him by
following his route.

In so doing we have put ourselves at something of an em-
barrassment in that Brethren literature provides nothing that
parallels S.K.'s technical conception of *den Enkelte*. The conclusion to be drawn is, however, not that S.K.'s category is *un*-
sectarian. It is rather that S.K. started "farther back," based
his thought on a more fundamental proposition than did
the Brethren or sectaries generally. Nonetheless, we will discover that the first characteristics S.K. derived from *den
Enkelte* are rather precisely paralleled in Brethrenism. The
suggestion, then, is strong that some sort of "individualism"
is also the *unspoken* assumption of the sectaries and that what
S.K. has accomplished is to give formulation to the "metaphysics" of sectarianism.

But it might be objected that Martin Luther himself had a
strong conception of individualistic religion and that this in
itself, therefore, dare not be classified a sectarian trait. Here is
raised a broader issue which should be considered. Not only
as regards "individualism," but in connection with any number of other Kierkegaardian motifs as well, Luther could be
quoted in support. But this fact does not invalidate the contention that the motif is also truly sectarian in character. For
one thing, it cannot simply be taken for granted that because
he was the founder Martin Luther symbolizes only "churchly"
Protestantism; in some respects this decidedly is not the case.
We noted earlier that scholars have found sectarian as well as
churchly traits in him.

But indeed we should not even expect sectarianism to be
completely different from "churchism"; both are Protestant
and thus will show many affinities. However, in some cases,
such as the strong critique of infant baptism, the Kierkegaard-sectarian view will run diametrically counter to Luther.
In some cases, such as *Gemeinschaft* being central in the doc-

trine of the church, the emphasis would be largely absent in Luther although not necessarily opposed by him. In cases such as "individualism" Luther could be cited in agreement, but the motif is much more central and emphatic in sectarianism. In cases, such as the equality of all men before God, Luther and sectarianism would be in full agreement, but the sectaries would prove more radical and sweeping in applying the doctrine to the life and structure of the church. And finally, in some cases the sectarian motif, although not greatly dissimilar to churchly teaching, nevertheless appears as part of a somewhat different pattern, is approached out of a somewhat different context.

In short, the uniqueness of the sectarian point of view does not depend on the uniqueness of every one of its motifs—nor even of any *one* of those motifs. It is rather the pattern as a whole, the consistent recurrence of differences in emphasis, the developing of an angle of vision, that in the end will distinguish Protestant sectarianism from its churchly counterpart.

As we begin with S.K.'s category of *den Enkelte,* we find that the very act of beginning is complicated by confusion and disagreement on how to translate the term that identifies the category. We are going to suggest that the best secondary exposition of S.K.'s conception is that by Martin Buber; and the English translator of that exposition is the person who has forced the question. He notes: "The German which I have rendered by the cumbrous and none too clear phrase 'the Single One' is *der Einzelne,* which is a fairly precise rendering of Kierkegaard's *hiin Enkelte.* It is a pity that in the English translations of Kierkegaard no effort seems to have been made by the translators to avoid the use of the word 'individual,' which is highly misleading. For every man is *individuum,* but not everyone is an *Einzelner* or *Enkelte.*"[5] Even so, Smith's decision must be questioned. *Der Einzelne,* the

[5] A note by the translator, Ronald Gregor Smith, in Martin Buber, *Between Man and Man* (Boston: Beacon Press, 1947), p. 207, n. 9.

German term used by Buber, is the customary German translation of the Danish original, and thus Buber is not responsible for any innovation. However, this translation itself begins to distort the meaning of S.K.'s Danish—and in the direction that Buber will go in criticizing Kierkegaard. Smith's "the Single One," then, though a close enough rendition of the German, distorts the meaning just one step further in the same direction.

Perhaps the problem best can be approached by starting with the German, moving back to the Danish, and then going to the English. The basic German root *einzeln* means single, sole, solitary, individual, isolated, detached. And there is a closely related German root that can clarify the matter by way of contrast; it is *einfach*, meaning simple, single, not complex or mixed, indivisible. The difference is a subtle one but quite significant. *Einzeln* defines the "one" in terms of his relation (more accurately, lack of relation) to "others," comes at the "one" by cutting him out of the herd, setting him apart. *Einfach*, on the other hand, defines the "one" in terms of his own essential "integrity," focusing on that which makes him a true integer, without regard to the presence or absence of others.

Danish allows the same sort of distinction. In Danish *ene* means alone, by oneself; *eneboer* is a hermit or recluse; *enebarn* is an only child; *ener* means one, unit; and *eneste* means only, single, sole. These clearly belong with *einzeln*. But *enkel* means plain, simple; *enkelhed* is simplicity; *enkelt* is single, simple, individual, the opposite of *dobbelt*. *Enkelt* is closer to *einfach* than to *einzeln*.

"The Single One," i.e. Smith's English translation, compounds the *einzeln* propensity by using two words that stress "apartness."[6] Much better would be "the Simple One" (although that has other connotations which would never do), or

---

[6] Since translating Buber's work Smith has made a switch. Now, in his *Smith Journals*, he consistently translates *den Enkelte* as "the single person"—a decided improvement! Also, he makes the very point that

"Simply, the One" (which is too awkward to be feasible). But from the standpoint of etymology alone, "the individual" is a very acceptable rendering. "Individual" means one in substance or essence; existing as a separate indivisible entity; an object which is determined by properties peculiar to itself and cannot be subdivided into others of the same kind.

And particularly if "individual" be read not so much as that which *can* not be divided but rather as that which *is* not divided, then it is a very close equivalent of S.K.'s *den Enkelte*. Smith's objection that a man necessarily is *individuum* and therefore cannot be thought of as becoming such is a complete misunderstanding. Clearly, S.K. was saying precisely that a person needs to become *individuum*, undivided, at one with himself, and not that he should cut himself off from the race. If, as S.K. very emphatically did say, "Purity of heart is to will one thing," than as he very well might have said, "Purity of existence is to *be* one thing"—"for he who is not himself a unity is never really anything wholly and decisively."[7] We support the customary translation of *den Enkelte* as "the individual," although to do this immediately creates difficulties of another order.

Martin Buber has pointed out that in current usage "individualism" carries two major types of implication: (1) what we might call *self-centeredness*, or *autonomy*—of which he explicitly absolves S.K.'s *den Enkelte*—and (2) *atomism*, *einzeln-ness, solitariness*— of which he explicitly accuses S.K.[8] As regards the first category, individualism implies self-assertion, self-reliance, self-realization, self-development, improving one's self, finding one's self, creating one's self.[9] But Buber

we here want to make, that Buber overdid it in accusing S.K.'s *den Enkelte* of isolationism. *Smith Journals*, p. 11, n. 2.

[7] *Purity of Heart*, p. 184.

[8] Martin Buber, "The Question to the Single One" (first published in 1936) in *Between Man and Man*, pp. 40ff.

[9] Martin Buber, *I and Thou* (first published 1923), 2d ed., trans. Ronald Gregor Smith (New York: Scribner's, 1958), pp. 63-64.

sees that these have nothing to do with S.K.'s *den Enkelte*.[10]
Indeed, S.K. himself had taken pains to repel such "heroic-
aesthetic individualism" in a very significant statement:

"In every one of the pseudonymous works this theme of 'the
individual' comes to evidence in one way or another; but there
the individual is predominantly the pre-eminent individual in
the aesthetic sense, the distinguished person, etc. In every one
of my edifying works the theme of 'the individual' comes to
evidence, and as officially as possible; but there the individual
is what every man is or can be. . . . But I believe that people
have for the most part paid attention only to 'the individual'
of the pseudonyms and have confounded me as a matter of
course with the pseudonyms."[11]

S.K. may be the father of existentialism, but obviously one
must be cautious about identifying his *den Enkelte* with the
"existentialist hero" of his present-day disciples.

In a later chapter we shall attempt to defend *den Enkelte*
against Buber's charge that it entails isolation and atomism;
here our concern is to establish only that "the individual" is
as good a translation of the Danish as has been proposed—if
one is careful not to allow the implications of "individualism"
and "individuality" that are current in much of modern philosophy and psychology and even in common parlance. Actually, S.K.'s *den Enkelte* is very close to the "I" of Buber's
primary word "I-Thou"[12] and thus to the concept "person"[13]
as it is used by a number of contemporary theologians.[14]

But how all-important the idea of *den Enkelte* was to S.K.

[10] Buber, "The Question to the Single One" in *Between Man and
Man*, p. 44.

[11] The second of "Two Notes on 'the Individual' " in *Point of View*,
p. 124.

[12] That Buber's concept, at least to some extent, was derived from
S.K. is apparent. See Maurice Friedman, *Martin Buber, The Life of
Dialogue* (New York: Harper, 1955), p. 35.

[13] That S.K. did in fact come very near to defining the concept "person" is seen in his statements quoted on pp. 122-23 below.

[14] These more recent formulations afford no particular help in translating *den Enkelte*, though they do aid in understanding it. One of the

is indicated by his statement: "I live, and with God's help I shall die in the belief that when death has carried me away ... He will place the imprint of providence upon my life so that it will help men to become aware of God and to see how thoughtlessly they hinder themselves from leading the highest life, a life in communion with God."[15] As shall become apparent, *den Enkelte* is for all intents and purposes a synonym for "a life in communion with God," but unfortunately it cannot be said that S.K.'s prayer has been answered, that his life has borne this imprint in the eyes of most men. S.K. has yet to be truly appreciated for the witness he was most concerned to make; and that appreciation must begin with a profound understanding of what he meant by *den Enkelte*.

The primary point—and one that Buber notes well, although too few other scholars do—is that *den Enkelte* is first and last, through and through, an absolutely *religious* conception. Buber calls it "a theological anthropology,"[16] and indeed S.K. himself spoke of "the theological self, the self directly in the sight of God—and what an infinite reality this self acquires by being before God!"[17] Buber puts *den Enkelte* into the sharpest possible antithesis to the anthropology of existentialist philosophy, noting that this anthropology has been made possible only by "renouncing" (more accurately, by simply ignoring) S.K.'s basic presupposition.[18]

---

best expositions of "person" is by Hugh Vernon White, *Truth and the Person in Christian Theology* (New York: Oxford Un. Press, 1963), pp. 53ff. The sheer word "person" is no real improvement over "individual," because it must fight its way clear of "personalism" and "personality" just as "individual" must do with "individualism" and "individuality."

[15] *Dru Journals*, 765 (1848). Cf. *Smith Journals*, XI² A 19 (1854).

[16] Buber, "What Is Man?" in *Between Man and Man*, p. 163.

[17] *The Sickness unto Death* (bound behind *Fear and Trembling*), trans. Walter Lowrie, trans. revised by Howard Johnson (Garden City: Doubleday Anchor, 1954), p. 210.

[18] Buber, *op.cit.*, p. 163; see also pp. 171-72 where he makes specific the contrast between S.K. and Heidegger.

It is not because S.K. failed to make that presupposition explicit; he made such plain and pointed statements as:

"Every human life is planned religiously. To deny this is to throw everything into confusion and to annul the concept of individual, race, immortality."[19]

"Essentially it is the God-relationship that makes a man a man."[20]

"The fatalist . . . has lost God and therefore himself as well; for if he has no God, neither has he a self."[21]

"That man's life is wasted who . . . never became eternally and decisively conscious of himself as spirit, as self, or (what is the same thing) never became aware and in the deepest sense received an impression of the fact that there is a God, and that he, he himself, his self, exists before God."[22]

It was in *The Sickness unto Death* that S.K. indulged in his most abstract and philosophical discussion of "the self," calling it the relationship which the self has to itself. He seems to mean that basically I *am* the person I *understand* myself to be; my own image of my role and purpose determines who I am. Yet even here S.K. specified that such self-understanding is correct, eventuating in a true self, only when it is the understanding that first was held by God and hence revealed to me through my relationship with him. Thus "the self cannot of itself attain and remain in equilibrium and rest by itself, but only by relating itself to that Power which constituted the whole relationship [of the self to itself]."[23]

[19] *The Concept of Dread*, by Vigilius Haufniensis (pseud.), trans. Walter Lowrie (Princeton: Princeton Un. Press, 1944), p. 94. Though technically this book belongs to the pseudonymous-aesthetic works, we know that S.K. added the pseudonym at the last moment, after having written the book for publication under his own name.

[20] *Postscript*, p. 219. Amazingly, this statement is from the mouth of the pseudonym Johannes Climacus, an avowed non-Christian and nonreligious person.

[21] *The Sickness unto Death*, p. 173.

[22] *Ibid.*, pp. 159-60.   [23] *Ibid.*, p. 147.

The constitutive principle of *den Enkelte* is that he exists "before God." The Danish word *for*—here translated "before" —can mean "for the sake of" as well as "in the sight of," and undoubtedly both meanings were part of S.K.'s intention. And "before God" is not a late, "religious" modifier attached to an earlier, philosophic concept; in point of fact, existence "before God" was a Kierkegaardian theme prior to the development of *den Enkelte* as a technical term.[24]

"*Before God* to be oneself—for the accent rests upon 'before

[24] The phrase "before God" as a full-fledged concept appears in the sermon that concludes the second volume of *Either/Or* (p. 346). This establishes the earliness of the term in S.K.'s thought (1843), although the idea is, of course, normal and natural enough *in a sermon*. What is much more impressive is that the conception—though not the phrase—is found in "Equilibrium," the central essay of *Either/Or II* which supposedly is by Judge William, who represents specifically the *ethical* and not the *religious* stage of existence (pp. 221, 246).

It is indeed a rather major break of character for S.K. to allow his ethicist to express such an idea—a break which is further compounded when the Judge describes the choice of oneself as being "repentance"— just as it is out of character for the philosopher Climacus to say that it is the God-relationship that makes a man a man. These not infrequent "leaks" on S.K.'s part probably admit two different explanations. In the first place, unconsciously S.K. found simply that he could not say what he wanted to say without resorting to religious categories. And in the second place these may be part of his deliberate design to entice his readers out of aesthetics, out of ethics, out of philosophy, and into religion. These "leaks" are of positive value in proving S.K.'s contention that he was a religious author from the outset and that his entire authorship is to be understood within this frame of reference.

How and when *den Enkelte* became a specific Kierkegaardian category has been recounted by S.K. himself: "When I first used the category of 'the individual' in the Preface to the *Two Edifying Discourses* of 1843, it still had for me, as well, a personal meaning [i.e. in reference to Regina]; the idea itself was not so very clear to me at the time that, without this personal meaning, I would have employed it immediately. When I used it the second time, with greater force, in the foreword to the *Edifying Discourses in Various Spirits* [1847], then I realized that what I was doing was completely ideal." *Papirer*, X³ A 308, quoted in Dupre, *op.cit.*, p. 36n.

God,' since this is the source and origin of all individuality."[25] In as strong terms as possible, S.K. made it plain that "authentic existence" is found solely and exclusively before God: "There is only One who knows what He Himself is, that is God; and He knows also what every man in himself is, for it is precisely by being before God that every man is. The man who is not before God is not himself, for this a man can be only by being before Him who is in and for Himself. If one is oneself by being in Him who is in and for Himself, one can be in others and before others, but one cannot by being merely before others be oneself."[26]

If, as is the common understanding, existentialism is a philosophy that starts with the givenness of man's existence, his *Geworfenheit*, his "being-what-he-is"; and if, starting from this premise, some existentialists come to a theistic conclusion and others to a nontheistic one—if this is existentialism, then S.K. was not an existentialist, and *den Enkelte* has little if anything in common with existentialist individualism.

S.K. *begins* with God, not *arrives* at God as a conclusion derived from human existence. It is not too much to say that *den Enkelte* is an affirmation about the intention and strategy of God before it is an affirmation about the nature of man. Buber points in this direction but does not go as far as he could or should; he says of S.K.'s *den Enkelte*: "Not before a man can say *I* in perfect reality—that is, finding himself—can he in perfect reality say *Thou*—that is, to God."[27] But it is not that man on his own initiative chooses to be *den Enkelte* in order to address God; rather, God first has addressed man as *den Enkelte,* and man must then get into that role if he is to hear

[25] *Works of Love,* trans. with introduction and notes by Edna and Howard Hong (New York: Harper, 1962), p. 253.
[26] "The Anxiety of Lowliness" (Pt. I, Discourse 3) in *Christian Discourses,* trans. Walter Lowrie (New York: Oxford Un. Press, 1939), p. 43.
[27] Buber, "Question to the Single One" in *Between Man and Man,* p. 43.

and respond. *Den Enkelte* is first of all the character of God's address and only then the nature of man's response.

The "singleness" of *den Enkelte* comes about, then, because God chooses to address men singly, individually, one by one —*enkeltvis*, as the Danish language so appropriately puts it. Although S.K. did not so use it, the golden text for his *den Enkelte* could well be Isaiah 40:26.

> Lift up your eyes on high and see:
> who created these?
> He who brings out their host by number,
> calling them all by name:
> by the greatness of his might,
> and because he is strong in power
> not one is missing.

The text he did use was Matthew 10:29. "What is there said about the sparrows is yet completely the literal truth about mankind, that God knows each individual—indeed, that to be man is simply to belong to the genus which has the distinction that each individual is known *qua* individual by God and can know him."[28]

The entire motive of becoming *den Enkelte,* then, is not so much a matter of a man realizing *his* nature, finding *his* authenticity, as it is a matter of *response*. S.K. did not develop "responsibility" as a formal concept—this has been the work of our own day—but Buber properly derives and defines the term as a part of his exposition of S.K.[29] Briefly put, *den Enkelte* is a man who has become single (single-minded, single-willed, single-hearted, single-eyed) in response to and in order to respond to the individual summons of God's requirement and the individual chrism of his grace.

That this is a rather different concept of individuality, S.K. was quite aware. He made so bold as to say that in one sense

---

[28] *Papirer*, IX A 316 (1848) [my trans.—V.E.]; cf. X² A 231 (1849).
[29] Buber, *op.cit.*, p. 45.

Christ was a greater thief than Barrabas, because Christ stole from the human race its "very notion of what it is to be a man!"[30] And the extent of that theft nowhere becomes more evident than when we consider the character of *den Enkelte*'s consciousness of his individuality. Because that consciousness is achieved *before God*, it is "not with respect to his talents but with regard to his guilt."[31] S.K. approached this thought in several ways, but the core explanation as to why the self-understanding of *den Enkelte* must be of this sort is quite simple: "Christianity is God's thought. To be a man was, for God, an ideal which we can hardly even imagine; the fall was a guilt which involved a degradation, and in order to feel the painfulness of it one must have an impression of the ideal which went before."[32] When a man puts what he *is* alongside what God intends and calls him to be, *guilt* is the only possible resultant: "When thou art alone, . . . alone in individuality, or as a single individual, and face to face with God's holiness—then the cry ["God be merciful to me a sinner"] issues of itself. . . . From [the Pharisee] no cry was heard. What is the meaning of this? . . . It means that he was not before God."[33]

"Repentance" is the counterpart of guilt, and it appears as an essential aspect of individuality amazingly early in S.K.'s authorship and, even more amazingly, in the mouth of Judge William, the ethicist of *Either/Or*. When S.K. finds himself impelled to attribute a thoroughly religious concept to a non-religious pseudonym we can be sure that we are dealing with

[30] "Christ as Example" (Discourse II) in *Judge for Yourselves!* [bound behind *For Self-Examination*], trans. Walter Lowrie (New York: Oxford Un. Press, 1941), p. 187.

[31] "On the Occasion of a Confession" (Discourse I) in *Thoughts on Crucial Situations in Human Life*, trans. David F. Swenson, ed. Lillian Marvin Swenson (Minneapolis: Augsburg Publishing House, 1941), p. 27.

[32] *Dru Journals*, 1391 (1854).

[33] "Behold, We Have Left All . . ." (Pt. III, Discourse 2) in *Christian Discourses*, p. 374.

something crucial and basic: "There is also a love by which I love God, and there is only one word in the language which expresses it . . . it is repentance. . . . For only when I choose myself as guilty do I choose myself absolutely, if my absolute choice of myself is to be made in such a way that it is not identical with creating myself."[34] With this concept of repentance S.K. set an absolute distinction between *den Enkelte* and all existentialist thought about creating oneself. The distinction was pressed even harder when, toward the end of his career, S.K. made an extended analysis of the following thematic statement: "To become sober is *to come to oneself in self-knowledge, before God, as nothing before Him, yet infinitely, absolutely, under obligation. . . .* Only by being before God can a man entirely come to himself in the transparency of sobriety. . . . Christianity thinks that precisely to become nothing—before God—is the way, and that if it could occur to anyone to wish to be something before God, this is drunkenness."[35]

It does not follow that this repentance, or becoming nothing, is a negative act, a degradation, for it is actually the glory of the human spirit.[36] Indeed, *den Enkelte* eventuates as the most positive of conceptions, for his becoming nothing is but the counterpart on man's side of the forgiveness forthcoming from God's side: "Believing that his sins have been forgiven is the decisive crisis through which a human being becomes spirit; he who does not believe that is not spirit."[37] In the final analysis, then, *den Enkelte* is one who has become single in repentance in order to find the grace and forgiveness of God which is bestowed upon and can be received by only those who are single.

---

[34] *Either/Or II*, pp. 220-21.

[35] "To Become Sober" (Discourse I) in *Judge For Yourselves!*, pp. 120, 121-22, 123.

[36] "To Have Need of God Is Man's Highest Perfection" (Discourse I) in *Edifying Discourses*, Vol. IV, pp. 22ff.

[37] *Rohde Journals*, 189 (1848).

Because one becomes *den Enkelte* via self-abasement rather than self-aggrandizement, a very important implication follows: God justly can demand that every man become *den Enkelte*; it is equally possible for every man to become *den Enkelte*.[38] We shall later identify as one of his sectarian characteristics S.K.'s radical and emphatic affirmation of the equality of all men before God; we see here that it is an inevitable corollary of his concept of *den Enkelte*.

Den Enkelte is fundamentally a religious idea, but the matter can be put even more exactly. S.K. did not consider himself to be developing any new category but simply delineating the Christian gospel; *den Enkelte* is nothing more nor less than the Christian man. S.K. said it in so many words: "The formula for being a Christian is to be related to, to turn to, God personally, as a single person, quite literally as a single person."[39] He developed the conception not as a philosopher but as a Christian evangelist, and thus at points could go so far as to read "before God" as meaning, specifically, "before Christ."

In the first place, Christ was himself *den Enkelte* par excellence.[40] But he is much more than just an example from man's side; he is also the term of address from God's:

"The potentiation in consciousness of the self is in this instance knowledge of Christ, being a self face to face with Christ. . . . A self face to face with Christ is a self potentiated by the prodigious concession of God, potentiated by the prodigious emphasis which falls upon it for the fact that God also for the sake of this self let Himself to be born, became man, suffered, died. As was said in the foregoing, 'the more conception of God, the more of self,' so here it is true that the more conception of Christ, the more self. A self is qualitatively what its measure is. That Christ is the measure is

---

[38] *Purity of Heart*, pp. 184-85. Cf. *Smith Journals*, XI¹ A 384 (1854).

[39] *Smith Journals*, XI² A 135. Cf. *Point of View*, p. 89n; *Dru Journals*, 632 (1847); *Smith Journals*, XI¹ A 130, 227, 248 (1854); and *Postscript*, p. 47.

[40] *Dru Journals*, 1089 (1850).

on God's part attested as the expression for the immense reality a self possesses; for it is true for the first time in Christ that God is man's goal and measure, or measure and goal."[41]

That he exists before God with Christ as the measure of his selfhood has tremendous implications regarding the role and character of *den Enkelte*. To examine some of these is the work of our next chapter.

[41] *The Sickness unto Death*, pp. 244-45. Cf. "Lifted Up on High He Will Draw All Men unto Himself" (Pt. III, Reflection 2) in *Training in Christianity*, trans. Walter Lowrie (New York: Oxford Un. Press, 1941), pp. 159ff.

CHAPTER VI

THE CHARACTER OF
DEN ENKELTE

A number of S.K.'s major motifs are very closely related to his conception of *den Enkelte*; they can, indeed, be considered as the first-ranked characteristics of *den Enkelte*. As we treat them, definite parallels with Brethrenism will appear.

A. FREE PERSONAL DECISION

A golden key, it is said, fits every lock. But decision too and determination also unlock doors, and that is why they are called resolution; with resolution, or in resolution, the doors are opened to the noblest powers of the soul.[1]

The heading above could have been: Freedom of the Will. But this would be to say both too much and too little. Too much because neither S.K. nor the Brethren showed particular interest in aligning themselves with any party in the traditional theological controversy over the free or the bound will; the matter was much too crucial to be subjected to that sort of scholasticism. For them, freedom was the essential life blood of their entire ideology. And if something is that necessary, its actuality can be assumed—very simply *must* be as-

[1] *Rohde Journals*, 828 (1848).

sumed, for one has not time to wait out the argument. S.K. and the Brethren both believed in the freedom of the will, but they afford no help to those who would make a case for it.

But it is also too little to call our topic Freedom of the Will, because the crucial question was not whether the human will possesses the faculty of making a free choice between options. That would be a necessary affirmation for S.K. and the Brethren but hardly an adequate one. The end they had in view did not remain on the rather innocuous level of "choice" but became a matter of "resolution," "decision," "determination," "conviction," "venture," "commitment." Their affirmation was not "We believe that men can choose," but rather "We are confronted with the choice through which a man becomes a man."

S.K. and the existentialists are known as Apostles of Freedom; it is hardly necessary to *prove* that S.K. was an exponent of the view. However, for S.K. the subject of this freedom was *den Enkelte*, the one who *chooses* himself (more accurately, chooses God and in that choice chooses himself). The freedom of *den Enkelte*, as his entire existence, transpires only and always "before God." And because S.K.'s *den Enkelte* was a thoroughly religious conception, so was his understanding of *den Enkelte's* freedom thoroughly religious. Again, S.K.'s position will be seen to be in rather diametric opposition to that which commonly is understood as existentialist. It is upon this difference that our exposition will concentrate.

S.K. did value the human freedom to choose, the bare power of choice; it is basic.[2] But this natural ability gains its true significance only in the one choice of all choices, "the absolute venture," the choosing of oneself before God as *den Enkelte*. This idea was so central for S.K. that it appeared even as out-of-character "leaks" in the pseudonyms. Climacus said: "The

[2] Discourse III on "The Lilies of the Field" in *The Gospel of Suffering*, trans. David F. and Lillian Marvin Swenson (Minneapolis: Augsburg Publishing House, 1948), p. 228.

fact is that the individual becomes infinite only by virtue of making the absolute venture. Hence it is not the same individual who makes this venture among others, yielding as a consequence one more predicate attaching to one and the same individual. No, but in making the absolute venture he becomes another individual."[3] And it was Judge William, the ethicist, who specified that this choice—far from being a cool, reasoned nod in favor of this over that, a choice based on calculated probabilities—is rather a solemn and passionate commitment to God.[4] Thus "resolve," or "venture," stands a whole quality higher than mere choice, or freedom of the will; and it is the fact that it transpires before God that gives it its critical character. Therefore S.K. could call resolution "the only language in which God wills to have intercourse with man."[5]

This freedom to resolve is the most precious possession of the human spirit but also the most precarious, for it exists only as long as it is rightly used:

"The most tremendous thing which has been granted to man is: the choice, freedom. And if you desire to save it and preserve it there is only one way: in the very same second unconditionally and in complete resignation to give it back to God, and yourself with it. If the sight of what is granted to you tempts you, and if you give way to the temptation and look with egoistic desire upon the freedom of choice, then you lose your freedom. And your punishment is: to go on in a kind of confusion priding yourself on having—freedom of choice, but woe upon you, that is your judgment: You have freedom of choice, you say, and still you have not chosen God."[6]

Is there not something highly ironic—and profoundly significant—in the fact that precisely the sort of freedom prized

[3] *Postscript*, p. 379.
[4] *Stages on Life's Way*, p. 114.
[5] "On the Occasion of a Wedding" (Discourse II) in *Thoughts on Crucial Situations in Human Life*, pp. 68-69.
[6] *Dru Journals*, 1051 (1850).

as ultimate by the existentialists is branded by "the father of existentialism" as punishment and judgment? S.K. here staked the freedom of *den Enkelte* at an almost infinite distance from any and all concepts that carry overtones of autonomy, egocentricity, Prometheanism, or self-creation; but let it not be said that he has denigrated freedom in the process. From the standpoint of his totally religious perspective, the fact that human freedom is so completely bounded by and tied to God is in no sense a detriment but precisely the source of its glory; man's freedom is the more real and the more precious when guaranteed by God's involvement than it would be if unrestricted by his presence.

"Resolve," "venture," "decision," "choice"—these are all synonyms for the more familiar Kierkegaardian term "leap." Actually, "leap" is S.K.'s earlier terminology—almost the property of the pseudonyms. These later, more strictly religious terms probably are superior for communicating S.K.'s thought, because "leap" tends to carry connotations of blind abandon, almost of irresponsibility. Such ideas are not truly part of the concept at all. But the point behind this whole family of words is of great importance to S.K.'s witness, for it is through the absolute venture that a man becomes *den Enkelte*, and that venture is nothing more nor less than what the Christian gospel intends by *faith*. S.K.'s position on freedom was not a philosophic or even anthropologic affirmation but essentially an exposition of the New Testament: "Christianity and the New Testament understood something perfectly definite by believing; to believe is to venture out as decisively as it is possible for a man to do, breaking with everything a man naturally loves, breaking, in order to save his own soul, with that in which he naturally has his life."[7]

The nature of this venture—now put into its specifically Christian context (which is the end S.K. had in view all along)—was made more explicit:

[7] *Attack upon "Christendom,"* p. 191.

"There cannot be any *direct* transition from an historical fact to the foundation upon it of an eternal happiness. . . . How then do we proceed [in relation to Christ]? Thus. A man says to himself, a la Socrates: here is an historical fact which teaches me that in regard to my eternal happiness I must have recourse to Jesus Christ. Now I must certainly preserve myself from taking the wrong turning into scientific inquiry and research. . . . And so I say to myself: I choose; that historical fact means so much to me that I decide to stake my whole life upon that if. Then he lives; lives entirely full of the idea, risking his life for it: and his life is the proof that he believes. He did not have a few proofs, and so believed and then began to live. No, the very reverse. That is called risking; and without risk faith is an impossibility."[8]

It would be quite possible at this point to understand S.K. as trying to make the best of a bad situation: when one cannot *know*, he *has* to make the venture of faith; it would be nice if we could *prove* that Jesus Christ is salvation, but since we cannot, we simply will have to act as though he is. It would be quite possible, too, to understand S.K. as making the venture completely unmotivated, fortuitous, subjectivistic, based on nothing more than what the man decides he wants to believe. Both these implications are very wide from the mark, as S.K. made plain in the very important journal entry that follows:

"If I truly have a conviction (and that, we know, is an inner determination in the direction of spirit) my conviction to me is always stronger than reasons; actually, conviction is what *supports* the reasons, not the other way around. . . . One's conviction, or the fact that it is one's conviction: my, your, conviction (the personal) is decisive. One can deal with reasons half jokingly: Well, if you insist on reasons I don't mind giv-

[8] *Dru Journals,* 1044 (1850). Cf. "Christ as Example (Discourse II) in *Judge for Yourselves!,* p. 200.

ing you some; do you want 3 or 5 or 7, how many do you want? Still, I cannot say anything higher than this: I have faith! I believe! . . . My development, or any man's, proceeds like this: Maybe he too starts out with some reasons, but they represent the lower plane. Then he makes a choice; under the weight of responsibility before God a conviction will be born in him by God's help. . . . The matter becomes further personal, or it becomes a question of personality, i.e., one can only defend one's conviction ethically, personally, that is through the sacrifice one is willing to make for it and by the dauntlessness with which one maintains it. There is only one proof of the truth of Christianity: the inner proof, *argumentum spiritus sancti*. In the Epistle of St. John (5:9) this is hinted: 'If we receive the witness of men' (meaning all the historical evidence and considerations), 'the witness of God is greater' i.e. the inner testimony is greater. And in verse 10: 'He that believeth on the Son of God hath the witness in himself.' It is not the reasons that motivate belief in the Son of God, but the other way round, belief in the Son of God constitutes the evidence. It is the very motion of the Infinite, and it cannot be otherwise. Reasons do not motivate convictions; conviction motivates the reasons."[9]

Here in brief compass is an epistemology of religion, the epistemology of freedom's venture, i.e. of faith. Note that it is a supremely religious method of dealing with *religious truth*; S.K. certainly did not mean to suggest this as a procedure for arriving at scientific fact, or even for constructing theological dogma. This is an epistemology for matters of "infinite, personal, passionate interest,"[10] operative in that realm where the human spirit must deal with things of the spirit. And here, in faith's proper sphere, conviction, decision, and venture—enthusiasm (*enthousiasmos*), if you will—are more powerful, more effective, and more knowledgeable than reasons and

[9] *Rohde Journals*, 201 (1849).   [10] *Postscript*, p. 33.

evidence and intellectual cognition ever could be. The free venture of *den Enkelte* is the only possible—but also the best conceivable—way to God and to true selfhood.

Notice, too, that this venture is far from being a subjectivistic leap in the dark, even though there are no so-called objective reasons and evidences to form its rationale. S.K. was emphatic that, in the venture, *den Enkelte* finds and is found by "God's help," "the inner testimony," "*argumentum spiritus sancti*," "the very motion of the Infinite." And here is objectivity enough and to spare; God the Spirit is a reality apart from the man, standing over against him, capable, thus, of confronting, judging, correcting, and disciplining him quite independently of the man's own subjective inclinations and desires. Of course this is an entirely individualized objectivity that never can be "shared," i.e. the inner testimony received by one man will not accomplish a whit in easing the need or paving the way for the next person to make *his* personal venture. But this in no way affects the powerful objectivity of *den Enkelte's* relationship to God and thus of his "definition" of himself.

Quite simply, for S.K. faith *must* possess this character of venture and risk, because it is the committing of oneself in a person-to-Person relationship. No other understanding of God except that he is a Person even will begin to give coherence to Kierkegaard's thought—and not his religious thought only, but also his so-called philosophic thought. Nothing S.K. ever wrote is more fundamental than the following journal entries:

"Augustine has done incalculable harm. The whole of Christian doctrine through the centuries really rests upon him— and he has confused the concept of faith.

"Quite simply, Augustine resuscitated the platonic-aristotelian definition, the whole Greek philosophical pagan definition of faith. . . .

"For the Greeks faith is a concept which belongs to the

sphere of the intellect. . . . So faith is related to the probable, and we have the ascending scale of faith and knowledge.

"From the Christian point of view faith belongs to the existential: God did not appear in the character of a professor who has some doctrines which must first be believed and then understood.

"No, faith belongs to and has its home in the existential, and in all eternity it has nothing to do with knowledge as a comparative or a superlative.

"Faith expresses a relationship from personality to personality.

"Personality is not a sum of doctrines, nor is it something directly accessible. Personality is bent in on itself, it is a *clausum* [something closed] an *aduton* [innermost shrine], a *musterion* [mystery]. Personality is that which is within, hence the word *persona* (*personare*) is significant, it is that which is within to which a man, himself in turn a personality, may be related in faith. Between person and person no other relation is possible. Take the two most passionate lovers who have ever lived, and even if they are, as is said, one soul in two bodies, this can never come to anything more than that the one believes that the other loves him or her.

"In this purely personal relation between God as personal being and the believer as personal being, in *existence*, is to be found the concept of faith.

"[In the margin:] Hence the apostolic formula, 'the *obedience* of faith' (e.g. Romans 1:5), so that faith tends to the will and personality, not to intellectuality."[11]

But it is not enough simply to establish the concept that God is a Person.

"Let us suppose that someone, a professor, spends his whole life in study and learning in order to demonstrate the personality of God—and let us suppose that in the end he succeeds. What then? Then at the end of his life he will have

[11] *Smith Journals,* XI¹ A 237 (1854); cf. XI² A 380 (1854).

come to the beginning, or to the end of the introduction to the beginning. . . .

"No, God is personal, the matter is certain.

"But with this you are no farther forward. Here again there is a human aberration, it is imagined that when the professor has finally proved that God is personality, then he must be so without further ado for us all. . . .

"No, God is certainly personal, but it does not follow from this that he is personal without further ado for you. Take a human relationship: a superior personality is certainly a personality, but does he not have it in his power, in the face of his inferior, to be a personality in relation to him, or to be related objectively to him?[12] Yet it is clear that the superior is and remains a personality.

"So with God. He is certainly personality, but whether he wills to be this in relation to the single person depends on whether it pleases God. It is God's grace that in relation to you he desires to be personality; and if you squander his grace, he punishes you by relating himself objectively to you."[13]

And because faith is a living, existential relation between a human person and the God Person, it follows that the relationship will be of the nature of *authority*.

"Christianity came into the world on the basis of authority, its divine authority; therefore the authority is superior. But for a long time now the situation has been quite changed around: one seeks to prove and establish authority on grounds of reason. . . . A so-called philosophical Christianity has discovered that authority is imperfect, at best something for the

[12] I have taken the liberty of amending Smith's translation so as to make a rhetorical question out of what he transcribes as a flat, negative assertion: "he does not have it in his power. . . ." Smith is true to the Danish edition of the *Papirer*, which does not have the question mark. But whether the mistake was S.K.'s or his editor's, the sense of the passage as much as demands that the question be what S.K. had in mind. [V.E.]

[13] *Smith Journals*, XI[2] A 175 (1854).

plebs, and that perfection consists in getting rid of it. . . . And theology seeks to establish the authority of Christianity by reason, which is worse than any attack, since it confesses indirectly that there is no authority."[14]

Of course faith's venture certainly does represent a free, centered act on the part of the individual, but that is not to say that the act is self-contained, involving nothing but the person's private power and action. Indeed, in the venture the individual need free himself only far enough that God can get at him, as it were; once a man makes the effort, God stands by to energize and direct the leap. In no sense does *den Enkelte* become self-creating, because even with his strong emphasis upon human freedom S.K. also held a strong concept of *enabling*, and even *prevenient*, grace:

"It is as when one gives a present to a child and then, to please him, pretends that he is giving us what we had given him, which in fact was ours. But our relationship with God is not even of that kind, for God is also at the same time the One Who gives us the power to succeed. It would, therefore, be like the father and mother who themselves help the child to write a congratulatory letter for their anniversary, which letter will be received as a present on the anniversary day."[15]

The role here assigned to grace explains why S.K. could as much as guarantee that he who leaps will leap correctly:

"For one can guarantee to make a Christian of every man he can get to come under this category [i.e. *den Enkelte*]—insofar as one man can do this for another, or we may say rather, that he can vouch for it that such a man will become a Christian. As a single individual he is alone, alone in the whole world, alone before God—and with that there is no question about obedience! All doubt . . . is just simply disobedience to God."[16]

[14] *Smith Journals*, XI[1] A 436 (1854).

[15] *Papirer*, VIII[1] A 342 (1847), quoted in Dupre, *op.cit.*, p. 110.

[16] The second of "Two Notes on 'the Individual'" in *Point of View*, p. 135.

The work of the Holy Spirit—although not usually posed under that name—is an integral part of S.K.'s concept of freedom, even if this aspect of the matter customarily is disregarded by his interpreters. But with this inclusion it is made very apparent that, for all his notorious subjectivity, S.K.'s basic thought is oriented toward and involved in a Reality that is objective and transcendental in the highest sense possible.

As did S.K., so did the Brethren believe in (or rather, assume) the freedom of the will, although they were as little concerned to prove the point as he was. Certainly it is the case that all Protestants, churchly as well as sectarian, are eager to preserve an emphasis both on the sovereignty of God and on faith as personal decision. At the same time it is rather clear that the sectarian tradition, with its insistence upon adult baptism, conversion, etc., has been more emphatic on the latter point than has the churchly. And in this regard it is unimpeachable that, historically, the sectaries were more inclined to uphold a doctrine of freedom of the will while the churches tended toward predestination and the bound will.

Implicit hints rather than explicit discussion make it plain that the Brethren were part of the sectarian, free-will tradition, even though they came out of a Calvinist background.[17] In the only Brethren word at all resembling a "theological" statement on the issue, Mack Junior took a position not intrinsically different from S.K.'s, striving to attribute all possible credit to the work of grace *yet without impinging on the decisive role of human freedom*: "God, indeed, can require of His creatures whatever He wishes. But when He does require something of us, He first influences the will—if one accepts it

---

[17] Of course by the time we get down to S.K. in the nineteenth century it is not unusual to find even "churchly" theologians advocating the free-will position. S.K.'s view, therefore, does in no sense prove him a sectary, although at the same time we shall see that he *uses* man's freedom in much the same existential way that the Brethren sectaries did.

—so that the person wills as He wills. Thus He also effects and gives the accomplishment according to His pleasure. And then things are good; God is pleased and the person is blessed."[18] The crucial little parenthesis "if one accepts it" amounts to the same thing as the child following his parents' suggestion and letting them help him write a congratulatory letter. From one standpoint this does not amount to much in the way of freedom, but as *real* freedom it marks a substantial move away from the doctrine of the bound will. The Brethren-Kierkegaardian view is far from the utter and infinite freedom of existentialism, but it is also far from churchly predestinarianism.

The heart of the matter, for Mack, came at the same place it did for S.K. Mack said: "The covenant of God under the economy of the New Testament demands genuinely voluntary lovers of God and His truth."[19] It can be put no more forthrightly—and S.K. would have been the first to applaud: The affirmation of human freedom is primarily and eminently a demand of the gospel, not a necessary concept of philosophical theology nor even an empirical observation regarding the human situation.

Thus the Brethren were not content, any more than S.K. was, to stop simply with the assertion that human freedom exists; they hurried on to the idea of faith as freedom committed through the absolute venture. Mack Junior, although speaking much less precisely than S.K., made the same point:

"To have faith and to believe are to be distinguished, just as to live and to act...." Here we must clarify Mack's terminology, for it is in some respects the precise opposite of that to which we are accustomed in English. Modern theology uses "faith" (with overtones of commitment and trust) as superior to

[18] Alexander Mack, Jr., *Appendix to the Refuted Anabaptists* [first published Ephrata, 1788], in a typescript translation by N. P. Springer (Mennonite Historical Library, Goshen, Ind., 1952), p. 3.

[19] Mack Junior, *Apology*, p. 15.

"belief" (mere intellectual assent to cognitive propositions), but this is not at all the distinction Mack had in mind. He is contrasting "to *have* faith," which is in the *passive* voice, thus that which is held merely as an inanimate possession, with "to believe," which is in the *active* voice, thus a dynamic, creative work of the believer. The contrast is the same as that between "to live," i.e. merely to be alive, in existence, with "to act." Mack continues:

" 'Behold the kingdom of God is within you (Luke 17:21).' Now, where the kingdom of God is in a person, there also is faith—nevertheless, with great disparity. With many it lies as dead and obscure as the fire in a cold stone; with others it lies as a little spark in the ashes; conversely, with others as a rather large coal."

Here lies the crux of the sectarian protest against the concept of faith as *practiced*, if not *taught*, by the churches—which protest led even to the denial of the Reformation principle of *sola fide*. The difference ultimately is a semantic one as to what is intended by the word "faith," and it may well be that the sectaries stood closer to what Luther intended by *sola fide* than the churchmen did. But whether the debate over the word "faith" was legitimate or not, the distinction is a real one. Mack is resisting any concept of faith that makes it an almost natural endowment, one that is achieved, at any rate, simply by being born in a Christian country and following the accepted social pattern of church life. The most that can be said for faith on this level is that it is *potential* faith, which, by being acted upon, lived by, ventured, can be fanned into true faith. Mack continues:

"But with everyone something must first happen[20] inwardly or outwardly—the commonest way is inwardly and outwardly together—something real first must happen so that

[20] S.K. expressed this idea with the term "predicament," or "situation"; see "Christ as Example" (Discourse II) in *Judge for Yourselves!*, p. 200. Cf. S.K. as quoted below, p. 174.

the person might come to believe, or to demonstrate, that faith is not his belonging but that, much more, lack of faith [*Unglaube*] is the element in which he chooses to live and die. In that connection Paul witnesses (Acts 17 [16?] :31) that God charges every person to believe."[21]

But the Brethren emphasis on faith as free venture comes through most characteristically as poetic exhortation rather than prosaic theologizing. Mack Junior, again, is the author:

> When now a child of man
>   In this short life
> Considers now and then
>   To whom he shall give himself,
> God or his Enemy,
>   So is the number of days
> For this great choice
>   Appointed by his Friend. . . .
> God Himself makes him brave
>   So that he conquers,
> Reveals to him the noble crown,
>   And metes out for him the time,
> That in this conflict he
>   May bring off the prize.[22]

Here is the theme of choice and its importance, the fact that God himself aids and enables one in the choice, and a new emphasis regarding the time factor involved. This last forms a specific parallel with S.K.; he developed the idea of what he called "the moment," or "the instant." This is the hour of decision, the *kairos* destined for the venture of faith. When fulfilled in the venture, "the moment" is the point at which eternity enters time, at which a man comes into existence before God. And the moment always is *now*. Yesterday has

21 Mack Junior, *Apology*, p. 62.
22 Mack Junior, a poem on suicide (c. 1770), in Heckman, *op.cit.*, pp. 136ff., stanzas 18, 20 [trans. amended—V.E.].

proved too early; it was allowed to pass without being used. Tomorrow will be too late; the longer one delays choosing the more likely that he will continue to delay and so never choose. Today is the day, this the moment God offers and has destined for the absolute venture.

In Brethren thought this idea is best represented in the poetry of Jacob Stoll; the urgency of decision becomes the next thing to an obsession with him. "O, the time of grace is urgent!/Therefore, buy it well."[23] Into two lines Stoll managed to cram his three favorite phrases: "this time of grace," "the time so urgent," and "buying the time." One of his best hymns is built on the recurrent line: "O, how is the time so urgent?"[24] But the most "Kierkegaardian" passage of all is his hymn "The Single Choice":

> Each person is what he chooses
> As being his desire and joy;
> Each person is what he strives for
> As his enjoyment.
> There must be some significance
> To what one chooses as his portion;
> And shall it prove, then,
> To be only vanity?
> So what shall now be my choice?
> What shall my portion signify?
> Thee, Jesus, my crown,
> Thee will I prize eternally.
>
> Of two things, choose one;
> Indeed, more you cannot have;

[23] Jacob Stoll, *Geistliches Gewurz-Gartlein* (Ephrata, 1806), pp. 135-36 [my trans.—V.E.].

[24] *Ibid.*, p. 163. The second stanza of this hymn appears in the German and in a modern translation as 428 in the current *Brethren Hymnal*. There it is attributed to Mack Senior. Although we have not been able to trace that attribution to its source, the likelihood seems to be that Stoll is the author of the lines.

And if you choose nothing,
The world does bury you,
And it eventually passes away
With all its lusts,
And what here pleased you
Will fill your breast with sorrow.[25]

B. *ANTIINTELLECTUALISM*

The Christian thesis is not intelligere ut credam, nor is it credere ut intelligam. No, it is: Act according to the precepts and commandments of Christ, do the will of the Father—and you shall have faith. Christianity does not lie in the least in the sphere of the intellect.[1]

For the simple heart it is simply: thou shalt believe. For the understanding intellect it is: it is against reason, but thou shalt believe. Here the "thou shalt" is much stronger because it is opposed to something.[2]

"Antiintellectualism," or "irrationalism," is a Kierkegaardian hallmark universally recognized and almost as widely analyzed, popularized, criticized and/or apotheosized. It will not be necessary for us either to duplicate or to compete with these efforts; it suffices to note a few things that many commentators overlook and to make audible the sectarian tenor of S.K.'s position.

One observation common to most Kierkegaard scholars but which deserves repeating is that S.K. nowhere denied reason a proper sphere or a competency in that sphere. And that sphere is broad, as broad as the world—but no broader. Reason does *not* have authority or competence in the supermundane dimensions of man's existence where he chooses himself and

---

[25] *Ibid.*, p. 185 [my trans.—V.E.].

[1] *Smith Journals*, XI¹ A 339 (1854).
[2] *Papirer*, X¹ A 187 (1849), quoted in Dupre, *op.cit.*, p. 128.

knows himself before God. S.K. belittled reason only where it presumed to encroach upon matters of faith. S.K. maintained that reason cannot provide adequate answers for problems of "infinite, personal, passionate interest"; he did not question the rights and capabilities of reason per se. Thus S.K. was not an "irrationalist" either in principle or in practice, and the last thing he wanted to be is precisely what his existentialist disciples have made of him, the founder of a philosophy which proves philosophically that philosophy is impossible.[3]

From this follows a second observation which is not as common to the commentators: S.K.'s contention against reason was a purely and thoroughly *religious* one. S.K. was *not* a philosopher who through his philosophic-rational investigations of reason discovered and gave rational definition to the limits of reason—as though reason were capable of mapping the territory into which it cannot go and then denying itself entry. S.K. was not a philosopher-theologian graciously "leaving room" for faith; he was a man of faith "making room" for faith against the incursions of intellectualism. If at times some of the pseudonymous works give this other impression, it is not because S.K. himself actually was operating out of a philosophic stance; rather, the religious maieuticer had "gone back" in the guise of a pseudonym to interest "philosophers" and entice them forward into religion. S.K.'s antiintellectualism—as every other of his major themes—is more accurately explicated when one starts from the true, religious premises of Søren Kierkegaard rather than the pseudo, philosophic premises of the *pseudo*nyms.

At base, S.K.'s antiintellectualism was directed not toward any defect or shortcoming within reason itself but toward the theological tendency to posit, justify, and defend Christianity on the grounds of its rational comprehensibility. Whether,

[3] *Papirer*, X⁶ B 114, pp. 143ff. (1849-50), quoted in Cornelio Fabro, "Faith and Reason in Kierkegaard's Dialectic" in *Critique*, pp. 178-79.

then, all theologizing is to be considered as coming under S.K.'s strictures depends entirely upon how broadly one applies the term "theology." So-called biblical theology, lay theology, applied theology, practical theology, etc., likely would not. What definitely would is philosophical theology, systematic theology, and any other theology that tends toward interpreting Christianity primarily in terms of its cognitive coherency—and certainly, in S.K.'s day and traditionally, this is what the very word "theology" suggested. Thus S.K. could make the acid comment: "Who speaks in honor of [faith]? Philosophy goes further. Theology sits rouged at the window and courts its favor, offering to sell her charms to philosophy."[4] And thus in the precise language of scholarship it is misleading to identify S.K. either as a philosopher or as a theologian, although in popular usage—where "philosopher" means simply "one who thinks about the meaning of life" and "theologian," "one who thinks about God and religion"—the terms are acceptable and, indeed, unavoidable.

It should be noted, and noted well, that the objection of both S.K. and the Brethren against theology did not have to do with the "content" of Christian doctrine. As S.K. said: "Doctrine, as normally expounded, is on the whole correct. Hence I am not quarreling about that."[5] In neither case are we dealing with a heterodoxy attacking orthodoxy in order to supplant orthodox beliefs with new ones of its own. Thus the antitheological bent of S.K. and the Brethren is something different from that of the Social Gospel, for example, in which the objection to theologizing was made suspect by the fact that the objectors were as much at odds with the basic content of orthodoxy as with the fact of its theologizing. The true Kierke-

---

[4] *Fear and Trembling* [bound with *The Sickness unto Death*], trans. Walter Lowrie, revised by Howard Johnson (Garden City: Doubleday Anchor, 1954), p. 43. The words are those of Johannes *de silentio* (pseud.); the sentiment can safely be ascribed to S.K. Cf. p. 5 above. Cf. also *Smith Journals*, XI[1] A 557 (1854).

[5] *Papirer*, X[3] A 635 (1850), quoted in Diem, *Dialectic*, p. 81.

gaard-sectarian concern is not so much that the churches hold *wrong beliefs* (beliefs in the sense of the basic, propositional definitions of the faith) as that they foster *anemic belief* (belief in the sense of decisive, ventured commitment). The live threat to Christianity is not heresy (to which theologizing might be an appropriate response, if it would confine itself simply to teaching correct beliefs rather than striving to prove or justify them) but indifference (which theologizing tends to compound by suggesting that what Christianity basically requires is intellectual comprehension and assent).

Thus S.K. was deeply troubled over the fact that theology tends to obscure rather than elucidate the true nature of Christianity. His statement quoted below is most significant because of its date; in 1836-1837 S.K. was but twenty-four years old, six years away from the opening of his authorship. Yet here appears a protest that could as well be part of the *Attack* of 1855:

"Every Christian concept has been so sublimated, so completely volatilized into a sea of fog that it is impossible to recognize it again. To such concepts as faith, incarnation, tradition, inspiration, which in Christianity must be referred to a particular historical fact, it has seemed good to philosophers to give an entirely different general meaning whereby faith becomes immediate certainty, which at bottom is neither more nor less than the vital fluid of the life of the mind, its atmosphere; tradition has become the summary of a certain world experience, whilst inspiration has become nothing but the result of God having breathed the spirit of life into man, and incarnation nothing else than the existence of one or other ideas in one or more individuals."[6]

This statement, and the continuing Kierkegaardian position of which it is an expression, carries some very interesting implications regarding the way S.K. has been used in modern

[6] *Dru Journals*, 88, p. 35 (1836-1837).

theology. There is not necessarily any discrepancy at all between the fact that Emil Brunner calls S.K. "the greatest
Christian thinker of modern times"[7] and the fact that Karl
Barth gives S.K. no attention whatsoever in his history of
nineteenth century theology.[8] S.K. could have been what
Brunner says he was without being an appropriate subject for
Barth's *theological* history. Either Brunner's, or Barth's, or
both assessments of S.K. are actually more consistent than the
approach of a Tillich or a Bultmann which draws heavily
upon S.K. in the process of constructing a philosophical theology which almost certainly would come under Kierkegaardian condemnation.[9] It would, perhaps, be both more accurate and more fair to posit an "either/or" rather than a liaison between all those who indulge in formal systematics and
the man who said: "In relation to Christianity, systematic philosophy is merely skilled in the use of all sorts of diplomatic
phraseology, which deceives the unsuspicious. Christianity as
understood by the speculative philosopher is something different from Christianity as expounded for the simple."[10]

In accord with his avowed position, S.K. did not write theology in the traditional sense, and it is only by a perverse sort
of exegesis that one can make him talk like a theologian. It is
difficult to pin him down on the "normal" issues of theology,
simply because he did not address himself to them. Indeed,
it is apparent that he made a studied attempt to avoid custom-

---

[7] Brunner, *Truth as Encounter*, p. 112.

[8] Karl Barth, *Protestant Thought: From Rousseau to Ritschl*, trans.
Brian Cozens (New York: Harper, 1959).

[9] Kenneth Hamilton recently has published a full-length study of
Tillich's theology, *The System and the Gospel* (New York: Macmillan,
1963), in which he deliberately uses S.K. as a norm against which to
criticize Tillich, going so far as to characterize him as an "anti-
Kierkegaard."

[10] *Postscript*, p. 200. These words of Climacus safely can be ascribed
to S.K. In fact, by virtue of its being designed specifically as a bridge
between the aesthetic and the religious works, *Postscript* comes as close
to being direct communication as a pseudonym can be.

ary theological terminology (such as "Trinity," "incarnation," "natures") even though it is equally apparent that he accepted the basic ideas with which the terms have to do.

An interesting example in this regard also provides a striking parallel with Brethrenism. In the course of his thought S.K., obviously, treated all three Persons of the Godhead time and again; but in all of his voluminous writings there is only one discussion of the Trinity as such, and this an unpublished journal entry. Even here, however, S.K. showed no interest at all in what the Godhead is in and for itself, what its essential nature may be or what the internal relations among the three Persons. The question he discussed is: what is the economy of the three Persons as they relate to the individual in the process of his finding salvation? His conclusion, very briefly put, was: One begins with an immediate relationship to God the Father but soon finds the disparity too exacting and so is referred by the Father to the Son as Model. Now, the Model is found to be impossibly high and so the Model refers the man to Himself as Redeemer. However, even in the Redeemer the demands of the Model still stand, and so the Son refers the man to the Spirit as a source of present help, guidance, and comfort. Then, and only then, is the Spirit ready to lead one to the Son and the Son to the Father.[11]

Although in the course of their writings the eighteenth century Brethren obviously treated all three Persons of the Godhead, there appears only one discussion of the Trinity as such. But even here they showed no interest in what the Godhead is in and for itself, etc. But Christian Longenecker addressed himself to the question: what is the economy of the three Persons as they relate to the individual in the process of his finding salvation? His conclusion was: One first meets God through a confrontation with the Father in his holiness. As a consequence the man is so struck by his own sinfulness that he shuns intimacy and finds forgiveness incredible.

[11] *Dru Journals*, 1282 (1852).

Therefore, the "tug of the Father directs him to the throne of grace and brings him to the Son." "Now the Son will cleanse his flesh and spirit of all defilement and give him a new leader, namely, the Holy Spirit." And then the man discovers that "he *can* love God."[12]

The major significance of this parallel does not lie particularly in the results; there may be more of a difference than our brief summaries would indicate. Rather, the impressive factors of the comparison are these: In the first place, neither S.K. nor Longenecker was heterodox, but their *approach* to orthodoxy was unorthodox, to say the least. Both recognized the importance of a correct understanding of Christian doctrine; in neither S.K. nor the Brethren is there any hint of an "it doesn't matter what you believe" attitude. But on the other hand, both S.K. and the Brethren saw doctrine as *correct* only insofar as it was *edifying*, relevant to one's immediate existence. The test of true doctrine is whether it edifies, not whether it is logically consistent. Just as soon as doctrine wandered toward the abstract and theoretical, S.K. and the Brethren lost all interest.

The position of both S.K. and the Brethren surely can be described as antiintellectual; it accurately could be called nontheological if one confines the term "theology" to formal, speculative, systematic thought; it would be inaccurate to call the position doctrinally heedless or promiscuous; and it would be entirely out of order to term it irrational.

Viewed from his radically religious perspective, S.K.'s antiintellectualism shows up at point after point in widely varying connections; in fact, it is seen to be the necessary negative that proceeds from any number of his positive motifs:

(1) Thus, because the concept of *den Enkelte* is a thrust in the direction of the personal, the concrete, the specific, the

---

[12] Christian Longenecker, "On the True Conversion and New Birth" [an essay from his book, *Eine Vertheidigung der Wahrheit* (Ephrata, 1806)], trans. Vernard Eller, *Brethren Life and Thought*, VII, 2 (Spring 1962), 23-26.

particular—any movement in the direction of abstraction and generality is to be condemned: "[People] regard Christianity as a sum of doctrinal statements and lecture upon them, just as they do upon ancient philosophy, the Hebrew language, or any other scientific discipline, treating the relation to them of the hearers or learners as entirely indifferent. Substantially this is paganism. The Christian position clearly is that the personal relationship to Christianity is the decisive thing."[13] Doctrine, if it is to touch *den Enkelte* where he lives, must be edification directed to that individual, not theory directed to the forum of learning.[14] And because God is a Person, *den Enkelte*'s relationship to him must involve infinitely more than just intellectual cognition.[15]

(2) We are dealing with S.K.'s antiintellectualism immediately following our discussion of his concept of faith because the connection is very close. If faith is venture in the radical sense defined above, then it can in no way be rational calculation. The two are opposed movements, for reflection proceeds, not by leaping into seventy thousand fathoms of water, but by building a pier out from the shore, welding cautious deduction to proven premise every inch of the way:

"If I really have powers of reflection and am in a situation in which I have to act decisively—what then? My powers of reflection will show me exactly as many possibilities *pro* as *contra*. . . . There is nothing more impossible, or more self-contradictory than to act (decisively, infinitely) by virtue of reflection. If anyone asserts that they have done so they only give themselves away and show that either they have no powers of reflection (because the reflection which has not a *pro* for every *contra* is not reflection at all, the essence of it being its duality) or else they do not know what it means to act."[16]

---

[13] "Our Salvation Is Now Nearer . . ." (Part III, Discourse 5) in *Christian Discourses*, pp. 221-22.

[14] *The Concept of Dread*, p. 14.

[15] See the quotations on pp. 120-25 above. Cf. *Smith Journals*, XI² A 86 (1854).

[16] *Dru Journals*, 871 (1849).

(3) Immediately following this discussion of antiintellectualism will come a section on S.K.'s understanding of "inwardness," or "subjectivity." The relationship again is very
close. Christianity becomes actual for a person only when it
has driven radically inward, affecting his very being, touching
the deepest wellsprings of his life; and cognitive propositions
simply do not penetrate to this level. What follows is S.K.'s
best and most succinct statement of an idea to which he devoted major attention. Would that in their effort to exegete
S.K.'s "subjectivity" all his commentators might start with this
little-used passage rather than confining their attention to
words of the nonreligious pseudonyms:

"The truth, in the sense in which Christ was the truth, is
not a sum of sentences, not a definition of concepts, etc., but a
life. Truth in its very being is not the duplication of being in
terms of thought, which yields only the thought of being. . . .
No, truth in its very being is the reduplication in me, in thee,
in him, so that my, that thy, that his life, approximately, in the
striving to attain it, expresses the truth, so that my, that thy,
that his life, approximately, in the striving to attain it, is the
very being of truth, is a *life*, as the truth was in Christ, for He
was the truth. And hence, Christianly understood, the truth
consists not in knowing the truth but in being the truth. . . .
No man knows more of the truth than what he is of the truth.
. . . Only then do I truly know the truth when it becomes a
life in me. . . . And hence one sees what a monstrous error it
is, very nearly the greatest possible error, to impart Christianity by lecturing."[17]

At least something of the same thought was expressed in an
anonymous tract which almost certainly comes from an
eighteenth century Brethren source. In concluding his appeal,
the author requests non-Christians to renounce their own
sophistical judgments of the matters presented and pray God
for a beginning of experience, saying, "A completely small

[17] "Lifted Up On High . . ." (Part III, Reflection 5) in *Training in
Christianity*, pp. 200-01, 202.

experience of the Way which Christ himself is is better than a great fancy [*Einbildung*] of the Way which Christ himself is."[18] Is this not an embryonic way of saying that truth "is a *life*, as the truth was in Christ" and not "the duplication of being in terms of thought"?

(4) The point at which the Brethren most fully justified and defended their antiintellectualism was as the negative counterpart of obedience. S.K. also had a strong emphasis on obedience and also saw that intellectualism is the enemy. "To reflect" is essentially opposed to "to obey," for reflection involves questioning, the demanding of an explanation, the holding back of commitment: "It is very far from being true that the longer a man deliberates and deliberates, the nearer he comes to God; on the contrary, the truth is that the longer the deliberation becomes while the choice is postponed, the farther he removes himself from God. . . . The ungodly calmness with which the irresolute man would begin in the case of God (for he would begin with doubt), precisely this is insubordination; for thereby God is deposed from the throne, from being the Lord."[19]

In their earliest theological work, through the writing of Mack Senior, the Brethren also emphasized that obedience must take precedence over intellectualizing: "It is very good to look only to the express word of the Lord Jesus and to His own perfect example. If people would just follow after Him in the obedience of faith, taking reason captive in obedience to the Lord Jesus, they would not be led astray by the high-

---

[18] *Ein Geringer Schein* . . . (Germantown, 1747), p. 24. For a description of this work, a translation of parts of it, the argument for its Brethren authorship, and the suggestion that Mack Junior may have been the writer, see Vernard Eller, "Friends, Brethren, and Separatists . . . ," *Brethren Life and Thought*, VII, 4 (Autumn 1962), 47ff.

[19] "The Anxiety of Irresolution . . ." (Part I, Discourse 7) in *Christian Discourses*, p. 90.

sounding talk of men."[20] A generation later, the second
Alexander Mack discussed the matter in more detail, in response to a specific accusation that the Brethren shrink from
the use of reason: "The baptism-minded ones [the "Dunkers"]
wish to have no other system than the words of their Savior,
as they stand written in the New Testament, which words
never give place to reason, and not only as well-ringing gold,
which can withstand the most severe inspection, but also will
stand when heaven and earth pass away. . . . Under heaven
there is to be found no higher honor for our small reason than
where it may shine in the bonds and fetters of heavenly wisdom, and that, on the contrary, where it is met outside this
captivity, it is outside its city of refuge."[21] Certainly there
may be an aspect of naivete to this "if people would just follow after Him," but if it has not become clear already, it presently will, that S.K., for one, always would rather be identified with naive obedience than with sophisticated theologizing.

(5) Another major characteristic of both S.K. and the
Brethren is their "devotional immediacy," i.e. the sense of
God's living presence and their intimate fellowship with him.
Of course, to treat God primarily in terms of rational cognition would be to kill that sense of immediacy forthwith; thus,
this is another grounds for antiintellectualism. As S.K. put it:
"That which a simple soul, in the happy impulse of the pious
heart, feels no need of understanding in an elaborate way,
since he simply seizes the Good immediately, is grasped by the
clever one only at the cost of much time and much grief."[22]
And in a word that is much more profound than its bantering
tone might indicate: "The best proof for the immortality of
the soul, that God exists, etc., is really the impression one gets
in one's childhood, and consequently the proof which, in con-

[20] Alexander Mack, Sr., *Rights and Ordinances* [first published Germany, 1715] in Durnbaugh, *Origins*, p. 395.
[21] Mack Junior, *Apology*, p. 61.   [22] *Purity of Heart*, p. 55.

tradistinction to the learned and highfalutin proofs, can be described thus: it is quite certain, because my father told me so."[23]

(6) One of S.K.'s strongest protests against intellectualism came in connection with his insistence on the equality of all men before God. Clearly, if one's ability to theologize is a necessary aspect of his becoming a Christian, then many a person is damned for his low native ability: "Are you, my reader, perhaps what is called an educated person? Well, I too am educated. But if you think to come closer to this Highest by the help of *education*, you make a great mistake. . . . Christianity is by no means *the highest* of education. . . . Alas, have not this education and the enthusiasm with which it is coveted rather developed a new kind of distinction, a distinction between the educated and the non-educated."[24]

From the Brethren side, Mack Junior, who shared S.K.'s concern about the equality before God, also saw that intellectual distinctions dare not be allowed to stand within Christianity: "Great people can certainly make great deductions, but little people, for all that, have often learned so much out of the Bible which even great people have missed."[25]

It should be plain that although neither S.K. nor the Brethren had much use for formal, rationalistic theology, they were not opposed to thinking and reason per se. Far from being philosophical irrationalists, they were Christians interested in preserving the simplicity and accessibility of the gospel. Indeed, their antiintellectualism was not even an independent and self-explanatory doctrine but only the negative corollary of the positive points they truly were concerned to make. Thus, on the one hand, *Mag. artium Hr.* Søren Aabÿe Kierkegaard, "father" of philosophies, theologies, and psychologies

[23] *Dru Journals*, 785 (1848).
[24] *Works of Love*, p. 71. Cf. *Postscript*, p. 143. Cf. also *Rohde Journals*, 118 (1846).
[25] Mack Junior, *Apology*, p. 37.

whose number cannot yet be counted, and on the other hand, the simple, uneducated Brethren—these two were nonetheless of a mind regarding the place (more accurately, lack of place) of intellectualism within Christianity.

C. INWARDNESS / SUBJECTIVITY

Christianity is spirit, spirit is inwardness, inwardness is subjectivity, subjectivity is essentially passion, and in its maximum an infinite, personal, passionate interest in one's eternal happiness. As soon as subjectivity is eliminated, and passion eliminated from subjectivity, and the infinite interest eliminated from passion, there is in general no decision at all, neither in this problem nor in any other. All decisiveness, all essential decisiveness is rooted in subjectivity.[1]

Because the choice through which *den Enkelte* chooses himself before God is not the calculated nod of the intellect but a daring venture of the self, "subjectivity," the involvement of the total person to the roots of his existence, was bound to be a major emphasis with S.K. "Subjectivity" has tended to become the technical term by which this theme is identified (although only because the commentators insist in centering on *Postscript*). Actually, "inwardness" is the better term; S.K. used it more widely, particularly as he moved out of the pseudonymous and into his religious writings. "Subjectivity" carries with it philosophic connotations, "inwardness" religious ones; and as we have not neglected to mention already, S.K. was a *religious* author.

It proves most interesting to trace this motif in Kierkegaard, because we discover a movement that does not often appear. There is, of course, the very familiar pattern of the "feigned movement," the movement from the pseudonyms, with their more abstract presentation, through the gradual revelation of

[1] *Postscript*, p. 33.

the true and thoroughly Christian grounding of the idea. But it also seems clear that we have here a case in which S.K.'s own thought changed and developed; there are lacking the usual clues and "leaks" that give away the fact that S.K. had in mind more than he was allowing the pseudonyms to say. Basically the movement represents the building of a dialectic —not the mere *presentation* of a dialectic in which the author knows what the second pole is to be before he delineates the first, but the *creation* of a dialectic; we *see* S.K. discover the second pole.

"Inwardness" is the first pole. Its *negative*, its contradictory, its perverted counterpart, is "hiddenness" (or, in other cases, "superficial emotionalism"). This is *not* the second pole. Involved here is a most important principle regarding Kierkegaardian dialectic. The relationship between a thing and its contradictory, between a positive and its negative, is *never* to be understood as dialectical; rather, the positive is to be wholly affirmed and the negative wholly rejected. The word "antithesis" is most confusing in this regard; it customarily is used to identify the second pole of a dialectic (although, more precisely, that of a Hegelian dialectic of philosophical *concepts*, which is something far different from the Kierkegaardian dialectic of existential *life modes*).[2] But antithesis

[2] There is a further distinction between the Hegelian and the Kierkegaardian dialectics which constantly should be borne in mind. Because the Hegelian dialectic operates with intellectual concepts, and because concepts are essentially stable, fixed, defined, and thus inanimate, "synthesis" is made possible. Once achieved, the "synthesis" is itself a concept, a third concept which is just as fixed and stable as its parents had been. And once that synthesis is accomplished, the prior dialectic becomes completely relaxed; the parent concepts are transcended and supplanted; the synthesis itself stands ready to perform as a new thesis. But in the existential dialectic of Kierkegaard, "synthesis" would negate the whole idea, for the pattern derives its dynamic precisely from the living and continuing tension between the two positives. To resolve the paradox or to stabilize the situation by defining a middle-ground compromise would be to rob the relationship of its life and vitality. The goal of such dialectic explicitly is *not* to

also has come to mean "the opposite," or "the contradictory." However, for S.K. the second pole is never the contradictory, or antithesis, of the first, because both poles must be "of the truth," i.e. worthy of being affirmed, even though "the whole truth" is achieved only as *both* poles are affirmed in concert. Therefore, the Kierkegaardian dialectic always consists of two positives (never a positive and its negative) which are paradoxical yet essentially complementary.

The second pole that forms a true dialectic with the pole of "inwardness" is that which constitutes the theme of our next section, "fruitbearing and obedience." The negative, or contradictory, of obedience is "works-righteousness," which will be examined in the further section following. But with inwardness, as with every dialectical motif, S.K.'s thought and witness have not been well understood until the complementary pole also is in view; the doctrine of inwardness is truly Kierkegaardian only when balanced against the doctrine of outward obedience.

We are here dealing with the very fundamental dialectic of "inner-outer." This same dialectic, as was suggested in an earlier chapter, was bred into the eighteenth century Brethren by virtue of their parentage; the powerful inwardness of Pietism came into conjunction with the equally powerful obedi-

---

transcend or synthesize the dichotomy but to keep *both* poles distinctly in view through constant alternation, through the attempt at simultaneity, through the ever gaining and regaining of balance.

From the above follows a very important implication: The characteristic Kierkegaardian theme of "either/or" is *not* part of S.K.'s conception of "dialectic"—as many commentators would have it. "Either/or" is the proper approach to a thing and its contradictory, to items which are essentially incompatible; to fail to make the decisive choice here is to sin. But on the other hand, (although S.K. does not so use the term) "both/and" is the only proper approach to polar dialectic; at this point to make an "either/or" choice or to synthesize would be to sin by destroying the dialectic. Precisely here, then, lies the crucial issue of the Kierkegaardian method: to recognize contradictories and meet them with an "either/or"; to recognize dialectics and meet them with a "both/and."

ence-fruitbearing emphasis of Anabaptism. But with S.K. the achievement of this dialectic (not simply in his thought but even more particularly in his life) was a most painful and agonizing struggle. All of his natural propensities—his genius, his melancholy, his delicate health, his introvertedness—all pointed him toward inwardness. It is no surprise, then, to discover in his writings the earliness, the strength, and the pervasiveness of this theme. But both in the authorship and in the biography, actually to witness S.K. move in a direction absolutely counter to that in which every natural factor drove him, into a complementary "outwardness," this is probably the most touching experience in the study of Kierkegaard. He claimed that this movement against the wind happened—and could happen—only by the hand of divine governance; and who would say him nay?

Our analysis begins, however, by focusing particularly upon inwardness. S.K.'s conception was rooted deeply in his understanding of the nature of God, the nature of man, and the nature of their relationship to one another. He stated the case in one of his early Edifying Discourses: "God is faithful, and does not leave Himself without testimony. But God is Spirit, and therefore can give only spiritual testimony, that is in the inner man; every external testimony from God, if one could imagine such a thing, is only a deception."[3] And Climacus put the matter most succinctly when he said: "God is a subject, and therefore exists only for subjectivity in inwardness."[4] These two quotations speak volumes; and S.K. wrote volumes in his effort to elucidate and establish the point.

It is as important to understand what S.K. did *not* say here as what he did say. "Every external testimony is a deception." Taken in the total context of his authorship it becomes obvious

---

[3] "Strengthened in the Inward Man" (Discourse 5) in *Edifying Discourses*, Vol. I, p. 103.

[4] *Postscript*, p. 178.

that S.K. did not mean to deny that God can and does use external events through which to reveal himself to and communicate with man. S.K. was too firmly rooted in the Bible to go this direction; he knew that there, indeed, God is presented as speaking through historical events much more than through inner voices and visions. S.K. was saying, rather, that external events, even when directed by God, can become "spiritual testimony" only when received by the *inner* man. Examined outwardly, these events can be proved only to be outward, historical events; received inwardly—and only when received inwardly—they are heard as the voice of God. A variation of the "inner-outer" dialectic clearly is at work.

Mack Senior emphasized the same understanding, applying the dialectic to the Scriptures as a specific instance:

"No one may say to a believer that he should and must believe and obey the Scriptures, because no one can be a believer without the Holy Spirit, who must create the belief. Now, the Scriptures are only an outward testimony of those things which were once taught and commanded by the Holy Spirit. . . . All believers are united in it, for the Holy Spirit teaches them inwardly just as the Scriptures teach them outwardly. . . . Outwardly, [one] reads the Scriptures in faith and hears the inner word of life which gives him strength and power to follow Jesus."[5]

We are dealing with two variations of, or contrapuntal movements within, the one, overall "inner-outer" dialectic. God's outward works must become man's inward testimony; in turn, man's inward experience must find expression in outward action. Such two-way alternation is the hallmark of effective dialectic. In his concluding sentence Mack suggested the "outer-inner-outer" movement in its totality. However, both Mack and S.K. were emphatic that there is no faith apart

[5] Mack Senior, *Rights and Ordinances*, in Durnbaugh, *Origins*, pp. 384-85. Cf. those parts of the same passage quoted on p. 74 above.

from inwardness, that this is the only site at which a man can meet God. Why? Because "God is a subject, and therefore exists only for subjectivity in inwardness."

S.K.'s wording is crucial: "God is *a* subject." This is an entirely different thing than to say that God is subjectivity, or that he is an aspect of my subjectivity; the presence of the indefinite article "a" prohibits any such interpretation. The obvious intention is: God is *a* subject; I am *a* subject; these are *two* subjects, two *different* subjects existing independently and over against each other no matter how intimate the communion between them may become.[6] Perhaps it follows that God thus is made an entity alongside other entities, but for S.K. there was no alternative.

"Therefore God exists only *for* subjectivity in inwardness." And this is an entirely different thing than to say that God exists *in* subjectivity, or that his existence is located in my subjectivity. Louis Dupre put it well when he said, "Subjectivity is not to be confused with subjectivism. . . . Indeed, [subjectivity] fosters the fullest objectivity."[7] Not simply on the grounds of the statement under examination but of his entire authorship it can be said that S.K. (and for that matter, the Brethren as well) absolutely distinguished themselves from two major nondialectic types of "subjectivism." One is the traditional mystic approach that looks for "the God within"—to the neglect of the inner testimony derived from God's *outward* works. The other is contemporary existentialist theology, which, ironically enough, understands itself to be the heir of S.K., but which, in one way or another, identifies God with man's own inwardness and undercuts the objectivity of God's outward acts by recasting them into symbols of inward process.

The inwardness of both S.K. and the Brethren was preserved from either fate by maintenance of the dialectic. Thus the "inner" of God's immanence was played off against the

---

[6] See again the quotation on p. 123 above.
[7] Dupre, *op.cit.*, p. 183.

"outer" of his transcendence. The God who chooses to meet man only in his inwardness (because this is the appropriate site for encounter between "subjects," or "persons") is nevertheless the God who is "Wholly Other."[8] The God who "exists only for subjectivity" nevertheless revealed himself supremely in an objectively historical life recounted in an objectively historical book. The God who speaks to man only in his lonely inwardness nevertheless demands that that conversation be given outward expression in acts of obedience and fruit-bearing.

But because God, man, and their relationship are of this sort, S.K. felt it to be one of the greatest needs of his age that the life of faith become more inward and deep. He sometimes put the matter in more general and abstract terms:

"All religiousness consists in inwardness, in enthusiasm, in strong emotion, in the qualitative tension by the springs of subjectivity. When one beholds people as they are for the most part, one cannot deny that they have some religiousness, some concern to be enlightened and instructed about religious things, but without allowing these things to affect them too closely. . . . I find no better comparison for their religiousness than the exercises in the field of maneuvers. As these exercises are related to battle or to being in battle (where there is danger, which in the field of maneuvers is absent), so is distance-religiousness related to inward religiousness."[9]

Sometimes, too, S.K. put inwardness into the authentic context of its Christian-biblical grounding—as when he cited Matthew 15:1-12, wherein Jesus castigates the Pharisees. "Christ is here regarded in general as [a] teacher . . . [who]

---

[8] It is interesting, is it not, that Barth chose to emphasize one pole of S.K.'s dialectic and Tillich the other, and yet that often both have been lumped together as "dialectic theologians!"

[9] *On Authority and Revelation: The Book on Adler*, hereafter referred to as *The Book on Adler*, translated with an introduction and notes by Walter Lowrie (Princeton: Princeton University Press, 1955), p. 155.

insists upon inwardness in contrast with all empty externalism, a teacher who transforms externalism into inwardness.
Such is the collision, a collision which recurs again and again
in Christendom; briefly expressed it is the collision of pietism
with the established order."[10] Highly significant is S.K.'s
identification of inwardness with pietism (whether he had in
mind the specific historical movement or only the broad tendency of piety) and his aligning of himself with it. Indeed, the
inwardness of both S.K. and the Brethren appears as a rather
clear and direct influence from their Pietistic backgrounds.

The aspects of inwardness presented thus far form a stable
element of S.K.'s thought; there is no particular change in this
emphasis, except for the usual revelation of its essentially
Christian character. When S.K. moved on to stress the second
pole of the dialectic, he did in no way alter or deemphasize
this conviction about inwardness. However, in the pseudonyms there is another aspect of inwardness which in time
very definitely did change, to the point of being consciously
renounced and condemned as the *negative* of true inwardness.
This was "secrecy," "invisibility," or "hiddenness." The note
is very strong in the pseudonyms. In *Fear and Trembling* perhaps the most notable characteristic of the "knight of faith" is
that there is absolutely no outward sign by which he can be
distinguished from other men. And the principle is stated
definitively by Johannes Climacus.[11]

But although it is the pseudonyms who most strongly emphasize *secret* inwardness, it seems certain that this was S.K.'s
own honest opinion. There is no evidence that, in this instance, the edifying author actually stood beyond the pseudonym. And given S.K.'s conviction about the utter necessity of
inwardness, plus the "inward" proclivities of his own introverted psyche, it is very plausible that he should have taken

[10] "Blessed Is He Who Is Not Offended in Me" (Part II) in *Training in Christianity*, p. 87.
[11] *Postscript*, p. 424.

such a position. Indeed, he had a very valid religious motive for his belief. Secret inwardness was not thought of as *opposed* to obedience and fruitbearing; this pole of the dialectic simply had not yet come into view. *Secret* inwardness was opposed to the hypocrisy that demands an outward sign seen by men in order that one's inwardness not go unnoticed and uncredited. Surely, secret inwardness is the cure for Pharisaism and is indubitably an authentic New Testament teaching.

But it is interesting to trace S.K.'s growing realization that there was another side to the coin and, consequently, his development of a true dialectic. The signs of awakening appear already in *Postscript*, almost alongside the most insistent demands for secrecy:

"The medieval spirit [i.e. monastic asceticism] did not have complete confidence in its inwardness until this became an outwardness. [S.K. elsewhere made it clear that this may not have been motivated by the hypocrisy of wanting to be seen of men but by the more excusable weakness of wanting to transmute the strenuous solitude and insubstantiality of inwardness into safe and sure objectivities.] But the less outwardness, the more inwardness, and an inwardness expressed through its opposite (the outwardness of being wholly like all others, and that there is outwardly nothing to see) is the highest inwardness [To this point, S.K. simply has reiterated the case for secrecy, but he continues with a parenthesis which in the course of the authorship grew in emphasis until it supplanted the demand for secrecy and reduced *it* to parenthetical status.]—provided it is there. This qualification must always be added, and also the warning that the less outwardness the easier the deception. . . . Had I lived in the Middle Ages, I could never have chosen to enter a cloister. And why not? Because anyone who entered a cloister was in the Middle Ages accounted a saint, and that in all seriousness. . . . If a cloister were set up in a modern environment the entrants would be regarded as mad. . . . This I regard as an extraordinary advantage. To be considered mad is something like; it is encouraging, it protects the inwardness of the absolute relationship."[12]

Probably without quite realizing what he had accomplished, S.K. here, in the first place, made impossible further insistence on secrecy. "Secret inwardness is the highest inwardness—*provided it is there.*" S.K. first had detected pharisaic, monastic, or pietistic hypocrisy, i.e. the desire for externalities that will prove one's inwardness, and had countered with the demand for secrecy. Now he began to sense a different sort of hypocrisy, that of established Christendom. In time the emphasis became conscious: "Protestant ministers made the discovery that up and down the land there are true Christians living, who are true Christians in all secrecy—and indeed, in the end we are all true Christians in hidden inwardness, we are all models. How charming! If the New Testament is to decide what is meant by a true Christian, then to be a true Christian in all secrecy, comfortably and enjoyably, is as impossible as firing a cannon in all secrecy."[13]

But in the second place, in this same early quotation from *Postscript* S.K. paved the way for a dialectic relationship which could protect against both types of hypocrisy simultaneously. If the outward expressions of inwardness were such that rather than evoking the praise and admiration of the world they called up its enmity, then, of course, outward works would lose their illegitimate appeal. This too, in due course, became a conscious emphasis: "Christianity in the New Testament has more hidden inwardness than you find in Protestantism, but that is not enough for it, it wants to be recognizable in a paradoxical form, and it is at this point that all the Christian conflicts arise."[14] And thus the way was open

---

[12] *Postscript*, pp. 370, 372. Here and elsewhere the material in parentheses is part of S.K.'s original, and only the material in brackets represents my additions—V.E.

[13] *Smith Journals*, XI[1] A 106 (1854).

[14] *Smith Journals*, XI[2] A 80 (1854).

to bring in outward obedience as the dialectic corollary of inward faith; and thus were the Kierkegaardian motifs of nonconformity to the world, the scandal of Christianity, and suffering for the faith drawn into the basic pattern of that dialectic.

All this is but hinted in the quotation from *Postscript*; the actual development took time and agony. A further step, in which the value and need of secrecy strove for preservation but in which the outward also gained in standing, came a few years later in a most penetrating analysis from *The Book on Adler*:

"Alas, the need of giving an inward resolution a striking outward expression is often an illusion. . . . Not rarely there is a suspicious incongruity between inward decision (the strength of resolution, salvation, healing) and the outward signs of decision. . . . That the outward expression is not always the inward is true not only of the ironists who intentionally deceive by a false outward expression, but it is true also of the immediate natures who unconsciously deceive themselves, yea sometimes feel a need of self-deception. . . . A man of some seriousness would rather hide the decision and test himself in silent inwardness in order to see whether it might not deceptively be true that he the *weak* one felt the need of a *strong* outward expression of resolution. . . . But if the change has really come about, then it is permissible, then one always may change little by little the outward expression, if one has quite seriously been on the watch lest the change might be *before others in the outward*, not *before God in the inward*."[15]

This statement has some implications that form an interesting parallel with Brethrenism, for the sort of "striking outward exhibition of decision" that S.K. deprecates here does not really touch the concept of outward obedience and fruitbearing to which both S.K. and the Brethren came. Indeed, we shall see that their understanding of obedience involved a change in

[15] *The Book on Adler*, p. 151. Cf. *Purity of Heart*, pp. 43ff.

one's mode of life, the sort of conformance to the will of God which only could be attained deliberately, gradually, studiedly. S.K. did not specify, but his "striking outward exhibition" would seem to point to the phenomenon of an *actual* outwardness that *appears* as the deepest sort of inwardness, or put conversely, the kind of inwardness that comes closest to being outwardness. This is revivalism, ecstaticism, emotionalized conversion, enthusiasm (in the popular and not the strictly etymological sense). *Emotion* itself, of course, is something basically inward, but *emotionalism* inevitably focuses on the outward manifestation.

It is not only of interest but quite significant that although both S.K. and the Brethren were strong in their emphasis on inwardness, devotional immediacy, and the like, both were equally strong in their suspicion of revivalism and hyperemotionalism. It is rather plain that there was nothing of this tendency in S.K.;[16] but the same is true of the Brethren. Their tradition was quite staid and dignified, particularly in comparison with the excesses of Radical Pietism and of many groups in colonial and frontier America. During the nineteenth century the Annual Conference actually prohibited the holding of revival meetings. But earlier, one aspect of the Brethren break with the Radicals was the rejection of their emotionalism; and in eighteenth century America, "awakened souls" among the Brethren almost inevitably fled to the more congenial atmosphere of the Ephrata Cloisters.

Although not for a moment denying the place of genuine emotion (S.K.'s "passion") as a concomitant of inwardness, the thing that guarded either S.K. or the Brethren (or the Anabaptist tradition in general) from going the way of revivalism was the dialectical balance with obedient fruitbearing. If hum-

---

[16] At the same time, it should not be overlooked that S.K. as much as said that he would rather court emotionalism with the sects than passionlessness with the church. See above, pp. 32-33.

ble, day-by-day obedience is the authentic outward correlate of true Christian inwardness, then a quick, highly charged emotionalism is no acceptable substitute. Something of this thought was revealed in a letter by Mack Junior. His correspondent, John Price (a descendant of the John Price mentioned earlier), had delayed being baptized because he could point to no concrete assurance of his sins having been forgiven. Mack responded:

"It must indeed be accepted gratefully when the Lord by the inward joyful strength and comforting voice of the Good Shepherd gives to the soul a sure marrow- and bone-penetrating assurance that his sins are now forgiven and that his name is written down in heaven. However, it seems to me that our prayer should be more to the effect that the Lord may keep us from sin and may lead us into the pleasure of His will, in order that our will, our desire, and our entire pleasure may become a daily burnt-offering to the pure love of God."[17]

This would seem well qualified as a specific instance of S.K.'s stated preference for step-by-step transformation as over against "the striking outward exhibition." Yet the entire discussion also becomes important from another standpoint. Inwardness is a strong emphasis among the sects (although not by that token entirely absent in the churches), but contrary to the popular impression, revivalism is not necessarily the form in which that inwardness expresses itself and indeed not the normative form for classic sectarianism; the complementary emphasis on obedience tended to check emotional excesses.

But the difficulty that hampered S.K. in moving out of *secret* inwardness into the full-fledged dialectic was not an intellectual one; the doctrinal solution undoubtedly would have come much more quickly and easily had not S.K. encountered within himself a *personal* compulsion toward secrecy. He spoke in one

---

[17] Mack Junior, a letter to John Price (Dec. 29, 1772), quoted in Brumbaugh, *op.cit.*, p. 240.

place of a despairing feeling of being shut up that was "inward-ness with a jammed lock."[18] This was S.K.'s own cross; and how hard it was to bear, those of a different psychology scarcely can imagine. For S.K. to venture out of his secret inwardness was a tremendous personal achievement, but once he saw that it must be done, he saw also that he had a personal obligation to his readers:

"And yet perhaps it is my duty to God [to speak openly about my own religious experience], and my hidden inwardness something which God countenanced my having until I had grown strong enough to talk about it."[19]

"*Hidden inwardness*, that is what must be rejected—all the lying, hypocritical, conceited confusion which "hidden in-wardness" has brought about. . . . It is to a certain extent true of me that I was unfortunate enough to go about and conceal a hidden inwardness. For that very reason, because there was some truth in me, I am the one who was given the task of throwing some light on this point."[20]

Without in the slightest deemphasizing the need for inward-ness as such, and without approving the pharisaical hypocrisy that requires outward credit for its inwardness, S.K. now felt obliged to damn *hidden* inwardness just as strongly as he had insisted upon it earlier.[21]

But the truest picture of S.K.'s position comes not through his polemic against hidden inwardness but in his presentation of the complete inner-outer dialectic. This was done most effec-tively when he used Christian love as a specific example:

"As the quiet lake is fed deep down by the flow of hidden springs, which no eye sees, so a human being's love is grounded, still more deeply, in God's love. . . . Yet this hidden life of love is knowable *by its fruits*—yes, there is a need in love to be recognizable by its fruits. . . . For one is not to work in

[18] *The Sickness unto Death*, p. 206.
[19] *Dru Journals*, 894 (1849).   [20] *Ibid.*, 1226 (1851).
[21] *Ibid.*, 831 (1848), quoted above, p. 33; 1003 (1849); and 1123 (1850).

order that love becomes known by its fruits but to work to make love capable of being recognized by its fruits. . . .

"What love does, it is; what it is, it does—at one and the same moment; simultaneously as it goes beyond itself (in an outward direction) it is in itself (in an inward direction), and simultaneously as it is in itself, it thereby goes beyond itself in such a way that this going beyond and this inward turning, this inward turning and this going beyond, are simultaneously one and the same."[22]

Essentially the same inner-outer alternation was applied by the Brethren in a wide variety of instances. In fact, it is, as we have seen, the basic pattern of early Brethrenism. Mack Senior suggested the double movement of "outer-inner-outer." Michael Frantz made rather wide use of the dialectic.[23] But perhaps the most extensive and self-conscious presentation of the pattern came in a poem by Mack Junior. He used the dialectic as S.K. did, pinpointing the same two types of hypocrisy, when he said:

> The outward service of God is correct
> Where one is not the servant of sin;
> The inward is supremely good
> Where one does not deceive himself.
> For how do all appearances help us
> Where we are not true Christians?[24]

The statements of this dialectic by S.K. and by the Brethren form a rather clear parallel—not that this makes it the exclusive property of S.K. and sectarianism, yet S.K. must have felt that the emphasis runs at least somewhat counter to churchly thought or he would not have been so polemic in asserting it.

[22] *Works of Love*, pp. 27, 28, 31, 261.
[23] Michael Frantz, *Einfaltige Lehr-Betrachtungen* . . . (Germantown: Sauer Press, 1770), in the long lead poem, see stanzas 125-26, 359-60; cf. pp. 39-40.
[24] Mack Junior, a poem from *Geistliche Magazien*, No. 34, c. 1767, in Heckman, *op.cit.*, p. 126 [trans. amended—V.E.]; cf. the lines following those quoted.

But because, for S.K., this matter involved a deeply personal "jammed lock" rather than simply a doctrinal formulation, his most significant demonstration came not in the form of statements but of decisive actions. First, in a preliminary way by challenging the *Corsair* and then by launching a full-scale attack upon Christendom, S.K. deliberately and with full knowledge of what it would cost chose to give his inwardness outward expression—an expression, indeed, that was conspicuous and flagrant in its very outwardness. The Attacker of Christendom is at some remove from the incognito Knight of Faith; and the basic significance of the battle stance that concluded S.K.'s career is that he was determined to practice what he had been preaching, namely: What a Christian *believes*, he *is*; what he *is*, he *does*; what he actually believes *is* what he is and does. Thus when S.K. took signal action, he not only had formulated but had lived the most fundamental dialectic of Christianity—and this on the part of a man totally unqualified by nature to achieve it. Only when inwardness is coupled with outward obedience is S.K.'s doctrine understood, and only when he had matched the hidden depths of his faith with an equivalent action was his witness complete.

D. FRUITBEARING / OBEDIENCE

My thesis is not that what is thus proclaimed in official Christianity ought not to be regarded as Christian. No, my thesis is that proclamation in itself is not Christianity. What I am concerned about is the "how," the personal enforcement of the proclamation; without that, Christianity is not Christianity.[1]

My duty is to serve truth; its essential form: obedience.[2]

Our examination of the inner-outer dialectic already has pointed us to the theme of this section, but we have yet to real-

[1] *Papirer* [Diem's citation of locus is in error], quoted in Diem, *Dialectic*, p. 145, n. 30.
[2] *Dru Journals*, 712 (1847).

ize the extent of this fruitbearing-obedience emphasis in S.K. and the fact that it is not brought in merely for purposes of completing a dialectic but actually stands as one of S.K.'s strongest and most pervasive motifs.

The double term of the heading is necessary to suggest the full scope of the thought of both S.K. and the Brethren. The very word "fruitbearing" suggests that outward action, or "personal enforcement," as S.K. called it above, is the natural outgrowth, the proper and necessary consummation of true inwardness. "Obedience," on the other hand, suggests adherence to a directive, a command, or a counsel which has come to one from another; it connotes submission to a superior will. Although, in their abstract definitions, these two conceptions are quite distinguishable, and although both must be kept in view if either S.K. or the Brethren are accurately to be understood, nevertheless in practice the two ideas tend to merge. The fact is that the "fruit" which is the natural product of true Christian inwardness is loving and joyous "obedience" to God.

That there is this close connection between fruitbearing and obedience says a great deal about the character of the obedience that S.K. and the Brethren had in mind. S.K. got to the heart of the matter when, in the guise of Judge William, he offered an etymological analysis of the word "duty" (which is, of course, the direct corollary of "obedience"). The Danish word for "duty" is *Pligt*, apparently derived from *paa ligget*, "upon lying," i.e. "that which lies upon." "It is strange that the word duty can suggest an outward relation, inasmuch as the very derivation of the word [*Pligt*] indicates an inward relation; for what is incumbent upon me, not as this fortuitous individual but in accordance with my true nature, that surely stands in the most inward relation to myself. For duty is not an imposition [*Paalaeg*, literally, "that which *is laid* upon"] but something which is incumbent [*paaligger*, literally, "that which *lies* upon"]."[3] Obedience, then, comes as the desired and desirable

---

[3] *Either/Or II*, p. 259.

fruit of faith, something valued in and for itself, something germane to one's existence as *den Enkelte*. Obedience definitely is *not* understood as a grudging concession, as something which, unfortunately, must be given in order to merit the rewards that are consequent to the painful sacrifice of one's own will. Paul Minear has pointed to this aspect of S.K.'s doctrine in his article which presents gratitude to God as a major Kierkegaardian motif. He suggests that S.K. saw obedience as motivated basically by thanksgiving for grace.[4]

The positive, happy quality of obedience was lifted up by S.K. in a statement which forms an amazing parallel to what Mack Senior had written over a hundred years earlier. S.K. said: "Be therefore as the child when it profoundly feels that it has over against itself a will in relation to which nothing avails except obedience—when you submit to be disciplined by His unchangeable will, so as to renounce inconstancy and changeableness and caprice and self-will: then you will steadily rest more and more securely, and more and more blessedly in the unchangeableness of God."[5] Mack wrote: "[God] does not need the service of men. . . . [But] in order to redeem man from his perilous condition, God ordered through his Son that [certain] simple things be done. If a man does them in true faith and in obedience holds his reason captive, he will gradually become single-minded and childlike. It is just in this single-mindedness that the soul again finds rest, peace, and security."[6] Clearly, "obedience" is a necessary concomitant of the concept *den Enkelte*, for it is precisely through obedience that one becomes single.

Although a number of the Brethren spoke to the theme of

[4] Paul Minear, "Thanksgiving as a Synthesis of the Temporal and the Eternal," in *Critique*, pp. 297ff.

[5] "God's Unchangeableness," a discourse appended to *For Self-Examination* [bound with *Judge for Yourselves!*], trans. Walter Lowrie (New York: Oxford University Press, 1941), p. 238.

[6] Mack Senior, *Rights and Ordinances*, in Durnbaugh, *Origins*, p. 355.

joyous obedience, it was Mack Junior who best expressed the
thought—in verse:

> Indeed, the world speaks: "Christ's teachings
> Are not so to be understood
> As though one were bound
> To follow him in all things;
> [For instance,] in poverty,
> That certainly would be too much!" ...
> [Yet] all the words of his teachings
> Taste to [Christians] like sweet sugar.
> Their desire, indeed, their adornment and honor
> Are his footsteps. ...
> All that [Christians] learn from him
> Tastes sweeter than honey;
> Christ's spirit and word are ever
> Their freedom and law.[7]

A concept of obedience that couples "law" and "freedom"—as
Mack did in his concluding line—on first thought may seem a
manifest contradiction, yet this gets directly to the point that
both the Brethren and S.K. were concerned to make. Only
through perfect submission and obedience to God does *den
Enkelte* become *free* to achieve the simplicity and singleness
of his own authentic existence.

From S.K.'s side, his most outstanding word regarding joyous obedience was: "The Christian serves with perfect obedience only one Master. ... This life is a hymn of praise; for only
by obedience can a man praise God, and best of all by perfect
obedience. ... The hymn is not something higher than obedience, but obedience is the only true hymn of praise; in obedience the hymn consists, and if the hymn is truth, it is

---

[7] Mack Junior, a poem appended to *Der Kleine Kempis* (Germantown: Peter Leibert, 1795), in Heckman, *op.cit.*, pp. 37-39, stanzas 4,
6, 8 [trans. amended—V.E.].

obedience."[8] Yet more moving than even these beautiful lines is
S.K.'s personal testimony to the effect that "I have had more
joy in the relation of obedience to God than in thoughts that
I have produced . . . [and] indescribable bliss when I turned to
Him and did my work in unconditional obedience."[9]

In one sense the remainder of this study is an exposition of
what S.K. and the Brethren felt to be the specific content of
their religious duty, that in which Christian obedience was to
consist. But what will become very obvious there perhaps
should be given initial consideration at this point. In the first
place this obedience is never understood as being directed toward any other human being or group; it is not submission to
any formal discipline or program. There is no spiritual superior, no order, no church that commands allegiance. This sectarian (and thoroughly Protestant) concept of obedience is at
a considerable remove from that of monasticism or any such
regimen.

In the second place, although this obedience is very closely
related to inwardness, it retains an entirely objective focus.
Obedience is never taken to signify "fidelity to my own true
nature," "response to my own higher possibilities," or anything
so esoteric as this. The Brethren, of course, would have been incapable of such sophistication; S.K. disdained it. Their concept of obedience necessarily assumed the presence of a
"wholly Other" possessing a will and intention of his own and
capable of communicating it to man.

Ultimately, then, both S.K. and the Brethren saw the source
of authority, the seat of command, as being threefold. Primarily, one seeks to be obedient to the individual intention, the
"custom-cut" will that God has in mind for each particular
person, for *den Enkelte*. But the matter does not end on this
level, as it does in atomistic spiritualism. *Objective* help has

[8] "The Anxiety of Irresolution . . ." (Part I, Discourse 7) in *Christian Discourses*, pp. 87-88.
[9] *Point of View*, p. 68.

been provided for discovering and interpreting this *subjective* revelation—this in the life example and the teachings of Jesus Christ (to be examined in Chapter XII). The third seat of command, or rather the third link in the one chain of command, is, then, the document that preserves and transmits the gospel record, namely, the New Testament (to be treated in Chapter XIII). And the crucial culmination of the matter is this: in neither Brethren nor Kierkegaardian thought does obedience amount to a rather general and abstract quality of mind, a wholly inward submission to God; rather, it everywhere implies and customarily is spelled out in terms of the actual, concrete fulfillment of specified commands.

S.K. was adamant on this score, expressing it in some of his shortest and sharpest thrusts:

"God is willing to understand only one sort of sincerity, namely, that a man's life expresses what he says."[10]

"All my labor with respect to knowing has no effect upon my life, upon its lusts, its passions, its selfishness; it leaves me entirely unchanged—it is my action which changes my life. . . . Thy understanding [is] constantly to be expressed as action, warm, full, and whole, issuing instantly the instant thou hast understood something."[11]

And the Brethren had been just as convinced as S.K. was. When his Radical Pietist opponents put to Mack Senior a question regarding the necessity of outward actions in relation to inward experience, he gave the blunt answer: "The spiritual rebirth is nothing else than true and genuine obedience toward God and all of his commandments."[12]

As S.K. and the Brethren saw obedience as absolutely neces-

[10] "Watch Thy Foot . . ." (Part III, Discourse 1) in *Christian Discourses*, p. 175.

[11] "To Become Sober" (Discourse I) in *Judge for Yourselves!*, pp. 131, 137. Cf. *Purity of Heart*, p. 111; *Rohde Journals*, 160 (1846); *Dru Journals*, 804 (1848); and *Smith Journals*, XI² A 204 (1854).

[12] Mack Senior, *Basic Questions* [first published Germany, 1713], in Durnbaugh, *Origins*, p. 338. Cf. Michael Frantz, *op.cit.*, stanzas 112-13.

sary to the Christian life, so did they see the quality of that obedience as being absolutely unconditional. It is impossible to overstate the case that S.K. put in these terms:

"[God] demands obedience, unconditional obedience. If thou art not obedient in everything unconditionally, then thou lovest Him not, and if thou lovest Him not—then thou dost hate Him. . . . [It is inconceivable] that a little disobedience . . . might not be absolute disobedience, . . . that the least, the very least disobedience, might in truth have any other name than . . . contempt of God. . . . Reflect that every sin is disobedience, and every disobedience sin."[13]

Here, too, is one of the deep springs of the Kierkegaardian-sectarian protest against intellectualism; and S.K.'s statement raises a fundamental issue regarding the theological situation pertaining in our own day and age. There would appear to be a rather major divergence between S.K. and his "heirs." "People try to persuade us that the objections against Christianity spring from doubt. That is a complete misunderstanding. The objections against Christianity spring from insubordination, the dislike of obedience, rebellion against all authority. As a result people have hitherto been beating the air in their struggle against objections, because they have fought intellectually with doubt instead of fighting morally with rebellion."[14] Quite explicitly, the "demythologizing" efforts of current existentialist theology presuppose that it is problems of intellectual formulation of the faith that have alienated modern man from Christianity; S.K. was of a different mind, and consequently his "theology" was of a much different character. S.K. con-

[13] "No Man Can Serve Two Masters" (Discourse II) in *The Lilies of the Field* . . . which is appended to *Christian Discourses*, pp. 335, 338, 346. Cf. "The Anxiety of High Place" (Part I, Discourse 2) in *Christian Discourses*, p. 54; and *Works of Love*, p. 36. Cf. also *Smith Journals*, XI¹ A 5 (1854).

[14] *Dru Journals*, 630 (1847). Cf. "Lifted Up On High" (Part III, Reflection 5) in *Training in Christianity*, p. 222.

sidered that even the church (to say nothing of the world) was in a state of mutiny, despite the lip service that was paid. He saw only one means of bringing it to a stop: "I wonder if every individual is not duty bound toward God to stop the mutiny, not, of course, with shouts and conceited importance, not by domineering and wanting to force others to obey God, but by unconditionally obeying as an individual."[15]

The Brethren emphasis on obedience was every bit as forceful as S.K.'s. In fact this was *the* thrust of Mack Senior's *Rights and Ordinances*—to the point that he came perilously close to advocating a form of works-righteousness. He could make such statements as:

"If you had been obedient in everything to me for ten or even more years, and I requested you to pick up a piece of straw, and you did not want to do it, I would have to consider you a disobedient child. Even if you said a thousand times, 'Father, I will do everything; I will work hard; I will go wherever you send me, but it does not seem necessary to me to pick up the piece of straw because it neither helps you nor me,' I would say to you, 'You are a disobedient wretch.'"[16]

"God looks only upon obedience, and believers are bound to obey the Word. Then they will achieve eternal life by obedience."[17]

"What Jesus has ordained cannot be intentionally changed or broken by any person without loss of eternal salvation."[18]

It may be helpful to know that the author of the above lines was also a believer in the eventual salvation of all men and, as we shall see, that both the Brethren and S.K. took considerable pains to avoid the implications of works-righteousness; but

---

[15] *Works of Love*, pp. 121-22.

[16] Mack Senior, *Rights and Ordinances*, in Durnbaugh, *Origins*, p. 354.

[17] *Ibid.*, p. 353.

[18] Mack Senior, a letter to Count Charles August (Sept. 1711), in Durnbaugh, *Origins*, p. 164.

these considerations in no way blunted their understanding of the Christian demand for unconditional obedience.

A further facet of the Brethren-Kierkegaardian concept calls for notice. This was a uniquely *Christian* concept, not only because it is Jesus Christ who is to be obeyed, but because he was himself the supreme example of obedience.[19] And the fact that Christ was the pattern for obedience led to the conclusion that obedience necessarily will entail suffering. S.K. observed that "if it were possible for man to learn obedience toward God without suffering, then would Christ, as human, not have needed to learn it from suffering."[20] The Brethren fully concurred in understanding this relationship as an essential one. In the public letter which they circulated prior to the first baptism, the note was struck: "We must publicly profess what Christ Jesus taught and did without hesitation or fear of men. We need not be ashamed and must above all suffer and endure all things with rejoicing."[21] And almost a century later, Jacob Stoll asked the rhetorical question:

> Does he who is indeed obedient
>   And follows Him in lowliness and submission—. . .
> Does he nevertheless experience
>   Persecution, ridicule, and shame?[22]

It is difficult to give a true impression of how central and all-pervasive is the emphasis on obedience in S.K.'s religious works. It must suffice to note that five or six of his discourses treat obedience per se, quite apart from those that center upon following Christ, the duty to love, and such closely related

[19] "The Anxiety of Irresolution . . ." (Pt. I, Discourse 3) in *Christian Discourses*, p. 87.

[20] ". . . The School of Suffering Educates for Eternity" (Discourse III) in *The Gospel of Suffering*, p. 53.

[21] "First Eight Brethren to Palatine Pietists" (1708) in Durnbaugh, *Origins*, p. 116.

[22] Jacob Stoll, *op.cit.*, p. 20.

topics. Once S.K. got past the idea of *hidden* inwardness, obedience became one of his major motifs.

Both in character and in emphasis, the Brethren doctrine was of a piece with S.K.'s, being beautifully summarized in a poem by Mack Junior:

> But whenever the love of Christ
> Can penetrate a man's poor heart,
> He begins of himself
> To sing a new song.
> He seeks not pretences, forms, nor appearances;
> He will be only eagerly obedient.
> Obedience is the stone
> Despised by all the world.
> Obedience alone is
> That for which faith aspires.
> Obedience is the treasure
> Buried deep in the field.[23]

But the most eloquent witness to this aspect of Brethrenism comes not out of any Brethren writings but from two outsiders contemporary with the early Brethren. One was Elhanan Winchester, the outstanding leader of colonial universalism, the other, Morgan Edwards, the equally outstanding Baptist pastor and church historian. Winchester wrote:

"Such Christians as [the Dunkers] are I have never seen. So averse are they to all sin, and to many things that other Christians esteem lawful, that they . . . [and he proceeds to list the things that Brethren do and do not do]. They walk in the commandments and ordinances of the Lord blameless, both in public and in private. . . . Whatever they believe their Saviour has commanded, they practice, without inquiring or regarding what others do. I remember the Rev. Morgan Ed-

---

[23] Mack Junior, a poem from *Geistliche Magazien*, No. 34, c. 1767, in Heckman, *op.cit.*, p. 125 [trans. amended—V.E.].

wards, formerly minister of the Baptist Church in Philadelphia, once said to me, 'God will always have a visible people on earth, and these are His people at present, above any others in the world.' "[24]

E. *FAITH AND WORKS*

Christianity's requirement is: Thy life
shall as strenuously as possible
give expression to works—
and then one thing more is required:
that thou humble thyself and admit,
"But none the less I am saved by grace."[1]

Anyone who promotes as emphatic a doctrine of works (which is precisely what "obedience" amounts to) as did S.K. and the Brethren inevitably opens himself to the risk and the accusation of works-righteousness. Protestant sectarianism continually had to face the charge. Fortunately, as it turned out, the Brethren were pushed hard on this score and thus were forced to clarify and define their own position, something they likely would not have done except under the spur of controversy.

In S.K.'s case, he was enough of a thinker to see the problem on his own and so address himself to it. It may well be that he gave more attention to this matter than has any other Protestant theologian. So impressive was his achievement that a *Roman Catholic* scholar has named as one of S.K.'s foremost contributions the solid integration of a doctrine of works into Reformation *sola fide* theology; Louis Dupre recognizes and expounds S.K.'s understanding of works as being a uniquely

---

[24] Elhanan Winchester, *The Universal Restoration* [1788], quoted in Henry Ritz Holsinger, *Holsinger's History of the Tunkers, Etc.* (Lathrop, Calif.: Pacific Press, 1901), p. 805.

---

[1] ". . . The Mirror of the Word" (Discourse II) in *For Self-Examination*, p. 42.

Protestant doctrine, explicitly refusing to claim it as a Catholic tendency.[2]

The Brethren, of course, hardly were capable of matching S.K.'s accomplishment, but they did reach after the same sort of solution. And if a central emphasis on works is a sectarian characteristic, the attempt to relate it to grace is a mark of *Protestant* sectarianism. With both S.K. and the Brethren, the fact that their emphasis on fruitful obedience was coupled with an equal emphasis on inwardness was itself some protection against a legalistic works-righteousness; at least their works would have to involve more than empty and merely outward acts. Yet it was necessary that they go further and explicitly posit salvation upon grace through faith, but doing it in such a way as not to blunt the demand for works of obedience. We shall see how this was accomplished.

It was inevitable—and appropriate—that baptism became for the Brethren the crux over which the issue should be joined. For one thing, baptism is the first work of the Christian life, first, that is, in chronological sequence, if not in preeminence. Second, it is apparent that baptism has some sort of connection with salvation, and thus if any work runs the risk of becoming a "saving work," it is certainly this one. And third, except as a "saving work" baptism would seem the most useless work of all. It fits precisely Alexander Mack's description of the command to "pick up a straw." Unlike works of charity or even those of self-discipline, baptism would seem to be of no use to either God or man—unless one did claim it as a grounds of salvation.

On the face of the matter, then, the purest Protestants would be the "spiritualists" who had altogether rejected such outward sacramental works; and they did indeed claim such status for themselves, accusing the churches as well as the sects of following works-righteousness. And it should be recalled that the Brethren came into being precisely out of such a spir-

[2] Dupre, *op.cit.*, pp. xi, 165-72.

itualist milieu and precisely through the readoption of baptism and other such works. In their very origin and from their very colleagues, then, the Brethren had to answer the charge that they were deserting the true faith in favor of works-righteousness.

We already have seen that Mack Senior, in stressing the necessity of obedience, had come very near suggesting that one is saved by his obedience. Even before making such statements, however, he had responded to the Radical Pietist charge and made it abundantly clear that he did not believe in works-righteousness but in salvation by faith alone. Both his assertions regarding obedience and regarding *sola fide* must be kept in the picture, because together they form the dialectic of grace *and* works.

Mack's reply to the Radicals' accusation that Brethren baptism was a saving work was in this way: First, salvation is through faith (it would be more accurate to say "only through faith" rather than "through faith alone"). "We do indeed believe and profess that eternal life is not promised because of baptism, but only through faith in Christ (John 3:15, 18)." But by its very nature, true faith cannot exist alone, its natural and necessary concomitant is the desire to obey. "Why should a believer not wish to do the will of him in whom he believes? If it is the will of Christ that a believer should be baptized, then it is also the will of the believer." Strictly speaking, it is not the outward obedience that is the essential corollary of faith but the *desire* to obey. "If he thus wills and believes as Christ wills, he is saved, even if it were impossible for him to receive baptism."[3]

Obedience, then, is the proof, or test, of the sincerity and thus the reality of one's faith. "Salvation is not dependent upon the water, but only upon the faith, which must be proved

[3] The sentences quoted in this paragraph form a continuous passage in Mack Senior, *Basic Questions*, in Durnbaugh, *Origins*, p. 331, answer to Question 12.

by love and obedience."[4] This is not to suggest that the proof operates infallibly in both directions; Mack was far from suggesting that the mere fact that one submits to an external work proves that he possesses true inward faith. "That would indeed be a good baptism, if all those whom we baptize in water were truly reborn. [But] it cannot be proved that [even] all those baptized by Christ and the apostles turned out well."[5] The proof operates only in the other direction, i.e. anyone who deliberately disdains to submit to the explicit commands of God *cannot* be in a state of true and saving faith: "We do not seek to earn salvation with these simple works, but by faith in Christ alone. If it is to be a saving faith, it must produce works of obedience. Where that faith is not present which produces obedience, . . . then no salvation is promised for a single work done without faith."[6] The fact of the matter is that the sectary Mack, for all his insistence and scrupulosity about outward works of obedience, was in a better position to defend his *sola fide* Protestantism than were the Reformers who retained a doctrine of baptismal regeneration and who, by virtue of its being *infant* baptism, would have had difficulty interpreting their baptism as being a work of voluntary obedience on the part of the believer.

Mack's was the fullest discussion of this matter among the eighteenth century Brethren, but there are enough hints among later writers to make it plain that this basic understanding was retained by the church.[7] And although the discussion tended to limit itself to baptism, clearly the same explanation could be applied to "works" in general.

S.K.'s solution of the faith-works dichotomy was not essentially different from that of the Brethren but went much

[4] *Ibid.*, p. 335, answer to Question 19.
[5] *Ibid.*, p. 338, answer to Question 28.
[6] *Ibid.*, p. 335, answer to Question 21.
[7] Michael Frantz, *op.cit.*, stanzas 395-432; *Eine Geringer Schein*, pp. 4-5, 24-25; Mack Junior, *Apology*, pp. 25-26, and *Appendix to the Refuted Anabaptists*, p. 7; Christian Longenecker, *op.cit.*, pp. 24-26.

further, simply because S.K. was more skillful in handling dialectic. S.K. not only alternated his emphasis between the two poles but showed how each pole, by its very character, *impels* a movement toward its counterpart. Here is true Kierkegaardian dialectic in its most dynamic form, not the logical, mechanical progression from thesis to antithesis to synthesis, etc., but the motion of a particle suspended in a magnetic field, pulled both ways, pushed both ways, forced to recognize the attraction of both poles and yet unable to give itself to either pole, every movement simply establishing the conditions for a countermovement.

Such a relationship between faith and works is basic to S.K.'s entire discussion; as his norm he specified that "for every increase in the degree of grace the law must also be made more severe in inwardness—otherwise worldliness breaks in and takes 'grace' in vain."[8] Precisely here is found one of S.K.'s fundamental criticisms of Martin Luther and the Reformation, a point to which he continually returned.[9] Certainly the medieval doctrine and practice of meritorious works-righteousness marked a perversion of the Christian faith; certainly it was proper that Luther endeavor to correct this situation with a radically new emphasis on grace; certainly Luther had no intention of eliminating the role of works. But the nature of churchly Protestantism's corrective was such that the dialectic got as badly out of balance in the "grace" direction as it had been in the "works" direction.

S.K. complained that Luther either did not or could not think dialectically; and a comparison of the two authors makes evident the nature of S.K.'s dissatisfaction. Luther tended to define and explicate "faith" and then turn to define "works" in *contradistinction* (rather than in *relation*) to "faith." A legitimate role was assigned to each, although they

---

[8] *Dru Journals*, 1207 (1851).

[9] Dupre, *op.cit.*, presents and treats considerable of this material on pp. 166ff.

were compartmentalized to the point that one encountered something of a disjuncture in moving from one to the other. Thus, to illustrate S.K.'s contention at the risk of oversimplifying Luther, the Reformer's presentation almost amounted to a panegyric on faith always followed by a footnote to the effect that works dare not be neglected. And in later editions (speaking figuratively) it was next to inevitable that the footnotes would tend to drop out.

S.K.'s dialectical approach, on the other hand, strove to establish the *continuity* between true faith and true works. The gospel is not served by soft-pedaling works in order to enhance grace; "for every increase in the degree of grace the law must also be made more severe." Indeed, when they are properly related, emphasis on one will work to the immediate enhancement of the other; neither can be overemphasized as long as they are tied together in close dialectical conjunction. And it was just this tie that S.K. sought to provide.

In the first place, works must never be stressed in such a way as to detract from the cruciality of grace: "But in spite of the fact that it is wise to stress the need for discipleship, even though—instructed by the error of the Middle Ages—in a new and different sense, yet above all the matter must not be so viewed that Christ appears merely as our example and not as our Savior, as though the spiritually mature, at any rate, did not need the atonement. No, no, no—and for this reason: the more mature one is, so much the more will one discover that one needs the divine atonement and grace. No, atonement and grace is and remains the decisive thing."[10]

In short, churchly Protestantism needs correction but not by any method that would endanger its basic insight. However, S.K. saw (and this is the heart of his contribution) that there is a truly Christian conception of works which directly and emphatically *feeds into* a conception of grace rather than detracting from it.

[10] *Papirer*, X⁴ A 491 (1852), quoted in Diem, *Dialectic*, p. 114.

The best presentation of this idea came in a journal entry which might well qualify as the one most basic and succinct statement of S.K.'s faith and witness. If only this one page survived out of all S.K.'s writings, theoretically at least, the entire content of his religious thought could be constructed. Almost every one of the Kierkegaardian motifs to be treated in this present study are either mentioned, implied, or made plausible by this passage. We quote only a part:

"How does a man become a Christian? Very simple. Take any Christian principle of action—dare to follow it. The action which you would make actual also will be characterized by its unconditionedness, for this is the mark of all true Christianity. At the same instant, in this action you will collide with the outer world in which to a certain degree your life essentially consists. The collision will now become such that . . . you need Christianity in order to hold out in this collision—unless you want to rely on the good that you do, although in this tension you likewise will discover that, quite contrary to your own idealism, you are still a wretched weakling so that you need grace unconditionally. Without *occasion*, without this occasion which isolates him almost to desperation and always in inverse proportion [i.e. the harder he works, the more he despairs], a man never comes to faith. This is also what Christ said and is the only proof possible for Christian truth: 'If anyone will do what I say, he shall learn what I say about myself [John 7:17].' . . . Dare once for truth's sake unconditionally to lay yourself open before everything; thus you shall indeed learn the truth of the Teacher, learn how He alone can save you from despairing or from going under."[11]

Only the man who earnestly has striven after works and consequently realized his own inability—only he is in position truly to appreciate and receive grace. But the total effect of

[11] *Papirer*, X³ A 470-71 (1850) [my trans.—V.E.]. Cf. *Papirer*, X⁴ A 349 (1851), quoted in Diem, *Dialectic*, p. 180; and *Dru Journals*, 1248 (1852).

this procedure is not as negative as it might appear; quite the contrary:

"So it is with the unconditional requirement [of works]; if I must lift it, I am crushed. But this is not the intention of the Gospel, its intention is that I, through humiliation, shall be lifted up in faith and worship—and then I am as light as a bird. . . . Thou canst not worship God by good works, still less by crimes, and just as little by sinking into a soft slumber and doing nothing. No, in order to worship aright and rightly to have joy in worshipping, a man must so comport himself: he strives with might and main, spares himself neither day nor night, strives to produce as many as possible of what upright men, humanly speaking, might call 'good works.' Then when he takes them and, deeply humbled before God, beholds them transformed to wretchedness and vileness, that is to worship God—and that is exaltation."[12]

This is the conception of works that *feeds into* grace; S.K. also understood the more usual conception of works that *proceed from* grace. There is no conflict between the two ideas; the dialectical movement continually must go both ways. For one thing, faith desires to express itself in works of obedience and service—not, indeed, to *earn* anything but as a simple expression of gratitude. S.K. used the analogy of a lover's desire to do something for his beloved.[13] Also, he saw that the conviction that all things come of grace, that God does everything, is no real detriment to works. He spoke of the seamstress who discovered that it was God and not herself who did spin and sew. But far from killing her initiative, she knew that God could sew only as she sewed; she redoubled her efforts for the joy of witnessing and experiencing that it is God who sews every stitch.[14] And finally, S.K. saw that when

[12] "Christ as Example . . ." (Discourse II) in *Judge for Yourselves!*, pp. 165, 166.

[13] *Dru Journals*, 1272 (1852).

[14] "Christ as Example . . ." (Discourse II) in *Judge for Yourselves!*, p. 192.

works are motivated by grace they possess a much more powerful dynamic than when they are required by law, even if
for the sake of one's salvation:

"[As a child] it bored me much to copy father's letters, but
he only had to say to me: all right then, I will do them myself. I was immediately willing. Oh, if he had scolded, alas,
there would simply have been a row; but this was moving. In
the same way many a self-denial may come difficult to a man
and embitter him if it is imposed by law, but the Saviour's
look and his words: Everything is given to thee, it is nothing
but grace, only look upon me and my suffering which won
this grace: yes, that is moving!"[15]

In his doctrine of inwardness, his undeviating emphasis
upon faith and grace, S.K. made himself staunchly and securely a *Protestant*; but when he deserted his earlier concept
of *hidden* inwardness and espoused a strong doctrine of
works, yet doing it in such a way that every insistence upon
outward obedience served simply to magnify the role of grace
—when he did this, he made himself not a crypto-Catholic but
a Protestant's Protestant.

F. DEVOTIONAL IMMEDIACY

*I have, quite literally, lived with God
as one lives with one's father.*[1]

*This God-relationship of mine
is the "happy love" in a life which has been
in many ways troubled and unhappy.*[2]

*O my God, I have really nothing to ask Thee for;
even shouldst Thou promise
to fulfill every wish,*

---

[15] *Dru Journals*, 1283 (1852).

---

[1] *Dru Journals*, 771 (1848).
[2] *Point of View*, p. 64.

I really do not know what to ask for,
only that I may remain with Thee,
as near Thee as possible in this time of our separation
one from the other,
and wholly with Thee in all eternity.[3]

We are here to deal with one of the most obvious characteristics of both S.K. and the Brethren, although also one that is
most difficult to specify and document, for we have to do, not
with a doctrine but a mood, a set of mind. And yet this is one
of the most important concomitants of S.K.'s concept of *den
Enkelte*. It is a quality which, in both the Brethren and S.K.,
can be identified rather positively as an inheritance out of their
respective Pietist backgrounds. This is the quality which, in
the Brethren, has been named and discussed as "mysticism."[4]
It is the strain in S.K. which led *Time* Magazine to identify
him as a mystic[5] and Walter Lowrie more cautiously to suggest that "his constant 'practice of the presence of God' almost
justifies the common notion that he was a mystic."[6]

The appellation "mystic" might be an acceptable one for
either S.K. or the Brethren, if only there were a very clear understanding as to what the term implies. But because there
definitely is not, it seems wise to forego the label. The motif
we are identifying certainly does have something in common
with what is found in the classic traditions of mysticism, but
those traditions also include other elements that were assidu-
ously avoided by S.K., the Brethren, and most Protestant

[3] "The True Man of Prayer . . ." (Discourse IV) in *Edifying Discourses*, Vol. IV, p. 132.

[4] Floyd Mallott, in particular, has developed this theme; see his
Studies in Brethren History, pp. 13-14, 19.

[5] The statement from *Time* is quoted on the dust jackets of the
Princeton University Press editions of S.K.'s *Authority and Revelation*
and *Philosophical Fragments*. The full appellation given him is "philosopher and mystic"; the philosopher obloquy we have refuted already;
the mystic, we have now to deal with.

[6] Walter Lowrie, the translator's appendix to S.K.'s *Repetition*
(Princeton: Princeton Un. Press, 1941), p. 211.

sectaries. If, for instance, he is to be called a mystic, the term must be so defined that it can allow for the fact that S.K.—in the person of Judge William—wrote a most trenchant ten-page analysis and critique of mysticism[7] and under his own name made such statements as: "[Mysticism] has not the patience to wait upon God's revealing," and "[Mysticism wants to] take the Kingdom of God by force."[8]

Likewise, in neither S.K. nor the Brethren is there any hint of a hypostatic union with God that would weaken one's consciousness of individuality; rather, with them one's sense of being *den Enkelte* is heightened. There is no intellectualistic tendency that would experience God as the consummation of philosophic contemplation; the presence of God is experienced immediately, directly, and simply. There is no self-conscious and programmed straining after God; one has only to turn and speak to him. There is no inclination to depersonalize God into the traditional hyperboles of Beatific Vision, Sweetness, Illumination, Oneness, Infiniteness, Ecstasy, Ground of Being, etc.; God is considered and described almost exclusively in familiar, personal terms. Given such fundamental divergencies between the Brethren-Kierkegaardian type and much of what has constituted the classic traditions of mysticism, it seems wise simply to drop the term and here use "devotional immediacy," which can imply only what we desire.

The clearest demonstration of S.K.'s devotional immediacy comes in the fact that he was that rarity among "philosopher-theologians," one whose writings included *prayers* of such merit as to deserve being collected and printed under separate cover,[9] some of them even being set to music.[10] Likewise, the

[7] *Either/Or II*, pp. 245ff. There is no apparent reason why S.K. would reject or even modify Judge William's position; his own statements do, in fact, support it.

[8] *Papirer*, III A 8 (1840) and I A 168 (1836), both quoted by Croxall in his notes to *Johannes Climacus*, p. 47.

[9] Perry LeFevre's collection of *The Prayers of Kierkegaard* supports the point we are making not only as a collection but also in LeFevre's

Brethren parallel can be demonstrated merely by pointing to their passion for writing hymns and devotional poetry. Both S.K.'s prayers and the Brethren hymns are rather obviously flowerings of the same Pietist tradition of devotion.

It is perhaps unnecessary to bring in specific documentation regarding Brethren devotion; in the case of any group born out of the same historical milieu that produced Gerhard Tersteegen and the Moravian Brethren, argument would be needed only to explain the *lack* of such piety. There was no lack among the Brethren; they practiced and expressed a very close "walk with God" and desired only that it might become even closer.

With S.K. the case is somewhat different in that his Pietist connections are not as widely recognized, his fame as an "existentialist philosopher" having obscured this much more fundamental aspect of his life and thought. But in the first place, S.K. had a doctrinal frame of reference that would allow for and even encourage personal devotion. He could, on occasion, put the matter in more abstract, theological terms: "God is really the *terminus medius* in everything man undertakes; the difference between the religious and the purely human attitude is that the latter does not know it—Christianity is therefore the highest union between God and man because it has made the union conscious."[11] He could, on other occasions, make the matter much more pointed and moving, although still in the "objective" terms of third-person discourse:

"Christianity teaches that this particular individual whatever in other respects this individual may be, man, woman, serving-maid, minister of state, merchant, barber, student, etc. —this individual exists *before God*—this individual who per-

---

discussion of S.K. as a man of prayer; his chapter well could serve as this part of our study.

[10] Samuel Barber has composed a cantata, *The Prayers of Kierkegaard*.

[11] *Dru Journals*, 487 (1844).

haps would be vain for having once in his life talked with the
King, this man who is not a little proud of living on intimate
terms with that person or the other, this man exists before
God, can talk with God any moment he will, sure to be heard
by Him; in short, this man is invited to live on the most intimate terms with God! Furthermore, for this man's sake
God came to the world, let himself be born, suffers and dies;
and this suffering God almost begs and entreats this man to
accept the help which is offered to him!"[12]

However, this immediacy ceased to be simply doctrinal and
began to become truly devotional only as S.K. assumed the
role of pastor, speaking directly to a hearer regarding his own
condition: "Now if you have truly realized that God is present
here and you are in his presence, . . . it will be noticeable in
you. One should be able to tell from a man's behavior that he
is in love, one should be able to tell that he is in the power of
a great thought: how then should one not be able to tell that
he is in the presence of God."[13] The impression was heightened when S.K. spoke to God Himself: "If only Thou,
[O God,] dost find some willingness on the part of the single
individual, Thou art prompt to help, and first of all Thou art
the one who with more than human, yea, with divine patience,
dost sit and spell it out with the individual, that he may be
able rightly to understand the Word; and next Thou are the
one who, again with more than human, yea, with divine patience, dost take him as it were by the hand and help him
when he strives to do accordingly—Thou our Father in
heaven."[14] But the full picture of S.K.'s devotional immediacy
came only when it included testimony to his own personal
experience.

It is clear that S.K. considered this immediacy as a necessary
element in the Christian faith of every man and not simply a

[12] *The Sickness unto Death*, p. 216.
[13] *Dru Journals*, 1028 (1849).
[14] ". . . The Mirror of the Word" (Discourse I) in *For Self-Examination*, p. 39.

preference of his own, but nonetheless the character of that conviction is best seen in his personal application of it. For S.K., God was Father in the most actual sense possible: "My father died—and I got another in his stead: God in Heaven—and then I found out that, essentially, my first father had been my stepfather and only unessentially my first father."[15] God was S.K.'s father in the most central and profound aspects of his life:

"It is wonderful how God's love overwhelms me. . . . I continuously thank him for having done and for doing, yes, and for doing so indescribably much more for me than I ever expected. . . . [My life] was all embittered for me by the dark spot which ruined all; . . . God takes charge of our lives. He lets me weep before him in silent solitude, pour forth and again pour forth my pain, with the blessed consolation of knowing that he is concerned for me—and in the meanwhile he gives that life of pain a significance which almost overwhelms me."[16]

But it is also significant that God was S.K.'s father in life's trivialities as well: "And it is true indeed that in agreement with God, which I always try to be, I am able to be perfectly calm and childishly happy in behaving as I do behave. Like a child I can say to God (it comes so naturally to me) as I would say to my father: now I must have a little recreation so as to amuse myself—and then I amuse myself."[17] And the most sure and unshakeable reality of S.K.'s life was the *quality* of that fatherhood: "This is all I have known for certain, that God is love. Even if I have been mistaken on this or that point: God is nevertheless love, that I believe, and whoever believes that is not mistaken. If I have made a mistake it will be plain enough; so I repent—and God *is* love. He *is* love, not he *was* love, nor: he *will be* love, oh no, even that future was too slow for me, he *is* love."[18]

[15] *Rohde Journals*, 45 (1848).   [16] *Dru Journals*, 754 (1848).
[17] *Ibid.*, 1114 (1850).   [18] *Ibid.*, 1102 (1850).

None of the early Brethren produced the sort of journal that would display their sense of devotion in such intimacy, but it is clear that theirs was of the same tradition and quality. It is also clear that with both S.K. and the Brethren this sense of immediacy represented the heart and core of their faith and not an idiosyncratic adjunct to what is truly important, their "theology." Thus whenever S.K. wanted to talk to real men about really important matters concerning the real God, his language became highly anthropomorphic—brashly, blatantly, brazenly anthropomorphic—without the slightest indication that he considered himself to be speaking symbolically, mythologically, or metaphorically. In the Brethren this might be overlooked as naivete. S.K. knew, however, that such language is suspect in sophisticated theology. But he was writing neither as a theologian nor for theologians. He knew where he stood and took his stand deliberately:

"As it is the worst thing that can be said about a man that he is inhuman, so it is the worst and most abhorrent blasphemy to say about God that He is inhuman, even if it is supposed to be distinguished or bold to speak thus. No, the God to whom [man] prays is human, has a heart to feel in human fashion, an ear to hear the complaints of human beings. And even if He does not fulfill every wish, His dwelling place is still near at hand, and He is moved by the cries of the petitioner."[19]

There here becomes apparent a drastic enough divergence between S.K. and some of his successors that more than the customary categories are called for. If S.K.'s thought is existential (which certainly it is in some sense of the term), then it is not enough even to specify it as Theistic, or even Christian, existentialism. In order to recognize the major distinction between it and contemporary schools which bear the name and yet threaten to weaken, if not eliminate, the "personhood" of God, perhaps S.K.'s variety could be called Pietistic existen-

[19] "The True Man of Prayer . . ." (Discourse IV) in *Edifying Discourses*, Vol. IV, p. 126.

tialism. It probably is no accident that the two great contemporary theologians who best understood Kierkegaard and best appropriated his contributions in their own work were Martin Buber, with his strong background in Hasidism, i.e. Jewish pietism, and Emil Brunner, schooled by the Pietist Blumhardt of Boll.

A final note is important. Although in S.K. we find devotional immediacy raised to a high pitch, it should be recalled that it was in this same S.K. that Karl Barth found a "wholly Other" God with whom to counter the immanental immediacy of Liberalism. Devotional immediacy, in and of itself, is not subversive of God's dignity, sovereignty, or freedom; and neither S.K. nor the Brethren allowed it to become so.[20]

G. SELF-EXAMINATION

Now examine thyself—for that thou hast a right to do.
On the other hand, thou hast properly no right,
without self-examination,
to let thyself be deluded by "the others,"
or to delude thyself into the belief
that thou art a Christian—therefore examine thyself.[1]

The motif now before us is a close corollary of *den Enkelte,* inwardness, and devotional immediacy. As with devotional immediacy, in both S.K. and the Brethren it can be understood as a direct inheritance from Pietism. And again, it is as much a mood or quality of mind as it is a doctrine.

One of S.K.'s books bears the title *For Self-Examination;* many of the others could as well have. Likewise, the title of

---

[20] None of the above should be taken to imply that devotional immediacy is the sole prerogative of sectarianism. Obviously this is not the case, although it is nevertheless a fact that the emphasis has been more central and pervasive in sectarian than in churchly (and, particularly, theological) circles.

---

[1] *Training in Christianity*, p. 42.

the first and major section of Michael Frantz's long poem is "Mirror and Test of Himself."[2] The opening stanza reads:

> Lord Jesus, Thou my Alpha and Omega,
>   Thus my beginning and my end,
> I now have it in mind
>   To lament to Thee how it is with me.

Seventy-six stanzas later he was still on the theme:

> O! If I could rightly test myself,
>   Then no one would be judged as I would be;
> I should not rebuke others
>   Until I have first judged myself.

And Stanza Ninety-Three reads:

> Lord, help me test myself still more,
>   Because I am very obscure to myself;
> I can judge only on the basis of what I myself am,
>   A self fallen into serious judgment.[3]

In an issue of Sauer Junior's *Geistliche Magazien* there appeared a brief appendix (evidently by Sauer himself) on "the necessity of self-proving," in which it is said: "Out of all considerations that a man can have, none is so necessary as this: that one's present thoughts and deeds agree with eternity, wherein one ponders what will be the result of each deed, word, and thought with which we detain ourselves. . . . Also, we must give God's judgment unimpartially not only upon all our deeds but also upon each unnecessary word that we have spoken."[4] In addition to such specific references, Brethren devotional literature is pervaded throughout with this mood of

---

[2] The fact that this title is worded in the third person may indicate that it was contributed by the publisher rather than the author himself; it is accurate in any case.

[3] Michael Frantz, *op.cit.*, stanzas 1, 76, 93, respectively [my trans.— V.E.].

[4] Sauer Junior (presumably), in *Geistliche Magazien*, Series I, No. 17, c. 1765, p. 143 [my trans.—V.E.].

pietistic soul-searching; the certainty of God's presence continually reflected itself in questions about one's own responsiveness. Without doubt a similar mood of introspection could be found in many writers of the churchly tradition, yet it does seem to be more widely typical of the sectaries.

However, if the flavor is pervasive in Brethrenism, in S.K. it is so strong that some readers find it distasteful. Of course, S.K. did indulge in self-dissection, although this emphasis *in Kierkegaard studies* is not entirely of his doing. As we observed earlier, scholars have taken it upon themselves to set out and footnote every "self-examining" passage in S.K.'s works, even where he had not intended them to be read as such, and so too have his journals been edited in a way that makes this aspect more central than it actually was.

Nevertheless it is probably true that no one in history ever has been more acutely cognizant of and concerned about his own inner nature, development, and history than was Søren Kierkegaard. Reinhold Niebuhr has called him "the profoundest interpreter of the psychology of the religious life since Augustine";[5] and with S.K., as with Augustine, that psychology was learned from precisely one case study, himself.

S.K.'s penchant for self-examination was, of course, in part a purely personal propensity; but more than that, it was part and parcel of his religious orientation and tradition. Self-examination is a necessary concomitant of the Kierkegaardian concept of faith. As was his custom, S.K. could and did put the matter in general, semiphilosophic terms: "The law for the development of the self with respect to knowledge . . . is this, that the increasing degree of knowledge corresponds with the degree of self-knowledge, the more the self knows, the more it knows itself."[6] And as was even more customary with S.K., he did not leave the matter on the level of abstract state-

[5] Niebuhr's remark is quoted on the dust jackets of the Princeton University Press editions of *Philosophical Fragments* and *Authority and Revelation*.

[6] *The Sickness unto Death*, p. 164. Cf. *Works of Love*, pp. 331-32.

ment but made it more personal, more religious, more Christian: "It is indeed our aim to prompt the hearer to test his life, his Christianity, to be observant of where he is."[7]

A most important point regarding self-examination, although one that almost goes without saying, is that it must take place before God and with his help. Thus S.K. was an enthusiastic supporter of the office of confession—not auricular confession to a priest (in which S.K. would have had no interest) but the Lutheran practice of his day, which was a service of worship preceding communion, directed specifically to helping the individual make his personal confession to God. A number of S.K.'s discourses were designated for this occasion, and of confession, S.K. said: "Not God, but you, the maker of the confession, get to know something by your act of confession. Much that you are able to keep hidden in darkness, you first get to know by your opening it to the knowledge of the all-knowing One."[8]

Although apparently not attested from eighteenth century sources, the Brethren traditionally have followed much the same practice. Theirs was not called "confession" but precisely "the self-examination service" (based on Paul's "Let each man examine himself" [1 Cor. 11:28]). It took the form not only of a direct adjunct to the agape-communion service but also of an earlier visit by the deacons with each member of the congregation individually.

H. EQUALITY BEFORE GOD

...As no coin is so small that it cannot bear
the image of the emperor
so no man is so humble that he cannot bear God's image....[1]

---

[7] "Our Salvation Is Now Nearer . . ." (Pt. III, Discourse 5) in *Christian Discourses*, p. 222.

[8] *Purity of Heart*, p. 51.

---

[1] Discourse II on "What Is To Be Learnt from the Lilies" in *The Gospel of Suffering*, p. 234.

Whatever difference there may be between two persons,
even if humanly speaking it were most extreme,
God has it in his power to say:
"When I am present, certainly no one will presume to be
conscious of this difference, because that would be
standing and talking to each other in my presence
as if I were not present.[2]

Thou plain man!
The Christianity of the New Testament is infinitely high;
but observe that it is not high
in such a sense that it has to do with the difference
between man and man with respect to intellectual capacity, etc.
No, it is for all. . . . Thou plain man!
I have not separated my life from thine;
thou knowest it. . . .[3]

With its doctrine of "the priesthood of all believers" the Prot-estant Reformation made a tremendous stride toward estab-lishing the theological foundations for the equality of all men before God. However, the churchly wing of that Reformation did not make nearly comparable progress in adjusting the structure and life of the church to implement the theological affirmation. Thus in our own day the problem of the laity has become an urgent one. The sectarian wing of the Reforma-tion, on the other hand, took the doctrine more seriously and developed a form of church organization that did attempt to give existential expression to it. But the one Protestant who felt this demand of the gospel most deeply, who preached it most insistently, who interpreted it most radically, who was most alert to spotting violations of it—this Protestant, we pro-pose, was Søren Kierkegaard.

But first, the Brethren. Although sectarian to the core, the eighteenth century Brethren did not speak much about equal-

[2] *Works of Love,* p. 315.
[3] *The Attack upon "Christendom,"* p. 287.

ity; appropriate quotations are hard to come by. However, careful consideration makes it plain that this silence is not an indication of the absence of the doctrine but of its presence at so basic a level that it simply was taken for granted. The church (the *Gemeinde*) was so structured that this equality was a fact, and there was no reason to talk about it. The other sects and the spiritualist groups with which the Brethren had contact were all of a mind on this matter, and the Brethren so completely had shaken the dust of the "churches" from their feet that the question of equality did not come under discussion. But (a) that conception which, in the Brethren situation of acceptance, was so primary as to be unconscious and (b) that conception which, in the churchly situation of S.K., he felt to be so primary that it must be made painfully self-conscious—these two were yet the same conception.

The Brethren understanding of equality is not to be found in written statements but in the way they constituted the *Gemeinde* and its ministry—this actually being a much more compelling demonstration than a mass of assertions *about* equality would be. It is the Brethren concept of "clergy" that is most revealing. This, of course, does not cover the whole gamut of equality before God, but it does stand as the crux of the issue and as a symbol of the Brethren conception in general. The case is that the distinction between clergy and laity was a very fluid and informal one. In some ways it would be correct to say that every Dunker was a layman; in other respects it would have to be said that every Dunker was a priest; the most accurate formula probably should adopt a Pauline style: in Christ there is neither layman nor priest.

A real rarity in church history, the Brethren constituted a church founded entirely by laymen; in fact, the evidence is that it was well into the nineteenth century before anyone with previous ministerial background and training even joined the brotherhood. Certainly from the outset Alexander Mack carried the role of elder (bishop), but there is no record of how, when, or *if* the church ordained him; and what is even more amazing, no one ever has raised the question. Although well respected and beloved as the "founder" of the church, Mack's original gravestone bore only his initials (not even his full name) with the dates of his birth and death. The stone of Peter Becker, the "founder" of the church in America, was even more simple, an unshaped fieldstone on which was scratched "Anno 1758, P.B." The early Brethren did not run the risk of giving undue honor to men.

The customary practice seems to have been that the "clergy" were chosen by the *Gemeinde* as a whole, out of its own number, as need arose. Apparently there were not even nominations, any and all members being considered as eligible for office. There were, of course, no educational or professional requirements, as, likewise, no salary nor monetary recompense. Brumbaugh cites a document from the pen of Mack Junior reporting the rather astonishing fact that a *woman* served as an elder in the church during its earliest days at Schwarzenau.[4] All members, irrespective of office, were addressed simply as Brother So-and-So and Sister Whomever; and in some Brethren writings it comes almost as a shock to discover the men we commonly know as *St.* Paul and *St.* Peter referred to as Brother Paul and Brother Peter.

In a letter of 1747 Michael Frantz counseled specifically that laymen are free to administer baptism and the communion if no elders are present and if all things are done in order.[5] His statement gives the impression (undoubtedly correct) that the clerical office exists not for the sake of any peculiar authority or power it imparts but as a means of assisting the *Gemeinde* to conduct its life and worship in a dignified and worthy manner; Dunker "priests" did not so much *administer* the sacraments as they *superintended* their observance.

[4] Brumbaugh, *op.cit.*, pp. 68, 176-77.
[5] Michael Frantz, a letter dated Dec. 9, 1747, in Henry Kurtz, *The Brethren's Encyclopedia* (Columbiana, Ohio: 1867), pp. 133-34.

But the most interesting and perhaps most enlightening insight into the Brethren concept of equality came in connection with the very delicate problem of ministerial discipline; surely the clergy would have to assert its prerogatives here. But not so. In 1764 Mack Junior and Sauer Junior were co-elders of the Germantown congregation. At that time some of the members became unhappy over the fact that Sauer was printing catechisms for the Lutherans. It was not that they objected to his doing work for another denomination, but they could not quite see a Dunker elder putting his imprint on a book that advocated and defended infant baptism. The writ of censure (if that it can be called) presumably was drawn up by Mack Junior; the manuscript was in his possession. It must be one of the strangest specimens of its kind. It opens with a prayer to the effect that God will strengthen and use his servant Christopher Sauer; it closes with a strong endorsement of the Sauer Press, its work and witness. In between, the petitioners are almost apologetic as they explain that they find themselves constrained by their consciences to lay the matter upon Sauer's conscience. And in the end their only "demand" is a polite request that, if Sauer ever contemplates publishing another edition of the catechism, he kindly inform the church beforehand so that a "big meeting" of the brotherhood might be called to consider the issue.

But the aspect of this writ that bears upon equality is its signatures. One of the signers is Alexander Mack, Sauer's co-elder and unquestionably the leading figure of the sect. But Mack's signature neither leads the list as foremost in authority nor does it conclude the list as being the last word; it appears unobtrusively in the middle. Two others of the signers are known to have been deacons;[6] of the remaining two we know

[6] Whether, in eighteenth century Brethrenism, the deacon should be considered as a cleric or a layman is a very neat question. Deacons were inducted into office through a laying on of hands, although it is also true that every member was so ordained into the Christian life

not that much.[7] Clearly, ecclesiastical powers and prerogatives which would make one believer in any way superior to another simply were not part of Brethren thought. These Dunkers were concerned studiously to avoid any sort of either spiritual or governmental hierarchicalism, although it is important to note that they were concerned just as studiously to have the order and offices that would guard against anarchy and atomism.

We shall discover that S.K.'s doctrine of equality was developed in an entirely different context than that just traced for the Brethren. S.K.'s comments on the government and ministry of the church were entirely *negative*, directed *against* the evils he found in his own situation. Actually, he had no occasion to prescribe what the ministerial structure of a *Gemeinde* should be. Nevertheless, is not a significant agreement between the Dunkers and the Dane suggested in the fact

---

at the time of his baptism. When, in the late nineteenth century, the Brethren began to develop a trained, professionalized ministry, the diaconate clearly became a *lay* office; but in the eighteenth century, the lay-clergy distinction was of such little moment that the question about deacons could not even be formulated.

[7] The so-called writ of censure (which is entirely my own title) is preserved in English translation in Kurtz, *op.cit.*, pp. 137-41.

The sequel and climax to the story is this: To the original, 1764 manuscript of the writ was appended a note by Mack Junior, dated May 17, 1767. In it he asseverates that, although he still holds the views expressed in the writ, he does not want either his name or the writ itself to be made the authority for calling any "big meeting" that might endanger the *Gemeinschaft* of the church. In addition to his own, this "concluding unscientific postscript" bears the signatures of three more of the original four other signers of the writ. It seems quite unlikely that the writ was ever "served"; the Brethren put higher value upon the preservation of *Gemeinschaft* than upon correcting Sauer. At the same time, however, it is highly likely that the concern did get communicated to the offender; the catalog of the Sauer Press lists no further printings of catechisms until 1777, the year when control of the business passed from Sauer to his sons. Apparently Elder Sauer—as well as his petitioners—had some feeling for *Gemeinschaft*.

that, on his deathbed, S.K. asked for communion *from the hands of a layman*?[8]

Our observations regarding the Dunker *Gemeinde* make it obvious that the Brethren held a strong doctrine of the equality of all *believers* before God. It might be objected, however, that this does not cover the question regarding men universally. But in a very real sense all men *do* share in this equality in respect of the fact that all are potential believers. Indeed, it is upon precisely such a premise that S.K. will found his doctrine of equality, i.e. on each man's potentiality for becoming a Christian. Moreover, the Brethren doctrine of radical *love* for all men (to be examined in a succeeding chapter) certainly carries rather direct implications regarding the *equality* of these men before God.

However, the view which in Brethren thought was only implicit became in S.K. very explicit:

"But let me give utterance to this which in a sense is my very life, the content of my life for me, its fullness, its happiness, its peace and contentment. There are various philosophies of life which deal with the question of human dignity and human equality; Christianly, every man (the individual), absolutely every man, once again, absolutely every man is equally near to God. And how is he equally near? Loved by Him. So there is equality, infinite equality between man and man.[9]

"I set the problem, the problem which faces the whole age: equality between man and man. I put it into practice in Copenhagen. That is something more than writing a few words on the subject: I expressed it approximately with my life."[10]

It is quite true that in other places S.K. spoke just as emphatically about other themes being the center of his witness, but this indicates no particular vagary on his part. The themes

[8] *Dru Journals*, p. 551, quoted above, p. 25.
[9] The Preface to *For Self-Examination*, p. 5.
[10] *Dru Journals*, 877 (1849). Cf. S.K.'s statements quoted above, pp. 93-94, 142, 179-80.

that made up the core of his thought were so closely interrelated that emphasis on one necessarily emphasized the rest. Thus to become *den Enkelte*, to live in true inwardness, to be unconditionally obedient to God, to practice devotional immediacy, or to achieve complete equality before God—all ultimately appear as necessary aspects of the same spiritual existence. Nothing is to be gained by promoting any one of them as *the* true key to Kierkegaard. It is not improper that, in turn, he should speak as though each were the most fundamental.

The theme of equality can be traced throughout the authorship, even back into the pseudonyms,[11] although the true depth and grounding of S.K.'s conviction became evident only in the religious works. Climacus of the *Postscript* began to develop the religious aspect, yet doing it in rather abstract, theological terms.[12] However, when S.K. spoke directly and in his own name, it was made obvious that his interest was not in a theological proposition but in a religious reality, a Christian reality which he was fervently concerned to actualize. He derived the thought of equality in a number of ways. For instance, equality is the concomitant of *faith*: "Faith has a different quality; it is not only the highest good, but it is a good in which all men can share. . . . And this is the glory of faith, that it can only be had on this condition [that its possibility be conceded to all men]."[13] Just as fundamentally, equality is a concomitant of *love*: "He who praises art and science emphasizes the cleavage between the talented and untalented among men. But he who praises love equalizes all, not in a common poverty or a common mediocrity, but in the community of the highest."[14]

[11] *Either/Or I*, p. 116; *Either/Or II*, pp. 280, 297; *Stages upon Life's Way*, pp. 222, 226, 282, 297.

[12] *Postscript*, pp. 92, 502.

[13] "Faith's Expectation" (Discourse I) in *Edifying Discourses*, Vol. I, p. 10.

[14] *Works of Love*, p. 335; cf. p. 97. Cf. also the second of "Two Notes on 'the Individual' " in *Point of View*, p. 118.

But what is probably S.K.'s most basic statement is the one that follows. It merits being quoted in full, because it reveals so much both of the background and the implications of S.K.'s thought: It points to the ultimate, Christian source of equality, God's redeeming act in Christ. It relates equality to S.K.'s concept of *den Enkelte*. It reveals how equality lays the foundation for a strong doctrine of *Gemeinschaft*. And it very precisely distinguishes what this equality is from what it is not.

"[Christianity] has saved men from this sort of evil [the ungodliness which teaches one man to disclaim relationship with another] by deeply and eternally unforgettably stamping the imprint of kinship between man and man, because kinship of all men is secured by every individual's equal kinship with and relationship to God in Christ, because the Christian doctrine addresses itself equally to every individual and teaches him that God has created him and Christ has redeemed him. ... Before Christ just as in the sight of God there is no aggregate, no mass; the innumerable are for him numbered—they are unmitigated individuals. ... Christianity *has not taken distinctions away*—any more than Christ could or would pray God to *take the disciples out of the world*—and these remain one and the same thing. ... [Christianity] sees—and with real distress, that earthly busy-ness and the false prophets of secularism will in the name of Christianity conjure up the illusion of perfect equality, as if only the high and mighty make much of the distinctions of earthly existence, as if the poor were entitled to do everything in order to attain equality—only not by way of becoming Christians in earnestness and truth. I wonder if one can come closer to Christian likeness and equality that way? Christianity, then, will not take differences away, neither the distinction of poverty nor that of social position. But on the other hand, Christianity will not in partiality side with any temporal distinction, either the lowliest or the most acceptable in the eyes of the world."[15]

[15] *Works of Love*, pp. 80, 81.

This last is a point that S.K. emphasized as strongly as any he ever made; it was reiterated time and again in his writings. Christian equality before God is not the same thing as sociopolitical equality. Equality within the context of the Christian faith is an entirely different phenomenon than equality in the worldly context. To read implications back and forth from one sphere to the other leads only to confusion. S.K. put the matter very bluntly:

"No politics ever has, no politics ever can, no worldliness ever has, no worldliness ever can, think through or realize to its last consequences the thought of human equality. . . . For if complete equality were to be attained, worldliness would be at an end. But is it not a sort of obsession on the part of worldliness that it has got into its head the notion of wanting to enforce complete equality, and to enforce it by wordly means . . . in a worldly medium? It is only religion that can, with the help of eternity, carry human equality to the utmost limit. . . . And therefore (be it said to its honor and glory) religion is the true humanity."[16]

Closely related to S.K.'s thought on equality is his doctrine of nonconformity to the world (to be examined in a later chapter); and this linkage gives his thought a particularly sectarian bent. Although committed to a most radical view of equality, neither S.K., the Brethren, nor sectaries generally are to be considered as "*demo*crats" or as an integral part of the democratic tradition. They assigned no particular value to "the voice of the people" or to "the natural rights of man." They were out-and-out "*theo*crats," the only thing distinguishing them from usual theocratic thought being that they conceived of God's rule not as mediated through any sort of hierarchical structure but as apprehended personally and directly by each individual believer. The connection between sectarian Christian equalitarianism and democratic social equalitarian-

---

[16] The Preface to "Two Notes on 'the Individual'" in *Point of View*, pp. 107-08. Cf. *Works of Love*, p. 82, and *The Book of Adler*, p. xxi.

ism is not as close as it might seem; and our interpretation of history probably is oversimplified when, for instance, we take religious sectarianism to be a direct progenitor of American democracy. It is significant that the classic sects showed no particular inclination to get involved in secular politics and made no attempt to give their ideology expression through widespread social reforms; S.K. understood why.

He did not deny that the Christian understanding of equality might have implications regarding the worldly relationships of man's social and political life, but for him these never could amount to a simple equation between democracy (or any other social-political system) and Christianity. Thus he did not merely *fail* to draw these implications but deliberately *refused* to, in order to avoid confusing the categories. For S.K. any equality based elsewhere than "before God," any equality derived from the nature of man rather than the gracious action of God in Christ, any equality that must be enforced by law rather than being the expression of neighbor love, any equality dedicated to mutual self-interest rather than to mutual service—any such equality hardly can qualify as true equality, hardly dare be yoked with Christian equality. Obviously, the Kierkegaard-sectarian view bears little resemblance to the liberalism of the nineteenth and twentieth centuries that charted the advance of the kingdom by the spread of social equalitarianism; and the Brethren and other such groups deserted their true heritage to the extent that they were captured by this modern ideology.

Because democratic equalitarianism is a worldly rather than a truly Christian form, it is bound to include seeds of the demonic within itself. And S.K.—amazingly early in the historical development—saw precisely where the demonism lies. It is in what he called "soul-consuming uniformity,"[17] a proc-

---

[17] "Every Good Gift . . ." (Discourse III) in *Edifying Discourses*, Vol. II, p. 48; see the entire discourse for an extended discussion of the theme.

ess which proves to be a "leveling" rather than an "elevating" equalization: "The individual no longer belongs to God, to himself, to his beloved, to his art or to his science, he is conscious of belonging in all things to an abstraction to which he is subjected by reflection, just as a serf belongs to an estate. . . . There is no other reason for this [leveling] than that eternal responsibility, and the religious singling out of the individual before God, is ignored."[18] Whereas democratic equalitarianism includes tendencies toward the deadening conformity of mass man, the organization man, etc., the true Christian equality is preserved from such a fate in that the presence and pressure of God posits and guarantees the retention of *den Enkelte*. S.K., in his analysis of secular equalitarianism, foresaw the situation which in our day called forth the existentialist revolt. But this revolt, no less secular in its orientation than that against which it revolts, is no real answer, because in its autonomous assertion of individuality it inevitably undercuts human equality and *Gemeinschaft*. No, the only solution is S.K.'s, the *religious* concept of a man finding his true, elevated equality with all other men precisely by existing as *den Enkelte* . . . before God.

There is nothing in S.K. that would deny that democracy might be the best form of secular government; but he passionately would have resisted the suggestion that a state's achieving of social and political equality made it in any sense Christian. Secular equalitarianism must be justified and defended on its own secular premises; and whatever its achievements, it does not begin to approximate the Christian concept. And how great the tragedy when it happens—as it often has happened—that Christians become confused, lose sight of their true equality, and in its stead chase the phantom of worldly equalitarianism. "Therefore, be it said to its honor and glory, religion is the [only] true humanity."

But of equal importance and perhaps even greater contem-

[18] *The Present Age*, p. 53; cf. pp. 51ff. for an extended discussion.

porary relevance than S.K.'s pointing us to the true source of human equality is the incisive way in which he pinpointed and exposed the equality-killing distinctions that slip into the very practice of our faith. One of these is the idea of merit, or accomplishment, in God's sight—whether the "Catholic" ascetic accomplishments of self-discipline and mortification or the "Protestant" accomplishments of service to the cause of the kingdom. In either case the inevitable implication is that one person stands higher with God than another; but S.K. said: "If both in relation to the demand do all, then they do equally much. And if neither of them does all, then they do equally little. . . . Oh, how great is the mercy of the Eternal toward us! All the ruinous quarreling and comparison which swells up and injures, which sighs and envies, the Eternal does not recognize. Its claim rests equally on each, the greatest who ever lived, and the most insignificant."[19]

Another invidious distinction between man and man is that of intellect; and the full thrust and passion of S.K.'s anti-intellectualism cannot be appreciated until seen in this connection. In the following, Climacus hardly spoke as a pseudonym: "God is affronted by getting a group of hangers-on, an intermediary staff of clever brains; and humanity is affronted because the relationship to God is not identical for all men. . . . For the speculative philosopher and the plain man do not by any means know the same thing, when the plain man believes the paradox, and the speculative philosopher knows it to be abrogated."[20]

Closely related but cutting even deeper is S.K.'s observation about social-cultural distinctions, an observation that may be particularly appropriate when, in our day, a certain conception of "secular Christianity" is popular:

"Therefore this distinguished corruption teaches the man of distinction that he exists only for distinguished men, that he

[19] *Purity of Heart*, pp. 123, 125.
[20] *Postscript*, p. 204. Cf. *Attack upon "Christendom,"* p. 159.

shall live only in their social circle, that he must not exist for other men, just as they must not exist for him. But he must be circumspect, as it is called, in order with smoothness and dexterity to avoid getting people excited. . . . He must be prepared to employ extreme courtesy towards common people, but he must never associate with them as equals, for thereby expression would be given to his being—a human being—whereas he is a distinguished personage. And if he can do this easily, smoothly, tastefully, elusively and yet always keeping his secret (that those other men do not really exist for him and he does not exist for them), then this refined corruption will confirm him as being . . . a well-bred man. . . . In company with scholars or within an environment which insures and elevates his distinction as such, a scholar would perhaps be willing to lecture enthusiastically on the doctrine of the equality of all men, but this means a continued maintenance of the distinction."[21]

Although certainly neither intended nor applicable as a blanket indictment, S.K.'s words do point out a phenomenon that is readily apparent on the current scene. This is the lust for sophistication—whether it take the form of impressive jargon-juggling; the display of ecclesiastical elegance; the studied casualness of name-dropping and quote-lifting; the two-way pose that can pass one off as a man of God or of the world as the occasion demands; the "being in touch with the world" which ever risks getting lost in the world; the proficiency in theological and ecclesiastical gamemanship. S.K. understood that all such represents a living refutation of Christian equality before God.

In a way it is amazing that Søren Kierkegaard should be the one to arrive at this insight, for he was eminently qualified to play the role of the sophisticate himself; he had the intellect, the wit, the money, the taste, the connections, even a natural propensity for aloofness. But perhaps it was precisely because

[21] *Works of Love*, pp. 85, 87.

he knew the disease within himself that he was so able to diagnose and expose it. And most assuredly it was because S.K. knew the disease within himself that he was not content "to lecture enthusiastically on the doctrine of the equality of all men" but felt impelled to go out on the street and put it into practice: "I have been deeply and inwardly concerned to recognize each of the poor men who knew me, to greet every servant with whom I had even the slightest acquaintance, to remember the last time I saw him, whether he had been ill, and to enquire after him. I have never in my life, not even when I was most preoccupied with an idea, been so busy that I did not first find time to stop for a moment if a poor man spoke to me."[22]

Only when, alongside his eloquent words, one also sees the person of the queer, introverted, melancholy Kierkegaard painfully practicing neighbor love—only then does one truly understand what he meant by the equality of all men before God. In the words of our epigraph: "Thou plain man! I have not separated my life from thine; thou knowest it. . . ." S.K. could say this because he was convinced that God, as it were, had said it first.

[22] *Dru Journals*, 719 (1847); cf. 769 (1848), 1092 (1850), and 1367 (1854). Cf. also *Point of View*, pp. 48-49.

CHAPTER VII

THE PROBLEM OF SOCIALITY

Nobody wants to be this strenuous thing:

an individual; it demands an effort.

But everywhere services are readily offered through

the phony substitute: a few! Let us get together

and be a gathering, then we can probably manage.

Therein lies mankind's deepest demoralization.[1]

Spiritual superiority only sees the individual.

But, alas, ordinarily we human beings

are sensual and, therefore,

as soon as it is a gathering, the impression changes—

we see something abstract, the crowd,

and we become different.[2]

In giving to *den Enkelte* and its characteristics as dominant an emphasis as the foregoing chapters indicate he did, S.K. inevitably created a major problem, the problem of sociality. How is man to be understood and handled in his *social* relationships? If religion is essentially a matter of *den Enkelte* before God, at what point do "others" come into the picture?

[1] *Rohde Journals*, 129 (1854).   [2] *Ibid.*, 127 (1850).

Can *den Enkelte* in any sense join with or be joined to them without jeopardizing his own status as *den Enkelte*?

Obviously, S.K. will give attention to one type of sociality that is inimical to *den Enkelte*, a sociality which acts precisely as an escape from or substitute for the strenuous thing of being *den Enkelte*. Such groupings S.K. named "the crowd"; and his polemic against the crowd and crowd mentality was loud, bitter, and abundant. In one respect he even made it his *first* task to attack the crowd, for only by dissolving it could he get to individuals with his concept of *den Enkelte*.[3]

Within S.K.'s frame of reference, "the crowd" was an absolutely negative concept; it is "the Evil," as he called it,[4] the sworn enemy of *den Enkelte*. And the same negativity was attributed to the corollaries of "the crowd," which are: (a) "the public"; (b) "the press," i.e. journalism, the instrument through which "the public" both expresses and creates itself; (c) "the world," in its technical, New Testament sense; and (d) "the Establishment," which, we shall see, is tantamount to "church" in that its *established* character is the hallmark of the churchly concept.

S.K. allowed no place at all for crowd sociality; and because of the emphatic and pervasive character of his invective, many students have read him as renouncing all sociality whatever. Martin Buber is the prime example of such an interpreter, and his stature as one of the ranking theologians who best understood S.K. makes his charge all the more serious. It behooves us to give the matter very careful consideration.

Buber opened his essay on S.K. with the following paragraph, which includes what we will contend is a gross misunderstanding:

"Only by coming up against the category of the 'Single One' [*den Enkelte*], and by making it a concept of utmost clarity, did Søren Kierkegaard become the one who presented Chris-

---

[3] *Purity of Heart*, pp. 143-44.
[4] *Point of View*, p. 61.

tianity as a paradoxical problem for the single 'Christian.' He was able to do this owing to the radical nature of his solitariness. His 'Single One' cannot be understood without his solitariness, which differed in kind from the solitariness of one of the earlier Christian thinkers, such as Augustine or Pascal, whose name one would like to link with his. It is not irrelevant that beside Augustine stood a mother and beside Pascal a sister, who maintained the organic connexion with the world as only a woman as the envoy of elemental life can; whereas the central event of Kierkegaard's life and the core of the crystallization of his thought was the renunciation of Regina Olsen as representing woman and the world."[5]

And as he continued, Buber pressed this point to the extreme:

"This relation [between *den Enkelte* and God] is an exclusive one, the exclusive one, and this means, according to Kierkegaard, that it is the excluding relation, excluding all others; more precisely, that it is the relation which in virtue of its unique, essential life expels all other relations into the realm of the unessential.[6]

"Kierkegaard does not marry . . . because he wants to lead the unbelieving man of his age, who is entangled in the crowd, to becoming single, to the solitary life of faith, to being alone before God."[7]

This is how Buber read S.K., and it is not extravagant to suggest that one of Buber's motives in writing *I and Thou* was to correct the solitariness of S.K.'s *den Enkelte*. Buber himself, in contrast to S.K., would incorporate sociality as an integral aspect of *den Enkelte*: "God wants us to come to him by means of the Reginas he has created and not by renunciation of them. . . .[8]

"The Single One corresponds to God when he in his hu-

[5] Martin Buber, "The Question to the Single One," in *Between Man and Man*, p. 40.
[6] *Ibid.*, p. 50.   [7] *Ibid.*, p. 59.   [8] *Ibid.*, p. 52.

man way embraces the bit of the world offered to him as God embraces his creation in his divine way. He realizes the image when, as much as he can in a personal way, he says *Thou* with his being to the beings living around him."[9]

And his summation reads: " 'The Single One' is not the man who has to do with God essentially, and only unessentially with others, who is unconditionally concerned with God and conditionally with the body politic. The Single One is the man for whom the reality of relation with God as an exclusive relation includes and encompasses the possibility of relation with all otherness, and for whom the whole body politic, the reservoir of otherness, offers just enough otherness for him to pass his life with it."[10]

Quite clearly Buber has chosen the better part—*if he has represented S.K.'s part fairly.* We contend that he has not. We would not endeavor entirely to absolve S.K. of a certain *deficiency of emphasis* which at least makes possible the reading Buber gives him. However, we will maintain: first, that a positive doctrine of sociality is not lacking in S.K. Although perhaps insufficiently stressed, it is present as a real, integral, and even necessary part of his concept. Second, although not as well *emphasized*, the social aspect actually is better *structured* in S.K. than in Buber. Buber does little more than asseverate that all man-to-man relationships are encompassed in the man-to-God relationship. S.K. analyzed sociality in more detail and made it integral to his thought as one pole of a dialectic.

There is a further distinction in the ways that S.K. and Buber treat sociality; it is subtle and almost impossible to document, but it may be of profound significance nonetheless. Buber *starts* with man-to-man and man-to-nature relationships and builds them up toward the man-to-God relationship. The man-to-God relationship becomes the consummation and sum of human relationships. Of course, the sum is

[9] *Ibid.*, pp. 56-57.   [10] *Ibid.*, p. 65.

greater than the parts and ultimately is to be seen as the source of the parts; but basically it is through our experience with other *thous* that we come to know the *Eternal Thou*. "God wants us to come to him *by means of* the Reginas he has created. . . ." And the book *I and Thou* is organized over precisely this pattern.

It will shortly become evident, however, that S.K.'s thought proceeded conversely. He began with the God relationship and derived all human relationships from it; it is only from God and with the help of God that one can discover his neighbor at all. And S.K.'s approach would seem the more accurate, at least for Christian thought. Actually, S.K. anticipated the possibility of criticism such as Buber's and tried to forestall it:

"In spite of everything men ought to have learned about my maieutic carefulness, in addition to proceeding slowly and continually letting it seem as if I knew nothing more, not the next thing—now on the occasion of my new Edifying Discourse they will presumably bawl out that I do not know what comes next, that I know nothing about sociality. The fools! Yet on the other hand I owe it to myself to confess before God that in a certain sense there is some truth in it, only not as men understand it, namely that always when I have first presented one aspect sharply and clearly, then I affirm the validity of the other even more strongly. Now I have the theme of the next book. It will be called *Works of Love*."[11]

S.K.'s "confession before God" gets at both the truth and the falsehood of Buber's reading. Kierkegaard's life was not socially normal. As a genius in a provincial town he was bound to feel somewhat isolated; as a *melancholy* genius it

---

[11] *Papirer*, VIII¹ A 4 (1847), quoted by the translators Howard and Edna Hong in their introduction to S.K.'s *Works of Love*, pp. 15-16. The Hongs themselves comment: "Those who say that Kierkegaard had no consciousness of anything but a purely private individualistic ethic cannot digest this work [*Works of Love*], nor, when properly understood, his other ethical works, but least of all this."

was inevitable that he live as one apart. It is true that he never married, that he never (at least after he broke with his father) had any truly intimate companions, that he never belonged to any group that afforded him first-hand experience of true *Gemeinschaft*. This personal deficiency undoubtedly is one reason why S.K. did not give more attention and emphasis to a doctrine of sociality, although an equally valid explanation could be that the need of his age was first for a concept of individuality before a social emphasis could be properly understood. Nevertheless, it is almost certainly this personal deficiency that S.K. meant as being confessed before God.

But even this deficiency ought not be exaggerated; there are some facts that stand on the other side. Particularly as a young man, S.K. was something of a social butterfly. He moved in the top circles of Copenhagen society; as a wit and *bon vivant*, his presence was valued on social occasions; he was a connoisseur of the theater, music hall, and dinner table. Throughout his life he maintained these connections to some extent and was an acquaintance of the leading social, civic, and religious figures of Denmark. Also, at least until the time that the Corsair incident drove people away from him, S.K. cultivated many speaking friendships with the common people on the street. He made it a point to converse with, counsel with, and offer help to servants, peasants, workingmen, people from any and all classes of society. And although S.K. was not a husband and father, he was an uncle par excellence; his nieces and nephews knew him as an especially loving and interesting friend of children. The people who actually rubbed shoulders with S.K. would be hard put to recognize Buber's stark description of one who had renounced all bonds with the world. It is true that none of these relationships were of the deepest, most intimate sort, yet it is grossly unfair to make S.K. out as simply and obviously a "solitary."

But such evidence quite aside, it is even more unwarranted to use S.K.'s personal life as *the* key for interpreting his thought, particularly when S.K. made it clear that he was well aware of his personal abnormalities and was striving continually to compensate for them. Above all, S.K.'s renunciation of Regina is in no sense to be understood as a symbol of what S.K. required of *den Enkelte*; whatever its meaning, that break was of purely personal significance, appertaining to Søren Kierkegaard and to Søren Kierkegaard alone. Certainly it was a renunciation of Søren Kierkegaard's marriage but not by that token a renunciation of marriage per se. *Fear and Trembling* was the book most directly molded by the Regina incident, in which S.K. meditated on his renunciation under the figure of Abraham's sacrifice of Isaac, but the sacrifice is there presented as the absolutely *exceptional* demand, in deliberate *contradistinction* to universal obligation. Kierkegaard did *not* break with Regina as a representation "in concrete biography of the renunciation of an essential relation to the world as that which hinders being alone before God," and most certainly he did not then "express it as an imperative: let *everyone* do so."[12]

Because it was Buber who initiated a contrast between S.K. and Augustine, perhaps we are justified in tracing the comparison more closely. The parallel is actually much nearer than Buber guessed and the conclusion quite different from that at which he arrived. The counterpart of Monica (Augustine's mother) is not Regina but S.K.'s father Michael. In both cases there was a deeply devout parent "praying" a prodigal son back to Christianity. In both cases there was a joyous reconciliation with God and with the parent in God—Augustine at the age of thirty-three years, S.K. twenty-five. In both cases the parent died but very shortly after the reconciliation took place. In both cases the sons entered their illustrious careers some three or four years after their "conversions" (Augustine did *not* have a mother standing beside him during his career

[12] Buber, *op.cit.*, pp. 58, 55, respectively.

as a Christian). In both cases the conversion was accompanied by the "renunciation" of women of intimate association. Before his conversion Augustine had sent away the mistress with whom he had lived for some years and by whom he had had a son—this in preparation for a respectable marriage. At the time of his conversion Augustine sent away a second mistress —this in preparation for Christian celibacy. S.K. both made and broke his engagement to Regina within approximately a three year period following his conversion.

Both "renounced" women; the difference in the way they did this *is* instructive, although the instruction is not at all what Buber suggests. Augustine left his two mistresses in the interest of achieving his own sainthood, the first in order to become acceptable in the eyes of men, the second in the eyes of God. In his *Confessions* Augustine showed extreme concern over his own sinfulness and his desire for holiness, but he showed nothing of a comparable concern over his responsibility to these women with whom he had loved and lived, no particular concern over what happened to them, over what his renunciation did to them.

With S.K. the case was very different. Although it probably never will be made completely clear just why S.K. felt that it was God's will for him to break his engagement, there is no evidence that he understood it as a way of enhancing his own saintliness; it is clear that he was as much or more concerned for Regina as for himself, that the break was as much for her sake as for his own. Consequently S.K. was quite willing to play the role of devil rather than saint in order to ease her suffering; and one gets the feeling that he actually would have been willing to have been lost in order to ensure her salvation.

There were, of course, differences of circumstance, social mores, *et al.*, between the action of Augustine and S.K., and we have no intention of running down Augustine. But completely contrary to Buber, if with either man the event was the crystallization of a sweeping and doctrinaire renunciation of "women and the world," patently it was more so with Augustine than with S.K.

However, the fundamental error of those who would interpret *den Enkelte* as being entirely solitary is the misimpression that S.K.'s fulminations against "the crowd" necessarily included all sociality. A more precise view of his terminology will enable us to correct this misunderstanding and will open to us new vistas of his thought.

The key—which is always the one to try with S.K.—is dialectic. And regarding this problem of sociality, we find precisely the same pattern as was described earlier in connection with "inwardness *and* obedience," "faith *and* works." In this instance the relationships are somewhat more complex, and a diagram may help clarify the discussion.

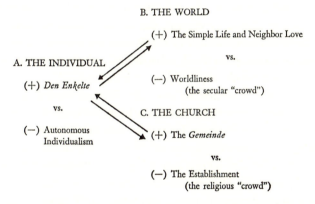

B. THE WORLD

(+) The Simple Life and Neighbor Love

vs.

A. THE INDIVIDUAL

(+) *Den Enkelte*

(−) Worldliness
(the secular "crowd")

vs.

C. THE CHURCH

(−) Autonomous
Individualism

(+) The *Gemeinde*

vs.

(−) The Establishment
(the religious "crowd")

The *A* column represents the first pole of the dialectic. *Den Enkelte*, of course, is the positive, religious concept of individualism as affirmed and promoted by S.K. The negative perversion, the contradictory—which is to be utterly rejected—is autonomous, self-asserting "individualism" (which S.K. identified and rejected as being of the Aesthetic Stage). The *B* column represents the other pole of the dialectic; under it is comprehended all sociality, any and all human associations for whatever purpose, constituted in whatever mode, on whatever principle. S.K. saw, however, that these can and should be divided into two distinct types. One social type is *B: The World*, using that term in the broadest possible sense to cover all associations except those of the church. The other social type is *C: The Church*, using that term also in the broadest possible sense to cover all associations of a religious nature. It would be wholly accurate to term *C* as *Religious Sociality* and *B* as *Secular Sociality*—except for the implication that therefore "secular" relationships lie outside the purview of religion. S.K. contended that one's life in the World must be lived before God just as certainly as his life in the Church; there is no distinction on this score. The distinction is, rather, that whereas the Church is constituted of man-to-man relationships for the sake of God, the World is constituted of man-to-man relationships for the sake of man; the primary orientation of the Church is vertical, that of the World, horizontal; a Christian's relationships of the World are *derived from* his prior relationship to God, whereas his relationships of the Church exist *for the sake of* his relationship to God.

Religious and secular sociality are different enough to call for individual treatment, and each forms its own distinct dialectic with *den Enkelte*. Under *B: The World*, the *positive* which S.K. affirmed consists of "The Simple Life," dealing with the world of nature and things, and "Neighbor Love," dealing with the human world of other persons. Opposed to this is the *negative*, the perversion, which is "Worldliness," or "Conformity to the World." The concept "crowd" includes the negative socialities of both the secular and the religious sphere; "crowd mentality" is what S.K. found to be the distinctive feature both of the World and the Establishment.

Admittedly, we have encountered terminological difficulty at this point. The word "world" properly can be used with three mutually exclusive meanings. In the *B* heading "the world" is an inclusive, nonevaluational term, although it is common usage thus to divide all of life between the Church and the World. But in the positive and the negative items subsumed under this "world" are two more "worlds" which complicate the situation no end. Here is found the contradiction between "the world" (*B*-positive) which God so loved that he gave his only Son (John 3:16) and "the world" (*B*-negative) which for us to love is proof that the love of the Father is not in us (1 John 2:15). These two "worlds" lie in even closer proximity in the sectarian shibboleth derived from John 17:16 and 18, i.e. "in the world but not of the world." "In the world" cannot mean merely "physically extant"; that would be too obvious to be significant; a Christian is not *called* to live in the world in this sense—he cannot help himself. No, the world the Christian is to be "in" is the world of "other people." The apostle who in one chapter of his epistle exhorted Christians not to love the world exhorted them in the succeeding chapter to love everyone in the world (1 John 2–3). And to love this world of people—an obligation which S.K. took very seriously—is, of course, to be related to them, to be a part of it.

On the other hand, the world which the Christian is not to be "of" is the world of goals and values as determined by the secular society which is not oriented toward the will of God. In short, one can love, accept, and identify with those who make up society without loving, accepting, or identifying with the standards of that society. The Christian can reject the evaluation men put upon things, thus rejecting both "the things of this world" and the possibility of being "a man of the world," without rejecting either "the world of things" or "the world of men." The distinction is a rather easy one to understand—a very difficult one to live. But because human language is not precise, S.K. explicitly could renounce and denounce the world, Martin Buber could come along later and accuse S.K. of renouncing the world, and yet what Buber says can be a grave misunderstanding. We intend to show that

S.K.'s strictures against "the world" are an instance of condemning only crowd sociality and thus by no means should be taken to imply solitariness and the rejection of all sociality.

Likewise, under *C: The Church*, the *positive* is "the *Gemeinde*" and the rejected *negative* is "the Establishment." Also, as above, terminological confusion again shows itself. The "church" of the *C* heading is a very broad and entirely neutral concept. The *C*-negative "church" is used in a "churchly" sense, as over against "sect." But in another sense, the *C*-positive *Gemeinde* is just as validly a church as any of the "churches" are.

The arrows on the chart illustrate the point that we have made earlier, that the dialectic relationship holds only between complementary positives; the intention is that the negatives be cancelled and obliterated.

There is a further observation regarding the dialectic pattern that holds equally true with our earlier examples as well as with this one. A real source of the power and efficacy of a dialectic lies in the fact that the positive of one pole stands precisely as the preventative or corrective of the negative of the opposite pole. Thus in the present instance a concept of *den Enkelte* is *the* cure for crowd mentality; and simple living, neighbor love, and *Gemeinschaft* are the cures for autonomous pretension. And thus in the earlier case obedience is the cure for either hiddenness or superficial emotionalism; and inwardness is the cure for works-righteousness.

Finally, the chart plots the sequence for this portion of our study. The present chapter has set the problem; Chapter VIII will treat the positions of S.K. and the Brethren regarding *B*-negative; Chapter IX, *B*-positive; Chapter X, *C*-negative; and Chapter XI, *C*-positive. Each chapter should be read in relation to the pattern as a whole.

CHAPTER VIII

THE WORLD WELL LOST

A. NONCONFORMITY TO THE WORLD

*To keep oneself pure and unspotted from the world
is the task and doctrine of Christianity—
would that we did it.*[1]

*What was said in paganism and Judaism,
that to see God is to die,
or at least to become blind or dumb
and the like, is expressed ethically in Christianity as a task:
to die to the world
is the condition for seeing God.*[2]

*Woe, woe to the Christian Church
if it would triumph in this world, for then it is not
the Church that triumphs, but the world has triumphed.
Then the heterogeneity of Christianity and the World
is done away with, the world has won, Christianity lost.
. . . And the day when Christianity
and the world become friends
Christianity is done away with.*[3]

[1] *Works of Love*, p. 84.
[2] *Smith Journals*, XI[2] A 113 (1854).
[3] "Lifted Up On High . . ." (Part III, Reflection 7) in *Training in Christianity*, p. 218.

The actual phrase "nonconformity to the world" (based on Romans 12:2) is not Kierkegaardian nor is it found in eighteenth century Brethren literature. In the *nineteenth* century it became the technical term by which the Brethren identified their doctrine, although by this time the doctrine itself had deteriorated until its primary emphasis was a legalistic prescription of a standard mode of dress and its secondary emphasis the legalistic prohibition of such things as jewelry, dancing, and card-playing. However, eighteenth century writings do not display this narrow moralism and do not so much as mention the wearing of a peculiar garb. The nineteenth century had the term, but the eighteenth century had much the better understanding of its meaning.

The closest the eighteenth century Brethren came to using the phrase itself was in a "big meeting" (probably the regular Annual Meeting of 1791) reported in the diary of Mack Junior. The principal query brought to that gathering was: "How could one, here in Germantown, resist by a united effort the very injurious evil which by conformation to the world is wrought upon the minds of the young, as we are living so near to the capital of the country."[4] Yet it is plain that the doctrine itself was part of Brethrenism from the beginning. Mack Senior had written: "This body or church is separated from the world, from sin, from all error, yes, from the entire old house of Adam—that is, according to the inner part of faith. ... However, this body or the church of Christ still walks outwardly in a state of humiliation in this wicked world."[5]

A prominent corollary of nonconformity—mentioned here by Mack and to be closely paralleled by S.K.—is that in contrast to the life of the world the life of the Christian is "a state of humiliation." This point was made with more emphasis in a hymn by John Price:

[4] Quoted in Brumbaugh, *op.cit.*, pp. 243-45.
[5] Mack Senior, *Rights and Ordinances*, in Durnbaugh, *Origins*, pp. 367-68.

Let us, with Lot, flee "the Sodom of this world." . . .
Let us not act as does the world
But seek only to be despised.
Let us not question this;
Let us look to heaven
And despise the tumult of the world,
Accepting all the disgrace.[6]

Nonconformity was a particularly strong theme with
Michael Frantz.[7] But it was Sauer Junior who picked up a
little different facet of the belief, this dealing with the Christian's relationship to worldly government. The Sauers felt
obliged to include in their almanacs the court calendar for the
year; they also felt obliged to accompany that calendar with a
little poem making it plain that the courts were no place for a
Christian to be found. We presume that Sauer Junior himself
was the author of the one for 1767:

[Christians] must, as [Christ's] servants,
    Proceed here according to His example
And highly honor His practices
    And claims, and stand within them.
Therefore they cannot become citizens
    Here in this vale of misery,
Because they are ransomed from the earth
    Through a great election of grace. . . .
They let cloak and mantle go,
    And rather do without clothing
Than in their years as pilgrims
    Mingle in the quarrels of the citizenry. . . .
They have never in anything opposed
    The authorities who are appointed. . . .

[6] John Price (d. ca. 1722), *Geistliche und Andachtige Lieder* [bound
as an appendix to *Der Wunderbahre Bussfertige Beichvatter*] (Germantown: Sauer Press, 1753), hymn 1, stanzas 4, 6.
[7] Michael Frantz, *op.cit.*, stanzas 170, 280-81, 315.

They will not readily sue anyone. . . .
   In poverty, shame, ridicule, and derision,
[The Christian] is known for his patience.
  The citizens of this world and time
  Can never be peaceful for long;
    Their self-interest teaches them to fight and quarrel;
They will have their rights and splendor.[8]

There are here several ideas that merit comment. Nonconformity follows as a direct corollary of *Nachfolge*, the imitation of Christ; this connection will show up as clearly in S.K. as in the Brethren. The Christian's life on earth customarily is typified in some such terms as "this vale of misery"; this is as true with S.K. as with the Brethren, although in neither case is it accurate to assume that this judgment leads to a "joyless" concept of the Christian faith. The note about the Christian not opposing appointed authorities is a very typical Brethren theme, actually an emphatic ingredient of the very doctrine of nonconformity. The Christian is to live *above* the law, and when the law would require him to do something contrary to the will of God he is to defy *that particular law*, but he has absolutely no intention of undermining the principle of law itself or questioning the right of secular authority to govern the world and to govern him to the extent that he is in the world. But the principle of the world is "self-interest," the struggle for one's own rights and privileges, and of this the Christian wants no part.

It was Mack Junior who picked up another basic point of contrast between the Christian and the world, the complete divergence as to what is valued as "treasure":

    Say, what is richer
    Than the poverty

---

[8] Sauer Junior (presumably), *"Eines Pilgers Gedancken vom Rechten,"* in *Der Hoch-Deutsch Americanische Calender* for 1767 (Germantown: Sauer Press, 1766), pp. 19-20 [my trans.—V.E.].

Which on the cross in Jesus' wounds
By the thief was found?
Christ's poverty
Makes us rich and free!
But whoever still tarries
With the treasure of the world,
He cannot find this treasure.[9]

And Jacob Stoll put the thought into stark and eloquent terms when he wrote:

Nothing is the lust of the world; nothing is the world;
Nothing is honor; nothing is gold;
Nothing are the dazzling things of this world—
Often they make the eyes dark.[10]

Kierkegaard, for his part, drove deep the cleavage in terms as intransigent as any used by the Brethren: " '*He must either hate the one and love the other, or he must hold to the one and despise the other.*' Consequently love to God is hatred to the world, and love for the world is hatred toward God; consequently this is the tremendous issue—either love or hate. Hence this is the place where the world's most terrible conflict is to be fought. And where is this place? In a man's heart."[11]

But, it immediately will be objected, there is a great difference. No matter how S.K. be quoted, it is quite obvious that, in sharp contrast to the simple Brethren, he was in many ways a prime example of worldly sophistication, as he said of himself, possessing "intellectual gifts (especially imagination and dialectic) and culture in superabundance."[12]

There is no denying that S.K. was such a person. His everyday mode of life was what men of the world would call "gra-

[9] Mack Junior, a poem "God Alone is Good," in Heckman, *op.cit.*, pp. 52-53, stanzas 5-6 [trans. amended—V.E.].
[10] Jacob Stoll, *op.cit.*, p. 189 [my trans.—V.E.]; cf. p. 107.
[11] Discourse III on "What Is To Be Learnt from the Lilies . . ." in *The Gospel of Suffering*, p. 227. Cf. S.K.'s words quoted above, p. 35.
[12] *Point of View*, p. 82.

cious," what the Brethren would have called "luxurious." In matters of art, music, theater, philosophy, learning—culture, in short—he was a crowning achievement of society, a "humanist," a *Christian* humanist par excellence. This aspect of S.K. is conspicuous, and it is clearly the case that many students have been drawn to him precisely because of his urbanity and sophistication: here is a model of culture *and* Christianity united in an attractive combination where each complements and enhances the other.[13] Walter Lowrie—who at this point definitely seems to be creating Kierkegaard in his own image —waxes eloquent about S.K.'s culture, concluding: "He remained a Humanist when he became a serious Christian, and for this reason, he was essentially a Catholic, as Father Przywara recognizes. And for this very reason Barth rejected him. It was owning to his Humanism that he disdained every sectarian movement however zealous."[14] Whether Lowrie fully understood Przywara and Barth is a question that need not detain us, and for the high Anglican Lowrie to find both humanism and Catholicism attractive in S.K. is not particularly surprising, but the question as to whether S.K. actually was a "humanist" demands the most careful consideration.

The very concept "humanism" is an ambiguous one and needs to be defined. Humanism can imply simply a deep concern for human welfare. In this sense Christianity is itself "the true humanity," as S.K. suggested; and he, along with every other Christian, was essentially a humanist. This, obviously, is not what Lowrie has in mind. In another sense, humanism is a faith, an alternative to Christianity that finds life's ultimate values not in God but in human achievement. In this sense neither S.K. nor any other Christian could be a humanist. Finally, and this certainly is what Lowrie intends,

[13] Note, for example, the place given to S.K. in Geddes MacGregor's plea for Christian humanism, *The Hemlock and the Cross* (Philadelphia: Lippincott, 1963).

[14] Walter Lowrie, in the translator's Appendix to S.K.'s *Repetition*, pp. 208-09.

Christian humanism is the position of those who value human culture *along with* their Christian faith, who see cultural values as integrally related to the faith, indeed as a vital part of the faith. It is in this sense that S.K. is identified as a humanist and in this sense that we are concerned to deny the attribution.

Part of the difficulty arises through an illegitimate identification of S.K. with his pseudonyms. The pseudonyms *were* humanists, openly and avowedly such, and for that matter not even *Christian* humanists. But S.K. was not his pseudonyms; in fact the pseudonyms were designed for the express purpose that S.K. might delineate a position *qualitatively lower* than that with which he personally would identify. The humanism of the pseudonyms is beside the point as to whether Søren Kierkegaard was a humanist or not.

More of the difficulty stems from a too-easy reading of the fact that S.K. *was* cultured—without inquiring about the *attitude* in which he held that culture. A careful study will show that S.K. had these things "as though not," as though he had them not.[15] And because S.K. had these things "as though not," because he attributed no real value or significance to them, he stands ideologically much closer to those who have them not than to those who do have them. The fact that he had all these "advantages" was, in S.K.'s own eyes, entirely incidental, worth nothing. As he saw it, the only real value of these gifts was that they enabled him to capture the attention of actual humanists that he might lead them out of humanism into Christianity. S.K. called himself "a spy in a higher service,"[16] and he meant it with the utmost seriousness. He was

---

[15] This Pauline concept is found in 1 Corinthians 7:29-31: "I mean, brethren, the appointed time has grown very short; from now on, let those who have wives live as though they had none, and those who mourn as though they were not mourning, and those who rejoice as though they were not rejoicing, and those who buy as though they had no goods, and those who deal with the world as though they had no dealings with it. For the form of this world is passing away."

[16] *Point of View*, p. 87.

not what he appeared, a man of the world; and it is tragic that the disguise has been taken for the real man.

S.K.'s most revealing statements in this regard cannot be fully appreciated unless one senses what Socrates meant to him. For S.K., Socrates represented the highest achievement of the human spirit; he stood as a symbol of the world at its best, the finest and noblest the world could offer. Kierkegaard was too modest to claim the following statement as his own, so he put it into quotation marks with a "so might the individual speak." However, the translator Lowrie (undoubtedly correctly) identifies it as a personal profession of faith—yet ultimately it militates against any identification of S.K. as a humanist: "I have admired that noble, simple wise man of ancient times [Socrates]; . . . but I have never believed on him, that never occurred to me. I count it also neither wise nor profound to institute a comparison between him, the simple wise man, and Him on whom I believe—that I count blasphemy." Would S.K. appreciate being treated in a volume entitled *The Hemlock and the Cross*? "As soon as I reflect upon the matter of my salvation, then is he, the simple wise man, a person highly indifferent to me, an insignificance, a naught."[17] And what of the hemlock, specifically? "Lo, to be executed, humanly speaking, innocently, and yet die with a witticism on his lips, that is a proud victory, that is the triumph of paganism; and it is also the highest victory in the relationship between man and man, that is, please note, if God is left out, if all of life and its greatest scenes are still at bottom a game, because God does not participate; for if He is present, then life is earnest."[18] When he deeply and seriously calls Socrates "a naught," calls his heroic death "at bottom a game," it seems

[17] "He Is Believed On in the World" (Part III, Discourse 7) in *Christian Discourses*, pp. 245-46.

[18] ". . . Courage Enables the Sufferer To Overcome the World . . ." (Discourse VII) in *The Gospel of Suffering*, p. 157. Cf. Discourse II on "What Is To Be Learnt from the Lilies" in *The Gospel of Suffering*, p. 212.

apparent that culture in general never could stand high enough with S.K. to justify his being called a "humanist," whether Christian or otherwise. "Among those born of women there has risen no one greater . . . ; yet he who is least in the kingdom of heaven is greater than he [Matthew 11:11]" —this is not the stance of humanist.

The real Kierkegaard was an antihumanist, staging the most effective critique of humanism ever made—and that directed particularly against so-called Christian humanism. He declared in so many words that his own aesthetic accomplishments were a feint[19] and evaluated the greatest of these in terms of the light it threw upon Christianity by way of contrast.[20] His considered judgment of Christian humanism was stated with utmost clarity: "It is not difficult to see that culture makes men insignificant, perfects them as copies, but abolishes individuality."[21] "[The] culture and civilization [which Christendom has produced through the centuries] has at the same time produced a development of rational understanding which is in the process of identifying being a Christian with culture, and with intelligence, desirous of a conceptual understanding of Christianity. This is where the struggle must come, and will be fought in the future."[22] "Fought in the future," S.K. said. Could it be that his critique has relevance when, under the aegis of an avant-garde concept of "secular Christianity," there is a theological movement which rather consciously is feeling after a new liaison with sophisticated culture? And if so, is it not ironic that one of the names often invoked in this movement is that of Søren Kierkegaard?

S.K.'s concern began to show itself as early as *Either/Or*, not too appropriately in the very mouth of "A," the aesthete:

"This is part of the confusion which in our age asserts itself

---

[19] *Point of View*, pp. 31ff., 39ff.
[20] *Ibid.*, p. 96.
[21] *Smith Journals*, XI^1 A 55 (1854).
[22] *Dru Journals*, 1288 (1853).

in so many ways: we look for a thing where we ought not to
look for it, and what is worse, we find it where we ought not
to find it; we wish to be edified in the theater, aesthetically
impressed in church, we would be converted by novels, get
enjoyment out of books of devotion, we want philosophy in
the pulpit, and the preacher in the professorial chair."[23]

S.K.'s later analyses were even more powerful:

"In established Christendom the natural man has managed
to have his own way. There is no endless contrast between the
Christian and the worldly. The relation of the Christian to the
worldly is conceived, at the most, as a potentialization (or
more exactly under the rubric, culture), always directly; it is
simply a direct comparative, the positive being civic rectitude.
. . . One starts with the worldly. Keeping an eye upon civic
rectitude (good—better—best), one makes oneself as com-
fortable as possible with everything one can scrape together in
the way of worldly goods—the Christian element being stirred
in with all this as an ingredient, a seasoner, which sometimes
serves merely to refine the relish. . . . Christianity is related directly to the world, it is a movement without budging from
the spot—that is to say, feigned movement."[24]

"Men have confused Christianity in many ways, but among
them is this way of calling it the highest, the deepest, and
thereby making it appear that the purely human was related
to Christianity as the high or the higher to the highest or the
supremely highest."[25]

It is a little difficult to understand why the author of such
lines should be classed as a Christian humanist.

S.K. was concerned to condemn not only the coarse, blatant,
repulsive sort of worldliness, but concentrated upon it in its
most attractive and elegant forms—which he was convinced
actually were the more sinister. Indeed, his critique would

[23] *Either/Or I*, p. 147.
[24] *Training in Christianity*, pp. 113-14.
[25] *Works of Love*, p. 70.

seem to constitute a blanket indictment of the world. In a sense it becomes that, but only because Christian values are so preeminent that *all* other values—which precisely is to say *worldly* values—come to be of evil in their tendency to attract or distract the ultimate loyalty of men. As S.K. put it: "[The world] is not absolutely evil, as it is sometimes passionately represented, nor is it untainted, but to a certain degree is both good and evil. But Christianly understood, this 'to a certain degree' is of evil."[26] S.K.'s was not a blind rage against the world; he saw clearly that the issue was one of ultimate loyalty, and he pointed his charges at specific evils. Interestingly enough, some of the qualities he attacked are the very ones that many readers value highly *in the writings of Søren Kierkegaard.*

For one thing, the entire tenor and mood of polite culture is opposed to that of Christianity: "Christianity should never be communicated in the medium of tranquillity (unless the person who does it would dare to affirm that now all and every one are Christians). That is why being busy with art, poetry, philosophy, science and lecturing constitutes a sin in the Christian sense—for how dare I indulge myself pottering about with such things in peace and quiet?"[27]

For another, S.K. would not be among those who in our day are so eager to look to the artists and literati as being unconscious, or at least incipient, prophets and theologians: "If, therefore, one occasionally presumes to understand his life with the help of the poet and with the help of Christianity's explanation, presumes the ability to understand these two explanations together—and then in such a way that meaning would come into his life—then he is under a delusion. The poet and Christianity explain things in opposite ways."[28]

And for still another, S.K. despised the quality which shows

---

[26] *Ibid.,* p. 127.
[27] *Rohde Journals,* 232 (1849).
[28] *Works of Love,* p. 63.

signs of becoming dominant in some sectors of contemporary theology: "What the world most highly and unanimously honors is cleverness or acting cleverly. But to act cleverly is precisely the most contemptuous of all. . . . To act cleverly is basically compromise, whereby one undeniably gets farthest along in the world, wins the world's goods and favor, the world's honor, because the world and the world's favor are, eternally understood, compromise. But neither the eternal nor the Holy Scriptures have ever taught any man to go far or farthest of all in the world."[29] The forthrightness, deliberate naivete, and simple honesty prized by the early Brethren would have appealed to S.K.

A very important element in S.K.'s thought was his social criticism, his insight into the dangers of technological and urban depersonalization, mass man, the tyranny of mob culture, etc. This part of S.K.'s message generally has been well heard and appreciated, and we need here note only that these insights grew out of his nonconformist viewpoint. But his basic position was thoroughly religious and Christian in character, and it is this aspect that is particularly germane to our study.

At heart, nonconformity to the world is simply the obverse of the doctrine of *den Enkelte*, for it is a person's incorporation into the world crowd that prevents him from existing singly before God.[30] Even so, although it is the world that keeps him from becoming *den Enkelte*, this is only because the man himself would have it that way.[31] And thus the choice of refusing to be conformed to the world and the free venture of faith in which *den Enkelte* chooses himself before God—these two are one and the same choice. S.K. put the matter in one of his most moving passages:

[29] *Ibid.*, p. 243.
[30] "To Win One's Soul in Patience" (Discourse IV) in *Edifying Discourses*, Vol. I, p. 76. Cf. *Smith Journals*, XI[1] A 16 (1854).
[31] *Dru Journals*, 614 (1846).

"A choice between God and the world. Do you know anything greater to set together for a choice! Do you know any more overwhelming and humbling expression for God's indulgence and pardon towards man, than that He sets Himself, in a certain sense, on an equal line of choice with the world, merely in order to allow the man to choose? . . . If God has condescended to be that which *may be chosen*, then man *must* also choose—God will not suffer Himself to be mocked. . . . No one is to be able to say: 'God and mammon, since they are not so unconditionally different, one may in his choice combine both'—for this is to refrain from choosing. . . . If anyone does not understand this, then it is because he will not understand that God is present in the moment of the choice, not in order to look on, but in order to be chosen. . . . But the right beginning begins with seeking the kingdom of God first; it begins therefore precisely with letting the world be lost."[32]

No matter how harsh S.K.'s diatribes against the world, no matter how complete his indictment of it, these proceed not from any sort of sadism, not from his melancholy, not from any judgment about the inherent evilness of the created world as such, but from a positive valuation of what God has offered in offering himself to man, then from a realization of the sort of absolute commitment and loyalty such an offer demands in response, and thus, finally, from the passionate hatred of anything that would obstruct such response. S.K.'s doctrine of nonconformity, when seen for what it is, shows up as highly positive rather than negative in its total impress.

Also, this consideration explains why having something "as though not" can be as effective as actually having it not. In many cases the thing is not evil in itself but only in the allegiance it attracts; thus to hold it "as though not," as a thing of no value, is effectually to depotentiate it as a threat to the God relationship. And for that matter one easily can love the

[32] Discourse III on "What Is To Be Learnt from the Lilies . . ." in *The Gospel of Suffering*, pp. 228-33.

world even while *possessing* few if any things of the world; "as though not" truly may be a more radical solution than "having them not." Thus "nonconformity to the world" is a much more accurate designation for S.K.'s position than would be "renunciation of the world."

Admittedly, nonconformity is a much more demanding and a much less stable position than renunciation; it requires a fine balance that is anything but easy to maintain, as is the case with every dialectic. But, for instance, what qualities and things can be retained "as though not" and what must be renounced as absolute evils? To what extent can one "have" and continue to "have" these things without coming to "value" them? At what point does honesty compel one actually to take leave of the thing in order to avoid its snares? Nonconformity, as all dialectic, can deteriorate so easily—and without it immediately becoming apparent what has happened. Thus, in the one direction, as S.K. contended was the case with his own church, everyone could and did "have" to his heart's content as long as he gave lip service to the principle of having "as though not." In the other direction, as was the case with *nineteenth* century Brethrenism, the demands of nonconformity could be met by the outward renunciation of a certain well-defined list of "things." S.K. and the eighteenth century Brethren, we suggest, represented the dialectic in its true character of tension and balance.

S.K. did not give a great deal of attention to following out his conception of nonconformity as it regards the Christian's relationship to the state. However, what he did say was very much in line with the sectarian Brethren position. In the first place, "Christianity has not wanted to hurl governments from the throne in order to set itself on the throne; in an external sense it has never striven for a place in the world, for it is not of this world."[33]

Second, nonconformity in regard to government necessarily

[33] *Works of Love*, p. 137.

involves the issue of freedom of conscience. This need not, however, imply a pleading before, or bringing pressure upon, government in an attempt to win the concession, as though this freedom were in the hands of the state to give rather than being the innate possession of the individual. Twentieth century Brethrenism has tended to misinterpret its sectarian heritage at this point. But S.K. delineated the posture precisely when he said:

"Ideally speaking it may be perfectly true that every man should be given freedom of conscience and freedom of belief, etc. . . . [But] the truth is that anyone who is so subjective that he only deliberates with God and with his own conscience, and is able to persevere, does not care a fig whether there are laws or regulations or not; to him it is only so much cobweb. . . . If it is really conscience, conscience alone, then your regulations be blowed—I should only laugh at them. . . . Ultimately no force can compel the spiritual, at the most it can oblige them to buy freedom at a higher price."[34]

This is exactly what it means to live above the law, submitting to it as an ordinance of God and a work becoming us to fulfill all righteousness—until a matter of conscience arises, a command of God—then "regulations be blowed," the Christian *takes* freedom of conscience whether the state sees fit to grant it or not.

In this connection one of the almost infallible hallmarks for distinguishing the sectarian view from the churchly is the interpretation of the Gospel incident in which the Pharisees asked Jesus about the tribute money. S.K. diverged radically from the Lutheran conception of the two realms and stated the sectarian understanding as well as it has ever been stated:

" 'Then give to the Emperor what belongs to the Emperor, and to God what is God's.' Infinite indifference! Whether the Emperor be called Herod or Shalmanezer, whether he be Roman or Japanese, is to Him the most indifferent of all

[34] *Dru Journals,* 1155 (1850).

things. But, on the other hand—the infinite yawning differ-ence which He posits between God and the Emperor: 'Give unto God what is God's!' For they with worldly wisdom would make it a question of religion, of duty to God, whether it was lawful to pay tribute to the Emperor. Worldliness is so eager to embellish itself as godliness, and in this case God and the Emperor are blended together in the question, as if these two had obviously and directly something to do with each other, as if perhaps they were rivals one of the other, and as if God were a sort of emperor—that is to say, the question takes God in vain and secularizes Him. But Christ draws the distinction."[35]

Alongside the state, of course, stands the established church. S.K.'s position toward it forms the theme of a later chapter, but there is an interrelationship with his doctrine of noncon-formity which can better be noted here. In the first place he was critical of the church for failing to promulgate noncon-formity.[36] But in the second place, and much more funda-mental, the very constitution of an established church makes impossible any real concept of nonconformity to the world, for "if every baptized person is a Christian and baptized Chris-tendom is pure Christianity, then the *world* does not exist at all in a Christian country."[37] The logic is unimpeachable; where the churchly ideology is followed consistently there is simply no way to define "the world," let alone produce an effective doctrine of nonconformity to it.

The interpretation of S.K. as a humanist, a man of the world, cannot be sustained; there is, however, a charge often leveled against him from the opposite quarter which also de-mands consideration—this the attribution to him of monastic asceticism. The problem is well posited in a statement by H. Richard Niebuhr, made in the course of his giving examples

[35] "Lifted Up On High . . ." (Part III, Discourse 3) in *Training in Christianity*, pp. 169-70.
[36] *Works of Love*, p. 62.
[37] *Ibid.*, p. 124.

of the "Christ *against* culture" ideology: "Monastic characteristics reappear in Protestant sectarians; and a Lutheran Kierkegaard attacks the Christendom of post-Reformation culture
with the same intransigence that marks a Wiclif's thrust
against medieval social faith."[38]

We, of course, concur heartily in this alignment of S.K. with
the Protestant sectaries; we object just as heartily to the identification of S.K. and the sectaries with monasticism. Niebuhr's suggestion is much more adequate than calling S.K. a
Christian humanist; and even his phrase "monastic characteristics" might be acceptable enough, if he would be quick to
allow the very basic distinctions between monasticism and the
Kierkegaard-sectarian position. That difference amounts to
our earlier distinction between "renunciation of the world"
and "nonconformity to the world": renunciation implies a
leave-taking from all possible uses of the world; nonconformity, rather, a change of attitude toward, or evaluation of, the
world. The difference is a very important one.

In the first place, nonconformity is in no way conceived as
an act of merit or a work of supererogation. This aspect of
Catholic monasticism simply was not in the thought of S.K. or
the Brethren. In the second place, nonconformity is not asceticism in the customary sense of the word. There are no implications of dualism, of an evil (or at least, lower) realm en-
compassing physical reality, the body with its earthly needs
and desires, which is then set over against the higher realm of
the spirit. There are no suggestions about chastising the body
for the good of the soul, about valuing punishment and deprivation for their own sakes, about giving up the comforts of life
as a sacrifice to God. Nonconformity is not conceived as a
sacrifice at all—any more than it is a "sacrifice" for a swim-
mer to shed his clothing before going in the water. He is
merely doing what he can to make possible and to enhance the
enjoyment of what he *wants* to do.

[38] H. Richard Niebuhr, *Christ and Culture*, p. 65.

Thus, in the third place, the most significant distinction is that the nonconformist, even while struggling to be "not of" the world, is equally determined to remain "in" the world. Although completely opposed to adopting the world's standard of values, S.K. did not so much as imply any leaving of the world. Certainly he did not renounce the world of other people, advocating any lessening of the responsibility to love, serve, share, and live with them—and in a chapter to come we will see that he made this a positive duty. Neither did he renounce man's life in the natural institutions of society: family, business, community, state, or church. He made it clear that none of these dare be organized or valued so as to compete with one's unconditional allegiance to God, but he did not say that any and every participation in these institutions constitutes illegitimate evaluation.[39]

Kierkegaard, both through the pseudonyms and in his own name, was explicit in discounting monasticism for its tendency to desert the world.[40] As we have noted he even brought this criticism against the Moravians, whom he otherwise credited with the purest Christianity he had seen.[41] He was, however, adamantly against the way in which the church strove to justify *its* worldliness by making invidious comparisons with these:

"And [Christ] remained in the world, He did not retire from the world, but He remained there to suffer. This is not

[39] We are compelled to recognize that at the very close of S.K.'s life, at scattered points in his private journals and in the periodicals that constitute the *Attack*, there appears a new note, or rather the *hint* of a new and frightening note. This material is not at all typical of, or even reconcilable with, the rest of his thought, but here appear signs of misanthropy, asceticism, and a masochistic desire for suffering. These notices appear so late and are so few that it is impossible to say what they signify, whether transitory lapses or the beginning of a tragic deterioration. In either case they hardly can be taken into account as part of the essential witness of Kierkegaard.

[40] *Stages upon Life's Way*, pp. 169-70; *Postscript*, p. 366; and "Christ as Example . . ." (Discourse II) in *Judge for Yourselves!*, p. 185.

[41] See S.K.'s words quoted above, p. 33.

quite the same thing as when in our age preachers inveigh against a certain sort of piety . . . which seeks a remote hiding-place, far from the world's noise and its distractions and its dangers, in order if possible in profound quiet to serve God alone. . . . Nowadays we do differently and better, we pious people, we remain in the world—and make a career in the world, shine in society, make ostentation of worldliness . . . just like the Pattern, who did not retire cravenly from the world! . . . No, it certainly is not the highest thing to seek a remote hiding-place where it might be possible to serve God alone; it is not the highest thing, as we can perceive in the Pattern; but even though it is not the highest (and really what business is it of ours that this other thing is not the highest?), it is nevertheless possible that not a single one of us in this coddled and secularized generation is capable of doing it."[42]

So S.K.'s position is equally distinguishable from churchly, humanistic world conformity on the one hand and monastic, ascetic world renunciation on the other; it would seem to be at one with the nonconformity of classic Protestant sectarianism.

The evidence is that the eighteenth century Brethren shared S.K.'s ideal and approximated it in practice. True, the *nineteenth* century Brethren did retreat to the "cloister" alternative, moving to the sequestered communities of the frontier to form what amounted to cultural and religious enclaves, although even this is not to imply that they thereby took up the total pattern of Catholic monasticism. But there is little indication that their eighteenth century predecessors had sought out seclusion. Admittedly they had fled Europe, although that was a case of persecution as much as forcing them out; and in America their rural situation and the language barrier did contrive to make them somewhat isolated. But if the examples of the Germantown leaders can be taken as a indication of their

---

[42] "Christ as Example . . ." (Discourse II) in *Judge for Yourselves!*, p. 179. Cf. *Smith Journals*, XI¹ A 263 (1854).

ideology, then the careers of men like Mack Junior and particularly the publisher Sauer Junior are evidence enough that these Dunkers had no intention of deserting the world.

"In the world but not *of* the world"—and the bond which most strongly ties the Christian into the world is the command to love. The positive explication of this theme will be the work of a succeeding chapter, but at one point S.K. stated the relationship so concisely that his words can be used both to sum up the discussion of nonconformity and to point ahead to its positive counterpart:

"[The Apostles] had the frightful experience that love is not loved, that it is hated, that it is mocked, that it is spat upon, that it is crucified, in this world. . . . So surely, they swore eternal enmity to this unloving world? Ah, yes, in a certain sense, but in another aspect, no, no; in their love for God, in order that they might abide in love, they banded themselves, so to speak, together with God to love this unloving world. . . . And so the Apostles resolved, in likeness with the Pattern, to love, to suffer, to be sacrificed, for the sake of saving the unloving world. And this is love."[43]

B. OATH-SWEARING

We hold the Holy Scriptures in high honor.
When e.g. an oath is to be particularly solemn
we swear by laying the hand upon the Holy Scripture
which forbids swearing.[1]

S.K. and the Brethren were in agreement on some specific items of nonconformity which, although in one sense rather minor, or at least subsidiary, are striking enough in their co-

[43] "It Is the Spirit that Giveth Life" (Discourse III) in *For Self-Examination,* pp. 103-04.

[1] "To Become Sober" (Discourse I) in *Judge for Yourselves!,* p. 128.

incidence to be worthy of notice. One such regards the swearing of legal oaths.

From the beginning the Brethren had understood the Sermon on the Mount (Matt. 5:33-37) as forbidding oath-swearing, and Brethren nonconformity in this matter is attested as early as Mack Senior's *Rights and Ordinances*.[2] Further attestation is found in Michael Frantz[3] and in Sauer Junior, whose persecution during the Revolutionary War was brought on, at least in part, by his refusal to swear the oath of allegiance required by the new government.[4] The church's position was stated officially in an Annual Meeting minute of 1785: "And as to the swearing of oaths, we believe the word of Christ, that in all things which we are to testify, we shall testify what is yea, or what is true with yea, and what is nay, or not true with nay; for whatever is more than these cometh of evil."[5]

S.K. did not give major attention to the matter of oath-swearing—as he hardly would have had occasion to do—and it is impossible to say whether he would have gone as far as the Brethren in actually refusing to take an oath. However, his passing references indicate that he viewed the problem as did the Brethren, and in fact did his viewing from the same perspective, a literal application of the Sermon on the Mount. In addition to the aside quoted as our headnote, S.K. elsewhere made the same point in another aside, saying that it is a contradiction to make "a man swear by laying his hand upon the New Testament, where it is written, Thou shalt not swear."[6]

[2] Mack Senior, *Rights and Ordinances*, in Durnbaugh, *Origins*, p. 376.

[3] Michael Frantz, *op.cit.*, stanzas 367ff.

[4] Sauer Junior, the account of his persecution, quoted in Brumbaugh, *op.cit.*, pp. 415ff.

[5] *Minutes of the Annual Meetings of the Church of the Brethren, 1778-1909*, hereafter referred to as *Annual Meeting Minutes* (Elgin, Ill.: Brethren Publishing House, 1909), minutes of 1785, art. 1, p. 10.

[6] *Attack upon "Christendom,"* p. 130. Cf. *For Self-Examination*, pp. 36-37.

These statements from S.K.'s religious phase align him with the Brethren in their reading of the New Testament, but just as significant, and even more interesting, are the earlier sentiments of the nonreligious pseudonym Climacus. Again merely in passing, as illustrative of another point (but for that very reason quite revealing), Climacus said: "But when a man has indulged in oaths for a long time, he returns at last to simple utterance, because all swearing is self-nugatory."[7] And one hundred pages later Climacus returned to give the theme a more extended, and now self-conscious, treatment:

"Only over-precipitate people, clouds without water and storm-driven mists, are quick to take an oath; because the fact is that they are unable to keep it, and therefore must perpetually be taking it. I, for my part, am of the opinion that 'never to forget this impression,' is something quite different from saying once in a solemn moment: 'I will never forget it.' The first is inwardness, the second is perhaps only a momentary inwardness. . . . Flighty and easily excitable souls are more prone to nothing than to the taking of a sacred promise, because the inner weakness needs the strong stimulus of the moment. To administer a sacred pledge to such a person is a very dubious thing."[8]

As in the previous statements S.K. related oath-swearing to a sectarian view of scriptural obedience, he here relates it to a sectarian view of inwardness.

The evidence is not extensive, but the very fact that S.K. identified himself even this far with a specific belief that is almost uniquely that of classic Protestant sectarianism—this fact is of some significance.

[7] *Postscript*, p. 113.
[8] *Ibid.*, pp. 214-15.

C. CELIBACY

That a woman [the woman who
was a sinner (Luke 7:36–50)]
is presented as a teacher, as a pattern of piety,
can astonish no one who knows
that piety or godliness
is in its very nature a womanly quality.[1]

Woman might be called "joie de vivre."
There is certainly a joie de vivre in man;
but fundamentally he is formed
to be spiritual and if he were alone
and left to himself he would not ... know how
to set about it, and would never really get as far as beginning.
But then the joie de vivre,
which is indefinite and vague
within him, appears outside him in another form,
in the form of woman who is joie de vivre;
and so the joy of life awakens.[2]

It is not often that one can catch S.K. in an out-and-out contradiction, but here is a bad one. Woman is either a symbol of godliness that can lead a man into spirituality, or else she is a symbol of *joie de vivre* that can lead a man into worldliness—S.K. was not quite sure which. Eighteenth century Brethren thought displayed something of the same, or at least a related, ambiguity. Apparently S.K. and the Brethren finally came out at opposite conclusions, S.K. supporting Christian celibacy, the Brethren Christian marriage. But the significance of the comparison lies not in the *divergence* of their conclusions but in the *agreement* of their confusions. The Kierkegaardian-Brethren *ambiguity* must be seen in contrast to the

[1] "The Woman that Was a Sinner," a discourse appended to *Training in Christianity*, p. 261.
[2] *Dru Journals*, 1321 (1854).

Roman Catholic *certainty* that celibacy is *required* for the higher righteousness of "spiritual Christians" and the churchly-Protestant *certainty* that celibacy is as much as *prohibited* for normal Christian spirituality.

We will advocate the position that S.K. concluded his life as a supporter of universal Christian celibacy, but we also will strongly resist the interpretation that would make S.K. such from the outset and then draw implications regarding his solitariness and world renunciation. Any such reading of the Regina incident cannot be reconciled with certain plain and forthright statements by S.K. For example: "I do not maintain, and have never maintained that I did not marry because it was supposed to be contrary to Christianity, as though my being unmarried were a form of Christian perfection. Oh, far from it. . . . My greatest pleasure would have been to have married the girl to whom I was engaged. . . . [But] I remained unmarried, and so had the opportunity of thinking over what Christianity really meant by praising the unmarried state."[3]

There is nothing in S.K. to indicate anything but that this asseveration was entirely honest and was his honest understanding throughout his life. Even when, in 1854-1855, at the very end of his career, S.K. seemingly took a view that would make celibacy a Christian *requirement*, the situation was not changed: S.K. did not arrive at this position until thirteen years after he had broken with Regina; he never mentioned Regina in the process of presenting this final opinion; and if there was any real connection between the breaking of the engagement in 1841 and the advocating of Christian celibacy in 1854, it is by no means clear what the nature or significance of that connection might be. In short, the Regina incident, far from being the key to Kierkegaard's witness, is of very questionable help in understanding S.K.'s religious views even of marriage, let alone the religious life as a whole. His relationship to Regina involved so many purely personal

[3] *Dru Journals*, 970 (1849). Cf. *Smith Journals*, XI[1] A 226 (1854).

factors that it hardly can be used as a source from which to derive a clear picture of his ideology.

We have called S.K.'s thoughts on marriage "confused"; this term is somewhat misleading if not unjust. S.K.'s was certainly a *changing* view but not by that token a chaotic one; if his statements are traced period by period a quite consistent pattern appears.

Phase I: The Regina incident and S.K.'s cogitations regarding it. This, as we have suggested, was predominantly a personal matter from which S.K. did not (and explicitly refused to) generalize concerning a Christian doctrine of celibacy per se. This phase is of little help to our study, although, as we shall see, it does lend some support to Phase IV.

Phase II: The aesthetic pseudonyms (in particular, those of *Either/Or I* and of the banquet in *Stages on Life's Way*). Here are both confused and inadequate views of marriage. Among these pseudonyms are "woman-lovers," analysts who approve of love, "woman-haters," and analysts who approve misogyny; and ultimately all of their views—those of the lovers as well as the haters—show up as inadequate and false. But this disorder ought not be laid to S.K.'s charge, for it was precisely his design to demonstrate that the aesthetic view is by nature confused and partial. Far from attempting to elucidate his own position, S.K. was deliberately using pseudonyms in order to assert that aesthetic analyses are futile.

Thus one cannot, as some would do, read, for example, the speeches of the banquet as an indication of S.K.'s own hatred of women—particularly when S.K. himself explicitly stated: "The five speeches, . . . which are all of them caricatures of the most holy, are written with the idea of bringing an essential, but nevertheless false, light to bear upon woman."[4] It is a very uncertain procedure to try to divine S.K.'s true opinion of women out of these pseudonyms; they were never intended to incorporate his view, and they present no consistent picture

[4] *Dru Journals*, 505 (1844).

within themselves. The only positive contribution this material can make to our quest is to say, "The answer is not with me," the truth about women and marriage lies not in the aesthetic sphere.

Phase III: The ethical pseudonym (in particular, Judge William, as he appears both in *Either/Or II* and *Stages*). We have rejected Phases I and II as being all but useless in leading us to S.K.'s true religious position regarding marriage; Phase III is much more helpful. Those commentators who tend to make Phases I and II normative and thus portray S.K. simply as a misogynist must overlook the fact that also within the writings of Søren Kierkegaard are to be found some of the most impressive pictures of conjugal happiness and some of the most profound analyses of the marriage relationship to occur anywhere. These commentators ignore the obvious fact that the banquet passage consciously is structured so that the mere appearance of the concrete and actual love relationship of Judge William and his wife immediately gives the lie to all the high-flown philosophizing of the banqueters.

Phase III presents as exalted a view of marriage as can be conceived, always from the mouth of Judge William, the ethicist, who makes such statements as these:

"What I am through her, that she is through me, and we are neither of us anything by ourselves but only in union. To her I am a man, for only a married man is a genuine man."[5]

"In paganism there was a god for love but none for marriage; in Christianity there is, if I may venture to say so, a God for marriage and none for love."[6]

"Marriage I regard as the highest *telos* of the individual human existence, it is so much the highest that the man who goes without it cancels with one stroke the whole of earthly life and retains only eternity and spiritual interests."[7]

[5] *Stages on Life's Way*, p. 101.
[6] *Ibid.*, p. 106.
[7] *Ibid.*, p. 107.

"I do not say that marriage is the highest, I know a higher; but woe to him who would skip over marriage without justification. . . . [Any exception] must occur in the direction of the religious, in the direction of spirit, in such a way that being spirit makes one forget that one is also man, not spirit alone like God."[8]

A very obvious difference between Phase III and Phase II is that Phase III has arrived at one consistent viewpoint. Likewise, this viewpoint displays insights that are much more profound, positive, and religious than those of even the greatest "lovers" of Phase II. Judge William is still a pseudonym (and this dare not be forgotten); Phase III does *not* present us with S.K.'s direct and final word.

A consideration of the general relationship between S.K.'s "stages of existence" will help elucidate the relationship between the specific "phases" that concern us here. S.K. held that a decisive "either/or" falls between the aesthetic and the ethical stages but that the progression from the ethical to the religious is much more gradual and continuous. Thus one must *choose between* Phase II and Phase III, between the banqueters on the one hand, Judge William and wife on the other. S.K. made this dichotomy very clear. It does not follow, however, that the same sort of choice is to be posited between the ethicist Judge William on the one hand and the religious view of S.K. himself on the other. Here the relationship we would expect (and which will prove to be the case) is that Judge William represents a truth which is nevertheless a partial truth; religious-Christian considerations will not cancel or supersede Judge William's position but definitely will supplement and modify it. It is highly significant to note that, in Judge William's third and fourth statements quoted above, there are explicit hints of other considerations yet to come.

Phase IV: The direct religious writings up until the *Attack*. In this phase are present two different conceptions which on

[8] *Ibid.*, p. 166.

first thought may seem contradictory but probably are not. In the first place there is the continuation of the Judge William line in which woman is praised as a spiritual helpmeet and example. The first of our two epigraphs is characteristic of the long passage of which it is a part—this from a discourse of 1850. Another such passage occurs in *For Self-Examination* (1851).[9] The comparative lateness of both these dates is significant.

But alongside this strain appears another, a specifically Christian note. One example will make S.K.'s thought plain:

"It is quite certain and true that Christianity is suspicious of marriage, and desires that along with the many married servants it has, it might also have an unmarried person, a single man; for Christianity knows very well that with woman and love all this weakliness and love of coddling arises in a man, and that insofar as the husband himself does not bethink himself of it, the wife ordinarily pleads it with ingenuous candor which is exceedingly dangerous for the husband, especially for one who is required in the strictest to serve Christianity."[10]

There would not seem to be any necessary opposition between the affirmation (1) that woman has an instinct for genuine religiousness which can be of inspiration to a man, and (2) that family life inevitably involves a man in worldly concerns that make it difficult for him to act completely and solely for God. In fact the recognition of *both* truths might well lead to S.K.'s customary dialectical treatment except that it proves somewhat awkward to apply the method to marriage. One hardly can be both married and not married at the same time; neither does rapid oscillation between the two quite achieve

[9] ". . . The Mirror of the Word" (Discourse I) in *For Self-Examination*, pp. 70ff. Cf. *Smith Journals*, XI² A 70 (1854); this late, right out of the midst of his misogynist phase, S.K. still can make complimentary statements about woman's religious role.

[10] *Training in Christianity* (Part II), p. 119. Cf. *Dru Journals*, 648, 768, 845, 920, 964.

the purpose; and even being married "as though not" is somewhat impractical, although this is precisely what Paul did advocate in 1 Corinthians 7:29.

The position S.K. actually took would seem to be as near to
dialectical as is feasible. His was a doctrine of "vocational
celibacy." *Ethically* understood, marriage is a moral imperative that applies universally (Phase III is *not* rejected). *Christianly* understood, marriage is proper and good, the "normal"
mode. However, the cause of true religion also *needs* (not,
"the law of the church *requires*") the contribution that only a
celibate can make. God *calls* a few Christians, the "exceptions," to a specialized service that needs the specialized qualifications found only in a celibate.

Though there may be some points of contact, this view
differs greatly from that of Roman Catholicism. With S.K. the
call is entirely a private matter between *den Enkelte* and God
and is so exceptional a case that no generalizations can be
drawn at all. *Den Enkelte* must bear the full responsibility for
having presumed "a teleological suspension of the ethical" (to
use the language of *Fear and Trembling*), being willing to
pay the price and risk the misunderstanding that such exceptions incur. This is a far different thing than a formal requirement of the church applied wholesale to an entire class of men
as a prerequisite for achieving an elevated spiritual status. No
merit accrues to the Kierkegaardian celibate; he has done no
more than the married Christian has done, because each has
sought simply to find the will of God for his particular life.
But as God may call one man to sacrifice his fortune to the
cause, another his social status, another perhaps his life, so may
he call still another to sacrifice his marriage. And S.K. clearly,
explicitly, and consistently interpreted his break with Regina
precisely in this frame of reference; he always thought of himself as "the exception" and did his utmost to prevent his action
from being generalized into a rule.

Up to this point, apart from the complicating factors of Phase I (i.e. his personal *actions* in regard to Regina), S.K.'s *thought* about Christian celibacy has followed the pattern that almost could be predicted; the development is of a piece with the rest of his religious thought. And Phase IV, which falls where we would expect to find the authentic Kierkegaardian witness, we take as being just that. This position is not typically churchly-Protestant; the fact that it so much as shows concern over the possibility of a *Christian* celibacy is a distinction, a distinction which, we intend to show, actually is sectarian in character.

Phase V: During the *Attack* (1854-1855). Contrary to S.K.'s usual pattern, during the closing months of his life, coincident with his attack upon Christendom, he seems to have drifted past sectarianism and into a view of marriage that can be adjudged only as "cultic." In several places in the periodicals that made up the *Attack* and more particularly in the unpublished journals of that period, S.K. condemned marriage and childbearing per se, making such statements as:

"The lower man is in the degree of consciousness, the more natural the [sexual] relationship. But the more intellectually developed a man is the more conscious life penetrates it and the closer one gets to the point where lies Christianity and whatever resembles it in religious and philosophic outlook, where continence becomes the expression of spirit."[11]

"*Christianly* it is anything but the greatest benefaction to bestow life upon the child. . . . *Christianly* it is egoism in the highest degree that because a man and a woman cannot control their lust another being must therefore sigh, perhaps for seventy years in this prisonhouse and vale of tears, and perhaps be lost eternally."[12]

"I came into being through a crime against God's will. The

[11] *Dru Journals*, 1331 (1854).
[12] *Attack upon "Christendom,"* p. 223; cf. pp. 163, 213-16, and 219-22.

offense, which in one sense, is not mine, though it makes me a criminal in the sight of God, was to give life."[13]

This is something *new*—new and shocking. Here is no natural development out of Phase IV; Phase IV suddenly and without warning has been turned upside down; what had been insisted upon as the exception now has become the rule. In addition, Phase V is not merely antimarriage, nor even misogynist, but deeply and terribly misanthropic. There are here implications that stand in direct contradiction to both the letter and mood of what we have seen as S.K.'s primary emphases. For instance, the first quotation above denies everything S.K. had said about antiintellectualism and the equality of all men before God. And what does this bitter hatred of life and of self do to the concepts of *den Enkelte*, devotional immediacy, neighbor love?

This dark note was a real note, but we would not give the impression that it marked the whole tenor either of the *Attack* or of the journals for this period. Such definitely is not the case; the scene did not suddenly turn dark but, rather, on the horizon appeared momentarily, from time to time, this black cloud no larger than a man's hand. What it presaged is impossible to say; it appeared too late and was too fleeting to provide grounds for accurate analysis. The existence of Phase V cannot be denied, but Phase IV is the only one that qualifies as the normative Kierkegaardian position on Christian celibacy, and it is far from representing the solitariness of a total renunciation of woman and the world.

If S.K.'s thought portrays a move from a churchlike assumption about marriage as a universal duty (Phase III), through sectarian dialecticism (Phase IV), into a cultic insistence on universal celibacy (Phase V), Brethren thought represents something of the same movement—in precisely the opposite direction.

[13] *Rohde Journals*, 239 (1855); cf. 31, 35 (both 1854). Cf. also *Dru Journals*, 1337, 1385, 1399 (all 1854).

Surprisingly enough, the original Brethren advocated and practiced a system of enforced celibacy (or continence in the case of couples that already were married). The chronicles of the Ephrata community included a brief description of Brethren beginnings at Schwarzenau which said: "[The Brethren] had their goods in common, and practiced continence, though it is said they did not persevere in this zeal longer than seven years, after which they turned to women again and to the ownership of property involved therein."[14] The Beisselites cited this information in the process of justifying their own practice of both communalism and continence; therefore, the entire notice would be highly suspect (as it is almost certainly mistaken regarding the seven year duration) except for the fact that it is supported by Mack Senior himself. One of the questions put to him by the Radical Pietists in 1713 asked whether the Brethren had not wavered by once rejecting the married state and then permitting it again. Mack answered: "It is true that we had to continue discussions on marriage, work, yes, and still other matters, after the [first] baptism. Before our baptism, when we were still among the [Radical] Pietists, we were not taught otherwise by those who were deemed great saints. Therefore, we had much contention until we abandoned the errors which we had absorbed."[15]

The fact that Mack Junior was born but four years after the church was founded and the statement above written five years after—this, plus the very tone of Mack's reply, all suggests that the period of strict Brethren celibacy was very much briefer than seven years, actually representing only the time needed for the group to get itself established and move out of the cultism from which it had come. Indeed, this cultic phase probably involved about the same length of time and the same

---

[14] Brothers Lamech and Agrippa (pseud.), *The Ephrata Chronicles,* or *Chronicon Ephratense* (first published Ephrata, 1786), trans. J. Max Hark (Lancaster, Pa., 1889), p. 2.

[15] Mack Senior, *Basic Questions,* in Durnbaugh, *Origins,* p. 341, answer to Question 37.

degree of fixedness in the Brethren as it did in S.K., the difference being, of course, that it lay at the beginning of the Brethren development and at the end of S.K.'s.

But the reinstitution of marriage did not terminate Brethren discussion of celibacy. In his *Rights and Ordinances* of 1715, Mack Senior said: "If the unmarried state is conducted in purity of the Spirit and of the flesh in true faith in Jesus, and is kept in true humility, it is better and higher. It is closer to the image of Christ to remain unmarried. Nevertheless, if an unmarried person marries, he commits no sin, provided it occurs in the Lord Jesus, and is performed in the true belief in Jesus Christ."[16] Although there are differences in approach and emphasis, Mack's is a dialectic-like solution quite similar in effect to S.K.'s Phase IV: both marriage and celibacy can be Christian; God purposes and calls some Christians for the one station and some for the other; no one can prescribe for the other person; neither should one vaunt himself over the other.

The most extended discussion of celibacy, following the same general line as Mack, is to be found in Michael Frantz (himself a married man, as Mack was). In his prolix poem he presented a discussion running for some forty-seven stanzas; what follows is a prose condensation and paraphrase:

"A person does not sin by marrying; neither should one try to prevent the godly marriage of his daughter or maid. Worldlings have wives and children without number and thus increase their demands for land and wealth; this has been the pattern since Adam and Eve. As the world has debauched God's other gifts, so marriage. Not all marriages are of God. However, marriage is clean and honorable for those who are called to it. Marriage, indeed, can even be a symbol of the inner relationship to the bridegroom Christ.

"Marriage should be classed along with fasting and praying, i.e., they easily can be misused. Whoever desires to prac-

---

[16] Mack Senior, *Rights and Ordinances*, in Durnbaugh, *Origins*, p. 390.

tice abstention within the marriage relationship should be very careful that his mate is of the same mind. Chastity is a good gift for those who have it and who practice it humbly and quietly. Whoever abstains in marriage should abstain in all things and not make a great deal of talk about it. Whoever despises marriage is following Satan; whoever abstains from marriage must take care not to abstain also from Christ's Spirit and the light of grace."[17]

The dialectic attempt to approve complementary positions and hold both in harmony is particularly marked in Frantz. It should be recalled that just as Mack had had to hold his position in the face of celibacy-promoting Radical Pietists, Frantz was working in the very congregation from which the celibate Beisselites but recently had gone out. Undoubtedly these external pressures helped to keep Christian celibacy a live alternative among the Brethren for as long as was the case. Following Michael Frantz, the matter does not appear again in eighteenth century Brethren literature, except for one interesting note. History tells us that Jacob Stoll, the poet-preacher of the latter part of the century, was engaged to be married at the time the church called him to the ministry. Along with his decision to accept that call he broke off his engagement and served as a celibate[18]—shades of (or rather, foreshadowings of) Søren Kierkegaard!

For the most part, however, the Brethren seem to have slipped back to the customary churchly way of simply assuming that anyone who can marry will, failing to give serious attention to as much as the possibility of a truly religious celibacy. Thus the Brethren path—just the reverse of S.K.'s—ran from cultism, through sectarianism, and into churchism.

---

[17] Michael Frantz, *op.cit.*, stanzas 194-240 [my trans. and paraphrase—V.E.]; cf. stanzas 46-47.

[18] *History of the Church of the Brethren of the Eastern District of Pennsylvania* (Lancaster, Pa.: 1915), pp. 362-63.

The customary approach of Kierkegaard scholarship is to treat S.K.'s position on marriage solely as a matter of his personal psychology. However, if one were to take S.K.'s own statements (those of both Phase IV and Phase V) simply and plainly at their face value, it would become quite obvious what *he* considered as the primary motive. In his New Testament S.K. found a number of counsels, commands, and examples that compel a serious consideration of religious celibacy. He frequently used phrases like those found in his statements quoted above: "Christianity is suspicious of marriage," and "what Christianity really meant by praising the unmarried state"; and these, for S.K., are the equivalent of saying, "The New Testament teaches . . ." In addition, he made specific reference both to the example of Jesus and the teachings of Paul.[19] But to a modern scholar it is inconceivable that anyone might take the Bible seriously enough to be bothered by the fact that it promotes celibacy. So, to the couch! If S.K. did not marry, it was because he was sexually maladjusted.

But our comparison with sectarianism can be instructive at this point, for with the sectaries it is obvious that biblical injunctions were the source of their restlessness. They were too deeply committed to scriptural obedience to take the churchly-Protestant option of ignoring a sizable group of texts. But on the other hand, because of their commitment to the equality of all men before God, neither could they take the Roman Catholic option of applying marriage-approving texts to the laity and celibacy-approving texts to a superior class of Christians. They were impelled, then, into the dialectic, vocational view, for which a strong case could be made that this is an accurate interpretation of the New Testament position. And it is just possible that S.K. too was being entirely honest when he indicated that he found a justification for celibacy within the New Testament.

[19] *Attack upon "Christendom,"* pp. 213-16, 219-22.

Ultimately, of course, neither S.K. nor the Brethren were able to maintain the balance that would give marriage *and* celibacy equal rights, equal honor, equal emphasis; this is a very difficult dialectic to hold. And it very well may be that in the end it was personal, psychological factors that determined that S.K. should lose his balance in the direction of a cultic insistence on celibacy. It would be foolish to deny the evidence of psychological abnormalities at play within the development of Søren Kierkegaard; but it is even more foolish to overlook the role that true religious conviction played in that life—and that conviction, in its impact regarding marriage, had a quality of sectarianism just as it did in regard to so many other things.

CHAPTER IX

THE WORLD WELL LOVED

The preceding chapter treated S.K.'s World Negative, those elements of secular sociality that the Christian is to renounce. We have seen, however, that even in regard to these conscious "negatives," S.K.'s renunciation was anything but a sweeping, out-of-hand rejection. The present chapter is the direct counterpart of the preceding one, this the treatment of S.K.'s World Positive, those elements of secular sociality that the Christian is to affirm and promote. The material is classed under two main headings: "The Simple Life" comprises the positive Christian relationship to the world of things, "Neighbor Love" to the world of people.

A. THE SIMPLE LIFE

When the prosperous man on a dark but star-lit night drives comfortably in his carriage and has the lanterns lighted, aye, then he is safe, he fears no difficulty, he carries his light with him, and it is not dark close around him; but precisely because he has the lanterns lighted, and has a strong light close to him, precisely for this reason he cannot see the stars, for his lights obscure the stars, which the poor peasant driving without lights can see gloriously in the dark but

> *starry night. So those deceived ones live in*
> *the temporal existence: either, occupied with*
> *the necessities of life, they are too busy to*
> *avail themselves of the view, or in their pros-*
> *perity and good days they have, as it were,*
> *lanterns lighted, and close about them every-*
> *thing is so satisfactory, so pleasant, so com-*
> *fortable—but the view is lacking, the pros-*
> *pect, the view of the stars.*[1]

Our present topic can be introduced in the form of a question. Put in terms of the parable above, it is: If the lanterns of
worldly interest obscure the view, what is the mode of existence that best reveals the stars? The Brethren answer was:
the simple life. As in the case of "nonconformity to the world,"
"the simple life" became a technical designation only in the
nineteenth century, although the emphasis had been present
from the sect's beginning. The same emphasis is to be found
in S.K., although, again, the phrase itself is not.

The simple life is a positive conception, its major focus being not so much upon what must be given up as upon what is
gained when one deliberately suppresses material values in
order to give preeminence to things of the spirit. The "constitutional precedent" for the Brethren teaching always has been
the well-known passage from the Sermon on the Mount,
Matthew 6:25–34, with its injunctions: "Take no thought for
your life"; "Be not anxious"; "Behold the fowls of the air";
"Consider the lilies of the field"; "Seek first God's kingdom
and his righteousness." And a glance at the index *Kierkegaard
and the Bible* makes it apparent that this same text is probably
the one biblical passage most used by S.K.; he gave full-
fledged exposition (not simply an allusion) to this selection, or

---

[1] ". . . Even When Temporal Sufferings Press Heaviest, the Blessedness of Eternity Outweighs Them" (Discourse VI) in *The Gospel of
Suffering*, p. 123.

to parts of it, at nineteen different points in his published works.[2]

The simple-life theme made its earliest appearance in Brethren literature in a hymn, "The Christian Pilgrim," found in the sect's first hymnal, compiled in Germany.[3] The idea was a favorite of Michael Frantz. In his long poem is a series of stanzas on the theme "An idol I have made for myself. . . ." The idols he lists are eating, drinking, splendid clothes, pride in the fact that one wears simple garb (note well!), crops, trees, houses, delight in natural creatures (livestock?).[4] But his best statement, giving greater accent to the positive, is in a shorter poem (only fourteen stanzas long) entitled "A Hymn of Brotherly Love and Community":

> In the quietness of God's will
> One indeed finds the most beautiful treasure—
> A treasure greater than all treasures—
> If the heart is a clean place.
> This treasure is only
> In hearts which are clean of the love of the world.
> One must beforehand sell everything,
> Then he can buy this treasure.
> He must indeed industriously pursue it,
> Dig for it day and night.
> If, then, one has sold everything,
> He will find the treasure directly in the act. . . .
> Whoever has a bare, small house—
> in accordance with what is necessary—
> His clothing and the bread of nourishment,
> Who has a stronger faith with love's gifts,

---

[2] Paul S. Minear and Paul S. Morimoto, *Kierkegaard and the Bible: An Index* (Princeton: Princeton Theological Seminary, 1953), p. 19.

[3] "The Christian Pilgrim," from *Geistreiches Gesang-Buch*, translated and reversified by Ralph W. Schlosser, in Durnbaugh, *Origins*, p. 412.

[4] Michael Frantz, *op.cit.*, the title poem, stanzas 35-41; cf. the prose piece, p. 46.

Free from guilt, wholly without need,
With children and wife, sound in body—
He thereby is truly blessed by God.[5]

Sauer Junior also wrote effectively concerning the simple life, saying at one point in a poem that a Christian does not presume to spread himself any further than he can cover with his own blankets.[6] But his most outstanding treatment of the subject was an article in one of his periodicals. In 1764 he established *Geistliche Magazien*, a little monthly of edification and exhortation which he distributed free of charge as a Christian service. In an issue of the first year appeared a brief essay on "The Usefulness of Poverty"; the fact that it was written as "an after-piece to fill up the remaining space" and refers to the lead article is evidence enough that Sauer Junior was himself the author. The following is a digest of its main themes:

"Men rebel against being poor. They do not consider their poverty as a position in which God has placed them and so use it according to his will. But if one accepted his position, he would thereby become free from it. And if he has fallen into the vicious sort of poverty, he should seek to escape the sin, not the poverty. If he will, he can become free in however little it is God has given him, knowing that He who cares for the birds certainly will not forsake him. His position even carries spiritual advantages: Not having gold, he is not responsible for his use of it. He is better off for not eating dainty foods. He does not do as much calling and so is healthier. Not being honored, he is correspondingly less often insulted—particularly behind his back. He does not have to worry about fashions and keeping up with the neighbors.

"The important thing is godliness, and the poor man has the easier road to it. Every man must at some time face suffering,

---

[5] *Ibid.*, p. 47, stanzas 8, 9, 11 [my trans.—V.E.].
[6] Sauer Junior, a poem accompanying the interest table in *Der Hoch-Deutsch Americanische Calendar* for 1761, p. 18.

and the poor man knows better how to do this because he has not trusted in temporal supports. One needs a sense of what are the true and what are the false values in life, and a poor man has fewer of the latter to renounce. The rich man, on the other hand, must give an account of his riches, how he obtained them, how he used them—as per the story of Dives and Lazarus. All men must become spiritually poor, and the poor man can do this more easily. In addition, rich men tend to use and exploit their neighbors.

"But ultimately, poverty can prove a blessing only to one who has been converted. When converted, God will direct one what to give up and will give him the power to do so. All men do not come to God in the same way; poverty is not the means of conversion for all men."[7]

It is obvious that the ideal of the simple life was a *comparative* and a *voluntary* poverty, neither grinding destitution nor a condition one accepts as a grudging necessity. It also seems clear that this is not the equivalent of what customarily is known as "the ascetic life." Material things are counted as good and not renounced as being evil; sacrifice is not valued in and for itself. The simple life is, rather, a life duly proportioned so that spiritual values are given the preeminence they deserve. Here, then, is a dialectic tension between the good of the gifts God has created and the good of God himself.

The heart of the Brethren position is strikingly illustrated by a little story told about Mack Junior.[8] As an old man this saint and patriarch of the church somewhere had acquired a silken lounging robe which he wore around the house. Some of the Brethren became concerned that such adornment did not fit well with the church's teaching regarding the simple life. Patriarch or not, a committee was delegated to wait upon

[7] Sauer Junior, "Die Nutzbarkeit der Armuth," *Geistliche Magazien,* Ser. I, No. 7 (c. 1764) 6off. [my trans.—V.E.].

[8] Freeman Ankrum, *Alexander Mack the Tunker and Descendants* (Masontown, Pa.: published by the author, 1943), pp. 27-28.

Brother Mack. These visitors found him at work in his garden, clothed in the very symbol of luxury they had come to condemn. Brother Mack rose to greet them, wiping his dirty hands on the very fabric of his splendor. Spontaneously the committee decided that even silk, if treated with such careless disdain, so obviously regarded "as though not," hardly posed a spiritual threat. An edifying conversation ensued; the point of the visit failed to get mentioned; and the committee reported back that Elder Mack still was well within the order of the church.

It quickly can be admitted that the Brethren would not have considered the comportment of Søren Kierkegaard as being within that order. He lived what we already have called a life of luxury, tending to pamper his rather extravagant whims in such matters as food, drink, clothing, housing, and personal regimen. However, neither was that mode of living ever advanced by S.K. as an example of what *he* intended by the simple life. S.K.'s words rather than his behavior must be the source for our study.

S.K.'s words on this theme were many; ten different discourses can be counted as dealing directly with the subject. And although it seems an unlikely combination, the emphasis shows up clearly in the pseudonyms. In fact, Climacus offers two very concise definitions of the doctrine, yet couched in anything but the language of devotion and edification:

"Now if for any individual an eternal happiness is his highest good, this will mean that all finite satisfactions are volitionally relegated to the status of what may have to be renounced in favor of an eternal happiness."[9]

"In order that the individual may sustain an absolute relationship to the absolute *telos* he must first have exercised himself in the renunciation of relative ends, and only then can there be a question of the ideal task: the simultaneous main-

[9] *Postscript*, p. 350.

tenance of an absolute relationship to the absolute, and a relative relationship to the relative."[10]

These are reiterations of the Brethren view, although it is
doubtful that any of the Brethren would have known what
Climacus was talking about, and it is clear that the definitions
themselves violate the first canon of the simple life, namely,
that it be *simple*. However, S.K. (not Climacus) earlier had
said the same thing in a much more appropriate way: " 'Let us
eat and drink, for tomorrow we die,' . . . is the cowardly joy of
the life of sensuality, the despicable order of things where one
lives in order to eat and drink, instead of eating and drinking
in order to live."[11] This statement goes to the heart of the matter, and S.K.'s development of the idea displays it as very similar to that of the Brethren.

His most effective presentation—unless it be the parable of
the carriage lanterns and the stars—is probably the parable of
the stock dove. He told of a wild dove of the forest which always was able to find adequate sustenance (because God provides for the birds of the air) but which, of course, never was
able to know for sure where the next meal was coming from,
or whether there would be a next meal. Thus not out of any
real deprivation but out of fear of future deprivation the wild
dove became jealous of the farmer's domesticated doves; they
lived assured by the presence of the farmer's abundant granary
and by the fact that the farmer fed them regularly from it. In
the end, anxiety over material security led the wild dove to
trade its forest freedom for the farmer's dovecot, and it
promptly found itself on the farmer's table.[12]

---

[10] *Ibid.*, p. 386.
[11] "Beside a Grave" (Discourse III) in *Thoughts on Crucial Situations in Human Life*, p. 90. This saying may not have been original
with S.K.; much the same thing had been said by Clement of Alexandria, c. A.D. 220.
[12] Discourse I on "What Is To Be Learnt from the Lilies" in *The
Gospel of Suffering*, pp. 184ff.

In his more formal explication S.K. saw that the first and most basic principle of the simple life is the *attitude* in which one holds his belongings:

"In connection with abundance, thought can take from the rich man the thought of *possession*, the thought that he owns and possesses his wealth and abundance as *his*. . . . He has no anxiety in gathering abundance, for he does not care to gather abundance; he has no anxiety in retaining, for it is easy enough to retain what one has not, and he is as one who has not; he has no anxiety for the fact that others possess more, for he is as one who possesses nothing; he knows without anxiety that others possess less, for he is as one who possesses nothing; and he has no anxiety about what he shall leave his heirs."[13]

It should be recalled that these words are addressed to the *wealthy* Christian and are intended to affirm that the sheer possession of material goods is not an absolute bar to one's being a Christian. At this point S.K.'s view is perhaps not completely incompatible with that often designated as "the Protestant ethic," an interpretation which has been at least somewhat typical of churchly thought. However, even here S.K. has begun to move beyond it, in that there is no talk about earning money to the glory of God or being called by God to accumulate wealth.

But S.K., as the Brethren, was not content to leave the simple life *only* on the level of an "as though not" attitude; this easily could become an invitation to hypocrisy. He went a step further:

"Christianity has never taught that to be literally a lowly man is synonymous with being a Christian, nor that from the literal condition of lowliness there is a direct transition as a matter of course to becoming a Christian; neither has it taught

[13] "The Anxiety of Abundance" (Part I, Discourse 2) in *Christian Discourses*, pp. 29-30.

that if the man of worldly position were to give up all his power, he therefore would be a Christian. But from literal lowliness to the point of becoming a Christian there is however only one step. The position of being literally a lowly man is by no means an unfavorable preparation for becoming a Christian."[14]

S.K. here aligned himself with the concluding paragraph of Sauer Junior's essay: poverty, in and of itself, is of no particular spiritual significance or value; neither is the way of poverty legalistically prescribed as the condition for becoming a Christian. Rather, the crux of the matter, S.K. saw, was in the *voluntary* quality of the discipline—voluntary in the radical sense that makes it an end in itself and not a "work" in the interests of a higher righteousness or an ascetic regimen, for "*voluntarily* to give up all is Christianity, . . . is to be convinced of the glory of the good which Christianity promises."[15]

In at least one place in his writings S.K. seemed to take a position even more radical than that of the simple life; he branded worldly goods as "themselves invidious":

"*All earthly and worldly goods are in themselves selfish, invidious; the possession of them, being invidious or envious, must of necessity make others poorer*: what I have, another cannot have; the more I have, the less another has. The unrighteous mammon (and this term might well be applied to all earthly goods, including worldly honor, power, etc.) is itself unrighteous, does injustice (irrespective of whether it is unlawfully acquired or possessed), cannot in and for itself be acquired or possessed equally. . . . Even though a man may be willing to communicate in his earthly goods—yet every instant when he is employed in acquiring them or is dwelling

---

[14] "The Anxiety of High Place" (Part I, Discourse 4) in *Christian Discourses*, p. 57.
[15] "Behold, We Have Left All . . ." (Part III, Discourse 2) in *Christian Discourses*, p. 186; cf. p. 195.

upon the possession of them he is selfish, as that thing is which he possesses or acquires. . . . In a sense this selfishness does not inhere in him, it inheres in the essential nature of the earthly goods. . . . No, the way, the perfect way of making rich is to communicate the goods of the spirit, being oneself, moreover, solely employed in acquiring and possessing these goods."[16]

Even here, in the most radical statement of his position, it should be noted that S.K.'s critique still has to do ultimately with the question of religious allegiance; it is not the materiality of "things" but the inevitable spiritual concomitants of their "possession" that concerned him. Thus, although his view is a long way indeed from the so-called Protestant ethic, it does not by that token fall into the category of Catholic "monasticism," as Lowrie would suggest.[17] It does not presuppose a matter/spirit dualism, meritorious sacrifice, or anything of the sort. Not "Protestant" and not Catholic, it does rather clearly and cleanly fall into the *tertium quid* of Protestant sectarianism.

The persuasive logic and strong New Testament overtones of S.K.'s argument make it hard to rebut, yet it is difficult to say just how he would have seen it working out in practice. On the face of it his thought would seem to point toward one form or another of voluntary Christian communalism.[18] And there is evidence that S.K. at least toyed with the idea. In dreaming about a truly Christian society he said: "The form of the world would be like—well, I know not with what I should liken it. It would resemble an enormous version of the

[16] ". . . The Poorer You Become the More You Can Make Others Rich" (Part II, Discourse 3) in *Christian Discourses*, pp. 120-21, 125.

[17] Walter Lowrie in the translator's footnote that accompanies the passage quoted above.

[18] We have designed our terminology precisely to avoid implications of the contemporary word "communism." The difference can be stated as diametrically as this: If "communism" is an economic system designed to give its adherents maximum acquisitions, Christian "communalism" is the *rejection* of economic *system* in an effort to *minimize* acquisition.

town of Christenfeld [which was an experiment in Christian communalism]."[19]

The same sources that cited the first, brief period of Brethren celibacy indicated that communalism was part of the same regimen.[20] Now communalism certainly is not a necessary or normative aspect of sectarianism per se, yet clearly it is within sectarianism that communal experiments tend to appear. Essentially neither S.K. nor the Brethren are to be identified as exponents of communalism; however, the very fact that both even were willing to entertain the notion is a mark of (1) the authority they attributed to scriptural commands and examples and (2) the radicalness of their view of the simple life.

B. NEIGHBOR LOVE

To love human beings is . . .
the only salutary consolation for both time
and eternity, and to love human beings is the only true
sign that you are a Christian.[1]

When it is a duty in loving
to love the men we see,
there is no limit to love. If the duty is to be fulfilled,
love must be limitless.
It is unchanged, no matter how the object becomes changed.[2]

---

[19] *The Book on Adler*, pp. xxv-xxvi. S.K. went on to press the distinction which our terminology intends to convey. He said that Communism would approve Christenfeld as the correct *worldly* way, Pietism as the correct *Christian* way; and that these are entirely different affirmations. The context indicates that S.K. was thinking more of the radical equalitarianism of Christenfeld than of its radical view of ownership, although, obviously, the two aspects are so closely related as to be inseparable.

[20] See above, p. 244.

---

[1] *Works of Love*, p. 347. In the text this quotation is put into the mouth of the Apostle John, but it is plain that the reason S.K. put it there is because he himself was so heartily in accord with it.

[2] *Ibid.*, p. 164.

It would be quite within the realm of plausible and defensible assertion to claim that, in *Works of Love*, Søren Kierkegaard has given us the greatest treatment of Christian love to have been produced since the New Testament. The great contemporary works by Nygren and de Rougemont (and Fromm) are so dependent upon S.K. and so anticipated by him that they hardly could be given priority.

The eighteenth century Brethren would have heartily endorsed the title of S.K.'s book and the reasoning which lay behind it, that true Christian love can be recognized and validated only when it shows itself in concrete acts, its very nature being to seek such expression. Thus the Brethren literature included little if anything in the way of abstract treatises, or even exhortations, about love in general but concerned itself immediately with the practical aspects of *works* of love.

Although not enlarged upon, clues are found within the Brethren writings which indicate that the concept of neighbor love was there derived in the same way as S.K. did. In a poem on 1 John 4:16, Jacob Stoll said:

> [Those who would know the love of God]
>   They, in their whole lives,
> Are at all times completely permeated
>   With this sort of pure love
> Toward God, their highest Good,
>   And out of tender love are moved
> Also to do good to their neighbors.
>   An attribute of pure love:
> It is of such noble power
>   That it can cleave to nothing;
> It seeks to live in God alone.[3]

To root neighbor love solely and completely in the God-relationship is, as we shall see, thoroughly Kierkegaardian; S.K.

---

[3] Jacob Stoll, *op.cit.*, p. 130 [my trans.—V.E.].

called God the middle term of the love relationship between *den Enkelte* and his neighbor.

And Michael Frantz carried the parallel even further when he specified that love is to do what God has commanded, help those in need, give to him who asks, loan without expecting return, feed enemies, etc.[4] In the first place, that "love is *to do*" is consonant with S.K.'s emphasis on the *works* of love. And in the second place, the suggestion that Christian love is motivated and moved primarily out of obedience to God's directive catches up the major theme of S.K.'s great work, that thou *shalt* love.

Frantz's listing of God's commands points to the source of the Brethren love ethic, the teachings of Jesus and particularly the Sermon on the Mount. As with the simple life, S.K. also followed the pattern here. It is interesting to note that what is probably S.K.'s earliest description of Christian love (1843) is almost a paraphrase of the Matthean passage, with allusions to going the second mile, turning the other cheek, giving the cloak also, forgiving seventy times seven.[5] Consultation of the Minear-Morimoto index supports the feeling that S.K. was attracted to these Sermon texts, although the attestation is not quite as spectacular nor S.K.'s expositions quite as extensive as was the case with the simple-life passage.[6]

As we examine the particular works of love that figured strongly in Brethrenism, the most dominant is the practice of charity. Michael Frantz signalized this in his "Hymn of Brotherly Love and Community":

> "Mine" and "thine" do not signify community
> > [*Gemeinschaft*];
> But a heart full of pure love does.
> "Mine" and "thine" create great disunity;

[4] Michael Frantz, *op.cit.*, p. 41.
[5] "Love Covereth a Multitude of Sins" (Discourse 3) in *Edifying Discourses*, Vol. I, p. 72.
[6] Minear and Morimoto, *op.cit.*, p. 19.

A heart full of love has everything in common.
Love and warmheartedness
  Are prepared to give help readily.
Whoever would have fellowship [*Gemeinschaft*]
                            with God
  And eat of the bread of life
Must share his gifts
  With the poor man when he comes in need. . . .
To give alms out of a pure heart,
  Which is a candle burning with love,
Is much better than treasures of gold.[7]

In 1760, when the Germantown congregation acquired a
dwelling to use as a meetinghouse, several rooms were reserved as a home for the aged or poverty-stricken; later the
house was used exclusively for that purpose.[8] In the Annual
Meetings of 1788 and 1793 the brotherhood as a whole set up
procedures by which alms could be distributed in an organized
and orderly fashion.[9] It must be admitted that the instances
cited above constitute charity directed more particularly to
"the brethren" than to neighbors as such. But while it is clear
that the Brethren saw their own members as being their first
responsibility, it is also clear that they drew no hard and fast
distinction in their charities. Indeed, the benevolences of Sauer
Junior were of such repute that he came to be known as "the
Bread Father of Germantown."[10] And this tradition has continued within Brethren life, as it has within other churches of
sectarian descent. The Brethren, along with the Mennonites
and Friends, have been leaders in the field of international relief and rehabilitation; and it is not by accident that these "his-
toric peace churches" are also the churches with a particular

[7] Michael Frantz, *op.cit.*, p. 47, stanzas 1, 2, 5 [my trans.—V.E.].

[8] Mallott, *op.cit.*, p. 62.

[9] *Annual Meeting Minutes*, 1788, art. 1, p. 11, and 1793, art. 1, pp.
15-16.

[10] Brumbaugh, *op.cit.*, p. 401.

reputation for service and outreach. Both emphases stem from the same radical love ethic of sectarianism.

A second work of love was the very early opposition of the Brethren to slavery. In his newspaper for February 15, 1761, Sauer Junior carried a strong editorial against the institution, quoting copiously from the antislavery tract by the Quaker Anthony Benezet (the Friends and the Brethren supported one another on this issue).[11] And in 1782 the church came out in an unequivocal stand: "It has been unanimously considered that it cannot be permitted in any wise by the church, that a member should or could purchase negroes, or keep them as slaves."[12] If the usual economy was in operation here, the Annual Meeting was simply giving official standing to what already was established as the practice of the church; the likelihood is that the Brethren never had held slaves or approved the traffic.

A third work of love was the Brethren refusal to initiate or press lawsuits. We already have noticed this practice in connection with nonconformity, but some of the poems Sauer Junior ran in conjunction with the almanac court calendars make it plain that love for the neighbor was also a primary motive; love for the one who has wronged me must take precedence even over the desire to win justice from him.

> My friend, do you now wish
>   To sue your friend?
> Does a painful gnawing
>   Stir in your breast?
> Your Jesus gives you counsel
>   That you should love your enemy
> And through His grace
>   Practice self-denial. . . .

[11] Sauer Junior (presumably), an editorial in the *Pennsylvania Bericht* for February 15, 1761, quoted in Brumbaugh, *op.cit.*, p. 420.
[12] *Annual Meeting Minutes*, 1782, p. 7; cf. 1797, art. 1, pp. 18-19.

Avenge yourself on the Enemy
 Who harms all men;
Avoid his deep-seated evil
 In all your deeds.

If you are now thus minded,
 You immediately will find the justice you seek,
And you do not need to capture
 Or bind any child of man.
Then Justice
 Already has him in custody,
And Mercy itself
 Gives the sentence power.

Do you seek the justice of time?
 Seek it in the justice of eternity;
Then you will find as well
 God and justice and the kingdom of heaven....
Whatever your neighbor has done,
 Come unto Me; I will make it good
And remove you out of yourself
 Into the highest grace and favor.[13]

A fourth and final work of love relates to the Brethren position on carnal warfare, so-called pacifism, more accurately called nonresistance or defenselessness. In some ways this matter becomes a particularly clear indicator of sectarian thought, not because every sect is invariably pacifist but because, traditionally, the teaching has had virtually no standing in churchly thought. There is, of course, nothing about conscientious objection to war that makes it more a true work of love than anything else we have listed, but here is a point at which it is rather easy to test just how radical one's love ethic is. It here becomes both costly and conspicuous to love the

[13] Sauer Junior (presumably), poems accompanying the court calendars in the *Hoch-Deutsch Americanische Calendar* for 1766, pp. 19-20, and for 1770, pp. 19-20, respectively [my trans.—V.E.].

neighbor, because both the world and the "churches" have
taught and required participation in war, not as an act contrary to Christian love but as one permitted by (if not actually
expressing) Christian love. Thus for one to adopt the nonresistant position (particularly in a state-church situation)
constitutes clear evidence that his love ethic is sufficiently
radical to distinguish it from traditional "churchism." A crucial question for us, then, will be: Was Kierkegaard a
"pacifist"?

The Brethren took such a stand from their beginning.[14] We
already have noted the price Sauer Junior paid for his convictions during the Revolutionary War. However, the most complete discussion from the first half of the century is to be found
in Michael Frantz's poem-treatise, where he introduced the
topic with these lines:

> It has never yet been heard
>   That a sheep defends itself against a wolf;
> A sheep that heeds the mind of Christ—
>   It follows, loves, believes Him.[15]

With this, Frantz began a twenty-stanza section entitled "Of
Worldly Belligerence"; what follows is a free summary and
paraphrase of some of that material: "A Christian does not resist evil with weapons or sword. Christ did not use war in
order to establish a worldly kingdom, and his love prohibits
his disciples from fighting. Both Isaiah and Christ teach
against hurting one's enemies. . . . God uses war as the rod of
his anger with which to punish the nations that go to war.
Thus warfare is not much of an adornment to so-called Christendom. One throws a rod into the fire after it has served its
usefulness—and thus it is rather easy to judge whether 'Chris-

[14] A comprehensive study of this tradition within Brethrenism is
Rufus Bowman's *The Church of the Brethren and War* (Elgin, Ill.:
Brethren Publishing House, 1944).
[15] Michael Frantz, *op.cit.*, stanza 327 [my trans.—V.E.].

tendom' is of Christ or not. . . . When the government requires preparation for war, the Christian must obey God
rather than man."[16]

Undoubtedly the most significant document regarding
eighteenth century Brethren nonresistance is a petition submitted *jointly* by the Mennonites and the Brethren to the
Pennsylvania House of Representatives on November 7, 1775.
At this time the war fever was rising to the point that conscientious objectors could begin to feel the hot breath of persecution. The plea read, in part:

"We find ourselves indebted to be thankful to our late
worthy Assembly, for . . . allowing those, who by the Doctrines of our Saviour Jesus Christ, are persuaded in their consciences to love their enemies, and not to resist evil, to enjoy
the liberty of their consciences. . . .

"The advice to those who do not find Freedom of conscience
to take up arms, that they ought to be helpful to those who
are in need and distressed circumstances, we receive with
cheerfulness towards all men of what station they may be—it
being our principle to feed the Hungry and give the Thirsty
drink;—we have dedicated ourselves to serve all men in everything that can be helpful to the preservation of Men's lives,
but we find no Freedom in giving, or doing, or assisting in
any thing by which Men's Lives are destroyed or hurt. We
beg the Patience of all those who believe we err in this point.

"We are always ready, according to Christ's Command to
Peter, to pay the Tribute, that we Offend no man, and so we
are willing to pay Taxes, and to render unto Caesar those
things that are Caesar's, and to God those things that are
God's, although we think ourselves very weak to give God his
due Favor, he being a Spirit and Life, and We only dust and
ashes.

"We are also willing to be subject to the higher powers, and
to give in the Measures Paul directs us. . . . We are not at

[16] *Ibid.*, stanzas 328-49.

Liberty in Conscience to take up arms to conquer our Enemies, but rather to pray to God, who has Power in Heaven and Earth, for us and them.

"We also crave the patience of all the inhabitants of this country,—what they think to see clearer in the Doctrine of the blessed Jesus Christ, we will leave to them and God, finding ourselves very poor; for Faith is to proceed out of the word of God, which is Life and Spirit, and a Power of God, and our consciences are to be instructed by the same, therefore we beg for patience."[17]

There are here several items of note. In as unecumenical an age as the eighteenth century, the fact that the Brethren and Mennonites could settle for a single statement says something about the character of the two groups. The strong biblical grounding of the nonresistant position is apparent throughout, but what is perhaps more impressive is the appeal to the rights of conscience. In the concluding sentence, indeed, scripture and conscience even are related to one another in the familiar pattern of the inner-outer dialectic. Also, something of S.K.'s understanding of how conscience says "Regulations be blowed!" is involved. Not that there is reflected any defiance of government, any disdain or even questioning of the state as a rightful authority; quite the reverse. And although in one sense the petitioners were requesting the rights of conscience, in a more profound sense this was not so at all. There is no suggestion that their action in any way would be contingent upon what the state decided; rather, "We are not at liberty in conscience . . . , i.e. we are going to do what we *have* to do, we hope that you will not deem it necessary to persecute us for it." This combination of deferential respect for governmental authority along with an absolute intransigence in matters of conscience—this is very typical of the classic sectarian position, as is the sectary's disavowal of any desire to force his under-

---

[17] *Votes of the House of Representatives of Pennsylvania, 1767-1776*, Vol. VI, p. 645, quoted in Bowman, *op.cit.*, pp. 79-81.

standing onto others, any more than he wants their understanding forced onto him. And finally, the positive emphasis upon service and concrete works of love shows up as a true and essential concomitant of the doctrine of nonresistance.

One other important statement of the Brethren position is a minute of the Annual Meeting of 1785: "We do not understand at all . . . that we can give ourselves up to do violence, or that we should submit to the higher powers in such manner as to make ourselves their instruments to shed men's blood, however it might be done. . . . For the love to God constrains to the obedience of his commandments, as John teaches, and as Christ requires and says, 'If ye love me, keep my commandments'; and his commandments aim throughout at nonresistance."[18]

It should be noted that these Brethren apologies include no hint of any Social Gospel romanticism regarding "the infinite worth of a human personality" nor modern Gandhian sociodynamics regarding "positive nonviolent action" as a technique for achieving social gains. The early Brethren pointed only to the divine command of neighbor love, the teachings and example of Jesus, and their own responsibility to obey— and found these warrant enough. S.K. would have appreciated (and did himself affect) this same blunt, unsophisticated approach.

In due course, after the evidence is in, we hope to identify S.K. as a sectarian pacifist, but as we proceed our primary interest is to demonstrate the radicalness of his love ethic. The affinity with sectarianism can be established with certainty that far, whether or not there is then agreement that this love ethic did in fact eventuate in nonresistance.

The simplest way to present S.K.'s views would be to direct the reader to *Works of Love*, or at least attempt a condensation and summary of that volume. However, our purposes will

---

[18] *Annual Meeting Minutes*, 1785, art. 2, pp. 8-10.

be served by lifting up only those points which are salient in making the comparison with sectarianism.

In the first place, the love of neighbor was, for S.K., thoroughly, completely, and exclusively, a *religious* conception and not a humanistic or even humanitarian one:

"Worldly wisdom thinks that love is a relationship between man and man. Christianity teaches that love is a relationship between: man–God–man, that is, that God is the middle term."[19]

"Man shall begin by loving the unseen, God, for thereby he himself shall learn what it is to love. But the fact that he really loves the unseen shall be indicated precisely by this, that he loves the brother he sees. . . . If you want to show that your life is intended as service to God, then let it serve men, yet continually with the thought of God."[20]

Love of neighbor is not essentially a human action; it does not lie within the human powers of initiation or consummation. Neighbor love can appear only as a consequence of one's relationship to God—and that not merely through learning the nature of neighbor love *from* God but only as God actually is present as the middle term in the love between *den Enkelte* and his neighbor. But notice also that this necessary connection between existing before God and loving one's neighbor is specified as holding in the reverse direction as well; not only must one be before God in order truly to love his neighbor, but just as necessarily, if one is truly before God he *must* love his neighbor, for "to love God is to love human beings."[21] Contrary to a common understanding, the very definition of the Kierkegaardian *den Enkelte*, far from excluding other people, actually includes them—and active works of love toward them—as an essential part of the concept. S.K. did not speak of *den Enkelte* coming into relation with God *by means*

---

[19] *Works of Love*, p. 112. In the text these lines are italicized as part of a thematic statement.
[20] *Ibid.*, p. 158.   [21] *Ibid.*, p. 354.

of his relations with his neighbors; rather, he made it emphatic that it is only out of one's prior relation to God that the concept "neighbor" emerges at all: "It is in fact Christian love which discovers and knows that one's neighbor exists and that —it is one and the same thing—everyone is one's neighbor. If it were not a duty to love [and this phrase presupposes God as the one whose command makes it a duty], then there would be no concept of neighbor at all."[22]

"Neighbor" is the key term in S.K.'s doctrine; to define "neighbor" is to define the *object* of Christian love, and to define that object is necessarily to define the *quality* of the love. This approach arrives at the same distinction achieved by Nygren's analysis of *eros* and *agape* and does it, perhaps, in a more concrete and existential way. The neighbor is, first of all, the one who is next to hand, the man one sees. This "athandedness" precludes Christian love from being a mere feeling, or sentiment, and compels it into the responsibility of demonstrating itself concretely as *works* of love. But the neighbor is also *whoever* happens to be next to hand, unconditionally, without discrimination as to who or what he is. "The neighbor"—this man, that man, whatever man—stands in direct antithesis to "the beloved"—this man *instead of* that man. The difference between *agape* and *eros* can be put no more pointedly: "Christian love teaches love of all men, unconditionally all. Just as decidedly as erotic love strains in the direction of the one and only beloved, just as decidedly and powerfully does Christian love press in the opposite direction. If in the context of Christian love one wishes to make an exception of a single person whom he does not want to love, such love is not 'also Christian love' but is decidedly not Christian love."[23] The Brethren did not define what they meant by

[22] *Ibid.*, p. 58. These lines are part of an opening précis that introduces a major section of the book.
[23] *Ibid.*, p. 63.

"neighbor," but their use of the term makes it plain that they would have welcomed S.K.'s definition.

Likewise, S.K. made it plain that he would have welcomed Michael Frantz's proposition that love is *to do*—and specifically, to do as in obedience to God's commands, which obedience is, then, the norm and standard of Christian love:

"Christianity says it is a duty to be in debt [the debt of loving one another] and thereby says it is an *act*—not an expression about, not a theoretical *conception of* love. . . . Although love in all its expressions turns itself out toward men, where it indeed has its object and its task, it nevertheless knows that here is not the place where it shall be judged. . . . It is God who, so to speak, brings up love in a man; but God does not do this in order that he might himself rejoice, as it were, in the sight; on the contrary, he does it in order to send love out into the world, continually occupied in the task. Yet earnestly reared love, Christian love, never for a moment forgets where it shall be judged."[24]

Because Christian love is not to be judged by the world on the basis of what it accomplishes in the world but by God on the basis of whether it was motivated by true obedience to him, it follows that S.K. would have had little patience with the modern sort of "prudential pacifism" which actually attempts to "sell" people on the way of love as the most effective method for achieving social goals. S.K. denounced in so many words any temptation to commend love as a "paying proposition": The true lover is one "who loves without making any demand of reciprocity, who grounds love and its blessedness precisely in not requiring reciprocity. . . . The true lover regards the very requirement of reciprocity to be a contamination, a devaluation, and loving without the reward of reciprocated love to be the highest blessedness."[25] So radical was the

---

[24] *Ibid.*, pp. 182-84.
[25] *Ibid.*, pp. 226, 227.

motive of S.K.'s love ethic that the neighbor is to be loved out of absolute obedience to a divine command, without any regard as to whether or how the loving "succeeds." Just as radical was his ethic in the *quality* of its love: "In a certain sense [the true lover's] life is completely squandered on existence, on the existence of others; without wishing to waste any time or any power on elevating himself, on being somebody, in self-sacrifice he is willing to perish, that is, he is completely and wholly transformed into being simply an active power in the hands of God."[26] And just as radical as in *motive* and *quality*, just so radical was S.K.'s ethic in its *extent*. That "the neighbor" included *all* men meant that it included one's *enemies*; S.K. emphasized—indeed, was insistent—that this was so.

Our own inclination would be to consider S.K.'s teaching regarding enemies as bearing directly upon his views of nonresistance and at this point claim his affinity with the defenseless Brethren. Certainly the Brethren themselves founded their nonresistance upon Jesus' teachings about the treatment of enemies. There is, however, a wide-spread school of thought that accepts a radical ethic of love, forgiveness, and defenselessness toward one's *personal* enemies (claiming that this was all that Jesus had in mind) while rejecting this ethic in regard to one's *official* enemies, those who threaten the state and social order rather than simply one's own person. Although all we know about S.K. makes it probable that he would have branded such a distinction as sophistical, out of recognition of the *possibility* we will forego the drawing of conclusions at this point. However, the evidence now to be presented certainly must be kept in mind as the background and context for the identification that is to follow.

S.K. understood that: "He who in truth loves his neighbor

[26] *Ibid.*, p. 260; cf. pp. 248-49, where S.K. as much as reiterates Michael Frantz's lines to the effect that there is no "mine" or "thine" in Christian love.

loves also his enemy. The distinction *friend or enemy* is a distinction in the object of love, but the object of love to one's neighbor is without distinction. One's neighbor is the absolutely unrecognizable distinction between man and man; it is eternal equality before God—enemies, too, have this equality."[27] It is, however, not simply that Christian love *does* include enemies but rather that it is the inclusion of enemies that establishes love as *Christian*: "One can only love one's enemies for God's sake or because one loves God. The sign that one loves God is therefore quite rightly dialectical, for 'immediately' one hates one's enemies. When a man loves his friends it is in no way clear that he therefore loves God; but when a man loves his enemies it is clear that he fears or loves God, and only thus can God be loved."[28]

Thus the command to love the enemy is an absolute one. Such love is not occasioned by the hidden good one can discover in that enemy, not by the potentialities for good one believes are there, not by the hope of reforming him for good, not even by the faith that there is "that of God in every man." All of these occasions may be true to the facts, and certainly God does use human love as a means of changing men for the better. But it is not the responsibility of the Christian lover to prove that this can or will happen, thus justifying his decision to love. To love is his bounden *duty*; how or whether that love is to bear fruit is God's concern.[29]

It is certain that S.K. shared with the sectarian Brethren a radical and absolutist love ethic. In the case of the Brethren this ethic eventuated in a nonresistant position regarding carnal warfare. Indeed, if modern Brethren wanted truly to understand their original heritage in this regard, the best source

---

[27] *Ibid.*, p. 79.   [28] *Dru Journals*, 818 (1848).
[29] *Works of Love*, pp. 168, 309ff. Cf. "Love Covereth a Multitude of Sins" (Discourse III) in *Edifying Discourses*, Vol. I, pp. 61ff. Cf. "But How Can the Burden Be Light . . ." (Discourse II) in *The Gospel of Suffering*, pp. 40-41.

to which they might be directed would be: Kierkegaard's *Works of Love*. But the question remains: Did S.K. himself see this ethic as implying nonresistance? It is difficult to know how he could have avoided the conclusion. When his position has been as thoroughly and consistently absolutist as it has been up to this point, it is hard to conceive of him relativizing it in regard to war—relativizing either the ethic itself to make it apply to individual but not to group action, or relativizing the concept "enemy" in order to distinguish between one's "personal" and "official" enemies, or relativizing the concept "love" in order to bring the bombing of a man's home, the killing of his wife and children, under the rubric of "a work of love."

To my knowledge the question of S.K.'s "pacifism" never has been submitted to scholarly research, and indeed the only opinion I have found is that of Robert Bretall. In introducing the selection from *Works of Love* in his *Kierkegaard Anthology*, he states: "We know, for example, that [S.K.] was no pacifist; but his only escape from pacifism would seem to be via the dubious distinction between individual and social morality. Otherwise, must not the man who is really in earnest about *The Works of Love* go on extenuating and forgiving the actions of a Hitler indefinitely?"[30] How Bretall "knows" that S.K. was not a pacifist he fails to specify. The only thing I have found that possibly could point to this conclusion is that for four days, as a seventeen-year-old undergraduate, S.K. belonged to the Royal Life Guards, the equivalent of our R.O.T.C. (He proved physically unqualified.) But this incident surely has no bearing on the question before us.

On the other hand I have found no statement which in and of itself would constitute unimpeachable proof that S.K. was a pacifist. But Bretall certainly is correct in suggesting that

[30] Robert Bretall, in the editor's introduction to the selection from *Works of Love* in *A Kierkegaard Anthology* (New York: Modern Library, 1946), p. 283.

Works of Love inevitably points toward such a conclusion, and this can be used as the basis for a very strong case of circumstantial evidence. Some of that evidence is as follows: "The means we use, . . . the way one fights for his idea, . . . the least means one allows oneself for the sake of realizing them, are equally important, absolutely equally important, as the object for which one fights and labors."[31] Under no circumstances would S.K. have defended war with an argument to the effect that the end justifies the means.

Neither would he have allowed the assumption that a decree of the state *ipso facto* carries Christian authority:

"Above all, save Christianity from the State. By its protection it smothers Christianity to death, as a fat lady with her corpus overlies her baby. And it teaches Christianity the most disgusting bad habits, as for example, under the name of Christianity to employ the power of the police."[32]

"The whole concept of a 'Christian' state is actually a self-contradiction, a humbug. . . . The state conducts itself according to the category: the race; Christianity according to the category: the individual—on this point alone one can see that they are heterogeneous. . . . But Christianity is infinitely exalted above the state."[33]

"In one sense Christianity is doubtless the most tolerant of all religions, inasmuch as most of all it abhors the use of physical power."[34]

By unconditionally rejecting the concept of a Christian state, and doubly so by specifying that one point of divergence between Christianity and the state is the use of physical coercion, S.K. cut himself off from any theory that would justify war by

---

[31] *The Book on Adler*, pp. 133-34. Cf. *Purity of Heart*, pp. 201ff.

[32] *Attack upon "Christendom,"* p. 140.

[33] *Papirer*, X² A 240 (1849) [my trans.—V.E.]. Notice the early date of this entry; it cannot be dismissed an an aberration of S.K.'s last years. But see *Smith Journals*, XI² A 374 (1854-1855) for an even stronger statement.

[34] *Attack upon "Christendom,"* p. 184.

granting the state authority in matters of Christian ethics. Thus prohibited are the traditional arguments of "just war," "the two realms," or whatever, all of which presuppose at least some form of a "Christian" state.

But the one argument S.K. would have been least likely to use is the very one Bretall puts forward, although Bretall's timidity in suggesting it is evidence that he realizes that it is not very plausible. Actually, it is unthinkable that S.K. would deny his entire ethical theory, which is based precisely upon *den Enkelte*, in order to introduce a new, *social* (crowd) ethic different from what he has interpreted as being the New Testament norm. Although not specifically in connection with war, S.K. in fact explicitly did renounce any such "social" ethic:

"If only there are many of us engaged in it, it is not wrong, what the many do is the will of God. . . . The thing to do is to become many, the whole lot of us, if we do that, then we are secured against the judgment of eternity. Yes, doubtless they are secured if it was only in eternity they became individuals. But they were and are before God constantly individuals."[35]

"The falsehood first of all is the notion that the crowd does what in fact only the *individual* in the crowd does, though it be every *individual*. For 'crowd' is an abstraction and has no hands: but each individual has ordinarily two hands, and so when an individual lays his two hands upon Caius Marius they are the two hands of the individual, certainly not those of his neighbor, and still less those of the . . . crowd which has no hands."[36]

If S.K. was not a pacifist, there would seem to be only one way he could have avoided it, a way he would not have been ashamed to have taken, to admit frankly that the Christian requirement was higher than man could attempt.

[35] *The Sickness unto Death*, p. 254.
[36] The first of "Two Notes on 'the Individual' " in *Point of View*, p. 113.

But the evidence is, rather, that he was at one with the sectarian Brethren, not only in their ethic of radical love (which is unimpeachable) but also in their position on war. At one point in his *Papirer* S.K. quoted Tertullian's comment to the effect that, in disarming Peter, Jesus took the sword from every Christian. The entry consists of the quotation and nothing more, although S.K.'s transcription of it must have signified approval rather than anything else.[37]

But the heart and core of S.K.'s "pacifism" is to be found in his development of the concept "martyr." It never was given a full-fledged presentation in any of his published works or even in the journals. By piecing together statements from a variety of sources, however, we can reconstruct a consistent and integrated picture of S.K.'s truly remarkable position. The dating of these materials makes it plain that S.K. formed the concept during the years 1847-1848 and under the direct influence of the war with Germany and the general political unrest in which Denmark was then involved.

The place to start is with a series of personal letters which S.K. wrote to J. L. A. Kolderup-Rosenvige during August 1848.[38] There is one matter that it would be useful to note beforehand and keep under consideration as we examine the material itself. The category S.K. lifted up and explicated was "the martyr," but this is not quite precise as a description of a role a Christian can set out to play, for one's martyrdom is not of his own doing. The Christian can take a position that invites martyrdom, and that far his duty may extend, but whether he actually then becomes martyred is hardly within his power. Therefore, when S.K. spoke of the Christian duty to be a

---

[37] *Papirer.* [I have lost track of the specific locus and been unable to relocate it.—V.E.]

[38] These are to be found in *Breve og Aktstykker Vedrøende Søren Kierkegaard* [*Letters and Documents concerning S.K.*], ed. Niels Thulstrup (Copenhagen: Munksgaard, 1953), pp. 200ff. [The translation involved in the analysis of these letters is my own—V.E.]

"martyr," the only portion of that role incumbent upon the individual was to become "a nonresistor," "a conscientious objector," "a defenseless Christian," one who refuses to fight and who, defenselessly, is willing to take the consequences of that refusal, even to the point of martyrdom.

S.K.'s correspondent was urging him to take an active voice and part in the politics of the war with Germany, the establishment of constitutional government in Denmark, and the turmoil that pervaded Europe at the time. S.K. declined, avowing that the situation was such as to make any contribution from him impossible (which in itself may be indicative of a sectarian disinclination against becoming too closely aligned with any particular political interest or party). At this point S.K. offered his analysis of the war and the general European situation. It should be remembered that in the following S.K. was speaking about a war in which his own homeland even then was being invaded. It is one thing, during times of peace, to be critical of wars in general or of other people's wars; it is quite a different matter to speak thus of wars that affect and involve one personally.

S.K. proposed the analogy of a real-life drama which apparently he actually had witnessed in one of the crowded residential quarters of Copenhagen:

"*First act*: Two dogs get into a fight. The event creates an enormous sensation; an incredible number of heads are stuck out of windows in order to see. Work can wait for a while; everyone leaves it in order to watch.

"*Second act*: Out of the street doors of the two houses lying nearest the battle step two women, each from her own door. These two women appear to be the dogs' owners. The one declares that it was the other's dog that started the imbroglio. Thereupon the women become so excited that they join battle. More I did not see—but the story easily can be continued.

"Therefore, the *third act*: Two men come up, the husbands of the respective women. The one declares that it was the other's wife who started it. Thereupon the two men become so excited that they join battle.

"Thus one can assume that more husbands and wives come until . . . now it is a European war. The cause is: Who started it? You see, this is the formula for war in the second degree. War in the first degree is war; in the second degree it is a war over who it was that started the first war."[39]

S.K. here identified the phenomenon which the nuclear age has forced into our vocabulary as *escalation*; and upon the basis of that observation he was suggesting that war neither is nor can be a valid instrument for achieving social justice, precisely because it cannot be controlled, cannot be confined to the real issue at question. We use the term "escalation"; S.K. coined one that is perhaps even more descriptive. He saw war and the events that lead to war as a "gyration," a whirl that spins faster and faster and faster until it disintegrates into a fling of fragments.

He used this figure as the basis for a subsequent letter; what follows is a paraphrase of it: Given the gyrating character of conflict, what society (particularly 1848 Europe) needs is not *movements* but *brakes*. Events are whirling wildly; it requires a *fixed point* to break up the turbination and bring it to a stop. (S.K. specified that it is *den Enkelte* who must play the role of the fixed point; and thus are suggested many points of contact between the line of thought he was developing here and his religious perspective as a whole.) *Revolution* cannot do the job, for the first revolution calls for a counterrevolution to halt it; the counterrevolt is a revolution which itself must be stopped, *et cetera ad infinitum*. This, for instance, was the pattern of the French Revolution. And in light of the above it follows that the fixed point cannot be something *out front* toward which one is driving but must be something that *lies behind*.[40]

Thus far S.K.; we interrupt the paraphrase in order to com-

[39] *Ibid.*, p. 201.   [40] *Ibid.*, pp. 205ff.

ment on this most seminal suggestion. S.K. will categorize as "political" any movement that drives toward a point out ahead, that proposes to *establish* an order different from the one that presently obtains, that would save the situation by *re-creating* it. A "religious" movement, on the other hand, is oriented toward a point that lies behind; that is, its basic character is simply obedience to the commands of God, conformance to the mind of Christ, without obligation to *accomplish* anything. Of course, outward accomplishment may come as a result of religious movement, but in the final analysis this is God's business; *den Enkelte*'s only concern is to be obedient, and that obedience is blessed quite apart from anything it may bring to pass.

S.K. here saw a distinction that makes it possible to define the sectarian doctrine of nonresistance with greater precision than has been possible before. According to the terms of the definition, "positive nonviolent action," which uses lobbying, demonstrations, sit-ins, etc., is still essentially "political" in character, as is any "pacifist" movement that sets itself the goal of building a peaceful world. These movements certainly mark a real gain over those that depend upon violence and coercion as their instrumentalities, but they are not strictly religious movements for all that.

Even so, to identify a movement as "political" is not *ipso facto* to declare it illicit, although it is to deny that there is anything intrinsically "Christian" about it. A political movement, even "positive nonviolent action," is basically a *technique*, an action directed toward the accomplishment of a specified goal. A religious movement is in no sense a technique, because it has its *telos* within itself. Being a technique, the validity of a political movement must be judged by what it accomplishes; a sit-in, for example, "succeeds" when the lunch counter is integrated. A religious movement, on the other hand, cannot be so judged, because it was never committed to succeed. God does not require *den Enkelte* to accomplish anything in a worldly sense (that involves so many factors that are beyond the man's control); God requires only unconditional obedience (which is precisely what each man does control).

Being a political technique, "positive nonviolent action" can commend itself equally to and be used to equal effect by a non-Christian Mahatma Gandhi or by an atheist Bertrand Russell or by a Christian Martin Luther King. It neither needs a Christian to use the technique, nor does the using of it qualify one as a Christian. The religious movement, on the other hand, is specifically Christian in that the sort of obedience it requires is precisely what S.K. also intended by "Christian faith." Being a technique, "positive nonviolent action," or any other political movement, could as well be directed toward an unworthy goal as a worthy one; there is nothing about the technique itself that dictates for what it is to be used. A religious movement, however, risks no such discrepancy, because it is directed toward a fixed, Christian point behind rather than toward any goal out front.

None of S.K.'s statements suggest that it would be anything but proper and perhaps even obligatory for a Christian to support political movements which are dedicated to the attainment of worthy political and social goals. His point, however, was that the fundamental problems of human conflict and violence ultimately will have to be solved by religious and not merely political means: "This is the distinction between political and religious movement. Every merely political movement, which thus is godless or lacking religiousness, is a whirling that cannot stop and that only fools itself with the fancy that it wants a fixed point in front, that it wants to stop with the help of a brake—because the fixed point, the only fixed point, lies behind. And therefore this is my view of the whole European confusion, that it cannot be stopped except by religiousness."[41] S.K. concluded this letter with the observa-

---

[41] *Ibid.*, p. 207. S.K.'s words in *Purity of Heart*, pp. 99ff., are very relevant at this point.

tion that the religious martyr is the prime example of the way to brake turbination; the martyr does not strive to move society toward a point out ahead but acts solely in relation to the fixed point behind.

These letters to Kolderup-Rosenvige add to our understanding of another statement written about the same time, this in one of S.K.'s prefaces to *The Book on Adler* (which he never published). In this case as with the letters, the war with Germany stands as the immediate context:

"To get eternity again requires blood, but blood of a different sort, not the blood of thousands of warriors, no, the precious blood of martyrs, of the individuals—the blood of martyrs, those mighty dead who are able to do what no living man can do who lets men be cut down by thousands, what these mighty dead themselves could not do while they lived but are able to do only as dead men: to constrain to obedience a furious mob, just because this furious mob in disobedience took the liberty of slaying the martyrs. For the proverb says 'He laughs best who laughs last'; but truly he conquers best who conquers last —so not he who conquers by slaughter—oh, dubious conquest!—but he who conquers by being put to death—an eternally certain conquest! And this sacrifice is the sacrifice of obedience, wherefore God looks with delight upon him, the obedient man, who offers himself as a sacrifice, whereas he gathers his wrath against disobedience which slays the sacrifice—this sacrifice, the victor, is the martyr; for not everyone who is put to death is a martyr. For tyrants (in the form of emperors, kings, popes, Jesuits, generals, diplomats) have hitherto in a decisive moment been able to rule and direct the world; but from the time the fourth estate [presumably, that is to say, the Christian martyrs as opposed to the three traditional estates of lords temporal, lords spiritual, and commoners] has come into the picture—when it has had time to settle itself in such a way that it is rightly understood—it will be seen that in the decisive moment only martyrs are able to rule the world. That is, no man will be able to rule the human race in such a moment, only Deity can do it with the help of the absolutely obedient men who at the same time are willing to suffer—but such a man is the martyr."[42]

A final statement—although written in 1847, a year earlier than the others, and although speaking of the apostles rather than the "martyr" per se—nevertheless climaxes S.K.'s insight into the dynamics of nonresistance:

"But the Apostles were indeed also constantly suffering; they not only *had sufferings,* for there can also be suffering where there is *acting,* but their entire course of action *was a suffering;* their conduct was a *yielding;* they did not preach rebellion against authority; on the contrary, they recognized its power, but in suffering they obeyed God rather than men. They did not plead to be excused from any punishment. They did not grumble because they suffered punishment, but though punished they continued to preach Christ. They did not wish to coerce anyone, but let themselves be oppressed, they triumphed precisely through letting themselves be oppressed. If this is not the relationship, then neither can courage perform miracles; for the miracle consists precisely in the fact that it looks to everyone like defeat, while to the Apostle it is victory."[43]

Of course, "suffering" here is used not so much in the sense of "experiencing pain" as of "allowing oneself to be acted upon" rather than acting upon another, "absorbing" as against "effecting." Thus "suffering" is the correlate of "the fixed point that lies behind," which is, in turn, the correlate of "absolute obedience." Thus, too, S.K.'s "suffering" becomes a rather precise equivalent of early Brethren "nonresistance" and "defenselessness."

---

[42] *The Book on Adler,* pp. xxiii-xxvi. Cf. *Dru Journals,* 856 (1848).

[43] ". . . Courage Enables the Sufferer to Overcome the World . . ." (Discourse VII) in *The Gospel of Suffering,* p. 155 [the italics are mine—V.E.].

As regards his love ethic, then, Søren Kierkegaard did not simply show "sectarian tendencies"; he offered the best presentation of the sectarian ethic that has been made—and that both in regard to its basic nature and motivation (this in *Works of Love*) and its political relevance and application (this in the concept "martyr").

C. UNIVERSAL SALVATION

How far Christianity is from being a living reality may best be seen in me. For even with my clear knowledge of it I am still not a Christian. Yet I still cannot help feeling that despite the abyss of nonsense in which we are stuck, we shall all of us be saved.[1]

We are here to deal with a belief that is only peripheral both in S.K. and the Brethren, although the fact that it even appears makes it worthy of mention. A doctrine of universal restoration has at least some connection with a radical love ethic, which is why we bring in the matter at this point. Also, although universalism hardly can be taken as a necessary or even characteristic hallmark of sectarianism, such universalism as has appeared in Protestant history does tend to be associated with the sects.

Morgan Edwards, the ecclesiastical observer who was on the scene, explicitly identified the eighteenth century Brethren with a doctrine of "general redemption and, withal, general salvation";[2] and there is sufficient evidence to make that identification unimpeachable.[3] However, the question as to how

---

[1] *Rohde Journals*, 180 (1854).

[2] See his full statement, above, p. 90.

[3] It is gathered and analyzed in Durnbaugh, "The Genius of the Early Brethren," *Brethren Life and Thought*, IV, 2 (Spring 1959), 13-14.

widely, how centrally, and how emphatically the doctrine was supported is still an open one. Particularly Michael Frantz,[4] but also John Naas[5] and Jacob Stoll,[6] can be quoted in apparent contradiction.[7] Indeed, there seems to be only one *Brethren* document that witnesses to the belief, although this one is very instructive. It comes in the course of the imaginary father-son dialogue of Mack Senior's *Rights and Ordinances*. The father has just presented a particularly vivid picture of the punishments of hell, at which point the son asks, "Do tell me, are these torments and tortures to last for eternity, without end?" And the father replies:

"According to the testimony of the Holy Scriptures, 'the smoke of their torment goes up for ever and ever' (Revelation 14:11). However, that it should last for eternity is not supported by Holy Scripture. It is not necessary to talk much about it or speculate about it. . . . Even if at some time the torment should end after long eternities, [the damned] will never attain that which the believers have achieved in the time of grace through Jesus Christ if they obey Him. Many who have heard about universal restoration commit the great folly not to deny themselves completely but rather hope for the restoration. This hope will most certainly come to naught when they enter the torment, and can see no end to it. . . .

"Therefore, it is much better to practice this simple truth that one should try to become worthy in the time of grace to escape the wrath of God and the torments of hell, rather than

---

[4] Frantz, *op.cit.*, stanzas 471-80, 498-500.
[5] Naas, in a hymn quoted by Brumbaugh, *op.cit.*, p. 127, stanza 10.
[6] Stoll, *op.cit.*, p. 54.
[7] The word "apparent" is here used advisedly. The Brethren doctrine did not deny the reality (and a very live awareness) of a punishment following death. Ultimately, then, the matter comes down to the rather fine distinction as to whether that punishment is *ever*lasting or only *long*lasting; and the terminology used by these three men is not in every case absolutely beyond dispute.

deliberate how or when it would be possible to escape from it again. . . . That is a much better and more blessed gospel which teaches how to escape the wrath of God than the gospel which teaches that eternal punishment has an end. Even though this is true, it should not be preached as a gospel to the godless. Unfortunately, in this day, everything is completely distorted by the great power of imagination of those people who teach and write books about restoration."[8]

Obviously it was not by accident that the eighteenth century Brethren were as much as "secret universalists"; to have allowed the doctrine to become central and conspicuous would have falsified it. The Brethren believed in universal restoration but were not "universalists" in the customary sense of the term.

And S.K.'s universalism, too, was precisely of this order. One journal entry has been quoted as the epigraph; another reads: "But I do not pretend to be better than others. What the old bishop said about me—that I talked as if everybody else was on the road to hell—is simply not true. No, if anyone wants to be able to say that I talk about going to hell, then I talk like this—'If the rest are all going to hell, then I am going along.' This is the way I speak if anyone is able to say in any sense that I talk about going to hell. But I do not believe it. On the contrary, I believe that we will all be saved—and I, too—something which arouses my deepest wonder."[9] And there is a third that points in at least something of the same direction.[10] Only this much and nothing more; but the interesting aspect of the case is that these journal entries come out of precisely the same period in which we discovered the dark cloud of morbidity and misanthropy. How this strange conjunction is to be explained we will not venture to guess.

---

[8] Mack Senior, *Rights and Ordinances*, in Durnbaugh, *Origins*, pp. 399-400.

[9] *Papirer*, XI³ B 57 (1854), quoted in Malantschuk, *op.cit.*, p. 95.

[10] *Smith Journals*, XI¹ A 296 (1854).

With both S.K. and the Brethren it seems likely that their universalism was a corollary of their sense of the immediacy of God's infinite love and of the equality of all men within that love. Thus whether or not their coincidence on this unemphasized detail is particularly significant in and of itself, it does tie in with the general pattern of sectarianism that we are developing.

CHAPTER X

THE CHURCH WELL LOST

Thus far we have examined S.K.'s position regarding secular sociality, both the World Negative which his faith impelled him to reject and the World Positive which his faith equally impelled him to accept, to love, and to serve. We proceed now to examine his stance regarding religious sociality, i.e. those social groups designed with specific reference to the relationship between man and God, namely the church. We look first at the Church Negative; this is the form of the church which S.K. felt to be dominated by crowd-mentality and thus (to use Brunner's phrase) "a disastrous misdevelopment" and mortal threat to the true Christian concept of *den Enkelte*. This church S.K. called "the Establishment," and the term was always used by him in a negative sense.

Perhaps some knowledge of the Danish church situation would be helpful as we strive to understand S.K.'s attitude toward it. A very good source in this regard is Kenneth Scott Latourette's *The Nineteenth Century in Europe*, Vol. II.[1]

Denmark was institutionally conservative in religion as in politics (not until 1848—in the midst of S.K.'s career—was the monarchy de-absolutized and put under the control of a constitution). The nation presented a picture of religious monolithism as tight and persistent as any in Europe. Latourette describes it thus:

---

[1] Kenneth Scott Latourette, *The Nineteenth Century in Europe*, Vol. II, *The Protestant and Eastern Churches* (New York: Harper, 1959), pp. 131-51.

"The Protestantism [of Scandinavia] was overwhelmingly Lutheran. At the outset of the nineteenth century it was almost exclusively so. . . . The Lutheran churches were the state churches, established by law, controlled by the civil government, and supported by public taxation. They were also national churches, the churches of the people, what the Germans would call *Volkskirchen* (folk churches). All the population were baptized and a very large proportion were confirmed as Lutherans. Religious instruction was given in the state schools. . . . Baptism and confirmation were compulsory [in Denmark], as was a church ceremony for marriage. Theoretically Communion was also obligatory."[2]

Particularly under the influences of the Enlightenment the formal legalism of this churchly structure had produced a marked decline in spiritual vitality; but interestingly enough, at the time of Kierkegaard, the church was experiencing something of a resurgence and renewal. The revival, however, was not of the sort that met S.K.'s approval. The two leading figures were Bishop Jakob Peter Mynster (1775-1854) and N. F. S. Grundtvig (1783-1872). Bishop Mynster, the ranking ecclesiastic of the Church of Denmark, was an urbane and sophisticated Christian humanist (in the anti-Kierkegaardian sense of the term) whose efforts served to popularize "religion" although—to S.K.'s mind—at the expense of New Testament Christianity. Grundtvig's movement was perhaps less worldly and more deeply spiritual than that of Mynster, but it also had an aspect that was anathema to S.K. Grundtvig did not stress the need for an individual relationship to God but was interested in a sacramental church life that would be the focus for a rebirth of ancient Danish culture. His was a strongly encultured (almost nationalized) concept of Christianity as a folk- or community-faith.

The presence of Mynster and Grundtvig—and S.K.'s focusing of his attack upon them—is significant in demonstrating

[2] *Ibid.*, pp. 131, 134.

that his basic concern was not so much with any current *apathy* in the church as with the fundamental wrongheadedness of its *constitution*.

S.K.'s critique of the church, of course, reached its culmination (although hardly its beginning) in the spectacular *Attack* of 1854-1855. And because this phase of S.K.'s career is so conspicuous and well known, there will be some tendency to equate S.K.'s "sectarianism" with his *Attack*. Certainly, something of that quality does show up strongly at this point, but it would be a misunderstanding to read either S.K.'s sectarianism or sectarianism in general as being in essence nothing more than a protest against the established church. Indeed, we find surprisingly little of such protest in Brethren literature—for the simple reason that even before becoming Brethren these people had so completely broken their ties with the state-church that it no longer existed for them. Sectarianism is a self-sufficient religious type and does not have to be defined negatively in relation to an established church. This chapter of our study, then, represents one expression of S.K.'s sectarianism but by no means its core. Indeed, the basic character of the Kierkegaardian perspective could be established apart from any consideration of the *Attack*.

Likewise, it would be wrong to give the impression that S.K.'s critique of the church and thus his essential sectarianism were confined to the last year or so of his life. The *Attack* did become overt at that time, but the basic content of the criticism had been in S.K.'s thinking and writing for many years previous.

By its very nature—and designedly so—that final *Attack* was sensational in the extreme, and a very possible impression is that S.K. was seeking sensationalism for its own sake, that he was feeding his own ego as much as or more than he was serving God. Perhaps one value of our putting the *Attack* within the total context of S.K.'s sectarianism is to give an indication of how deep and honest his convictions were. In his own heart and mind S.K. was certain that to become *den Enkelte* is the one and only way to become a Christian. Of course, there is the crowd-world which wishes to block this development, which would entice, or if need be force, a man to accept its interpretation of existence, its goals, its way of salvation. But this opposition comes as no particular surprise; the New Testament warned that the world was of this order. But to discover that the Christian church, the instrument designed and commissioned by Jesus Christ for the express purpose of helping a man to become *den Enkelte*—to discover that this church in actuality was a crowd-church in collusion with the crowd-world, seeking to entice, or if need be force, one to find his salvation by joining its crowd-institution—this struck S.K. as the most abominable sort of sacrilege:

"Man is 'a social animal,' and what he believes in is the power of union. So man's thought is, 'Let us all unite'—if it were possible, all the kingdoms and countries of the earth, with this pyramid-shaped union always rising higher and higher supporting at its summit a super-king, whom one may suppose to be nearest to God, in fact so near to God that God cares about him and takes notice of him. In Christian terms the true state of affairs is exactly the reverse of this. Such a super-king would be farthest from God, just as the whole pyramid enterprise is utterly repugnant to God. What is despised and rejected by men, one poor rejected fellow, an outcast, this is what in Christian terms is chosen by God, is nearest to him. He hates the whole business of pyramids."[3]

Thus, the disappointment, the frustration, the shock, the horror, the rage that characterized S.K.'s *Attack* were real. Those not sympathetic with his position can hardly appreciate that fact—although to get S.K. into the sectarian perspective may help make his feelings more plausible. Granted that in the *Attack* S.K. used the weapons of satire and mockery with

---

[3] *Smith Journals,* XI[1] A 330 (1854).

their accompaniments of exaggeration and hyperbole, nevertheless the intent behind the whole must be accepted as serious, dedicated, and utterly sincere.

A. THE ATTACK UPON CHRISTENDOM

The triumphant Church and established Christendom are falsehood, are the greatest misfortune that can befall the Church; they are its destruction, and at the same time are a punishment, for such a calamity cannot come about undeserved.[1]

Put off thy shoes from off thy feet, for the place whereon thou standest is holy ground, when thou standest in Christendom, where there are nothing but true Christians! Let God keep eternity for Himself, where taken all in all He hardly gets as many true Christians as there are at any one instant in Established Christendom where all are true Christians.[2]

Although dealing with S.K.'s *Attack* as a totality, the scope of this portion of our study is quite circumscribed. In an earlier chapter we gave some attention to the *Attack* in its historical aspects: how the concern developed in S.K., the strategy he followed, what he intended to accomplish, etc.; we will not reopen such matters here. Neither will we attempt to review all the criticisms S.K. directed against the Establishment; many of these were simply the obverse negatives of items we have

[1] "Lifted Up On High . . ." (Part III, Discourse 5) in *Training in Christianity*, p. 226.

[2] *Ibid.*, p. 212. For both a sober pronouncement and a highly satiric jibe to typify S.K.'s critique, we have made a point of going not to the *Attack* proper but to a work of some four years earlier.

treated and will treat independently (for example, the church *fails* to be obedient, to lift up Christ as Pattern, to teach non-conformity, etc.). Our present investigation will be confined to S.K.'s most basic contentions regarding the essential nature of the church. We will deal only with the ideological core of the *Attack*, with S.K.'s negative ecclesiological concern.

In this section there will appear no parallel quotations out of Brethren literature; it does not provide such. The explanation already has been suggested: by the time the Brethren began developing a literature the Establishment was for them a dead issue; there was nothing to be gained by continuing a dispute which they previously had settled once for all. Brethren writings do contain derogatory asides about the "churches" but nothing in the way of serious ecclesiological criticism. Nevertheless, given the entire sectarian context which we have been developing, it is obvious that when those who became Brethren made their break with the church it must have been for reasons very similar to those voiced by S.K. In other words, the parallel between S.K. and the Brethren holds even though we have not the materials for making it explicit.

One more prefatory comment is in place. In S.K.'s use of the term "the Establishment," a major referent is to the fact of the church's formal and constitutive relationship to the state. However, this was by no means the total, or even central, impress of what S.K. had in mind. A church is established primarily in reference to its "respectability," its "fashionableness," the fact that it is "built-in" as a normal and expected feature of the social order. Thus, the formal "disestablishment" of a state-church would be a step in the right direction but, in and of itself, could not be taken as a total answer to S.K.'s concern. Indeed, just as negative as "the Establishment" is his term "Christendom," which assumes that the community, the nation, i.e. society itself, has in some sense become *Christian*. Obviously, the church's liaison with the state, its social respectability, and its presupposition of a "Christendom" are but three expressions of a common ideology. The three stand or fall together; S.K.'s interest was that they fall.

"Ideally and essentially viewed, . . . *the question* [is] whether a so-called Christendom, or rather a fallen Christendom, openly or more hiddenly, now by attack now by defense, has abolished Christianity."[3] Is Christianity, i.e. the faith once delivered, ultimately compatible with Christendom, i.e. a Christianized society? That is the decisive question which S.K. put as early as 1848. The question implied his answer, although he soon stated it so as to leave no doubt: "That which should be reformed in our time is not church government and the like—but the concept Christendom."[4] In another 1848 writing S.K. made his contention against Christendom as pointed as possible; and even if he did not use the term, his accusation had "crowd-mentality" written all over it: "Yet all these people [i.e. even those who do not live in Christian categories], even those who assert that no God exists, are all of them Christians, call themselves Christians, are recognized as Christians by the State, are buried as Christians by the Church, are certified as Christians for eternity."[5] Thus, in the *Attack* proper (which our quotations would indicate had been in the making for at least six years), S.K. could word the statement which we quoted earlier but which is as significant as anything he ever said: "In the last resort, precisely to the concept 'Church' is to be traced the fundamental confusion both of Protestantism and of Catholicism—or is it to the concept 'Christendom'?"[6]

S.K.'s question about "church" *or* "Christendom" was asked simply for effect, because it is clear that the two are at base identical. The very concept "church" assumes Christendom as its context, just as Christendom assumes a "church" as its

[3] S.K.'s 1848 Preface to *The Book on Adler*, p. xx.
[4] *Papirer*, X^2 A 537 (1849) [my trans.—V.E.].
[5] *Point of View*, pp. 22-23.
[6] *Attack upon "Christendom,"* p. 34.

religious expression. The basic assumption behind the entire church-Christendom idea is that the community, the geographically based social unit, is in some real sense Christian— and that without specific consideration as to how far and in what sense the individuals who make up that community are Christian. The "church," then, represents the natural expression of the community in its religious aspect, just as the state represents the expression of its civil aspect. It makes sense, too, that the church and the state should be closely allied, because both are complementary expressions of the same Christian community. Almost as much a matter-of-course as a person's *citizenship* (99 out of 100 people in the community are citizens thereof simply by virtue of being there), is his *Christianity*. Within Christendom it can be assumed that any person (simply by virtue of his being there) is a church member; and if a church member, then a Christian; and if a Christian, then "certified for eternity." And infant baptism stands as the logical symbol of this view. With the infant, of course, there is no question about *his* intentions, desires, or commitments, but as a part of the community he also should be included within its religious expression, and through the rite of baptism his incorporation is so symbolized.

Although the above has been stated in such a way as to make plain the contrast we want to draw and hence may be overstated in some respects, yet assumptions of this general order are necessarily involved in the "church-in-Christendom" view. But just as the churchly position must make these assumptions either consciously or subconsciously, the sectarian position is that which explicitly denies them. "Christendom," a natural community which is nevertheless by nature *Christian*, is an impossible concept. The church cannot simply *be*, by virtue of the natural religiousness of the community finding its expression, but must *become*, must be "gathered" as individuals who *are* Christian (not simply who are assumed to be so because they are part of the community) deliberately band themselves together.

According to the churchly view, the community *is* (as a natural, *a priori*, social entity); the community *is* Christian (by virtue of its having been so organized at some time long past); the community *is* the church (by virtue of the community's giving formal expression to its Christianity); and the individual *is* a Christian (by virtue of the fact that he is a part of the Christian community and participates in the formal expression of its Christianity).

According to the sectarian view, Christianity is of such an order that it can be a criterion only of *den Enkelte*, not of the community. Therefore, a community of Christians, not a Christian community (which is an impossibility), constitutes the sectarian church. Necessarily, then, the community must *come to be*; the community of Christians must *be created* as those who are Christian (by virtue of a personal transaction with God in Christ) gather *to form* a community. And thus adult baptism—which involves personal attestation to the Christian-making transaction with God and a conscious affiliation with the community—is the only appropriate symbol of the sectarian church which ever and always must come to be. The "church"man *participates* in the church, in the Christian community that *is*; the sectary *creates* the church, creates community by joining with those of like precious faith.

The church is the communion of the saints; so be it. But the churchly view takes this to mean: the church is the corporate body of those who are saints by virtue of their affiliation with this holy institution. The sectarian view takes it to mean: the church is the *Gemeinschaft* of saints who have been made such through a personal transaction with Christ and who have banded together on the basis of this common experience. Or, at the risk of oversimplification, yet to put the distinction just as succinctly as possible: In the churchly view, "the church" as an institution is prior, the cause, and "the Christian" posterior, the consequence. In the sectarian view, "the Christian" (*den Enkelte*) is prior and the *Gemeinde* is posterior. Thus a Protestant "church" is defined as being where the Word is truly preached and the sacraments rightly administered (the primary emphasis being on the doctrinal "rightness" of the institution). But a Protestant sect would have to be defined as being where those are gathered who truly hear the Word and rightly receive the sacraments (the primary emphasis being on the religious "rightness" of *den Enkelte*).

That S.K. had in mind some such distinction is made apparent in the following, very significant statement:

"In the definition of the Church which we find in the Augsburg Confession, namely that it is that communion of the saints where the Word is rightly taught and the sacraments correctly administered, it is simply the two latter clauses about doctrine and the sacraments which have been correctly understood (i.e. incorrectly), while the former clause has been overlooked: the communion of the saints, in which description the emphasis lies on the existential; in this way the Church has been turned into a communion where doctrine is correct and the sacraments correctly administered, but where the lives of the individual members are a matter of indifference (or where the existential element is neglected): this is nothing but heathenism."[7]

Earlier S.K. had written: ". . . [People] have conceived of the truth of Christianity as a result, as what might be called a surplus, a dividend, for in the case of truth as the way [i.e. where Christianity is a mode of existence which must be reduplicated in *den Enkelte*] the emphasis falls precisely upon the fact that there is no surplus, no dividend, which accrues to the successor from the predecessor, that there is no result."[8]

This statement points us back to one we quoted earlier (al-

[7] *Papirer*, X⁴ A 246 (1851), quoted in Diem, *Dialectic*, p. 178.
[8] "Lifted Up On High . . ." (Part III, Reflection 5) in *Training in Christianity*, p. 205.

though it comes out of the same passage in S.K.), this the one on page 139 above, in which he specifies that "the truth, in the sense in which Christ was the truth, is not a sum of sentences, but a *life*." Together, then, these suggest an analogy which we can use to epitomize the distinction between the churchly and the sectarian understanding of church.

"Church"men see the church as being a *commissary*; sectaries see it as being a *caravan*. The treasure, the truth, of a commissary is something it *has*, something it possesses, something then that, through proper transaction, it can dispense to the "customers." Conversely, the treasure or truth of a caravan is not anything it has but something it is *in*, when it is proceeding toward its proper destination in proper fashion.

The existence of a commissary hinges upon its being *established*, its being licensed, authorized, stocked—thus the churchly emphasis on its divine commission, on proper orders and ordination, on the possession of orthodox doctrine and efficacious sacraments. And, to put it bluntly, once a commissary receives legitimization it "has it made"; how many customers may come (whether any at all), how they receive the commodities, and how they use and are affected by them—ultimately these considerations have no bearing on whether the institution is a "true" commissary.

But the existence of a caravan involves qualifications of an entirely different order. There is no sense in which a caravan can be "established"; indeed, it is a caravan only so long as it is *on the way*; as soon as it stops, gets lost, or is dispersed it is no longer a caravan. Here too the existence and condition of the constituency (not now "customers" but "fellow hikers") is essential to the very concept: a caravan can travel (and thus be a "caravan") only as each and every person in it does his own traveling; the number of people who can be "carried" is strictly limited. And whereas with a commissary it is largely incidental whether or not the different customers make common cause or even know one another, with a caravan it is only the "togetherness" of the going that makes going possible at all; thus the centrality of *Gemeinschaft* in the sectarian understanding of the church.

S.K. also came at the matter from a different angle. The "church" presupposes Christendom; but the very concept "Christendom" necessarily implies that the character of "the world" has changed drastically since New Testament times, that the world which then stood in diametric opposition to Christianity is now allied with it. And if this has happened, it follows that the church itself has changed character just as drastically in adapting to the changed situation:

"[One] error is the specious notion which has arisen in the course of the ages, that in a way we are all Christians. For if this is posited, the Church militant seems an impossibility. Wherever there seems to be, or people assume that there is, an established Christendom, there is an attempt to construct a triumphant Church, even if this word is not used; for the Church militant is in process of becoming, *established* Christendom simply *is*, does not become. . . . What Christ said about His kingdom not being of this world was not said with special reference to those times when He uttered this saying; it is an eternally valid utterance about the relation of Christ's kingdom to this world, and so it is valid for every age. As soon as Christ's kingdom comes to terms with the world, Christianity is abolished. . . . To be a Christian in [the] militant Church means to express what it is to be a Christian within an environment which is the opposite to Christian. To be a Christian in a triumphant, an established Christendom, means to express what it is to be a Christian within an environment which is synonymous, homogeneous with Christianity. . . . At the precise place where suffering would have come if I had been living in a militant Church, now comes reward; there, where scorn and derision would overtake me if I had been living in a militant Church, now honor and esteem beckon to me; there, where death would be unavoidable, I now celebrate the highest triumph."[9]

In this regard S.K. saw the alliance between church and state as a particularly vicious thing, saying, "If [the Establishment] wishes the help of Government, it betrays the fact that it is not the Christianity of the New Testament."[10] And again: "Nothing, nothing, nothing, no error, no crime is so absolutely repugnant to God as everything which is official; and why? because the official is impersonal and therefore the deepest insult which can be offered to a personality."[11]

A basic, thematic pattern is beginning to emerge here, a pattern which ties together a great deal of what S.K. had to say and which suggests sectarianism as clearly as anything in his thought. There are two fundamental world-views which stand in complete opposition to each other. The one is the *Christian* view, and its basic categories are: (a) *den Enkelte*, (b) the personal, and (c) "becoming," i.e. that which is in process, which is militant. The other is the *worldly* view, and its corresponding categories are: (a) the crowd, (b) the impersonal, and (c) "extant," i.e. that which simply *is*, which is established. And clearly, the sort of church most concerned to press this distinction between itself and the world is the sect.

The state is by nature (and properly so) a worldly institution; the church is not of this world; therefore the two are hardly such as can be either combined or even closely allied: "The 'Church' ought really to represent 'becoming'; the 'State,' on the other hand, 'establishment.' That is why it is so dangerous when Church and State grow together and are identified. . . . 'Becoming' is more spiritual than 'existing'; the

[9] *Ibid.*, pp. 206-08. This entire discourse is germane to the topic—as is the passage on pp. 89ff. in Part II of the same volume. Cf. "It Is Blessed Indeed—To Suffer Derision . . ." (Pt. III, Discourse 6) in *Christian Discourses*, p. 235.

[10] *Attack upon "Christendom,"* p. 63.

[11] *Dru Journals*, 1309 (1854). Cf. *Smith Journals*, XI[1] A 68 (1854).

servants of the Church ought not therefore to be officials, probably not married, but those *expediti*[12] who are fitted to serve 'becoming.' "[13]

The reason S.K.'s *Attack* did not include a multitude of suggestions about what the Danish Church should do, how it should go about reforming itself, now seems apparent. It was not, as Diem suggests,[14] that S.K., without intending any radical changes, simply was staging a demonstration which might encourage the church to examine itself and deepen its spiritual life. Rather, S.K.'s concern and criticism ran so deep that any sort of "program of reform" would not even have touched the issue. Not *reformation* but *reformulation* was what was required. S.K. hardly would have settled for less, so his only alternative was to attack the church on as deep a level as possible and then, for his own part, divorce himself from it.

This pattern was precisely that of Brethren sectarianism: The Brethren-to-be left the church out of the conviction that it was not a Christian church. Later, and only later, did they proceed to the work of reformulation, to the organizing of a different *kind* of church. Whether or not S.K. ever would have proceeded to a similar step is, of course, impossible to say; he died too soon. But that his *Attack* pointed toward reformulation and a different *kind* of church seems evident.

B. LUTHER CRITICISM

When Luther introduced the idea of the Reformation,
what happened? Even he, the great reformer,
became impatient, he did not reduplicate strongly enough—
he accepted the help of the princes, i.e., he really

---

[12] The *expediti* were crack troops of the Roman army, highly trained and disciplined, carrying the very minimum of gear so that they could move into trouble spots quickly and decisively. They were the ancient counterpart of storm troopers, commandos, or the Green Berets of the U.S. Special Forces.

[13] *Dru Journals*, 941 (1849).

[14] Diem, *Dialectic*, p. 157.

became a politician, to whom victory is more important
than "how" one is victorious.[1]

That S.K. was not content to attack simply the Danish Lutheran Church of the nineteenth century but carried the battle
back to Luther himself, that he thus took on churchly Protestantism at its pristine best, that he would criticize the Reformation itself—all this suggests rather strongly that S.K. was
interested in something deeper than just reformation. And
though the wording of his accusation does not make it immediately apparent, we shall discover that S.K.'s quarrel with
Luther had to do precisely with the fact that Luther stopped
with *reformation* of the church rather than proceeding to a
Christian *reformulation* of it. S.K. spoke to Luther as a typical
(though unusually competent) sectary to the founder of
churchly Protestantism.

It will not be necessary to make anything like a comprehensive study of S.K. and Luther. Suffice it to say that S.K.
had no basic differences with the reformer regarding Protestant doctrine per se. Indeed, he did at points express appreciation for the fact that Luther understood the faith in a way
quite superior to that of contemporary theology.[2] True, S.K.
was critical about Luther's lack of dialectical balance on such
matters as faith and works, but these matters were not of ultimate significance. However, the fundamental criticism to
which he returned again and again is the one stated in the
epigraph, namely that Luther became a "politician." Elsewhere S.K. accused him of having ruined his own Reformation, first by becoming "a political hero" and then "a jolly man
of the world."[3] And finally S.K. charged that by coming out

---

[1] *Dru Journals,* 1166 (1850).

[2] Thus he could say: "Thank God for Luther! He is still always a
big help against the puffed up and almost demented dogmatic and
objective conceit with which we go far in abolishing Christianity."
(*Papirer,* X² A 231 [1849] my trans.—V.E.)

[3] *Dru Journals,* 1119 (1850). Cf. S.K.'s statement quoted above, p. 33.

as a success rather than a martyr Luther confused the basic concept of what a reformer should be.[4]

The terms "politician" and "martyr" lead us back to the Kierkegaardian distinction between religious and political movements, and we need now to apply that typology not simply to the problem of war but to the very nature of the church.[5] Rather than being the religious martyr who was oriented solely to the fixed point behind, interested only in becoming obedient, Luther acted as a politician striving to accomplish a new order within society, driving toward a point out front, namely the establishment of a Protestant church. Thus, as S.K. put it, Luther became more interested in the victory of his cause, i.e. the accomplishment of his end, than in the "how" of that victory, i.e. the "how" of strict obedience that leaves the result entirely in the hands of God.

In what follows, S.K.'s statements do not concern Luther per se, but the line of thought is relevant—and highly sectarian as well. *Why* did Luther become a politician? The answer is simple. As a "church"man, Luther saw the church as an institution, a commissary. Thus, whatever might be done in the way of reformation, it was, of course, absolutely essential that the institution itself be preserved. That is no feasible reformation which loses the church in the process of reforming it. Therefore, Luther's program actually came to be: to reform or change the church into conformance with the gospel ideal *insofar as that could be done without endangering the very existence of the institution.* It is the presence of this conditional (although essential) clause that gave the Reformation the pragmatic, political character to which S.K. objected. It was this consideration that led Luther to "accept the help of the princes," to shrewdly exploit the political situation, to com-

---

[4] *Dru Journals,* 1304 (1854).

[5] In the letter where S.K. established this concept (see above, p. 281), he also specified the Reformation as a movement that appeared religious but proved to be political.

promise some of his religious insights.[6] None of this is to be read as dishonesty or hypocrisy on Luther's part. *If* the church is essentially an institution, that institution must be preserved; and rather clearly, these things had to be done in order to preserve it.

S.K. put the matter this way: "Politics consists of never venturing more than is possible at any moment, never going beyond what is humanly probable. In Christianity, if there is no venturing out, beyond what is probable, God is absolutely not with us; without of course its following that he is with us whenever we venture farther out than what is probable."[7]

Now the sectary too is vitally concerned to preserve the church, but consider that by the very nature of its constitution a caravan can be preserved only by venturing; to stop, dig in, and establish fortifications might save something, but whatever was saved would be so only by ceasing to exist *as a caravan.* Thus the only way for a sectary to preserve his church is to become as radically obedient as possible and leave the preserving to God. He, in all conscience, *must* do the one thing that the "church"man, in all conscience, *cannot* do: risk the martyrdom of the church itself in the interests of unconditional obedience. S.K. saw what was at stake here:

"Somewhere in a modern author (I think Böhringer) I have read something like the following observation. He is speaking of one of the critical points in the history of the church, and says that for the church only one of two things was to be done: either it had to admit plainly that the Christian church did not exist (but that would be suicide) or it had to put a bold face on it and claim that it was the true Christian church.

---

[6] For instance, in his *The German Mass and Order of Worship* (Holman, *Works*, Vol. VI, p. 173), Luther describes "the kind of service which a truly Evangelical Church Order should have." What follows is as accurate a description of a "gathered church," a sectarian *Gemeinde,* as could be drawn. But in conclusion Luther as much as admits that he has not formed that sort of a church because it would not "work."

[7] *Smith Journals,* XI¹ A 502 (1854).

"So it would be suicide? Yes, truly, suicide, and yet an action well-pleasing to God. For that would mean that there is enough truth to kill oneself to make room for the truth, instead of stifling it with its beastly expansion which impudently claims to be Christianity. But the church had neither the courage nor the truth to do this, to accomplish his heroic suicide—it preferred to kill Christianity with its lies. But precisely what that author describes as preposterous, as something that the church could not think of doing, is what must be done."[8]

S.K. is here making explicit an aspect of the sectarian ideal which perhaps the classic sectaries themselves were not able to enunciate quite this clearly, namely that nonresistance, or defenselessness, is not simply a position regarding the Christian and war but marks the basic stance and orientation of the church's entire existence. The following statement S.K. applied simply to *den Enkelte* but it would hold for the church as well: "That the Christian is sacrificed is also expressed in the image which Christ constantly uses, and which is repeated here: to be salt. For to be salt means not to be for oneself, but to be for others, that is, to be sacrificed. 'Salt' has no being for itself, but is purely teleological, and to be determined purely teleologically means to be sacrificed."[9] Call it "salt" or call it a "caravan," either figure points toward the sect as a church striving to be determined purely teleologically—and that teleology is to give itself unreservedly in radical obedience to God.

Both S.K.'s and Luther's views on preserving the church are entirely consistent and sincere. *If* the church is what the "church"man sees it to be, then sectarian radicalism is a real and present threat to the very existence of the Christian *church*. But *if* the church is what the sectary sees it to be, then Luther-type "politics" are a real and present threat to the very existence of the *Christian* church. Which view is correct, it is

[8] *Smith Journals,* XI² A 325 (1854).
[9] *Smith Journals,* XI¹ A 7 (1854).

not for us to say. However, his critique of Luther makes it quite plain that, regarding the nature of the church, S.K. was a sectary and not a Lutheran.

C. CLERICALISM

[The modern parson] is a skillful, active, and quick man,
who finds it perfectly easy,
with the aid of attractive conversation and bearing,
to introduce a little Christianity—but as little as possible.[1]

[The priest's] whole existence as a combination
of civil servant and disciple of Christ
is entirely inadmissible,
directly contrary to Christ's ordinance.[2]

[The priest] walks in long robes,
which Christ, however, does not exactly recommend
when both in Mark and Luke He says, . . .
"Beware of those who go about in long robes."[3]

A major aspect of S.K.'s criticism of the church was his anti-clericalism. Again in this case there is no Brethren material that forms a direct counterpart. However, a correlation can be made by noting that the Brethren form of the ministry specifically (and without doubt deliberately) *avoided* just those usages of which S.K. was most critical.

S.K. questioned the very constitution of the state-church ministry, asking, "Can one be a teacher of Christianity by royal authorization?"[4] He saw that the arrangement leads to a truly serious conflict of interests. The matter of financial support becomes a problem: "Only in one case can a teacher of Christianity, who is bound by an oath to the New Testament, defend himself for being maintained by the state—namely,

---

[1] *Smith Journals,* XI^1 A 69 (1854).
[2] *Attack upon "Christendom,"* p. 228.
[3] *Ibid.,* p. 27.
[4] *Ibid.,* p. 46.

when he has been arrested, and, let it be noted, arrested for the sake of Christianity. . . ."[5]

"If one cannot impart to men so much of a picture of the importance of Christianity that they pay willingly, neither should anyone take their money. Christianity is too high-born to patronize the state."[6]

In contrast to the clergy of his own day, S.K. looked back to the situation of the early church: "But there was a time when Christianity was preached by witnesses for the truth—there were no livings in those days, inasmuch as Christianity (incredible as it is!) had come in without any help from livings. . . . O ye revered figures whom Christianity so touched and moved that it and ye conquered your hearts, and ye resolved, and kept the resolve to preach Christianity in poverty and lowliness, [this was] genuine preaching."[7] The Brethren practiced the very thing that S.K. seems to have had in mind; they recognized the right of the minister to accept contributions toward his support and yet their leaders regularly served on a purely volunteer basis.

S.K. also took the clergy soundly to task for another aspect of their "professionalism," their tendency to substitute theologizing and rhetoric for a demonstrated way of life. Such preaching completely misses the point:

"The speaker who does not know how the task looks in daily life and in the living-room might just as well keep still, for Sunday glimpses into eternity lead to nothing but wind. To be sure, the religious orator is not to remain in the living-room, he must know how to hold fast the total category of his sphere, but he must also be able to begin everywhere. And it is in the living-room that the battle must be fought, lest the religious conflict degenerate into a parade of the guard once a

[5] *Smith Journals*, XI[2] A 352 (1854).

[6] *Papirer*, X[2] A 240 (1849) [my trans.—V.E.].

[7] "To Become Sober" (Discourse I) in *Judge for Yourselves!*, pp. 140, 142.

week; in the living-room must the battle be fought, not fantastically in the church, so that the clergyman is fighting windmills and the spectators watch the show; in the living-room the battle must be fought, for the victory consists precisely in the living-room becoming a sanctuary."[8]

Here is a "secular Christianity," although definitely not one that threatens to become incognito in its worldliness or to become "of the world" in the process of being "in the world."

"Living-room sermons" require a peculiarly qualified preacher. His basic qualification is one that churchly orthodoxy specifically disavowed but which was central in sectarianism. Not the credentials of his ordination, not his eloquence, not his theological skill or doctrinal correctness, but the quality of his experience and life, sectaries would say, is the primary requisite of the minister. Kierkegaard too took his stand clearly in this tradition: "Christianity not being a doctrine, it is not a matter of indifference, as in the case of a doctrine, *who* expounds it if only (objectively) he says the right thing. No, Christ did not appoint professors, but followers. If Christianity (precisely because it is not a doctrine) is not reduplicated in the life of the person expounding it, then he does not expound Christianity, for Christianity is a message about living and can only be expounded by being realized in men's lives."[9] Obviously again, the Brethren minister would seem to have come close to the Kierkegaardian ideal. His church actually was a living-room (if not a barn); he had neither the ability nor the inclination to indulge in speculative theology; and he had been chosen minister by the friends and neighbors who knew him best, and that precisely because of the quality of his Christian life.

---

[8] *Postscript*, pp. 415-16. Climacus purportedly is the author, but there is no doubt that the words belong to the Christian Kierkegaard rather than to his non-Christian pseudonym.

[9] *Rohde Journals*, 141 (1848); cf. 138 and 219. Cf. *Smith Journals*, XI² A 402 (1854). Cf. *Johannes Climacus*, pp. 135-36, and ". . . The Mirror of the Word" (Discourse I) in *For Self-Examination*, pp. 36-37.

Finally, as part of the same pattern, S.K. denounced clerical vestments. As surprisingly early as 1847, he wrote: "I am well aware that in the matter of canonicals some prelates use broadcloth, others silk, velvet, bombazine, etc. but I wonder if the true Christian canonicals are not these: Being derided in a good cause, being scorned and spat on, the degree thereof would indicate the clergyman's order of rank. . . . But to preach about Christ decked out in finery and furbelows to a crowd of curious gapers! Disgusting!"[10] And in the *Attack* proper, the fusillade was made just that much more devastating:

"The decisive point is that when the teacher acquires 'canonicals,' a peculiar dress, professional attire, you have official worship—and that is what Christ will not have. Long robes, splendid churches, etc., all this hangs together, and it is the human falsification of the Christianity of the New Testament. . . . It is not true of the clerical order as it is of other orders, that there is nothing evil about the order; no, the clerical order is, Christianly considered, in and for itself of the Evil, is a demoralization, a human egoism, which inverts Christianity to exactly the opposite of that which Christ had made it."[11]

It will suffice to note that the vestments of a Brethren cleric consisted of a clean pair of overalls (or the eighteenth century equivalent).

D. INFANT BAPTISM

[*A young husband who normally feels no need at all for religion gets in a family way; the baby must be baptized.*] *So they notify the priest, the midwife arrives with the baby, a young lady holds the infant's bonnet coquettishly, several young men who also*

[10] *Rohde Journals*, 218 (1847).
[11] *Attack upon "Christendom,"* p. 175.

*have no religion render the presumptive
father the service of having, as godfathers,
the Evangelical Christian religion, and assume obligation for the Christian upbringing
of the child, while a silken priest with a
graceful gesture sprinkles water three times
on the dear little baby and dries his hands
gracefully with the towel—And this they
dare to present to God under the name of
Christian baptism. Baptism—it was with this
sacred ceremony the Savior of the world was
consecrated for His life's work, and after
Him the disciples, men who had well
reached the age of discretion and who then,
dead to this life (therefore were immersed
three times, signifying that they were baptized into communion with Christ's death),
promised to be willing to live as sacrificed
men in this world of falsehood and evil.*[1]

That, as he did here, S.K. affirmed "the age of discretion" as
the proper time for baptism, and that (oh, favor beyond all
meed!) he should specify *trine immersion* as the proper mode
—this is sufficient to endear S.K. to Dunker hearts for all time.
But of course, there is more that must be said—particularly in
light of such a deflating comment as that of the non-Dunker
Walter Lowrie: "The many Baptist sects will welcome
[S.K.'s] criticism of infant baptism (although in fact S.K. was
not disposed to discard it)."[2] But neither the "Baptist sects"
nor S.K.'s opinion of infant baptism really can be put off with
so brief a parenthesis.

Lowrie is correct in suggesting that, at the point where S.K.
made his most extended analysis of infant baptism, in *Post-*

---

[1] *Attack upon "Christendom,"* p. 205.
[2] Walter Lowrie, the translator's Introduction to *Attack upon "Christendom,"* p. xv.

script, he was not disposed *to demand that it be discarded* (to make Lowrie's wording a little more accurate). But *Postscript* is a rather early work (1845–1846), written before S.K. had faced up to the true extent of his alienation from the church. And given his reluctance to say anything which might suggest that the church could make everything right simply by introducing certain reforms (such as dropping infant baptism), it is little wonder that S.K., at that time, did not come out with a flat denunciation of infant baptism.

However, if due weight is attributed to the depth of his critique (even in 1846) and then to the statements he made after he had given up the church as a bad cause, the picture is somewhat different. One such later statement is that quoted as our epigraph. Another reads: "Infant baptism: it is easy to see that this is really connected with the knavish cunning with which mankind has tried to cheat God of Christianity by turning it into Epicureanism."[3] And again: "Now everything is turned into twaddle by passing off an infant as a Christian."[4] These are not the words of a proponent. Clearly, the burden of proof is not upon the Baptist sects but upon Lowrie to show that the later Kierkegaard did in fact (or even to show how he conscientiously could) favor the retention of infant baptism.

The point at issue goes far beyond determining the correct *mode* for the observance of a common Christian rite. The difference between infant and adult baptism is a radical one, involving opposed concepts of the church. It was a mark of insight that historically the matter was seen as decisive enough that certain sectarian groups—such as the Anabaptists, the Baptists, and the Dunkers—were labeled and identified on the basis of their baptismal practice. For the truth is that infant and adult baptism are two different rites, symbolizing two different actions, presupposing two different definitions of the parties involved. Either baptism is right and proper within

[3] *Smith Journals,* XI¹ A 546 (1854).
[4] *Smith Journals,* XI¹ A 39 (1854); cf. XI² A 25 (1854).

the context of its own concept of the church; neither makes sense apart from that context.

From the churchly view, baptism is primarily an act of the church, the baptizer (rather than of the individual, the one being baptized). In this act the institution incorporates the person into itself in order that, during the course of his life, he may enjoy the blessings and graces which the institution (commissary) communicates. Because the church is the religious expression of the Christian community, because the child, clearly, is a member of that community, and because it is through his participation in this sacred institution that grace is mediated and he becomes a Christian—because this is the case, infancy obviously is the due and normal time for baptism. *If* the church is essentially an institution, infant baptism is manifestly correct.

However, according to the sectarian view, baptism is primarily an act of *den Enkelte*, the one being baptized (rather than an act of the church per se). In this act *den Enkelte* attests to the reality of *his* personal, immediate relationship to God, to the fact of what has already happened and is happening in *his* life, to the faith that is present in *him*. In this act, also, he covenants with God regarding the life of loyalty and obedience which *he* intends and desires to live, the road he intends to travel. And finally, he also covenants with his fellow Christians to be *a constituent member of the caravan* (not a subject of the institution). Because this is what is involved, it is clear that a person who has reached the age of discretion and responsibility is the only fit applicant for baptism. *If* the church is essentially a *Gemeinde*, only adult baptism is correct.

The sect baptizes *Christians* as a profession, attestation, and seal of their Christianity; and in that baptism the church is *created*. The church (the *Gemeinde*) originally came into being as Christians joined with one another, and it must ever continue to come into being as contemporary Christians join with one another anew. Even so, it is completely correct to call the church the body of Christ and to acclaim him as its creator, for it is, of course, his work that creates Christians in the first place, his call that brings them together, and his living lordship in their midst that imparts the quality of *Gemeinschaft* to their gathering.

The "church," on the other hand, baptizes *potential* Christians (actually, potential *persons*, who by that token are potential *Christians*) in order to set up the conditions through which the church, as a divinely pre-established repository, can administer the graces of correct doctrine and true sacraments which will make them Christians.

Just this striking is the difference between the infant baptism of the classic churchly tradition and the adult baptism of the classic sectarian tradition. It will become quite apparent that S.K.'s uneasiness over infant baptism arose from the fact that he held a sectarian "theology of baptism" which he could not reconcile with the churchly "mode of baptism."

The Brethren, of course, could be quoted at great length regarding baptism; this was the doctrine in which they were most conspicuously at odds both with the "church"men on their right and with the "spirituals" on their left and regarding which they therefore did the most writing and explaining. It will be sufficient here to note a few significant points. In the first place, baptism was essentially an act of obedience and an outward attestation of an inner process—no suggestion of baptismal regeneration was involved.[5]

In the second place, the delay of baptism until the age of discretion[6] did not mean—as the sectaries were often accused—

[5] See above, pp. 170ff.

[6] The practice of the eighteenth century Brethren would indicate that they considered that age to be somewhere around sixteen to eighteen years. Modern Brethren have the age pushed down to little more than half that—to the place where the biting words of S.K. begin to apply: "Confirmation then is easily seen to be far deeper nonsense than infant baptism, precisely because confirmation claims to supply what was lacking in infant baptism: a real personality which

that their children were denied salvation. As an Annual Meeting minute put it, "The children of the faithful belong to the flock of Christ just as naturally as the lambs belong to the flock of sheep."[7] And Mack Senior explained in more detail, using the analogy of circumcision, although in a way quite different from its traditional use as an argument for infant baptism. He pointed out that:

"The circumcision of the Old Testament was demanded only of male infants on the eighth day. If then, a child died before that time, he would not have violated God's commandment. Doubtless many died before the eighth day, and they were certainly not rejected, as little as the female infants, who were not circumcised at all, and despite this were under the promise. Therefore, if a child dies without water baptism, that will not be disadvantageous for it, because this has not been commanded of the child. It has not yet experienced the 'eighth day'—that is, the day on which it could have repented and believed in the Lord Jesus, and could have been baptized upon this, its faith. . . . The children are in a state of grace because of the merit of Jesus Christ, and they will be saved out of grace."[8]

Ultimately, then, there is no issue between the churchly and the sectarian views as to (1) whether or not children can be saved; (2) whether or not the church has a concern, responsibility, and ministry for children; or even (3) whether or not it is proper to have a ceremony symbolizing the church's adoption of the child. The question is whether this sort of ceremony is what the New Testament intended as baptism. Thus the very serious-sounding charge made by Ian Henderson would bother a sectary not at all, nor would it need have

---

can consciously assume responsibility for a vow which had to do with the decision of an eternal blessedness." (*Attack upon "Christendom,"* p. 218.)

[7] *Annual Meeting Minutes,* 1789, art. 2, p. 12.

[8] Mack Senior, *Rights and Ordinances,* in Durnbaugh, *Origins,* p. 352.

bothered S.K. Henderson says: "A view of Christianity like Kierkegaard's which confessedly has little place for children . . . seems hardly to be true to what we know of Jesus of Nazareth."[9] Indeed, it would be quite accurate to carry this further and say that Christianity has *no* place for children. However, this is not at all to say that *Jesus Christ* has no place for children; any sectary would be eager to affirm that Christ's love and favor extends to them without condition. Nevertheless, it does seem true to what we know of Jesus of Nazareth to suggest that *Christianity*, i.e. the Christian *faith*, is accessible only to those who are capable of *faith*.

Thus the thing that the Brethren, and particularly S.K., resisted most was not so much the bare rite of infant baptism as the implication that the infant's being baptized does, at least in some sense and to some degree, make him a Christian. In this light, S.K.'s original position (as presented in *Postscript*) is seen to be consistent—if not quite realistic. He was willing to retain the rite if the implication about the infant's becoming a Christian were dropped. His later statements—made after he realized that his quarrel with the church was too deep to be resolved through compromises—would indicate that he then understood (1) that the implication was an intrinsic and inevitable aspect of the rite itself, and (2) that if the implication were dropped, the residual rite would bear little if any relationship to what the New Testament calls Christian baptism.

It is interesting to discover in an early, pseudonymous work such as *Postscript* an extensive and recurring discussion of infant baptism.[10] Actually, the entire treatment is out of place, for it is hardly in character that a worldly philosopher Clim-

[9] Ian Henderson, *Myth in the New Testament* (Chicago: Henry Regnery Co., 1952), p. 24.

[10] Passages dealing essentially with infant baptism are to be found on pp. 42-44, 260, 325-29, 332-34, 340-41, and 520-39; thus six passages of significant length total some thirty pages. Yet only a few brief references to baptism are found outside of *Postscript*.

acus should become so agitated concerning a churchly rite. But obviously, S.K. had lost sight of his pseudonym, and at times it must be said that he lost sight of his readers as well. Thus we find a rare situation in Kierkegaardian literature. Right or wrong, S.K. almost always spoke with precision, forthrightness, and authority; he was perhaps the writer least inclined to hedge, to qualify, to muddle his ideas. And yet here, in his alternate denunciation and defense of infant baptism, the impression is given that he was as much feeling his own way as he was communicating solid convictions to his readers. Plainly, S.K. was deeply bothered about the doctrinal implications of infant baptism.

This very unrest fits perfectly the pattern through which sectarianism normally develops. Almost invariably it is in connection with infant baptism that the incipient sectary begins to feel acute dissatisfaction with the church—usually some considerable time before he realizes that it is actually a doctrine regarding the basic nature of the church itself that is at stake. It would not be amiss to date these passages as marking the onset of S.K.'s sectarian birth-pangs.

However, the position S.K. there developed at such length (and with a great deal of repetition) actually is very simple:

"In times when people became Christians as adults, and were baptized in mature years, one might with some assurance speak as if Christianity had some significance for the baptized. . . . But when the rite of baptism is relegated to the second week after birth . . . it is impossible to deny that membership in the visible Church constitutes a very doubtful proof that this member is really a Christian."[11]

"That time, or existence in time, should be sufficient to decide an eternal happiness is in general so paradoxical that paganism cannot conceive its possibility. But that the whole matter should be decided in the course of five minutes, two weeks after birth, seems almost a little too much of the paradoxical."[12]

[11] *Postscript*, p. 326. [12] *Ibid.*, pp. 328-29.

These statements (plus much more of the same) certainly constitute a very harsh indictment of infant baptism *as it was customarily interpreted*. Nevertheless, in *Postscript*, S.K. did not call for the abolition of infant baptism—although he did have difficulty in justifying its retention. Yet to that end he presented three arguments:[13] (1) Infant baptism is defensible as "an anticipation of the possibility" that the child someday will become a Christian. But S.K. would have had to admit that the anticipation is only of a "possibility"—sheer possibility. According to S.K.'s thought it would be just as "possible" for one who was not baptized as an infant to become a Christian as for one who was. Indeed, the rite of baptism itself (apart from the child's later education) would not even affect the "probability"; it is just as probable that the unbaptized child of *sectarian* parents will become a Christian as that the baptized child of *churchly* parents will. S.K. made no attempt to relate his "anticipation of the possibility" to New Testament teachings regarding baptism; it would be a mistake to try.

(2) Infant baptism is defensible "as an attempt to prevent the dreadful laceration that the parents might have their blessedness attached to one thing, and the children not to the same." But this is about the most unKierkegaardian thing S.K. ever wrote. S.K. knew and stressed that the salvation of the Christian is based solely upon his personal appropriation of the Christian faith. The salvation of the infant—which the sectary would insist is nevertheless real—*cannot* be upon this same basis, for babies are incapable of the personal appropriation which is faith. Therefore, what S.K.'s suggestion amounts to is that, for the sake of people's feelings, the church should continue to live out and to symbolize something that is not quite true—and that is not like Søren Kierkegaard.

(3) Infant baptism is superior to adult baptism precisely be-

---

[13] These are given on pp. 340-41 of *Postscript* and then reiterated on pp. 531-32.

cause it is such an impossible symbol of becoming a Christian. S.K. did not word his argument quite this way, but it came to just this. When thoroughly analyzed, the position is seen to be strange indeed: that sacrament or symbol is best which is at the farthest remove from and bears the least possible connection to the inner experience it symbolizes. It must be recalled that *Postscript* comes from the period when S.K. still was promoting the idea of "hidden inwardness," i.e. that true Christianity is an entirely inward process that carries no external indicators whatsoever. Therefore, if one gets his baptism out of the way before it can possibly represent his becoming a Christian, then when he actually does become such he can do so in complete inwardness without the temptation to "sectarian externality" that an outward baptism would present.

Considerable confusion is evident here—which needed to be rejected along with the whole doctrine of hidden inwardness. The observation that adult baptism *can* be "a sectarian externality" signifying an inward reality which *may* not actually be present—this certainly is no argument in favor of infant baptism, which S.K. himself insisted *customarily* signified an inward reality which *could not possibly* be present. Indeed, the only logical conclusion to this hidden-inwardness line of reasoning is not the *retention* of infant baptism but the *elimination* of all baptism, all sacraments, all public worship, all organized religion—any external that implies the presence of Christian faith.

Taken all in all, S.K.'s "defense" of infant baptism sounds very much like that of a thinker who was already far gone into sectarianism but fighting desperately to resist his fate. Yet even if this defense were accepted uncritically and as fully valid, still the major thrust of S.K.'s discussion was expressed in some very sectarian-sounding statements made years after the *Postscript* struggle:

"The notion of being a Christian because one is born of

Christian parents is the fundamental delusion from which a multitude of others stem."[14]

"The truth is, one cannot become a Christian as a child; that is just as impossible as for a child to beget children. Becoming a Christian presupposes (according to the New Testament) being fully a man, what one might call in a physical sense maturity of manhood—in order then to become a Christian by breaking with everything to which one naturally clings. Becoming a Christian presupposes (according to the New Testament) a personal consciousness of sin and of oneself as a sinner."[15]

E. CREEDALISM

If a man is to be a Christian, it is doubtless requisite for him to believe something definite; *but it is just as certainly requisite for him to be* quite definite *that "he" believes. In the same degree that thou dost direct attention exclusively to the definite things a man must believe, in that same degree dost thou get away from faith.*[1]

Neither S.K. nor the eighteenth century Brethren spoke at any length concerning their opinions of creeds; yet at this point occurs the most impressive instance of correspondence to be found in our entire study.

It is well established that the Brethren absolutely refused to subscribe to any creed or to formulate anything like a formal confession of faith. The historian Morgan Edwards at-

---

[14] *The Book on Adler*, p. 182, note.

[15] *Attack upon "Christendom,"* p. 212. Cf. *Smith Journals*, XI² A 81 (1854).

---

[1] "He Is Believed On in the World" (Pt. III, Discourse 7) in *Christian Discourses*, p. 248. S.K. was not here addressing himself to the matter of creeds, but the anti-creedal implications are inescapable.

tested to this fact,[2] and another contemporary historian, Robert Proud, said: "When [the Brethren] are asked about the articles of their faith, they say they know of no others but what are contained in this book [i.e. the New Testament]; and therefore can give none."[3]

Brethren writings from the eighteenth century include no specific discussion of the matter, although from hints, from later teachings, and from a knowledge of the ideological context, it is easy to reconstruct what the original position must have been. It was not the *content* of the classical creeds that bothered the Brethren; their faith was orthodox (or better, sufficiently orthodox that the creedal content offered no difficulty). And in any case, heterodox inclinations would not have prevented them from formulating confessions of their own. Rather, their objections concerned the implications that follow from the very form and character of creeds per se.

In the first place, affirmation of a creed tends to become a substitute for true inwardness, tends to distort faith from existential venture into mere intellectual cognition, tends to undercut the importance of obedience and fruitbearing. As stated in an Annual Meeting minute of 1789: "[We] do not spare any labor and toil to convince [the children of the members] by our teaching and life, not after the manner which is almost too common nowadays, where the young are made to learn something by heart, and then to rehearse it in a light, thoughtless manner, and then are permitted to go on in life as thoughtless as before—but [we desire] that they may give themselves up to God in an earnest life."[4]

Most of what S.K. had to say about creeds relates at this point: "The objective faith, what does that mean? It means

---

[2] See Edwards' statement quoted above, p. 90.

[3] Robert Proud, *History of Pennsylvania* . . . [written 1776-80] (Philadelphia: 1798), Vol. II, Pt. IV, p. 345, quoted in Brumbaugh, *op.cit.*, p. 524.

[4] *Annual Meeting Minutes*, 1789, art. 2, p. 13.

a sum of doctrinal propositions. But suppose Christianity were nothing of the kind; suppose on the contrary it were inwardness."[5] And a few pages later he stated: "To know a confession of faith by rote is paganism, because Christianity is inwardness."[6] It is interesting to note, too, that in all of his voluminous writings S.K. made very few references to any of the creeds, confessions, or symbols, and seems deliberately to have avoided the use of creedal language and terminology.

In the second place, the Brethren also opposed creeds as being a threat to the primacy of scripture as the sole rule of faith and practice. They saw the creeds as later, purely human inventions, the work of a tradition which threatens to impinge upon the biblical revelation. Thus Mack Senior, although not discussing creeds as such, could say: "How wretched it is to appeal to testimonies of men and to look to men who are considered holy and wise, so that one is led to think or say: 'Truly, if they taught in this way and believed according to the Scriptures, we shall believe it also!' "[7] S.K. said almost the same thing:

"Yet, from a Christian standpoint, this talk about our fathers' faith is a misunderstanding, at all times a misunderstanding: for this can never be described as something decisive. For the Christian, the only thing that matters is the New Testament, with which every generation has to begin. And the confusing factor, which has produced 'Christendom' and led Christianity back to Judaism, is that in the course of time each generation, instead of beginning with the New Testament, has begun with 'our fathers' faith,' with holding fast to our fathers' faith. Always this knavery of bringing in history and the category of the human race instead of ideality and the single person, which is the Christian category."[8]

[5] *Postscript*, p. 193. The fact that Climacus is the author presents no problem here.

[6] *Ibid.*, p. 201; cf. pp. 41-42. Cf. *Smith Journals*, XI[2] A 172 (1854).

[7] Mack Senior, *Rights and Ordinances*, in Durnbaugh, *Origins*, p. 396.

[8] *Smith Journals*, XI[1] A 392 (1854).

A third, and very deep, objection of the Brethren was the fact that creeds and creedal definitions represent the attempt to stop theological and exegetical development at a given stage, to crystallize the faith into a fixed and unchanging system fastened into place with precise and formal statements. This, in Brethren eyes, was to betray the living character of revelation, to deny the teaching work of the Holy Spirit, to presume a finality of human understanding that is not and cannot be the case. The pages that follow will document the belief both of the Brethren and of S.K. in this regard.

But the accidental element that makes our Kierkegaard-Brethren comparison so intriguing at this point is the fact that S.K. was aware of Brethren non-creedalism and approved it. Although it is highly improbable that S.K. would have so much as heard about the little Dunker sect on the Pennsylvania frontier, the improbable did happen. S.K. did not hear much, but on the strength of a very slight notice he gained a deep insight into the essential nature of Brethrenism. And what he did see, he highly approved.

The story is this. In 1851, S.K. read Benjamin Franklin's *Leben und Schriften*, a German translation of Franklin's works done by one Binzer. A whole series of S.K.'s journal entries are comments upon that book. But in Franklin's *Autobiography*, S.K. came across this passage:

"These embarrassments that the Quakers suffered from having established and published it as one of their principles, that no kind of war was lawful, and which, being once published, they could not, afterwards, however they might change their minds, easily get rid of, reminds me of what I think a more prudent conduct in another sect among us, that of the Dunkers. I was acquainted with one of its founders, Michael Welfare, soon after it appeared. He complained to me that they were viciously calumniated by the zealots of other persuasions, and charged with abominable principles and practices, to which they were utter strangers. I told him this had always been the case with new sects, and that to put a stop to

such abuse, I imagined it might be well to publish the articles
of their belief, and the rules of their discipline. He said it had
been proposed among them, but not agreed to, for this reason:
'When we were first drawn together as a society,' says he, 'it
had pleased God to enlighten our minds so far as to see that
some things, which we once esteemed truths, were errors; and
others, which we had esteemed errors, were real truths. From
time to time He has been pleased to afford us further light,
and our principles have been improving, and our errors di-
minishing. Now we are not sure that we are arrived at the
end of this progression, and at the perfection of spiritual or
theological knowledge; and we fear that, if we should once
print our confession of faith, we should feel ourselves as if
bound and confined by it, and perhaps be unwilling to receive
further improvement, and our successors still more so, as con-
ceiving what we their elders and founders had done, to be
something sacred, never to be departed from.'

"This modesty in a sect is perhaps a singular instance in the
history of mankind, every other sect supposing itself in possession of all truth, and that those who differ are so far in the
wrong; like a man traveling in foggy weather, those at some
distance before him on the road he sees wrapped up in the fog,
as well as those behind him, and also the people in the fields
on each side, but near him all appears clear, though in truth
he is as much in the fog as any of them."[9]

[9] *Benjamin Franklin's Autobiography*, ed. Samuel Thurber (New
York: Allyn and Bacon, 1929), pp. 144-45.
    Franklin was confused on one point. Michael Welfare (the German
name was "Wohlfahrt") was a monastic from the Ephrata Cloisters
and not properly a Dunker. However, although on some points it
would be highly misleading to identify the two groups, on the point
of non-creedalism no damage is done; the Brethren and the Beisselites
were of one mind. The outstanding example of Wohlfahrt's principle
in practice among the Brethren is Mack Junior's open letter on feetwashing (above, pp. 84ff.).
    The above statement is probably the only kind thing Franklin ever
said about the Brethren. As a printer, Sauer Senior was a competitor

Upon reading this passage, S.K. wrote the following entry in his journal: "Franklin (in his *Leben und Schriften* v. Binzer, 2nd vol.) mentions a sect, the Dunkers, who would not compose a written creed—so as not to hinder themselves in free development. Franklin finds this very excellent, since otherwise sectaries distinguish themselves simply by matching their opponents. Now, 'the latest' can be true enough; but nevertheless, these sectaries are by this token also again *expediti*.[10] This is inexplicably the case—however they may have succeeded on that score in forming a sect."[11]

This statement is so compact as to be almost cryptic, but actually, S.K. saw much deeper into Brethrenism than did the reporter upon whom he depended for his information. In the first place, we already have seen that to be Christian *expediti* marks a very high ideal in S.K.'s thought, the same thing, really, as being a "caravan" church. His remark about sectaries simply matching their opponents is a report of Franklin's opinion and not necessarily an expression of his own. The next clause—"Now, 'the latest' can be true enough"—is where S.K. rejected and went beyond Franklin's interpretation. He had read enough of Franklin to identify him correctly as a free-thinking child of the Enlightenment who, although he might welcome Christian morality and ethics, would pride himself on his rational and "scientific" modernity and thus have little use for anything relating to dogma, tradition, and orthodoxy. Thus the aspect of non-creedalism that appealed

---

of Franklin's—a serious enough competitor that Franklin tried to force him out of business by buying up all available ink supplies. Sauer circumvented him by making his own ink. Also, at a later time, Franklin published a tract demolishing the German sectaries for their nonresistant lack of cooperation in the Indian wars.

[10] Regarding this term, see above, the note on p. 301.

[11] *Papirer*, X⁴ A 73 (1851) [my trans.—V.E.]. A somewhat fuller account than is given here, describing how I came to make this find, etc., is my article "Kierkegaard Knew the Brethren!—Sort of," *Brethren Life and Thought*, VIII (Winter 1963), 57-60.

to Franklin, S.K. saw, was the freedom to adopt current modes of thought, to keep one's religion in pace with the world. But of course, this decidedly was not the orientation of either S.K. or the Brethren; and S.K. was able to recognize a kindred spirit—in spite of Franklin's non-sectarian exegesis.

Thus S.K.'s phrase must be taken to mean, "Now I suppose it is possible—although not very probable—that Franklin's implicit assumption about modern thinking being the truest could, at least occasionally, hit the mark. The possibility dare not be ruled out, although certainly the principle itself is a very unreliable one. *But nevertheless,* these Dunkers are not the modish friends of fashion, as Franklin would have it; they are *expediti,* freeing themselves from creeds not in order to follow the world but to follow in obedience the teachings of their Lord and Master and the leading of the Holy Spirit." What little S.K. did know of Brethren sectarianism, he seems to have seen as reflecting his own faith.

F. SACRAMENTALISM

It is because of the place we have assigned to the sacraments, and the use we have made of them, that Christianity has been reduced to Judaism. And it is very true—probably the truest statement about Christendom—that, as Pascal says, it is a union of people who, by means of the sacraments, excuse themselves from their duty to love God.[1]

Christendom's Christianity takes Christianity merely as a gift. That is why it makes so much ado about the sacraments (in the superstitious sense), and pretends not to know that the sacrament carries an obligation.[2]

[1] *Papirer,* XI¹ A 556 (1854), quoted in Dupre, *op.cit.,* pp. 106-07.
[2] *Smith Journals,* XI² A 387 (1854).

To demonstrate that S.K.'s sacramental theory was sectarian rather than churchly in viewpoint involves something of a problem in that the churchly tradition itself shows so much divergency on this point. Thus, although there is no difficulty whatever in distinguishing between the sacramental thought of sectarianism and Lutheranism, it is very difficult to establish any significant difference between that of sectarianism and Calvinism. However, because S.K. came out of a *Lutheran* background, it is of some value to our study to see just how far from *his* churchly tradition he had come.

Neither S.K. nor the Brethren gave any detailed attention to sacramental theory, yet some aspects of their thought are plain. Both treasured the sacraments as a vital and valuable part of the Christian faith. To a large degree, the very separation of the Brethren sect from out of the Radical Pietist milieu was motivated by the desire to regain and reestablish the sacraments which Radical Pietism had dropped. And the "filling out" of the Lord's Supper, making it a re-enactment of the upper room occasion by putting the eucharist into the context of a full evening's service with a period of self-examination, the feetwashing, and the agape meal—this certainly points toward a high evaluation of the sacraments.

Likewise with S.K.: his works include fifteen separate discourses that are designated as meditations relating to the communion and/or the service of confession that accompanied it. Nowhere does S.K. say anything that could be interpreted as derogatory of the sacraments themselves, although—as in the epigraph above—he could be very harsh on the church for the way it used (i.e. misused) them.

Thus, although in both the Brethren and S.K. we find a high respect for the sacraments per se (which is not unsectarian), we also find a highly anti-sacramental interpretation (which is notably sectarian). Regarding baptism, we already have seen that the Brethren explicitly rejected anything suggestive of baptismal regeneration or the spiritual efficacy of the water. They understood baptism, rather, as being primarily a work of obedience, an external, human sign witnessing to an inner operation of the Spirit. And although eighteenth century writings do not treat the issue, all the evidence suggests that the Brethren interpretation of the eucharist must have followed the same pattern. The Brethren impulse to drop the term "sacrament" and refer to these signs as "ordinances" is an accurate reflection of the ideological shift involved.

As to S.K., the evidence is anything but voluminous, but it points to the fact that he was anti-sacramental in the same sense that the Brethren were. Indeed, Louis Dupre says, "It should be obvious that sacraments in the Catholic, or even in the orthodox Lutheran, sense of the word are incompatible with Kierkegaard's theory."[3] And S.K. did, in fact, explicitly renounce the orthodox Lutheran concept: "People have put these words (John 6:35ff.) in conjunction with the Lord's Supper, they have developed a doctrine of the ubiquity of Christ's body, and with that they have in Christendom a fantastic notion of Christ."[4]

However, S.K.'s most significant statement was a positive one. It is nothing more than a hint, but a hint that gets to the heart of the matter: "Hence the Lord's Supper is called Communion with Him; it is not merely in remembrance of Him, not merely a pledge that thou hast communion with Him, but it is the communion, the communion which thou shalt endeavour to maintain in thy daily life by more and more living thyself out of thyself and living thyself into Him."[5] The sacraments involve (or are intended to involve) an absolutely real communion with God. In this sense the Kierkegaard-sectarian view is truly a high one; and given the powerful sectarian stress on devotional immediacy, the oft-repeated churchly charge that the sectaries reduced the sacraments to "mere memorials" is patently not the case.

---

[3] Dupre, *op.cit.*, p. 106.

[4] *Training in Christianity* (Pt. II), p. 101.

[5] "Love Shall Hide the Multitude of Sins" in *For Self-Examination*, pp. 24-25.

But the sense in which S.K. was truly anti-sacramental shows up in his identification of the communion of the altar with "the communion which thou shalt endeavour to maintain in thy daily life." In short, there is ultimately but one mode of man's relationship to God: *den Enkelte* existing before God in the venture of faith. The so-called sacraments are instruments divinely instituted and designed to intensify and focus this one relationship which must constantly constitute and control the Christian life. In the taking of the sacraments, then, the experience of the communicant may be different in degree but not in kind from what it is normally. And thus would seem to be excluded the special sacramental relationship of Christ's corporeal body being received orally by anyone who partakes. This is the basic distinction between churchly "sacraments" and sectarian "ordinances"; S.K. stood on the sectarian side.

G. RELIGIONLESSNESS

The law for God's nearness and farness is . . . that the more the phenomenon, the appearance, expresses that God cannot possibly be there, the nearer he is. And inversely, the more the phenomenon, the appearance, expresses that God is quite near, the more distant he is.[1]

Up to this point we have been insistent that first and foremost S.K. was a *religious* thinker. Now, without going back on what has been said, we want to be equally insistent that "religious thinker" is about the worst possible choice of label for S.K., seeing that one of the most fundamental characteristics of his thought is precisely its "religionlessness."

What has happened is that the word "religion" has switched

[1] *Smith Journals*, XI[2] A 51 (1854).

meanings on us. We had to call S.K.'s thought "religious" in order to distinguish it from "theological"—the point being that his interest almost exclusively was to help men into a personal, existential relationship to God rather than simply give intellectual formulation to the Christian faith. But as soon as we understand "religion" in the negative sense in which Barth and Bonhoeffer have forced it into our vocabulary, then S.K. must be seen as joining them—better, as being way ahead of them (and our current "radical theologians" so-called)—in religionlessness.

Although S.K. did not use the term "religionlessness," a moment's thought will make it evident that what we have seen S.K. protesting in this chapter on "the church well lost" is precisely what Bonhoeffer and company signify by "religion." "Religion," now, denotes any and all thought and practice which implies that man has some sort of control over God's end of his God-relationship, that he can dictate the terms of that relationship, that he has the wherewithal to turn God on and off or channel God's grace to suit his own convenience.

But S.K. did not stop with what we have examined thus far, simply a protest against various manifestations of religiousness; he saw to the heart of the basic principle involved. Indeed, we submit that he saw more clearly than Bonhoeffer, even though it is Bonhoeffer rather than S.K. who came up with the term "religionlessness" and so launched a movement. It is in a group of journal entries (which clearly hang together as a series) that S.K. presented his thought; these are found in the *Smith Journals*, XI^2 A 50-56 (1854).

Bonhoeffer based his idea of religionlessness upon (or at least tied it to) the very problematical thesis that modern man somehow has "come of age"—which also has the effect of making it merely a twentieth century phase of the gospel. S.K., on the other hand, saw religionlessness as being the necessary implication of God's sovereignty (or his "majesty," to use the term he preferred). He explicates it, then, as a basic theme of the biblical revelation, without regard to what may or may not be the sensibilities of contemporary man. (Also, if S.K. is right, the latest fillip of pronouncing God dead is seen to be, not the zenith of religionlessness, but just the opposite, the height of religious presumption which leaves man completely and absolutely in control of whatever of the Christian faith is left.)

As we have noted, for S.K., even the human *person* is, above all, a free and integral agent. How much more is it the case, then, that God, the primordial *Person*, is—whatever else may be said of him—"a free spirit"? While it is true that God (particularly as he is seen in Jesus Christ) in love and service has given himself for man to the uttermost, this is not to say that he has given himself over to man's *control*. If we may put it thus: God is servant of all but lackey of none. And man's religious effort at domesticating God then takes on the aspect of small children designing a birdhouse which, *to their minds,* any bird would fall over himself to live in. But birds, thank God, still retain enough independent judgment not to let themselves be suckered into living as children think birds ought to live; and God, thank God, is at least as bright as the birds he created. God, therefore, is not about to let himself be geared into a bunch of "holy visibilities" which would have the effect of man's putting Him in His place.

Now it becomes clear why S.K.—and the sectaries—were so opposed to the "commissary concept" of the church; it is essentially a "religious" view. The church is a *holy* institution, authorized by a *holy* book, housed in *holy* buildings, managed by a *holy* officialdom as they dispense the commodities of *holy* sacrament and *holy* beliefs—and the whole holy bit is under human control. And this is why S.K. took bead on the concepts of (1) the church as an *institution* [pp. 288ff. above]; (2) the Bible as a legal franchise: "It is very remarkable how ingenious, how inventive, how sophistical, how persevering in

learned investigations certain men may be, merely to get a
Bible text to appeal to. On the other hand, they do not seem to
observe that this precisely is to make a fool of God, to treat
him as a poor devil who has been foolish enough to commit
something to writing and now must put up with what the
lawyers will make of it."[2] (3) church buildings as houses of
God: "[Christendom] plays at Christianity ... in theaters built
for the purpose, called houses of God—very apt, if it is the
same sense as one defines a storm-house as a house intended
to keep storms out. No, God does not need a house—the world
of reality is what he wishes to be with."[3] (4) the clergy as
God's official representatives [pp. 306ff. above]; (5) the sacraments as carrying intrinsic spiritual benefit and power
[pp. 309ff. and 325ff. above]; and (6) the creeds as guarantees
of correct belief [pp. 319ff. above].

And the basic principle of religionlessness which stands behind these separate protests S.K. put in these words:

"God is Spirit. As Spirit God is related *paradoxically* to
appearance (phenomenon), but paradoxically he can in turn
come so near to reality that he is right in the midst of it, in
the midst of the streets of Jerusalem. . . .

"If I were to suggest a feeble analogy, I should say that at
certain times in human history, when everything was in confusion, there have arisen rulers who have ruled, if I may say
so, in shirt-sleeves. This is a much higher majesty than that of
an emperor who is directly recognizable: here is something
paradoxical, that the rulers are recognized because they go
about in their shirt-sleeves. It follows from this—and we
should not omit it—that if one imagined such a ruler later
getting established as an emperor who was directly recognizable as such, then one should have to laugh (the comical nature of direct recognizability) if he thought he had become
something more, for in fact he had become something less.

[2] *Postscript*, p. 534.
[3] *Smith Journals*, XI[2] A 50 (1854).

"Therefore God can be related only paradoxically to appearance, but then he also comes so near that he can stand in the midst of reality before our very noses. . . .

"*The more the phenomenon, the appearance, expresses that God cannot possibly be there, the nearer he is.* So in Christ. And just at the moment when the appearance expressed that not only was it impossible that this man should be the God-man—no, when the appearance expressed that men even denied that he was a man (see, what a man!), at that moment God's reality was the nearest it has ever been. . . .

"*The law for God's farness* (and this is the history of Christianity) is therefore that everything that strengthens the appearance makes God distant. At the time when there were no churches, but the handful of Christians gathered as refugees and persecuted people in catacombs, God was nearer to reality. Then came churches, so many churches, such large and splendid churches—and to the same degree God is made distant. For God's nearness is related inversely to the appearance, and this increase (churches, many churches, splendid churches) is an increase in appearance. When Christianity was not a doctrine, when it was a few poor propositions, but these were expressed in life, then God was nearer to reality than when Christianity became a doctrine. And with each increase and embellishment, etc., of doctrine, God removes himself the more. For doctrine and its spread mean an increase in the direction of appearance, and God is related inversely to appearance. When there were no priests, but the Christians were all brothers, then God was nearer to reality than when there were priests, many priests, a powerful priesthood. For priests are an increase in the direction of appearance, and God is related inversely to the phenomenon. . . .

"And this is the history of Christendom: by strengthening the appearance it puts a distance between itself and God, or else (as in certain circumstances one speaks of removing someone in a refined manner) the history of Christendom consists of removing God more and more, in a refined manner, by building churches and splendid buildings, by elaborating monstrous edifices of doctrine, along with an endless horde of priests.

"So Christendom practically means the greatest possible distance from God."[4]

Here is a religionlessness more radical than that of Bonhoeffer, both in its basic dynamic and in the thoroughness and consistency of its application (Bonhoeffer somehow managed to preach religionlessness without its affecting his rather churchly view of the church, his sacramentalism, his support of infant baptism, etc.). And here, note well, is not a religionlessness sponsored by twentieth century man in the interests of winning his own freedom (whether from old and outmoded concepts of God or from any and all concepts of God) but a religionlessness sponsored from eternity by God himself in the interests of God's preserving his own independence so that he is free to be *for man* in his own way, at the time and place of his own choosing.

And right here S.K. has stated the fundamental motif of sectarianism more precisely than it ever has been stated before, because, in essence, classic Protestant sectarianism is nothing more nor less than the attempt to recapture the New Testament ideal of religionless Christianity.

[4] *Smith Journals*, XI² A 51 (1854).

CHAPTER XI

THE CHURCH WELL LOVED

This chapter completes the five dealing with S.K. and sociality; and the pattern developed in Chapter VII shows up nowhere more clearly than here. We have examined the Crowd-World that S.K. renounced, the Neighbor-World he accepted and loved, the Crowd-Church he attacked—and now comes the keystone of the entire structure. It is at this point that the whole must tie together—or else the whole falls apart.

The problem—the terms of which S.K. already has set and to which he must give answer—can be put rather concisely. S.K. must devise (or better, describe) a religious (yet religionless) sociality, i.e. a church, a grouping of men associated with one another for the sake of their relationship to God. His social concept will need to be closely related to his concept of *den Enkelte*, because it is plain that for S.K. a man cannot be related to God except as *den Enkelte*. Likewise, this sociality must studiously avoid each and every aspect of crowd-mentality which S.K. attacked so vigorously in the Establishment, for this of course represents a direct threat to *den Enkelte*. In short, S.K. must provide a concept of sociality that is real and meaningful and yet one that, rather than compromising his concept of *den Enkelte*, can stand in a true dialectic relationship to it. Thus the crux of the problem of sociality necessarily falls here, within the religious sphere, rather than earlier, for no other reason than that *den Enkelte* itself is essentially a religious concept.

This was S.K.'s problem; and many commentators feel that it was precisely this problem that he failed to answer (or to answer adequately). The defect—if actual—would be a serious one, for then S.K.'s concept of *den Enkelte* would lead to a churchless atomism, an alternative that is as little acceptable to the sectaries as to the "church"men. However, we intend to show that there was no defect in the *quality* of S.K.'s answer. Indeed, we will maintain that he offered as profound an analysis concerning the nature of the sectarian church (the *Gemeinde*) as has ever been made and that this constitutes one of the most valuable contributions of Kierkegaardian thought.[1] The defect lies solely in the fact that S.K. hid his light under a bushel (as he did regarding the political relevancy of nonresistance), in this case confining the crucial statements to a few hitherto untranslated entries in the journals and dropping only some broad hints in the published works themselves.

A. GEMEINDE / MENIGHED / COMMUNITY

Religiously *speaking, there is no such thing as a public, but only individuals. . . . And insofar as there is, in a religious sense such a thing as a "congregation," this is a concept which does not conflict with "the individual," and which is by no means to be confounded with what may have* political *importance: the public, the crowd, the numerical, etc.*[2]

[1] The sociologist Ferdinand Tönnies (*Gemeinschaft und Gesellschaft,* 1887) is usually credited with having formulated the classic typology of human sociality. He developed his theory at much greater length and applied it much more broadly, but S.K. preceded him in point of time; and a strong case could be made that, aided by his concept of *den Enkelte*, S.K. drew the distinction even more fundamentally and more seminally than did Tönnies.

[2] "The Accounting" (1849) in *Point of View*, p. 149 (with the footnote accompanying).

Because sectarianism lays great stress upon the individual believer, and because it is so deeply critical of the churchly concept of corporation, or institution, the temptation might be to
epitomize sectarianism simply as individualistic Christianity
and churchism as social Christianity. But such a distinction
falls far wide of the mark, for it overlooks the fact that a hallmark of the sects is their sense of *Gemeinschaft*. Although it
is very true that sectarianism is insistent *against* one sort of
sociality, this truth always must be supplemented by the recognition that sectaries are equally insistent *in favor of* another
sort of sociality.

The terms that denote the two types are "church" (the rejected sociality) and *Gemeinde* (the approved sociality). We
should pause to clarify this terminology. *Gemeinde* (German), *Menighed* (Danish), and "community" (English)
would seem to be precise equivalents in the three languages.
Each is constructed over the root that means "common" and
points toward the definition: "a group of persons drawn together on the basis of something they have in *common*." It
follows that the quality of *Gemeinschaft* will be in proportion
to the extensiveness, intensiveness, and evaluation of the common factor that constitutes the group. Thus a community
based solely on the geographical proximity of its residents is
not likely to be very strong in *Gemeinschaft*; one based upon
a common concern for the public school, such as a PTA, gives
promise of being somewhat stronger; etc. The *Gemeinde* that
should display the most profound *Gemeinschaft* is that based
upon the commonality of a redemptive relationship to God in
Jesus Christ, i.e. the Christian church. Therefore, although
etymologically speaking *Gemeinde* and *Gemeinschaft* have
no necessary religious connotations, we will proceed to use
them in a highly religious sense.

Ultimately, Christian *Gemeinschaft* amounts to "the love of
the brethren," the love of the brethren for one another, which
is consequent upon God's love for them and upon the mutual

love they hold for Him. Obviously, true *Gemeinschaft* necessarily involves the intimate, face-to-face relationships of comparatively small groups sharing "life together"; the mere
recitation of a common creed or attendance at a common service of worship can hardly represent *Gemeinschaft* at its deepest
level. By its very nature *Gemeinschaft* cannot be a purely formal concept; it must exist as an existential reality or not at all.

Early Brethren literature is dominated by the theme; clearly,
it was not by accident that the Brethren came to be identified
as "the Brethren." For them, the element that made the church
the church was precisely *Gemeinschaft* in Christ—not the
possession of true doctrine and efficacious sacraments. Of
course, both doctrine and sacraments play their roles in creating *Gemeinschaft*, but until they do eventuate in *Gemeinschaft* they have failed to perform one of their major functions. Indeed, it is worthwhile to note that, by filling out the
Lord's Supper with the feetwashing and the agape meal, the
Brethren explicitly were giving symbolic expression to the fact
that true communion with Christ in his body *must* involve
and produce *Gemeinschaft* with the brethren, a symbolism
that is not nearly as clear when the eucharist is left to stand
alone.

Although it will become plain that the Brethren and S.K.
held a common view of the *gemeinschaftlich* nature of the
church, their points of departure are different enough to add
real interest. The Brethren gave most attention to the character of *Gemeinschaft*, signalizing the quality of the love that
binds the brethren together, describing the means through
which this love finds expression. S.K. started farther back,
with what might be called the "metaphysics of the *Gemeinde*,"
i.e. an analysis of the basic spiritual economy that brings the
Gemeinde into being and gives it its distinctive character.
S.K.'s work can be of immense value in defining and understanding sectarian ecclesiology.

Rather than attempting a comprehensive survey of eighteenth century Brethren treatments, we will present only three outstanding commentaries on our theme; they communicate the thought and tone that pervade many Brethren writings. The earliest and fullest discussion—a truly notable piece of work for a Brethren author—is an essay (or possibly, sermon) by Michael Frantz, *An die Gemeinde*.[3] What follows is a paraphrased condensation, interspersed with observations and comments:

> Our communion [*Gemeinschaft*] is with God in Christ. We have nothing of our own but inherit all things through him, for all is Christ's and we are his. From God's good gifts we bring forth spiritual fruit. . . . Christ imparts his own nature to us; he knocks at our hearts and would sup with us. O! what a true love feast! Our communion is in suffering; suffering with the Jesus who bears the cross, we die with him, rise with him, and go with him to heaven.

Clearly, *Gemeinschaft* is not essentially the work of man—even of those who make up the *Gemeinde*. It finds its source in the grace of God that comes through Christ, and it is only as men are in fellowship with Him that *Gemeinschaft* is produced among themselves. Also, suffering for Christ and with Christ gives a strong impetus to *Gemeinschaft*.

> The communion of Christians is in eating, drinking, working, reading, speaking, etc.—in all these things being mindful of the Lord. Thus they have fellowship with one another, admonish, edify, and correct one another; together they follow, imitate, and praise God. They assemble in simplicity before their king to glorify him and to learn from his word. They become one heart and soul, because they have only one knowledge and one gospel basis of the truth they understand in common. So they serve one another with the

---

[3] The essay appears in the same volume with his long poem; Michael Frantz, *op.cit.*, pp. 35-46.

gifts they have received, obey one another in the fear of God, and practice humility.

Just as God's will and work affect a man's total life, so *Gemeinschaft* is practiced broadly, touching all aspects of life together; it is not confined to public worship or to one day a week.

Those of the community [*Gemeinde*] are members of one body and one of another; they suffer together and they rejoice together. As do man and wife, so do the children of God become one flesh; they are like him in love, purity, etc. For if their communion is with God, it cannot be with darkness. With his good gifts God also gives Christian virtues; and in the community men partake of God's very nature and thus show forth his virtues.

Gemeinschaft produces the most profound sort of unity between man and God and between man and man. And because of God's participation, this *Gemeinschaft* will always have a very high moral and ethical quality. It will also show the more active character of *works* of love:

True members of the community love their enemies, feed the hungry, etc. "Thine" and "mine" are no longer heard; one holds his goods to use in behalf of the neighbor (both the one within the community and the one outside). Everything he owns he holds simply as a trustee for the community; this is what it means to "lay it at the Apostles's feet" and follow the practice of the Book of Acts.[4] One will give without stint as long as he can be of help; for God demands back from us what he has given to us through Christ—and that with interest—although always out of love and not through compulsion.

[4] At this point I have transposed some of Frantz's material to give it a more logical progression—V.E.

It is clear that *Gemeinschaft* and neighbor love are closely related themes. And Frantz concluded with these words: "The community [*Gemeinde*] is from God; and whatever its accomplishments, God is to be thanked for them. Indeed, the unity of the one community is its common source in and common loyalty to God."

A second portrayal of Brethren *Gemeinschaft*—this more in the character of a demonstration than a disquisition—has to do with the Hummer incident. Catharine Hummer was a young woman, the daughter of one of the ministers of the congregation at White Oak. In 1762 she developed a propensity for ecstatic trances in which she enjoyed visions. These immediately made her a sensation—and also a focus of strong contention throughout the brotherhood. Her father and others accepted and promoted the visions as divine communications; many condemned them as diabolical.[5] The matter became an issue of dispute before the Annual Meeting of 1763, but the conference refused to rule on the visions either one way or the other. The wording of the minute makes it plain that the Brethren saw *Gemeinschaft* as taking precedence over all other considerations, saw it, indeed, as the only basis for any ultimate resolution of the problem:

"If there are on both sides conviction and acknowledgment, then we advise out of brotherly love, that on both sides all judgments and harsh expressions might be entirely laid down, though we have not the same opinion of that noted (singular) occurrence, so that those who think well of it, should not judge those who are of the contrary opinion, and those who do not esteem it, should not despise those who expect to derive some use and benefit from it.

"For the rest, we advise you, beloved brethren, receive one another as Christ has received you, and pardon one another

---

[5] For two complementary accounts, see Brumbaugh, *op.cit.*, pp. 520-23, and Mallott, *op.cit.*, pp. 76-77. Cf. Catharine Hummer's letter to Mack Junior in Holsinger, *op.cit.*, pp. 779ff.

as Christ has pardoned us also, and let us everywhere consider that all disputing, judging, and despising should be entirely laid aside, and thus remain, that everyone leave to the other his own opinion, in the fear of the Lord, and altogether for conscience's sake. . . . If now one or the other should think we have not sufficiently judged the occurrence, let him consider, that we cannot see the least cause for a separation for conscience's sake. Hence, we have felt constrained not to criticize or judge this (strange) affair, but rather to advise everyone to a godly impartiality and patience."[6]

There is much about this statement that is reminiscent of the "writ of censure" which the Germantown brethren did *not* serve on Sauer Junior,[7] and together they underline an important feature of *Gemeinschaft*. *Gemeinschaft* does presuppose an openness toward God and a love toward the brethren, but it does not demand that the brethren possess a uniformity in their apprehension of God—whether affecting doctrine, gifts, church order, or whatever. Indeed, the surest way to kill the unity of *Gemeinschaft* is to enforce uniformity. *Gemeinschaft* can exist only as *den Enkelte* is left free in conscience to find God's leading *for him* and thus make his own peculiar contribution to the *Gemeinde*. The *Gemeinde* will step in to discipline or to ban only when it has reason to believe that the individual has deserted his sincerity toward God and/or his love of the brethren.

This line of thought leads directly to the third and undoubtedly greatest portrayal of Brethren *Gemeinschaft*, namely Mack Junior's open letter on feetwashing which was examined earlier.[8] We will not review that document except to recall that it catches up much of the thought presented above and then goes on to suggest a *"gemeinschaftlich* epistemology"*: "Above all, preserve love, for then we shall preserve

[6] A minute dated May 28, 1763, recorded in Kurtz, *op.cit.*, pp. 135-37.
[7] See above, pp. 190f.
[8] See above, pp. 83ff.

light." A *Gemeinde* is the most effective receptor for divine truth and leading; and the religious insight received will be complete and true only so long as it is held and practiced within a setting of *Gemeinschaft*.

It must be admitted from the outset that S.K. had not the "feel" for *Gemeinschaft* that the early Brethren did; he showed no similar appreciation of its power, its depth, its efficacy as a way to truth. S.K. *saw* (intellectually) the *Gemeinde* as a possibility, indeed, as the only proper alternative for a Christian church, but he did not *know* (existentially) *Gemeinschaft*. However, it is not difficult to explain either S.K.'s deficiency of feeling or the fact that he "hid" the insight he did have.

(1) S.K. simply had neither the temperament nor the opportunity to learn true *Gemeinschaft*; everything was against him on this score. Indeed, it is amazing that he saw as far as he did; a melancholy genius with jammed-lock inwardness is not the most promising material for the practice of community.

(2) S.K. himself suggested another consideration. He was not at the place on the sectarian cycle where a strong emphasis on the *Gemeinde* would have been appropriate. His job—his proper job—was "to oppose a given factor wrongly promulgated"[9]; first the *Attack*, and then (if "then" had ever come) might be the right time to talk about a *Gemeinde*.

(3) A final consideration is important although not readily apparent. S.K. was hampered in developing his concept of *Menighed* (*Gemeinde*) simply because N. F. S. Grundtvig already had appropriated the term and ruined it. Grundtvig made the word the touchstone of his movement, although using it to denote only a sentimentalized, nationalized, enculturated concept which did not mark any real move out of churchism at all. But as a consequence, one finds in S.K. such

[9] "Regarding the 'Two Notes,'" a postscript dated March 1855, only a few months preceding his death, in *Point of View*, pp. 137-38.

statements as the following: "Such a conception as that of 'the congregation' [*Menigheden*], about which people in these days especially have been so busy, is really, as applied to this life, an impatient anticipation of eternity. . . . 'The congregation' therefore belongs properly to eternity; 'the congregation' is at rest what 'the individual' is in unrest. But this life is precisely the time of testing, the time of unrest, hence 'the congregation' has not its abiding place in time but only in eternity."[10]

The fact that S.K. here put *Menighed* into diametric opposition to *den Enkelte*, whereas in his crucial statements he put them into correlation, and that he made *Menighed* the equivalent of the "triumphant church," the Establishment, precisely that which is not "caravan"—all this clearly indicates that S.K. here was using *Menighed* only in Grundtvig's sense and entirely counter to his own. This, of course, makes confusion all but inevitable and would have frustrated any effort S.K. might have made to communicate his own insights about the *Gemeinde*.

So much as apology for the fact that S.K.'s treatment of *Gemeinschaft* was not more extensive; we proceed to the demonstration of our thesis that his treatment was very intensive. Amazingly early in S.K.'s writings there appeared notices indicative of his feeling of a need for a doctrine of *Gemeinschaft* and a reaching after the same; for example: "How dreadful it is when everything historical vanishes before a diseased probing of one's own miserable history! Who is to show us the middle course between being devoured by one's own reflection, as though one were the only man who ever had existed or ever would exist, and—seeking a worthless consolation in the *commune naufragium* of mankind? That is really what the doctrine of an *ecclesia* should do."[11] Although statements

---

[10] "Lifted Up On High . . ." (Pt. III, Reflection 5) in *Training in Christianity*, p. 217.
[11] *Dru Journals*, 163 (1837); cf. 85 (1836) and 192 (1838).

such as this by no means constitute a full-fledged doctrine, they do reflect both a dissatisfaction with the usual crowd-institutions and the hint that there must be something better. S.K. was getting the problem formulated even before he opened his authorship in 1843.

But the answer to which S.K. eventually came must itself be read against the background of his understanding of the role that *Gemeinschaft* (in the general sense of the term) plays in the very constitution and life of mankind:

"All through the ages everyone who has thought deeply over the nature of man has recognized in him this need for community. . . . In the busy, teeming crowd, which as community is both too much and too little, man becomes weary of society, but the cure is not in making the discovery that God's thought [i.e. that Adam needed community] was incorrect. . . . So deeply is this need grounded in the nature of man that since the creation of the first man there has been no change, no new discovery made; this self-same first observation has only been confirmed in various ways, from generation to generation varied in expression, in presentation, in turns of thought. So deeply is this need grounded in the nature of man and so *essentially* does it belong to being a human being that even He who was One with the Father and in the communion of love with the Father and Spirit, He who loved the whole race, our Lord Jesus Christ, even He felt in a human way this need to love and be loved by an individual human being."[12]

This statement, of course, stands in direct contradiction to the understanding of S.K. that many scholars would foster. Granted this was not a major, or even typical, theme with S.K., but it was an authentic one. Any exegesis of *den Enkelte* that would exclude and prohibit the role of *Gemeinschaft* is not true to S.K.; he must have and will have *den Enkelte* in society and in a church.

We come, then, to S.K.'s doctrine of religious *Gemeinschaft*

[12] *Works of Love*, pp. 153-54.

—which is his ecclesiology.[13] The basic and all-controlling principle is that the *Gemeinde* must be something categorically different from a "crowd," which by its very constitution is religiously negative—indeed, religiously prohibitive.[14] The *Gemeinde*, therefore, must be so formed that both in point of order and of value *den Enkelte* takes precedence over the group itself:

"It is not the individual's relationship to the congregation which determines his relationship to God, but his relationship to God which determines his relationship to the congregation. [This sentence recalls much of what was said in the previous chapter regarding the churchly and the sectarian views of the church, baptism, etc.] Ultimately, in addition, there is a supreme relationship in which 'the individual' is absolutely higher than the 'congregation.' . . . [When] a person first of all and qualitatively [is] an 'individual' . . . the concept 'Christian congregation' is secured as qualitatively different from 'public,' 'many,' etc."[15]

Given this as his determinative principle, S.K. could then proceed to explicate *Gemeinschaft*. What follows is his definitive statement on the subject:

[The journal entry bears the title:] The Difference Between "Crowd," "Public"—and "Community" (*Menighed*).

"In 'the public' and the like, the individual is nothing; there is no individual; 'the numerical' is the constitution and law of its genesis, a *generatio aequivoca* [an equivocal beginning]. Detached from 'the public' the individual is nothing, and in the public—more deeply understood—he actually has nothing either.

---

[13] The pages that follow include several rather lengthy passages from S.K.'s journals. They are reproduced *in toto* (or at least, at length), first, because they are crucial statements of a little recognized aspect of S.K.'s thought, and second, because they are not elsewhere available in English translation.

[14] *The Present Age*, pp. 61-63.

[15] *Papirer*, X⁵ B 208, p. 392 (1849), quoted by the translators in a footnote in *Works of Love*, p. 362.

"In community, the individual is; the individual is dialectically decisive as *prius* in order to form community, and in community the qualitative individual is essential and can at any instant become higher than 'the community,' namely, as soon as 'the others' fall away from the idea."

S.K. has here stated the principle that accounts for the characteristic sectarian emphases on the right of conscience, non-creedalism, and anti-authoritarianism in all its aspects. He continues:

"The binding force of community is: that each is an individual—and thus the idea. The public's bond—or rather, its looseness—is: that the numerical is everything. Each individual, in community, guarantees the community; the public is a chimera. The individual, in community, is a microcosm which qualitatively reduplicates the macrocosm; in this respect it is very true, '*unum noris omnes*' [referring to the saying from Terrence, 'To know one is to know all']. In the public, no individual is; the whole is nothing. Here it is impossible to say, '*unum noris omnes*,' for no 'one' is here. A community is certainly more than a sum, but it is in truth a sum of units. The public is nonsense: a sum of negative units, of units which are not units, which become units in the sum, whereas the sum should become sum in the units."[16]

The thought about *den Enkelte* guaranteeing the *Gemeinde* and being "a microcosm which qualitatively reduplicates the macrocosm" gets directly to the heart of the sectarian understanding of the church; and the matter has never been better put. In the sect, ideally any member—and not simply the pope, or a bishop, or a priest, or a clergyman, or a theologian—demonstrates on a small scale within himself *every* power, *every* attribute, *every* grace that the church itself can demonstrate. And within this context, the sectarian teachings regarding such things as free personal decision, inwardness, obedience,

[16] *Papirer*, X² A 390 (1850) [my trans.—V.E.].

devotional immediacy, equality before God, and *Nachfolge* suddenly become obvious: the church can be no more Christian than are the individuals who make it up; the church becomes Christian as those who constitute it become Christian.

S.K. went on to show that it is precisely the stance of contradiction between Christianity and the world, between the *Gemeinde* and the public, that gives Christian *Gemeinschaft* its depth and power. Nonconformity and *Gemeinschaft* are two sides of the same coin. S.K.'s metaphor is a striking one:

"CHRISTIAN COMMUNITY: In order to indicate where it lies I see no better illustration than an analogy, although it actually is beyond comparison. The criminal world creates a little society for itself which lies on the other side of human society, a little society which also has an intense solidarity that is not entirely common to the world—perhaps because each person feels himself expelled from human society.

"So with the society of Christians. Each one, by accepting Christianity, in consequence of becoming a believer, i.e. by accepting—indeed, by basing his life upon—the Absurd, has told the world goodbye, has broken with the world. For this very reason there is a society among these who of their own free will have put themselves outside of society in the general sense; and their society is all the more intense because each of them feels how isolated he is from 'the world.' But as with the criminal club it must be precisely the case that no one can come into the club if he does not discover this, so with the society of Christians: it must be that no one comes into this society except precisely those who are known to have been polemical in the extreme against society in general. This, the Christian community, is a society consisting of qualitative 'individuals,' the fervor of which society is determined by this polemical attitude toward the great society of mankind.

"But when, as in the course of time and in the constant advance of nonsense, to be a Christian became identical with to be human, so did the Christian community become the human race—good night nurse! Now the Christian community is the public, and in every cultured cleric's eyes and finally in the eyes of the lay people, it is offensive to talk about 'the individual.' "[17]

Finally, S.K. addressed himself to what must be the decisive question for sectarian ecclesiology: Is the *Gemeinde* a *necessary* feature for the faith of *den Enkelte*? If the church is in no sense a "saving institution," and if *den Enkelte* possesses in himself all the attributes of the church, why can he not "go it alone"? Does faith require a *Gemeinde* as its context?

Surprisingly enough, the answer of S.K.—who probably never experienced true Christian *Gemeinschaft*, whose career marked a struggling free from the "church," and who died separated from both "church" and *Gemeinde*—was a strong affirmative. And as we shall see, that affirmation of the *Gemeinde* seems to have been based directly on the lack, the "sickness," he felt in his own *ungemeinschaftlich* experience: "Here, upon this point, properly lies the significance of religious sociality, namely, that as the fact of God's ideality becomes powerful to the individual (thus he cannot indeed desire an unmediated revelation of God, and reflection [i.e. thinking *about* God] catches him);[18] he now must have other men with whom he can talk about it. But one sees, therefore, that sociality is not the highest but is a concession as regards what it is to be man in his infirmity." It will become apparent that for S.K. to call sociality "a concession" was in no way intended as derogatory. Indeed, by far the greater part of the Christian faith represents God's "concession as regards what it is to be man in his infirmity." God's election of Israel, the Incarnation, particularly Christ's death on the cross—every manifestation of grace—all are concessions made necessary

---

[17] *Papirer*, X² A 478 (1850) [my trans.—V.E.].
[18] Here as always, the bracketed material is mine; all else (including the parentheses) is S.K.'s—V.E.

only because of man's sin and finitude. But concession or not, these things were necessary and are necessary for every man; and just so with sociality. S.K. continues:

"Here again, then, lies the significance of the fact that God relates himself to the whole race. The race (sociality) is thus a middle term between God and the individual.

"This is the retrogressive movement; but wherever there shall be preaching for revival, wherever the price will be hiked up, there individuality shall be maintained. And in point of order this is the more necessary movement, because men in general live slackly and lazily enough.

"The relief, on the other hand, is to apply sociality. It is not good for man to be alone, it is said, therefore woman was given to him for society. But it is beholden upon us to be alone —literally alone—with God. That the neighbor is not to stand in one's stead, this is terribly strenuous; therefore man seeks society. . . . Religious sociality, then, is God pointing away from himself, as it were. Being love, he nevertheless says, in effect: 'Yes, yes, my child, now let this [the seeking of relaxation in sociality] be for good; also remember that I am still God. How humble, how believing, how burning your prayer and devotion are even so [even though you cannot sustain a direct, immediate, unbroken relationship]; in this way neither can you nor should you be thinking of me at every moment.' "

The character and function of the *Gemeinde* here are coming into focus. The direct relationship of *den Enkelte* with God is too strenuous for any man to maintain or endure without interruption; the sheer finitude of our nature makes this inevitable. However, the full alternation between being in relationship to God and then being wholly out of relationship certainly would not be good. Thus God has set up the *Gemeinde* to help carry *den Enkelte* over the troughs. Here one is somewhat sustained in his relationship to God through the aid of his brethren (and the "caravan" analogy is nowhere more apropos). Here is made possible a "semi-" or "secondary" relationship to God which allows the tension to be relaxed without the connection being completely broken; *den Enkelte* now can supplement his talking *to* God with talking to his brethen *about* God.

And although S.K. did not speak to the point, there is an implication which should be followed up. It would not be correct to picture the situation as though *den Enkelte* rests *in* the *Gemeinde* during his troughs but rises *out of* it and *beyond* it during his peaks, for although it is during his troughs that he needs the *Gemeinde*, it is during his peaks that the *Gemeinde* needs him. In other words, *den Enkelte* must help to carry his brethren as well as being carried by them.

From all this, we can derive insight into the character of true *Gemeinschaft*. In its life and work the *Gemeinde* must strike the fine dialectical balance that truly bears up *den Enkelte*—but without infringing on his personal relationship to God. It must afford him true repose—but without encouraging him to stay in repose. It must provide him a truly helpful "secondary" relationship to God—but without letting this become a substitute for the "primary" relationship.

As S.K. continued this same passage, he made the point that to try—or even to desire—to bypass the *Gemeinde* in the interests of living solely as *den Enkelte*, far from being heroism, is actually presumption, a sin against God:

"Here lies a dangerous point, namely, that the highest culmination of true religiousness [a personal, intimate, and individual relationship with God] can indeed hang by a hair and also can come to be recognized as a presumption, because even the humblest consciousness of being less than a sparrow before God, of being a nothing—yes, this is good—but presumption still can lie within it, within this consciousness that would think upon God at every instant and be conscious of itself as existing before him. It is proper to be conscious of oneself as nothing before God, but it is asking too much to wish to have this consciousness at every instant—or, if I dare say so (in order to indicate the error, because it is like a love affair), to wish to see the beloved every instant, even if one understands deeply enough that before him one is nothing."

In the next succeeding journal entry, which clearly is to be read in continuity with the foregoing, S.K. proceeded to describe the fruits of such presumption, the sort of soul-sickness to which it gives rise. And it is here that S.K. may have been referring to his own experience:

"A particular, individual God-relationship (in which each individual relates himself to God) is still the goal and norm. . . . But when the particular God-relationship of the individual becomes sick [which, he has implied, is inevitable if the individual presumes to "go it alone"], then one sets up temporarily the middle term of sociality, or 'the other people.' This sickness can take indeed the almost physical character of melancholy and the like. [Is S.K. referring to his own melancholy?] But principally it is the passion which, through vanity, is mistaken about how the individual relates himself to God, imagining that he wishes to be or that he is the entirely exceptional individual, [S.K. often spoke of himself as "the exceptional individual"; is he here repenting of at least some aspects of that role?] thus troubling himself to do nothing but sit and play the coquette with God as it were. But the fact is that he cannot remain in unhealthy intoxication with the thought of how the individual relates himself to God—if he becomes sober with the help of that which is possible to everyone, which is indeed commanded to everyone [i.e. through a consciousness of sociality]."[19]

As S.K. continued this particular entry he also pointed out that this sickness in the God-relationship *might* be a temptation, leading *den Enkelte* to seek refuge in sociality before that was appropriate, so the passage may not be as confessional as it sounds. In any case, it is clear that S.K. recognized the *Gemeinde* as a real and necessary aspect of the Christian life.

[19] *Papirer*, IX A 315-16 (1848) [my trans.—V.E.].

And indeed, it may be that some of the tragedy of S.K.'s melancholy life came about through the fact that he was a convinced sectary who never found a *Gemeinde*.

But whether consciously or not, S.K. was here constructing one of his characteristic dialectics—perhaps the most fundamental of them all. *Den Enkelte* is a good and necessary concept—but not apart from the *Gemeinde*. The *Gemeinde* is a good and necessary concept—but not apart from *den Enkelte*. *Den Enkelte*, apart from the *Gemeinde,* contracts a sickness in his God-relationship, becomes melancholy and/or vain. The *Gemeinde*, if it loses sight of *den Enkelte,* also loses its *Gemeinschaft* and degenerates into a crowd. Although he failed to emphasize it as he might have, S.K.'s most basic premise was not "*den Enkelte* before God" but actually "*Enkelter* in *Gemeinschaft* before God."

CHAPTER XII

CHRIST AS SAVIOR
AND PATTERN

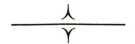

Jesus Christ was the foremost reality of S.K.'s faith and religious thought. Many scholars—at least among those of theological persuasion—have appreciated something of the centrality of that orientation; all too few have appreciated the *uniqueness* of S.K.'s Christological thought. His peculiar terms and concepts customarily have been picked up and treated without close examination, as though they already were understood—and that in accord with traditional modes of thought. Actually, however, S.K. was a pioneer in this field, offering a doctrine that is in many respects quite different and in some quite counter to customary Christology, although quite in line with the basic tenor of sectarian thought.

Traditional Christology inevitably has been marked by a profound dualism. This dualism takes many aspects, which can be indicated through a whole congeries of specific dualities; and these, in turn, can be arranged so that the left-hand terms are all obviously interrelated and the right-hand terms similarly. Thus they all stand as components of one general duality:

DIVINE NATURE .... HUMAN NATURE

PERSON .... WORK

SAVIOR	EXAMPLE AND/OR TEACHER
CHRIST OF FAITH	JESUS OF HISTORY
EXALTATION AND GLORY	HUMILIATION AND KENOSIS
IMMEDIATELY RECOGNIZABLE	INCOGNITO
PURE ATTRACTIVENESS	POSSIBILITY OF OFFENSE

Church theology traditionally has tended to stress the items of the first column to an extent somewhat detrimental to (although obviously not denying) those of the second. The exception to this rule is modern Liberalism, which concentrated on the first four items of the second column to the virtual exclusion of their first-column counterparts. But interesting to note, regarding the last three items, it tended to stay with the first rather than moving to the second column.

A primary and most obvious characteristic of S.K.'s Christological thought is that, without at all denying the truths of the first column, he endeavored to bring particular emphasis to those of the second in the attempt to restore a proper balance. In doing this, as we shall see, S.K. was in accord with sectarianism. But S.K. did not stop with a balancing of emphasis; his unique contribution was to weld the elements of each pair together in such a way that one could not be defined without involving the other. He concentrated upon the necessary relationship between them rather than upon their disjuncture. His tool for doing this was, of course, his dialectic method, i.e. interpreting the paired elements as complementary truths either of which is completely true only as both are solidly conjoined.

One example will illustrate S.K.'s technique. It concerns the relation of the divine and the human in Christ, and it is something he did entirely in passing, without calling attention to what he had accomplished. Creedal theology, of course, handles the matter with a doctrine of two natures in one person. Undeniably, the point of the doctrine is that the *two* natures are united in *one* person. Yet nevertheless, the very posit-

354

ing of the *two* natures is an invitation to distinguish between them, to identify that which is divine in Christ as separate from that which is human. And to do this is inevitably to create the problem of balance and set the stage for one nature to be emphasized over the other—which is precisely what happened in Christian thought.

S.K., on the other hand, made no use of this creedal solution—but not because he was intent on deserting orthodoxy. He chose to be unorthodox in the interest of achieving a purer orthodoxy. He consistently referred to Christ under the term "the God-Man," and he never allowed the slightest grounds for breaking that hyphen apart to examine the two halves independently. The God-Man is not some of God and some of Man; he is not two natures in union; there is no suggestion that either in his being or his actions there is that which can be identified as stemming from his deity as over against that which stems from his humanity. Precisely the significance of Christ's humanity is that it is *God* who has assumed it; and precisely the significance of Christ's deity is that it is revealed in *human* form. The two "natures" cannot get out of balance, because the concept has been so developed that it is impossible to describe either without affirming the other. More examples of a similar dialectic will appear on the pages to follow.

One of the very basic dualities of Christology is, certainly, that between Christ's role as Savior and as Pattern, or Example. S.K. provided a terminology with which to handle the distinction: "contemporaneousness" refers essentially to a man's approach to Christ as Savior, *Nachfolge* to him as Pattern. This distinction will be used to organize the discussion that follows. However, even here we shall discover that S.K., quite contrary to most theology, went a long way toward obliterating the distinction in practice. He did not simply identify the Savior with the Christ of Faith and the Pattern with the Jesus of History. Actually, "contemporaneousness" and *Nachfolge* come out as very similar spiritual economies di-

355

rected toward one and the same object, the God-Man Jesus Christ. And thus, in the end, the difference between them is found to be one merely of thought, whereas in practice the two necessarily and inevitably go together with nothing to be gained by trying to separate them.

A. CONTEMPORANEOUSNESS

[*Contemporaneousness*] *is the decisive thought! This thought is the central thought of my life. And I may say too with truth that I have had the honor of suffering for bringing this truth to light. Therefore I die gladly, with infinite gratitude to Governance that to me it was granted to be aware of this thought and to make others attentive to it. Not that I have discovered it. God forbid that I should be guilty of such presumption. No, the discovery is an old one, it is that of the New Testament.*[1]

S.K.'s conception of contemporaneousness with Christ is in no sense a complicated or difficult one. Yet it seems not to occur to many commentators that, although there are a number of routes and methods by which a believer might achieve contemporaneousness, S.K. was intent upon one and only one of these. It is not sufficient to cite the word "contemporaneousness" and then classify as Kierkegaardian anything and everything that might qualify under the term; a more thorough investigation is required to determine precisely with what (or who) it is that S.K. desires the believer to be contemporary and precisely how that contemporaneousness is to be attained.

But this investigation is not often enough made. For exam-

---

[1] *Attack upon "Christendom,"* p. 242.

ple, in an essay which was designed solely as a précis of S.K.'s *Training in Christianity* (his primary exposition of contemporaneousness), the reviewer fails to make a single statement which is clearly identifiable with S.K.'s doctrine and does make several which are quite contrary to it. He says, for instance: "The Christian is he who acknowledges Christ as a present reality." And again: "[Christ] is a living reality, seen through the eyes of faith, contemporaneous with each generation. His reality is such that it transcends both time and space."[2]

Now, of course, S.K. believed in the presence of the living Christ, but he never identified this presence as "contemporaneousness," and this presence was not his particular concern in *Training in Christianity*. There is a great deal of difference between saying that Christ is contemporary with us and saying that we are to become contemporary with him—the difference in who moves to meet whom and where the meeting takes place. S.K. consistently talked in terms of the latter alternative, his reviewer consistently in terms of the former.

Because there are these alternatives, perhaps the best way to get at S.K.'s intention is by eliminating the possibilities he did *not* intend. However, first there must be an understanding of *why* the necessity of contemporaneousness, *what* the meeting is designed to accomplish.

A saving relationship to Jesus Christ is, of course, one special case of faith in general—or rather, *the* special case of faith. Thus, faith in Christ—which is the goal of contemporaneousness with him—can best be understood in the light of our earlier discussion of faith.[3] There faith was defined as *den Enkelte*'s absolute venture of his total life and self, the "leap"

---

[2] The review of S.K.'s *Training in Christianity* in *Masterpieces of Christian Literature in Summary Form*, ed. Frank N. Magill (New York: Harper & Row, 1963), p. 721.

[3] See above, particularly pp. 119ff.

in which he cuts himself off from every earthly security, every human dependency, to float over 70,000 fathoms of water through trust in the God before whom he exists. This sort of venture is necessitated, is impelled, when *den Enkelte* encounters a claim to truth which, in the first place, is a matter of "infinite, personal, passionate interest," something which, for him, will make all the difference in the world whether it is true or false. In the second place, this matter is so paradoxical in nature that no amount of investigation, no amount of research, no amount of logic, no amount of reflection accomplishes one whit toward indicating whether the claim is indeed true or false. The problem is not that the claim is such as to prohibit investigation but that investigation invariably produces just as many "con's" as "pro's," for every proof that the claim is true an equally convincing proof that it cannot be true. One must *choose* (the matter is too crucial to let slide); one cannot *compute* an adjudication (the evidence is too ambiguous); therefore one can only *venture* absolutely, throwing himself upon God (which act is faith).

The situation that most completely fulfills this pattern is the event of Jesus Christ. He is *The* Paradox, the Absurd, and thus, at one and the same time, the Sign of Offense and the Object of Faith—indeed, he is the object *of faith* precisely because the possibility of becoming *offended* is always a very real one. The claim he both presents and represents is that this plain, ordinary, individual man (who thus obviously is *not* God) is in fact God. The claim dare not be ignored, for if it is true it does indeed make all the difference. If Jesus is in fact God, then to accept him is to accept God and, what is perhaps even more fateful, to reject him is to reject God. If Jesus is in fact God, to accept him is to find life, to reject him is to miss life and choose damnation. Clearly, if Jesus is in fact God, neutrality has been made impossible; to answer God's address with a shrug amounts to the same thing as defiance and rebellion. One *must* choose.

358

One must choose, but the outcome of that choice cannot be calculated on a rational basis—whether scientific, historical, or philosophical. Ultimately, neither investigation nor reflection proves of any use *in deciding the matter.* However, this is not the same as saying that investigation and reflection are of no use whatsoever; S.K. has been badly misunderstood on this score. Reason and research do have a role, the real and necessary role of determining whether the claim is truly a paradox or not, whether there is indeed evidence both "pro" and "con." Thus, regarding the claim "Napoleon was a man," research can say, "This claim is not a paradox but an evident fact; all the evidence is 'pro'; there was such a man and there is nothing to indicate that he was anything other than a man." Conversely, regarding the claim "Plymouth Rock is God," research can say, "This claim is not a paradox but an absurdity; all the evidence is 'con'; the rock is a rock and there is nothing to suggest that it might also be God." Finally, regarding the claim "Jesus Christ is God," research can say, "This claim, indeed, is a true paradox; there is strong and convincing evidence both pro and con; Jesus is either what the claim says he is or else he is a fraud—either God-Man or madman, but which, no amount of study or thought will accomplish a whit to decide."

Although research, stymied by contradictory evidence, cannot contribute to deciding the case, it does have an important role to play nonetheless. By separating the Absurd (i.e. the true Paradox) both from self-evident facts and from mere absurdities, research, as it were, holds the nose of *den Enkelte* right to the point where the venture must be made. Research is competent to elucidate (not settle) the claim, to marshal the "pro's" and "con's" involved in the historical situation itself. Research is competent to establish the source and locus of the paradox, to say that this claim is not simply an idea, a concept, a myth, a hypothesis, a proposition for discussion, but a hard, concrete, specific, and indissoluble lump in history—a fact which can be interpreted in either of two ways (either as a sign of offense or as an object of faith) but a solid fact for all that.[4]

Because paradox is the precondition of faith—indeed, it is the very occasion and context that produces faith and without which faith would be as impossible as unnecessary—because this is the case, for S.K., Christology must, above all, maintain the paradoxicality of Jesus Christ. And how is this to be done? Clearly, by welding the terms of the right-hand column solidly to their counterparts of the left-hand column in a dialectic that does not allow one to be defined without reference to the other; each "pro" must be tied inseparably to its "con."

Thus S.K. proposed the term "God-Man," a term which affirms Jesus' divine humanity (or human deity) but without positing a human nature *and* a divine nature in such a way that one tends to gain predominance over the other.

Thus, regarding the exalted Christ as against the humiliated Jesus, S.K. protested against the de-emphasis of the second term:

"Who is the Inviter [who said, "Come unto me . . . and I will give you rest"]? Jesus Christ. Which Jesus Christ? The Jesus Christ who sits in glory at the right hand of the Father? No. From the seat of His glory He has not spoken one word. Therefore it is Jesus Christ in His humiliation, in the state of humiliation, who spoke these words. . . . That He shall come in glory is to be expected, but it can be expected and believed only by one who has attached himself and continues to hold fast to Him as he actually existed. . . . What He said and taught, every word He has spoken, becomes *eo ipso* untrue when we make it appear as if it were Christ in glory who says it."[5]

---

[4] The pattern of thought presented here can be traced in S.K. by reference to the following condensed statements: (a) *Dru Journals,* 871 (1849); (b) the journal entries quoted in *A Kierkegaard Critique,* pp. 182-86; (c) *Dru Journals,* 1044 (1850); and (d) *Rohde Journals,* 201 (1849).

[5] *Training in Christianity* (Pt. I), pp. 26-27. Cf. *Smith Journals,* XI^2 A 343 (1854).

With this emphasis S.K. desired to correct the imbalance he found in the church of his own day; but lest his own correction itself become an imbalance, he spoke also as follows:

"[But] in case one could feel himself drawn to Christ and able to love Him only in His humiliation, in case such a man would refuse to hear anything about this exaltation when power and honor and glory are His—in case . . . he longs only for the spectacle of horror, to be with Him when He was scorned and persecuted—such a man's vision also is confused, he knows not Christ, neither loves Him at all. For melancholy is no closer to Christianity than light mindedness, both are equally worldly, equally remote from Christianity, both equally in need of conversion."[6]

And what his position actually came to, then, was this: "Whether in lowliness or in exaltation, [Christ] is one and the same; . . . Christ is not divided, He is one and the same. The choice is not between lowliness and exaltation; no, the choice is Christ; but Christ is composite, though one and the same, He is the humble one and the exalted."[7] Obviously, it is this character of being "composite though one and the same" that constitutes Christ's paradoxicality; and the "pro" of his exaltation (which would indicate that he is the God-Man) is made ambiguous by the "con" of his humiliation (which would indicate that he is not).

Thus, too, S.K. was not about to let the Christ of Faith become detached from the Historical Jesus:

"If Christianity is the historical truth, how then can it be the absolute? If it is the historical truth, it has happened at a certain time and place. If people say that it existed before it came into being and that it is like the harmonies [of which Leibniz spoke], then they are saying no more about it than any other idea, because it is also 'without father, mother, and genealogy'

[6] "Lifted Up On High . . ." (Pt. III, Reflection 1) in *Training in Christianity*, p. 154.
[7] "Lifted Up On High . . ." (Pt. III, Reflection 2) in *ibid.*, p. 160.

[Hebrews 7:3]. By insisting upon that, they enervate the essence of Christianity, because the historical is the essential point about it, whereas with other ideas the historical is the incidental."[8]

Thus, again, as regards Christ's recognizability as over against his incognito, S.K. would have both factors in operation concurrently and in tension with one another. S.K. has not been well understood on this point, and in an effort to go him one better, thinkers of the modern "kerygma theology" school[9] have ruined his initial insight. These theologians have picked up the truth of S.K.'s insistence upon Christ's incognito and made it mean that the "deity" of the historical Jesus must be absolutely invisible and indiscernible. The paradox, then, comes about in this wise: The life, career, and person of the earthly, historical Jesus constitutes the "con"; nothing is to be seen here except what would indicate that Jesus is simply and solely a man. Later, after the historical Jesus has left the scene, the "pro" comes along in the form of the early church's contention that this man was indeed God. But this was not S.K.'s position: in fact, he said: "The whole life of Christ on earth would have been mere play if He had been incognito to such a degree that He went through life totally unnoticed—and yet in a true sense He was incognito."[10]

In order to make the facts meet the pattern of the kerygma-school it is necessary to eliminate anything in the historical Jesus that might be read as "proofs" or "signs" of his deity, for these would betray his incognito. And this is precisely the

[8] *Papirer*, IV C 35, quoted by Ronald Grimsley, "Kierkegaard and Leibniz" in *The Journal of the History of Ideas*, XXVI (July-Sept. 1965), 395.

[9] By "kerygma theology" we intend those who would locate the essential paradox and the object of faith not primarily in the historical Jesus himself but in the early church's proclamation about him, i.e. in the kerygma. This description would cover such otherwise diverse thinkers as Karl Barth, Paul Tillich, Rudolf Bultmann, and many others.

[10] *Point of View*, p. 16.

point of Bultmann's demythologizing; any visible "supernaturalness," any outward miracle, any mark that would betray deity must be understood as belonging to the early church's affirmation of faith and by no means as a literal event concerning the historical Jesus. Whether or not it is legitimate to determine the historicity of an event through theological fiat, Bultmann's motive is creditable, for if supernatural demonstrations such as miracles can be pointed to as proofs of Jesus' deity, then the paradoxical precondition of faith has been destroyed.

S.K. would have agreed with Bultmann's principle but not with his application of it, for S.K. denied that miracles actually can play the role that Bultmann fears they do. Indeed, S.K. insisted that miracles are meet for his purpose, that their very nature reflects the ambiguity, the pairing of "pro" and "con," which truly heightens the paradox rather than destroying it. He pointed out that a miracle is understood as a miracle only by one who through an act of faith already has accepted the miracle-worker for what he claims to be. Otherwise, the so-called miracle is simply an inexplicable event which just as easily and just as logically can be explained as a fraud or delusion. For S.K., Jesus' miracles are very much to the point; they are ambiguous witnesses that attract attention and then, quite the opposite of providing a proof, force one to make a decision regarding the paradoxical miracle-worker.[11]

[11] See *Training in Christianity* (Pt. II), pp. 98-99, for S.K.'s discussion. I have had it in mind as certain that it was S.K. who presented the perfect illustration of this point of view, but I cannot locate the citation. However, if S.K. did not, he should have pointed out that even the ultimate miracle, the resurrection of Christ, was not received as a self-evident demonstration that Jesus was the God-Man. Certainly, to those who had made the venture of faith the resurrection *became* a "proof"—but only a proof *after the fact*, i.e. after the fact of faith itself, if such in any sense can be called a "proof." But it was, indeed, one of the very Gospels (Matthew) which suggested that the empty tomb could be read as a case of theft and fraud just as well as a case of resurrection and that, in fact, some of the first witnesses—

S.K.'s position would seem to have the better of Bultmann's at every point: first, in making it unnecessary to demythologize before one can get at the gospel in Gospels; second, in retaining the positive theological significance of miracle; and third, in saving us from the rather awkward position of, in effect, prohibiting God from showing himself in the world because it would be "untheological" of him to do so.

S.K. and Bultmann show a similar difference over the question of the historical Jesus' verbal claims to deity. Bultmann rejects all of these, on critical grounds as a Bible scholar but also as a theologian, because such claims, again, would compromise the incognito. S.K., on the other hand, accepts and welcomes these verbal claims as support for his interpretation. On the face of it, a plain and direct statement to the effect "I am God" constitutes a rather clear betrayal of Jesus' incognito —until one pauses to consider that the speaker is a mere man and therefore obviously *not* what he says he is. The speech is indeed all "pro," but the speaker is all "con," and thus that speech in the mouth of that speaker is paradoxical in the extreme.[12]

---

namely the soldiers guarding the tomb, who were just as close to the event and just as competent observers as any of the "believers"—chose the alternative of offense rather than faith. The empty tomb, although the sort of occurrence to attract attention and compel a decision one way or the other, involves just as much of "con" as it does of "pro," and it becomes a witness to Jesus' deity only to one who, through the venture of faith, already has chosen to be convinced that Jesus was One whom God *would* resurrect.

[12] For S.K.'s exposition, see *Training in Christianity* (Pt. II), pp. 134ff. In this case, critical scholarship since S.K.'s time has made it at least problematical whether the historical Jesus actually did make any verbal claims regarding his own deity. This finding would have the effect of cancelling this particular aspect of S.K.'s argument— although not by that token his argument as a whole. However, the most recent scholarship, i.e. post-Bultmannian scholarship, seems to be circling back, as it were, to undergird S.K. in a stronger way than he himself envisioned. The best of contemporary scholarship holds that, whether or not Jesus made any *verbal* claim for himself, his en-

Clearly, "incognito" meant something different to S.K. than it does to Bultmann and others of the kerygma-school. For S.K., it did not mean that the historical Jesus must be denied any and every indicator that would suggest his deity but only that every such indicator be accompanied with a counter-indication which would have the effect of balancing the account and leaving the verdict wide open—yet all the more urgent because of the evidence that is building up. In short, the kerygma-school sees the historical Jesus as nothing but incognito; S.K. saw him as incognito so dialectically welded to immediate recognizableness as to form a most irritating and inescapable paradox.

S.K.'s position avoids some of the most glaring weaknesses of the kerygma-school. For if the case is, as this school maintains, that nothing paradoxical is to be found in the historical Jesus but that the paradox comes into being only when the early church claims deity for him, then there is no compelling reason why that claim should attach to Jesus of Nazareth and not to someone else, or to anyone else, or even to no one at all. Yes, because essentially the paradox lies not in the historical person but in the claim, that claim would be just as effective in evoking faith if it concerned a figure of the imagination instead of an actual historical man.

And further, if ultimately the kerygma itself is the only paradox, then any contributions on the part of reason and research are absolutely excluded; there is no way of investigating whether this is a true Absurd or merely an absurdity. Research regarding the historical Jesus cannot possibly be of help, because it is decreed beforehand that only "con" evidence will be admitted, that anything that might look like "pro" evidence

---

tire ministry and message was in fact an *acted* claim to more than human authority. And if this be so, it puts the Kierkegaardian paradox on an even more fundamental level, for now Jesus becomes not simply a man (and thus not God) who *says* that he is God but rather a man (and thus not God) who *acts as though* he were God.

cannot be credited to the historical Jesus but must be attributed to the early church's kerygmatic claim. Thus, the kerygma-school does not possess a true Kierkegaardian paradox composed of pro-and-con evidence building up to an existential tension that compels one either to take offense or to make the venture of faith. It holds, rather, a mass of "con" *evidence* topped by a "pro" *claim* which brings with it absolutely no substantiation except the subjective power of "God's Word." But why this particular claim, coming as it were out of thin air, should be treated as the Absurd rather than merely an absurdity, no one is able to say. And what there is about a claim so lacking in solidity, in historical actuality and "presence," that should attract a man's attention, compel him to face up to it, and force him to decide one way or the other—again, no one is able to say. And yet—and yet Kierkegaard is the one who customarily gets accused of irrationality, subjectivism, and making faith into a wild and unmotivated leap in the dark.

Actually, S.K.'s dialectic Christology was deliberately polemic against several familiar types, of which kerygma-theology is only one. For instance, S.K. was strongly opposed to the traditional, creedal Christology which had held the field up until the development of scientific scholarship made possible "the quest of the historical Jesus." S.K. was critical of the Pre-Quest Christology for making the tacit assumption that the New Testament, the ecumenical councils, and the whole tradition of the church had settled the matter of Jesus' deity once for all, that the 1800 years since Christ had resolved any paradoxicality that may have been involved in his historical manifestation, and that, rather than making any decisive venture of faith, modern Christians had only to let themselves be carried on the tides of scripture, creed, and church.[13]

Even though S.K. lived and wrote before Liberalism's "Old

[13] Regarding this aspect of S.K.'s argument, see particularly *Training in Christianity* (Pt. I), pp. 28ff.

Quest" (the quest described in Schweitzer's classic study) had reached its heyday, the major thrust of his polemic was directed against this movement. The Old Quest was dedicated to "going beyond faith," to reaching Christianity via a sturdy bridge of scientific-historical evidence rather than a leap across a paradox. To this end the "truly historical" kernels of the Gospel tradition were threshed out of the chaff of "mere assertions of faith," and Christian doctrine was to be reared precisely upon these findings, as logical deductions drawn from proven facts of history. Of course, in S.K.'s view, such an approach would destroy Christ's incognito, his humiliation, his paradoxicality, his Person, and indeed the very possibility of faith and thus any true concept of Christianity.[14]

Then, within the memory—and indeed, the work—of men still living, Old-Quest Liberalism was challenged and conquered by so-called Neo-Orthodoxy, which, although quite varied in many respects, seems to have been pretty much of a mind as concerns its "No-Quest Christology." S.K. has been looked to as one of the "fathers" of Neo-Orthodoxy, and it is true that these theologians used (and used properly) S.K.'s "anti-historicism" to break up Old-Quest Liberalism. They did not, however, use (or use properly) Kierkegaardian concepts in constructing their own positive Christology, for S.K. was anything but a kerygmatic Christologian.

We already have suggested something of the difference between S.K. and the No-Quest school, but the matter can be made more pointed. Although writing even before the Old

---

[14] S.K.'s attack upon scientifically derived (i.e. historically and/or philosophically derived) Christianity is so pervasive as to be difficult to cite; in effect, the whole of *Philosophical Fragments, Postscript,* and *Training in Christianity* deals directly or indirectly with this issue.

It should be noted, too, that all of S.K.'s fulminations against "history" as an enemy of faith are directed toward this one sort of historiography which sets out to "go beyond faith." But there is nothing in S.K.'s thought that would outlaw or denigrate historical study per se, and as we shall see, he did specifically intend and make room for historiography of a proper sort.

Quest had reached its height, S.K. seems to have anticipated kerygma theology and risen to counter it. His crucial statement in this regard opened with the words: "Christianity is not a doctrine." But the fact of the matter is that the kerygma is precisely a doctrine and nothing else: in essence it is a proposition, a concept, an idea. Granted it is a proposition that has reference to an historical event; but when it is insisted that the content of that event is irrelevant, is not open to investigation, or, if investigated, is destined to produce only negative results —if this is the case, then the kerygma remains solely and exclusively a doctrine, and S.K.'s statement applies: "Christianity is not a doctrine. All the talk about offense in relation to Christianity as a doctrine is a misunderstanding, it is a device to mitigate the shock of offense at the scandal—as, for example, when one speaks of the offense of the *doctrine* of the God-Man and the *doctrine* of the Atonement. No, the offense is related either to Christ or to the fact of being oneself a Christian."[15]

A merely doctrinal paradox is not an adequate occasion for producing true faith. Such a paradox exists only on the intellectual, cognitive level, and here it can be argued away just as easily as it can be argued into being; an intellectual paradox can be resolved through intellectual gymnastics. And in actuality it can be disposed of even without this effort, simply by ignoring it. The common man is neither excited nor disturbed by a *doctrinal* paradox, this plaything of the theologians about which he could not care less. No, only a real, live, demanding Paradox with all its attention-catching "pro's" and "con's" is adequate to pull the existential tension to the point that energizes the venture of faith.

"Offense has essentially to do with the composite term God and man, or with the God-Man. Speculation naturally had the notion that it 'comprehended' God-Man—this one can easily

[15] *Training in Christianity* (Pt. II), pp. 108-09.

comprehend, for speculation and speculating about the God-Man leaves out temporal existence, contemporaneousness, and reality."[16]

"By force of lecturing they [modern thinkers] have transformed the God-Man into that speculative unity of God and man *sub specie aeterni*, manifested, that is to say, in the nullipresent medium of pure being, whereas in truth the God-Man is the unity of God and an individual man in an actual historical situation."[17]

Edit that last to read "speculative unity of God and man sub specie *hypothesis*" and "manifested in the nullipresent medium of *existential self-understanding*" and the statement becomes directly applicable to modern kerygma-Christology without changing S.K.'s point in the slightest.

Clearly, S.K.'s basic and crucial Christological move was to tie the act of faith securely to a specific, objective historical event—not by that token making faith a simple, straight-line deduction from historical evidence (the evidence is too ambiguous for that) but certainly neither by de-historicizing the event into a mere kerygmatic postulate. He staked out his position in so many words:

"Christianity exists before any Christian exists, it must exist in order that one may become a Christian, it contains the determinant by which one may test whether one has become a Christian, it maintains its objective subsistence apart from all believers, while at the same time it is the inwardness of the believer. In short, here there is no identity between the subjective and the objective. Though Christianity comes into the heart of never so many believers, every believer is conscious that it has not arisen in his heart, is conscious that the objective determinant of Christianity is not a reminiscence. . . . No, even if no one had perceived that God had revealed himself in a

[16] *Ibid.*, pp. 83-84.
[17] *Ibid.*, p. 123.

human form in Christ, he nevertheless has revealed himself. Hence it is that every contemporary (simply understood) has a responsibility if he does not perceive it."[18]

This one statement puts S.K. a pole away from modern existentialist theology. His position, for example, is the contrary of that of a Paul Tillich, who can say: "The believing reception of Jesus *as* the Christ, calls for equal emphasis. Without this reception the Christ would not have been the Christ." And again, "Since the Christ is not the Christ without the church, he has become the Christ."[19] A statement by Rudolf Bultmann, as another example, is also at a considerable remove from S.K.:

"This 'once for all' [of redemption in Christ] is not the uniqueness of an historical event but means that a particular historical event [which, by inference then, is *not* unique in and of itself], that is, Jesus Christ, is to be understood as the eschatological 'once for all.' As an eschatological event this 'once for all' is always present in the proclaimed word, not as a timeless truth, but as happening here and now. . . . The word of God is Word of God only as it happens here and now. The paradox is that the word which is always happening here and now is one and the same with the first word of the apostolic preaching crystallized in the Scriptures of the New Testament and delivered by men again and again."[20]

Bultmann may be the dominant figure of existentialist theology and S.K. may be known as the founder of existentialism, but their respective Christologies have very few points of contact. Bultmann's "eschatological event," his "event" which somehow becomes synonymous with "word," is not at all what S.K. would have meant by "event."[21] Bultmann's paradox is

[18] *The Book on Adler*, pp. 168-69.
[19] Paul Tillich, *Systematic Theology*, Vol. II (Chicago: Un. of Chicago Press, 1957), pp. 99 and 154 respectively; cf. pp. 135 and 180.
[20] Rudolf Bultmann, *Jesus Christ and Mythology* (New York: Scribner's, 1958), p. 82.
[21] Undoubtedly the German language has helped to make possible

not at all S.K.'s. And even Bultmann's object of faith (the kerygmatic word) is not at all S.K.'s (the historical God-Man). And thus the problem of contemporaneousness is completely different for Bultmann than for S.K.

But if, with S.K., the Christ of Faith is in fact the Historical Jesus *believed upon*—rather than, with Bultmann, the Kerygmatic Word *affirmed*—then inevitably a valid and even necessary role has been opened for historical research and criticism. As passionately opposed as he was to the sort of historical research that proposed to make faith unnecessary, S.K. did not at all resist this other implication but did himself elucidate it. As early as the pseudonymous *Philosophical Fragments* (1844), S.K. made the following, very seminal statements:

"The absolute fact is an historical fact, and as such it is the object of Faith. The historical aspect must indeed be accentuated, but not in such a way that it becomes decisive for the individual; . . . for a simple historical fact is not absolute, and has no power to force an absolute decision. [Thus is the Old Quest with its exclusive concentration on history disqualified.] But neither may the historical aspect of our fact be eliminated, for then we have only an eternal fact. [And thus is the No

---

this discrepancy. For S.K., "event" and/or "history" implied something wholly within the objective sphere, something that happened as it actually happened and was what it was—whether it was believed upon or even known about. The event, of course, becomes effective in my life only as I receive and interpret it through faith, but my faith does not change the objective "happenedness" of the event either one way or another. "Event" is simply and solely an affirmation of *Historischlichkeit*. Existentialism, on the other hand, has had the effect of subtly transposing "event" out of the objective sphere and into the subjective. History is thought of not primarily in terms of its *Historischlichkeit* (its happenedness) but of its *Geschichtlichkeit* (its meaningfulness). The reality of an event as "history" is tested, not by investigation as to whether it actually occurred out there, but by what the thought of it does to me in here. Thus "event" (what happened at that place at that time) becomes "eschatological event" (what hap-

Quest with its exclusive concentration on the kerygma disqualified.]"[22]

And again, he said: "As long as the Eternal and the historical are external to one another, the historical is merely an occasion." In this one sentence is hidden the key to the history of Christological thought. In Pre-Quest Orthodoxy, the Eternal and the historical were thought of in substantial terms, *a* divine nature and *a* human nature. They were necessarily compartmentalized and thus essentially external to one another, and so inevitably the Eternal came to overshadow the historical as being obviously pre-eminent. Thus the historical *did* become merely an occasion. In Old-Quest Liberalism, the Eternal's aspect of the case was virtually ignored and thus held external to the historical. Inevitably the quest of the historical Jesus failed to get anywhere, because it was studying merely the occasion. In No-Quest Neo-Orthodoxy, the Eternal and the historical were deliberately kept external to one another, and the historical consciously was treated as merely an occasion . . . for the kerygma of the Eternal. But as we repeat and complete S.K.'s statement, we see that he would have had none of these:

"As long as the Eternal and the historical are external to one another, the historical is merely an occasion. . . . But the Paradox unites the contradictories and is the historical made Eternal, and the Eternal made historical. . . . Faith is not a form of knowledge;[23] for all knowledge is either a knowledge of the Eternal, excluding the temporal and historical as indifferent [thus the abstract philosophizing of No-Quest existen-

---

pens to me here in this time), and "event" (happenedness) even becomes "word" (meaning), and the distinction between objective, outward action and subjective, inward reaction is completely obliterated.

[22] *Philosophical Fragments*, p. 125.

[23] S.K. is not meaning to say that faith excludes knowledge or is without cognitive content. He is saying that faith must be more than knowledge, or that faith is an entirely unique sort of knowledge which cannot be classified with any of our usual forms of knowledge.

tialism], or it is pure historical knowledge [thus the critical researches of the Old Quest]. No knowledge can have for its object the absurdity that the Eternal is the historical. . . . But the disciple is in Faith so related to his Teacher as to be *eternally* concerned [i.e. in an infinite, personal, passionate way] with [the Teacher's] *historical* existence."[24]

By positing this Christology which insists on a dialectic of *both* objective event *and* subjective word, *both* history *and* faith, *both* research *and* venture, S.K. was pointing toward the latest school of Christology, the so-called New Quest.[25] Indeed, the New Questers themselves have never outlined their program better or more succinctly than did Søren Kierkegaard a full century before the New Quest was as much as dreamed of: "The historicity of the redemption *must* be certain in the same sense as any other historical thing, but not more so, for otherwise the different spheres are confused. . . . The historical factual assumption necessary for the redemption must only be as certain as all other historical facts, but the passion of faith must decide the matter."[26]

Of course, S.K. did not *perform* the New Quest; he was not trained in biblical criticism, and indeed, the tools and methods

---

[24] *Philosophical Fragments*, pp. 75-76 [italics mine—V.E.].

[25] More than coincidence may be involved in the fact that the one leading theologian of the No-Quest period who has welcomed the New Quest and appropriated its basic position as his own is the same theologian whom we earlier named as the one with the best understanding of S.K., namely Emil Brunner (see his *Dogmatics III*, pp. 178ff.).

Our terminology here already may be becoming inadequate, for a split is showing up within the New Quest itself. Eduard Schweizer, for instance, would identify neither himself nor Günther Bornkamm (whose *Jesus of Nazareth* usually is considered the "firstfruits" of New Quest research) as being New Questers but would reserve that term for a group who, in his opinion, have only slightly modified the Bultmannian No-Quest position without actually moving out of it. If his analysis is correct, then we mean to identify S.K. with those non-Bultmannians who go even beyond the New Quest.

[26] *Dru Journals*, 602 (1846) [italics mine—V.E.].

now being used had not yet been discovered or developed. But be that as it may—and even though the New Questers have not taken their cue directly from S.K. but on their own are correcting the distortion that Bultmann imparted to the tradition which *he* derived from S.K.—nevertheless it is unimpeachable that Kierkegaard developed a theological rationale that explains and necessitates precisely the sort of historical quest that is going on today.

Indeed, it may well be that S.K. went further, that he can point the New Questers to their next step, to the implications that their work has for the preaching and teaching of the gospel. This he did in his doctrine of contemporaneousness.

By defining the object of faith as he did, by specifying that it is the *historical* Jesus believed upon, that the immediately recognizable elements in Christ always must be made ambiguous by his incognito, that offense always must be just as live and just as logical an alternative as faith—with this definition S.K. in effect already had determined the route that contemporaneousness must take.

"Contemporaneousness" is, of course, nothing more than the procedure by which *den Enkelte* meets the God-Man, confronts and is confronted by him in such a way that the venture of faith can take place. Actually, all worship, all ritual, all preaching, all theology is in one sense or another directed toward the achievement of contemporaneousness. However, S.K. held that there is only one mode of contemporaneousness which truly is appropriate and effective for the act of faith.

Plainly, all attempts at contemporaneousness can be classified into two major groups as regards the direction of the movement involved. Either Christ moves out of first century Palestine to become contemporary with *den Enkelte*, meeting him in the present time and situation; or else *den Enkelte* moves out of the present to become contemporary with Christ, meeting him in first century Palestine.[27]

[27] A third alternative—which may be an accurate picture of classical

Most approaches to contemporaneousness—and particularly the churchly ones—assume the first context: Christ comes to meet *den Enkelte*. However, given S.K.'s definition of the object of faith, this alternative poses some problems from the outset. For one thing, to what extent can the historical Jesus be moved out of his own locus and still be the *historical* Jesus? Were not his life, words, and actions closely enough related to the first century milieu that they must be seen against that background in order to be understood? And for another, the very fact that this Christ *can* move across the years to confront *den Enkelte* rather effectively eliminates any possibility of his being incognito; his very being *here* is positive proof that he is the God-Man and not a madman; there is no paradox in a contemporary Christ.

To get down to instances, then, the entire cultic apparatus of churchly worship obviously is designed to create contemporaneousness. Just as obviously, the meeting is thought of as taking place on the spot, i.e. in the church here and now. All of the symbolism, the liturgy, the vestments, the architecture, the music, and so forth—all point to the glorified, exalted Son of God; there is little if anything to remind one of the humble carpenter of first century Nazareth. Even the celebration of the eucharist is performed, not so as to remind or re-create before the congregation a meal eaten in an upper room in Jerusalem (this would be the dynamic of the opposite movement), but as a commemoration of the eternal Christ. Contemporaneousness with the Christ of the altar hardly will meet the conditions requisite for a Kierkegaardian venture of faith.

Also, creedal theology is designed to create contemporaneousness. However, it does not so much represent an attempt to

---

mysticism—is that both parties move and meet in a realm of the spirit where there is nothing in the way of time, space, location, or even concrete awareness of the persons involved. Obviously, S.K. would have had nothing to do with such a scheme.

understand the historical Jesus and/or the early church's faith in him *in terms of the first century situation* (i.e. biblical theology) as to explain Christ *in terms of the Greek thought forms that were contemporary at the time the creeds were formulated.* Thus it represents another case of bringing Christ to us rather than the reverse. And again the consequence is that very little of the historical Jesus shows through, his incognito is explained away, and there is nothing in him that would offend anyone. Contemporaneousness with the Christ of Nicaea and Chalcedon would not satisfy S.K.

Likewise, modern kerygmatic, existentialist theology is designed to create contemporaneousness, this indeed being its *forte.* If Christ's primary locus is in eschatological event, in the word of proclamation, in symbol, then contemporaneousness is not a problem. Contemporary with us is the only possible way in which Christ can exist, and as Paul Tillich has as much as said, it is our acceptance of his contemporaneousness that brings him into being.[28] But S.K. specifically denied that a paradoxical doctrine, or proposition, is a true paradox capable of occasioning true faith. Contemporaneousness with the Kerygmatic Word will not do.

A final mode within this first type of contemporaneousness holds particular interest because it involves a conscious attempt to do justice to the historical Jesus and not simply to the exalted or the proclaimed Christ. This "theology" was signalized in Charles Sheldon's popular classic *In His Steps* and is characterized by the shibboleth "What would Jesus do?" The theory is that contemporaneousness is to be achieved as a wholesale transplant of the Palestinian rabbi into the twentieth century where he can then function as tutor and guide. This approach proves singularly ineffectual, because in the process of transplantation either the historical Jesus must be subtly transmuted into a twentieth century man or else he

[28] See above, p. 370.

376

is so out of place as to be of no help at all. Contemporaneousness even with the historical Jesus, if the meeting must take place on our ground, hardly will meet S.K.'s conditions.

The other option is for us to become contemporary with Christ by going back to meet him in his own time and place. From the outset, this procedure shows more promise of satisfying the Kierkegaardian definition, and it is here S.K. will find his answer, although he will be far from approving every approach that comes under the category.

The old, Liberal "Quest of the Historical Jesus" was a sincere attempt to go back to first century Palestine and meet Jesus "as he really was." However, because this research was informed by certain hidden assumptions regarding what evidence would be admitted and what interpretations allowed, the final results were somewhat less than satisfactory. In his account of that Quest, Albert Schweitzer pointed out time and again where and how this occurred. Far from either seeking or finding a paradox, these scholars were intent specifically to remove all problematic elements and present a humane and idealistic Jesus worthy of recognition as the founder and norm of an enlightened culture-religion for modern man. In effect, the Old Quest set out to erase from the Gospels precisely those features that S.K. valued, those that might make Jesus paradoxical and a sign of offense.

The popular counterpart of the Old Quest, which has not been as easily put down (precisely because it is *popular* and thus not susceptible to scholarly refutation), is what might be called the Sunday-school, or Hollywood, approach. In Sunday school, this takes the form of children dressing up in bathrobes and beards, building models of a Palestinian home, etc. In Hollywood, it costs a bit more money to do the same thing. There is something commendable about all this, the desire to join the disciples, go with them to meet the Master, and believe on him as they did. But in this well-intentioned procedure, one element is distorted in such a way that the entire enterprise becomes falsified. Because of Christ's incognito, the first disciples could believe only after an agonizing struggle to surmount offense; they had to *dare* to accept Jesus as the God-Man under conditions in which this interpretation of the matter was by no means self-evident. Biblical movies present no such problem, for here the historical [sic] Jesus is surrounded with an aura of light, wears a pure white robe, speaks through an echo-chamber with harps in the background, looks like a Greek god (if not a Hebrew one), and hardly would have the audacity to say, "Blessed is he who is not offended in me!"

Any mode of contemporaneousness that proposes to overlook the incognito and possibility of offense achieves at most a pseudo-contemporaneity:

"Most people now living in Christendom live, we may be sure, in the vain persuasion that, had they lived contemporary with Christ, they would at once have known and recognized Him in spite of his unrecognizableness. They are quite unconscious that they thereby betray the fact that . . . this notion of theirs, notwithstanding that it is certainly meant as praise of Christ, is really blasphemy."[29]

"If the glory had been directly visible, so that everybody as a matter of course could see it, then it is false that Christ humbled Himself and took upon Him the form of a servant; it is superfluous to give warning against being offended, for how in the world could anybody be offended by glory attired in glory!"[30]

The fact of the matter is that S.K. branded as inadmissible the very approaches to Jesus that are most prominent in churchly teaching and worship.[31]

Contemporaneousness in S.K.'s sense of the term is a conscious effort of the imagination by which *den Enkelte* over-

[29] *Training in Christianity* (Pt. II), pp. 127-28.
[30] *Ibid.* (Pt. I), p. 69.
[31] *Christian Discourses* (Pt. III, Discourse 1), pp. 181-82; (Pt. IV, Discourse 1), pp. 266-67; and (Pt. IV, Discourse 4), pp. 284-86.

leaps the entire 1900-year tradition which the church has established regarding *its* faith and, free of inherited presuppositions, meets the historical Jesus, sees him with the eyes not simply of the first *Christians* but of the first eyewitnesses (crucifiers as well as disciples), and there, in the painful tension of that dilemma, makes his own choice as to whether Jesus is the God-Man who has an absolute claim to his life or a madman who should be avoided at all costs.

Of course, S.K. believed that there is also a living Lord who meets the believer *in the present*, but this movement takes place only posterior to and consequent upon the venture of faith; this presence is discernible only to the believer and is not itself the occasion which *produces* faith. S.K. consistently used the term "contemporaneousness" in reference to the first movement and not to the second. His intention, certainly, was not to prohibit or even inhibit the second but to establish the priority and absolute necessity of the first.

With this distinction in mind, even a cursory examination of *Training in Christianity* makes S.K.'s point unmistakable. Much of that book, indeed, is given over to a frankly imaginative reconstruction of how different contemporaries might have spoken about Jesus. And although the following quotations represent an attempt to cite the most compact and crucial statements of S.K.'s thesis, they are at the same time *typical* —completely typical—of his entire Christological approach:

"The past is not reality—for me: only the contemporary is reality for me. What thou dost live contemporaneous with is reality—for thee. And thus every man can be contemporary only with the age in which he lives—and then with one thing more: with Christ's life on earth."[32]

"But so long as there is a believer, such a one must, in order to become such, have been, and as a believer must continue to be, just as contemporary with [Christ's] presence on earth as

[32] *Training in Christianity* (Pt. I), p. 67.

were those [first] contemporaries. This contemporaneousness is the condition of faith, and more closely defined it is faith. O Lord Jesus Christ, would that we also might be contemporary with Thee, see Thee in Thy true form and in the actual environment in which Thou didst walk here on earth; not in the form in which an empty and meaningless tradition, or a thoughtless and superstitious, or a gossipy historical tradition, has deformed Thee."[33]

"The principal concern now is to be able to clear the ground, get rid of the eighteen hundred years, so that the Christian fact takes place now, as if it happened today. . . . This contemporaneousness, however, is to be understood as having the same significance that it had for people who lived at the same time that Christ was living. . . . However, the contemporaneousness here in question is not the *contemporaneousness of an apostle*, but is *merely the contemporaneousness which everyone who lived in Christ's time had*, the possibility in *the tension of contemporaneousness* of *being offended*, or *of grasping faith*."[34]

The clear implication is that the preaching, teaching, and worship of the church should be directed toward helping *den Enkelte* to make his own experiment in contemporaneousness. It was S.K.'s conviction, based on his own quite uncritical (i.e. not scientific-scholarly) reading of the Gospels, that anyone who tried such a "contemporary-reading" would meet the same Jesus that he had. The New-Quest research of our own day has the effect of confirming S.K.'s conviction. The Kierkegaardian picture of the Paradox will bear the full weight of the closest sort of scientific-historical scrutiny, because the New Quest, too, establishes the historical Jesus of Nazareth as having been a real, live, ordinary man (and thus obviously not God) who nevertheless spoke such a message,

[33] *Ibid.* (Pt. I), p. 9.
[34] *The Book on Adler*, pp. 62-63. Cf. *Training in Christianity* (Pt. I), pp. 40 and 43.

presumed such an authority, and acted in such a style as would indicate that he considered himself in possession of divine prerogatives. It would not be inaccurate to suggest that the New Quest *allows* (or even *compels*) the scholar and theologian to read the Gospels in the same terms that S.K. was sure the common man could and would if sophisticated scholarship and church tradition left him alone.

Needless to say, neither the Brethren nor sectaries in general ever have produced the sort of Christological thought that would match S.K.'s. Nevertheless, in an intuitive way they did have a "feel" for the historical Jesus, for his humiliation and incognito, for the possibility of offense—a feel which, it must be said, is not nearly as strong in the churchly tradition. S.K. himself realized that the simple, unlearned believer would understand contemporaneousness better than would the intellectual. In analyzing the case of Adler, the pastor who, after taking a rural parish, became spiritually deranged, S.K. suggested, half seriously, that perhaps the thing with which Adler could not cope was the meeting of true Christians:

"Magister Adler becomes a priest in the country, and so is brought into contact and into responsible relation with simple and ordinary people who, lacking a knowledge of Hegel, have, as perhaps men in the country still have, a serious though meager Christian instruction, so that, unacquainted with every volatilization of it, they simply believe in the Christian doctrine and have it before them as a present reality. For simple, believing men so deal with Christianity that they do not hold it historically at a distance of eighteen hundred years, still less fantastically at a mythical distance."[35]

The early Brethren fit S.K.'s description precisely. Mack Senior, for example, said:

"There is a time of humiliation and a time of exaltation. The Lord Jesus first appeared very humbly and lowly in this world in humble and willing submission to the will of His Father.

[35] *The Book on Adler*, p. 147.

The second time, however, He will appear in great power and glory as an exalted Christ. All souls who desire to be with Him in His exaltedness must certainly first accept Him as a humbled Christ. They must confess Him before men in all His commandments, and not be ashamed of them. In this way they will become humble in the humble commandments, and then finally they shall be exalted in due season. It will be impossible otherwise. For this reason, the church of the Lord has always been lowly and despised in this world. It has always been considered as filth."[36]

And Mack Junior came even closer to formulating a concept of contemporaneousness when, in speaking against infant baptism, he said:

"What did it avail a poor man in Israel in former times, when he could only hear of a fiery serpent, which was erected for his healing. He had to see the serpent; yes, he himself had to look at it, and not another for him; thus also it must not remain with the witnesses in this important matter; if we want to be thoroughly healed from our deep injury, then we must see Jesus crucified ourselves."[37]

It would not be accurate to say that the Brethren held S.K.'s *doctrine* of contemporaneousness; it would, however, be accurate to suggest that they would have welcomed the interpretation had they been exposed to it. They did not, as did S.K., talk *about* contemporaneousness with Christ; they did, rather, often, talk *as if they were* contemporaneous with Christ. Their

[36] Mack Senior, *Rights and Ordinances*, in Durnbaugh, *Origins*, p. 394. Sauer Junior made much the same point in his "Forward with Respect to Courts" in the *Hoch-Deutsch Americanische Calender* for 1760, p. 19.

[37] Mack Junior, *Apology*, p. 20. Mack Junior also wrote a poem on the crucifixion in which, as it were unconsciously, he constantly slipped back into terms of contemporaneousness, as though he were an eyewitness—and a guilty witness—at Calvary. And the way in which this is done would indicate that it was more Mack's *religious instincts* than his *poetic sensibilities* that were responsible. (See Heckman, *op.cit.*, pp. 100ff.)

mode of observing the Lord's Supper points toward contemporaneity. So do their "low" forms of worship and church architecture. So does the very simplicity of their demeanor and way of life. And so, particularly, does their central emphasis on *Nachfolge* (which is our next topic).

B. NACHFOLGE / EFTERFØLGELSE / IMITATION

"Imitation," "the following of Christ,"
this precisely is the point
where the human race winces, here it is principally
that the difficulty lies,
here is where the question really is decided
whether one will accept Christianity or not.[1]

Christianity is not a doctrine.
It is a belief, *and corresponding to it,*
a well-defined way of existence,
an imitation.[2]

For the proof of Christianity really consists in "following."[3]

Efterfølgelse is the Danish and Kierkegaardian term that is the precise equivalent of *Nachfolge*, the German and Brethren term. These have no such precise equivalent in English. They are often translated "discipleship," but this can suggest merely the adherence to a master's *teachings* or an acceptance of his *philosophy*, whereas, as S.K. put it, "To be a follower means that thy life has as great a likeness to His as it is possible for a man's life to have."[4] "Imitation" is perhaps the preferable translation—if one guards against the tinge of artificiality the word conveys and against the hint of works-righteousness that traditionally has accompanied *imitatio Christi*.

Nachfolge is certainly one of the major themes of all classic

---

[1] "Christ as Example" (Discourse 2) in *Judge for Yourselves!*, p. 197.
[2] *Papirer*, X³ A 454 (1850), quoted in Dupre, *op.cit.*, p. 172.
[3] "Christ Is the Way" (Discourse 2) in *For Self-Examination*, p. 88.
[4] *Training in Christianity* (Pt. II), p. 108.

Protestant sectarianism and might well be claimed as *the* central theme of eighteenth century Brethrenism—being, of course, very closely related to the theme of obedience/fruit bearing. More Brethren authors could be quoted at greater length concerning *Nachfolge* than any other motif we have treated. But rather than amassing evidence we will cite only the one best presentation, this a poem by Sauer Junior. (Its structure is such as to merit its being printed as poetry even though the translation is not metrical.)

> Whatever is opposed to Christ
>   Is the Antichrist.
> That which to our frivolous eyes
>   Appears as something to be valued,
> That is—as beautiful as it may be—
>   Directly counter to Christ.
>
> Christ was the friend of the poor;
>   We Christians are their enemies.
> He hated honor;
>   We give it heed.
> He did not love riches;
>   We are bound to them.
>
> He sought only to suffer;
>   We seek to avoid it.
> He was despised, laughed at;
>   We would be esteemed.
> He was as a little child;
>   We would be quickly grown.
>
> He was the people's laughingstock
>   And stood not on the throne.
> He hated lust and pleasure;
>   We love both of them.
> He lived in anxiety and need;
>   We relish the bread of pleasure.

He was blamed for his conduct;
  We would be approved.
He would be loving;
  We love only ourselves.
He considered it reasonable
    that we should follow him;
  We live in self-will.

"Deny yourself," he said;
  None of us does that.
"Each one shall constrain himself";
  We are opposed to constraint.
No one recognizes
  Works of love in these times.

At present, only God and no one else
  Would love and never compel.
We love what is high;
  He loved what is lowly here.
He would teach us humility;
  We will not listen.

He sought hardship;
  It makes us wail and cry.
He noticed the forsaken;
  We notice the elevated.
He approached the poor;
  We climb high.

He is full of goodness and love;
  We follow our inclinations.
He suffered many blows,
  In this was no man like him.
He would have us poor in spirit;
  We seek great gifts.

One should be in the Spirit alone
  And not according to nature.

385

Through such opposition,
Where the devil's power is so great,
Jesus' life and teachings now
Become wholly despised.[5]

At least one striking difference between Brethren *Nachfolge* and that of early twentieth century Liberalism becomes evident here. With the Brethren there was no tendency to read Jesus as the attractive exemplar of the humane ideals and graces that culture-religion exalts. Quite the opposite; the Brethren found in Jesus the possibility of offense and precisely those attributes that the natural man naturally despises. Thus in Sauer's poem there is implied an idea which S.K. was to make specific, namely, that the *following* of Christ—far from displacing, or substituting for, *faith* in him as Savior and Redeemer—serves to make it abundantly clear that one *must* have a Savior. Without the help of the Savior, the call to discipleship is as infeasible in prospect as impossible in achievement.

Kierkegaard could be quoted at even greater length regarding *Nachfolge* than could the Brethren—simply because he wrote more. The emphasis was just as central with him as with them—although S.K. undoubtedly had more "central emphases" than did the Brethren. And for him, *Nachfolge* meant essentially the same thing it meant for the Brethren: "To follow Christ, then, means denying one's self, and hence it means *walking the same way* as Christ walked in the humble form of a servant—needy, forsaken, mocked, not loving worldliness and not loved by the worldly minded."[6] This is what *Nachfolge* means, and this—S.K. was certain—is what is demanded of every Christian.[7]

[5] Sauer Junior (presumably), a poem without title, appearing as an independent feature in the *Hoch-Deutsch Americanische Calendar* for 1766, p. 24 [my trans.—V.E.].

[6] "The Joyfulness of Following Christ" (Discourse 1) in *The Gospel of Suffering*, p. 12.

[7] "Lifted Up On High . . ." (Pt. III, Reflection 6) in *Training in Christianity*, pp. 231-36.

But rather than simply multiplying the sort of quotations that did constitute several discourses and could be used to fill a volume, we present one very pertinent statement—pertinent because in it S.K. set his doctrine in its historical perspective, differentiating it clearly from earlier forms of "imitation":

"However great [the Middle Ages'] errors may have been, its conception of Christianity has a decisive superiority over that of our time. The Middle Ages conceived of Christianity with a view to action, life, the transformation of personal existence. This is its valuable side. It is another matter that there were some singular actions they especially emphasized, that they could think that fasting for its own sake was Christianity, and so too going into a monastery, bestowing everything upon the poor, not to speak of what we can hardly refer to without smiling, such as flagellation, crawling on the knees, standing upon one leg, etc., as if this were the true imitation of Christ. This was error. . . . What was worse than the first error did not fail to make its appearance, that they got the idea of meritoriousness, thought that they acquired merit before God by their good works. And the situation became worse than this: they even thought that by good works one might acquire merit to such a degree that it accrued not only to his advantage, but that like a capitalist or bondsman one might let it accrue to the advantage of others. And it became worse, it became a regular business. . . . Then Luther came forward. . . . But let us not forget that for all this Luther did not do away with the following of Christ, nor with voluntary imitation, as the effeminate coterie is so fain to make us believe. . . . The erroneous path from which Luther turned off was exaggeration with respect to works. And quite rightly, he was not at fault: a man is justified solely and only by faith. . . . But already the next generation slackened; it did not turn in horror from exaggeration in respect to works (of which Luther had had personal experience) into the path of faith. No, they transformed the Lutheran passion into a doctrine, and with this they diminished also the vital power of faith. . . . When the monastery is the misleading thing, faith must be introduced; when the 'professor' is the misleading thing, imitation must be introduced. . . . The 'disciple' is the standard: imitation and Christ as the Pattern must be introduced."[8]

It is manifestly false to call S.K. a Catholic on the basis of his doctrine of *Nachfolge*, to equate (or for that matter, even liken) his view with that of monastic imitation. Rather, the position for which S.K. here set the stage is a doctrine of *Nachfolge* which is thoroughly Protestant in character—indeed, without which Protestantism cannot even remain true to its own normative principles. And if the possibility of a truly Protestant *Nachfolge* was a real one for S.K., then it was equally real for the entire tradition of classic Protestant sectarianism. S.K. and the Brethren were at one in their demand for a *Nachfolge* in respect to Christ that would not threaten *faith* in respect to Christ. S.K.—because he was capable of doing so—went far beyond the Brethren in formulating the theological bases for such a position.

It comes as no surprise to discover that the technique S.K. used for relating Christ the Pattern to Christ the Savior was dialectic; he did so consciously: "I must take good care, or rather God will take good care for me, that I am not led astray by concentrating too one-sidedly on Christ as our pattern. The related term through which it becomes dialectical is Christ as gift, as He who bestows Himself upon us (to call to mind Luther's regular classification)."[9]

In a sense, S.K. already had cleared the site for his dialectic. In traditional theology, *faith* is directed primarily toward the Christ of Faith, concerns primarily the divine nature; *Nachfolge*, on the other hand, (if considered at all) is directed primarily toward the historical Jesus, concerns primarily the

---

[8] "Christ as Example" (Discourse 2) in *Judge for Yourselves!*, pp. 201, 202, 205, and 207.

[9] *Papirer*, X[1] A 246 (1849), quoted in Diem, *Dialectic*, pp. 160-61.

human nature. In this situation, then, the relating of faith and *Nachfolge* faces the complication of the two being oriented toward two somewhat different objects. S.K. did not have this problem; his one object was the God-Man. As we have seen, S.K. consistently used "contemporaneousness" to denote *den Enkelte's* approach to the God-Man to the end of believing upon him through *faith*; "*Nachfolge,*" on the other hand, denotes the approach to Him for purposes of *imitation*. Yet, in practice, both are identical approaches made to the one God-Man, i.e. imaginative efforts to see and hear Jesus Christ as he was during his life on earth. As S.K. set the terms, then, it is not necessary for either *den Enkelte* or the God-Man to change roles when their relationship alternates from that of "grace bestowed upon faith" to that of "instruction enjoined for *Nachfolge.*"

The first movement of the dialectic, as S.K. explicated it, consists of such a stringent interpretation of the demand for *Nachfolge* that one is, in effect, "chased" to grace:

"What is written in the Epistle to the Galatians 2, 19, 'I through the law have died to the law,' corresponds exactly to the explanation I am accustomed to give of our relation to the 'Model.' First one must realize that the model is a crushing demand. But thereupon the model, Christ, transforms itself into grace and mercy, and tries to take hold of you in order to bear you up. But so it is that through the Model you have died to the model."[10]

"By becoming contemporaneous with Christ your pattern, you discover that you never equal Him, not even in what you term your best moments. . . . Hence it follows that you learn to flee with profit to faith and grace. . . . Thus Christ as our example is He who most severely and endlessly judges— and at the same time is the One who has pity on you."[11]

[10] *Papirer*, X² A 170 (1849), quoted in Dupre, *op.cit.,* p. 179.
[11] *Papirer*, IX A 153 (1848), quoted in Diem, *Dialectic,* pp. 113-14. Cf. "But How Can the Burden Be Light . . ." (Discourse 2) in *The Gospel of Suffering,* p. 22.

Thus far S.K. has been in complete accord with much of so-called neo-orthodox ethics; but S.K. was not content to stop at this point, as Neo-Orthodoxy is inclined to do. Here is *Nachfolge*, but in a peculiarly truncated form: there is a demand for discipleship but never any hope of accomplishing it —indeed, it was never the Demander's intention that there should be accomplishment, his interest being simply to humiliate the individual into a realization of his need for grace. S.K. saw this implication and proceeded to correct it; the following is one of his most important statements:

"Which is it? Is God's meaning, in Christianity, simply to humble man through the model (that is to say putting before us the ideal) and to console him with 'Grace,' but in such a way that through Christianity there is expressed the fact that between God and man there is no relationship, that man must express his thankfulness like a dog to man, so that adoration becomes more and more true, and more and more pleasing to God, as it becomes less and less possible for man to imagine that he could be like the model? . . . Is that the meaning of Christianity? Or is it the very reverse, that God's will is to express that he desires to be in relation with man, and therefore desires the thanks and the adoration which is in spirit and in truth: imitation. The latter is certainly the meaning of Christianity. But the former is a cunning invention of us men (although it may have its better side) in order to escape from the real relation to God."[12]

S.K. would not be as quick to talk about an "impossible ideal" as is Reinhold Niebuhr, nor would he be as ready to insist that an *impossible* ideal is truly "relevant."

So S.K. did not stop with just half a dialectic, with a *Nachfolge* that only moves the individual into grace and leaves him fixed at that point. He inserted a countermovement from grace to *Nachfolge* which would have the effect of sustaining the alternation. Imitation, he saw, *proceeds from* grace as well

[12] *Dru Journals*, 1272 (1852). Cf. *Smith Journals*, XI¹ A 27 (1854).

as *leads to* it: "The true imitation is not produced by preaching on the theme: Thou shalt imitate Christ; but as a result of preaching about how much Christ has done for me. If a man grasps and feels that truly and profoundly then imitation will follow naturally."[13] Also, this "post-faith" *Nachfolge* is itself enabled and empowered by grace; it is the Savior who makes it possible for *den Enkelte* to follow the Pattern: "It is not enough to say that Christ is the model and we only need imitate Him. In the first place, I need His assistance in order to be like Him; and in the second place, inasmuch as He is the Savior and the Redeemer of humanity, I assuredly cannot imitate Him."[14]

And the case is that *Nachfolge protects* faith no less than faith *empowers Nachfolge*. It is not that faith is the be all and end all, with *Nachfolge* as an optional supplement. In a brief but pregnant phrase S.K. said that "human honesty [is] evinced by imitation."[15] A person's willingness to follow the Pattern is the proof and test of the reality of his faith in the Savior; *Nachfolge*, far from being the enemy of faith or a substitute for it, is precisely that which preserves faith's purity and prevents it from being misused by hypocrisy and carelessness.

Thus the God-Man's functions as Redeemer *and* Pattern are integrated in a most powerful dialectic, which dialectic was given very eloquent expression in the invocatory prayer with which S.K. opened his most important discourse on *Nachfolge*:

"Help us all and every one, Thou who art both willing and able to help, Thou who art both the Pattern and the Redeemer, and again both the Redeemer and the Pattern, so that when the striver sinks under the Pattern, then the Redeemer raises him up again, but at the same instant Thou art the Pattern, to

---

[13] *Dru Journals*, 1150 (1850).
[14] *Papirer*, X¹ A 132 (1849), quoted in Dupre, *op.cit.*, p. 176.
[15] *Attack upon "Christendom,"* p. 147.

keep him continually striving. Thou, our Redeemer, by Thy blessed suffering and death, hast made satisfaction for all and for everything; no eternal blessedness can be or shall be earned by desert—it has been deserved. Yet Thou didst leave behind Thee the trace of Thy footsteps, Thou the holy pattern of the human race and of each individual in it, so that, saved by Thy redemption, they might every instant have confidence and boldness to will to strive to follow Thee."[16]

C. SCANDAL AND SUFFERING

When one first begins to reflect upon Christianity it must certainly have been an occasion of scandal to one before one enters upon it. . . . That is why one is sickened by all the chatter of fussy go-betweens about Christ being the greatest hero, etc., etc.[1]

For, to say it short and sharp: this is the very definite utterance of the New Testament, that Christianity, and the fact that one is truly a Christian must be in the highest degree an "offense" to the natural man, that he must regard Christianity as the highest treason and the true Christian as the most scurvy traitor against humanity.[2]

One may learn more profoundly and more reliably what the highest is by considering

[16] "Christ as Example" (Discourse 2) in *Judge for Yourselves!*, p. 161.

---

[1] *Dru Journals*, 105 (1837). Note particularly this date; these words were written by a university student, six years before he opened his authorship.

[2] "To Become Sober" (Discourse 1) in *Judge for Yourselves!*, p. 154. These words come toward the close of S.K.'s career, 1852.

*suffering than by observing achievements,
where so much that is distracting is present.*[3]

*The situation is this: the more thou hast to
do with God, and the more He loves thee,
the more wilt thou become, humanly speaking, unhappy for this life, the more thou wilt
have to suffer in this life.*[4]

The themes (or moods) of scandal and suffering that pervade both the Brethren and the Kierkegaardian literature are
undoubtedly to be understood as derivatives of the concept of
following Christ who is the possibility of offense—this coupled
with the doctrine of nonconformity to the world. But however derived, the sectarian parallel is unmistakable.

Regarding the scandal of Christianity, the first document of
Brethrenism, the open letter inviting participation in the
inaugural baptism, stated: "For the world, however, Christ
and His disciples are a stumbling block and an annoyance,
and it takes offense at the Word on which they are founded."[5]
The preface to the first Brethren hymnal, compiled in Germany, referred to the fact that the Christian must be willing
to bear "the shame of Jesus with the people of God."[6] And
Mack Senior answered one of the Radical Pietist queries with
these words: "[Christ] does not say that men will flock to his
gospel by the thousands in such miserable times as these are,
unfortunately, when love has grown cold in many hearts. Indeed, even the well-meaning souls do not come very willingly
to the discipleship of Jesus, where all must be denied if Christ
is to be followed rightly."[7]

[3] *Purity of Heart*, p. 149.
[4] *Attack upon "Christendom,"* p. 189.
[5] "First Eight Brethren to Palatine Pietists" (1708), in Durnbaugh,
Origins, p. 118.
[6] Preface to *Geistreiches Gesang-Buch* (1720), in *ibid.*, pp. 407-08.
[7] Mack Senior, *Basic Questions* (1713), in *ibid.*, answer to Question
10, p. 330.

Although there would be no point in doing so, we could document this sense of scandal for the remaining eighty years of our period just as extensively as we have done for the first twelve. The Brethren well understood that Christianity appears scandalous to the eyes of natural man.

The theme was, if anything, even stronger in S.K. The whole of Part II of *Training in Christianity* is a detailed study of the sources of offense that are inherent in Christ and Christianity, and the notes echo throughout S.K.'s religious works. He could put the matter into the strongest language possible: "Everywhere where these words [i.e. Christ's warning about being offended] do not resound, or at least wherever the statement of Christianity is not at every point permeated by this thought—there Christianity is blasphemy."[8]

But the most pertinent aspect of S.K.'s thought on this subject was the emphasis that present-day acceptance of Christianity is actually an aggravation of the scandal and not a mitigation of it:

"But although by taking away the possibility of offense men have gotten the whole world Christianized, the curious thing always occurs—the world is offended by the real Christian. Here comes the offense, the possibility of which is after all inseparable from Christianity. Only the confusion is more distressing than ever, for at one time the world was offended by Christianity—that was the intention; but now the world imagines that it is Christian, that it has made Christianity its own without detecting anything of the possibility of offense— and then it is offended by the real Christian."[9]

S.K. never wrote anything more sectarian in tone than these words which many of the classical sectaries could have documented out of their own experience.

A close concomitant of Christianity as scandal is the suffering the Christian must endure for his faith; and early Breth-

---

[8] *The Sickness unto Death*, p. 259.
[9] *Works of Love*, pp. 193-94.

renism was just as completely pervaded with this theme as with the former. The anonymous Brethren tract *Ein Geringer Schein* gave major attention to the theme of Christian suffering and related it in an interesting way. The tract points out that Christ's baptism—and so ours—was threefold: (1) by water; (2) by the Spirit (symbolized in the dove); and (3) by suffering (symbolized in the cross). Christ called his suffering a baptism and predicted the same for his disciples, which they experienced in due course. The first Christians fulfilled this baptism with actual martyrdoms; "but those who have not come to an outward martyr's crown even so have here carried the death of Jesus in their bodies and are also, through an inner martyrdom, sharing in a crucifixion of their lusts through the baptism of blood."[10]

And a poem by Mack Junior pointed up an important aspect of the Brethren emphasis:

> And what is the difference, if one learns
>   Out of bitterness to make sweetness
> And on the cross's beam
>   To laugh with weeping eyes!
> Thus the spirit will be strengthened,
>   And the soul acquire,
> Through Him who died for it,
>   That which the whole world does not note.
>
> When grief makes us ill,
>   Let us earnestly think
> That He who guides all things
>   Will also guide our hearts
> That through His grace we may
>   Endure in grief
> And wisely learn to sow
>   The noble seed of tears.

[10] *Ein Geringer Schein*, pp. 6-9 [my trans.—V.E.].

We have while here
   No other joy for which to hope
Until our tribulations
   Reach their proper goal
When we are reconciled with God
   Through the death of His Son,
See our misery demolished,
   And are trained to love correctly.[11]

It should be noted that an emphasis on Christian suffering does not necessarily imply morbidity or joylessness; indeed, it is precisely through suffering that one overcomes the world, and this is a source of tremendous satisfaction and hope.

There probably is no author in Christian history who has written on the theme of suffering more extensively, more profoundly, and with more feeling than Søren Kierkegaard. He wrote one series of seven discourses under the title *The Gospel of Suffering* (originally part of a larger collection) and another series of seven entitled "Exultant Notes in the Conflict of Suffering" (Part II of *Christian Discourses*); and by collecting scattered discourses on the theme, one or two more such series could be compiled. Major discussions regarding the relation of suffering to religion and Christianity put in their appearance far back in the pseudonymous literature,[12] and almost every major work thereafter at least touches upon the subject. Beyond doubt, S.K.'s personal temperament and the fact that he was himself an authentic sufferer go far in explaining the presence and extent of this emphasis; but at the same time, it was an inherent and natural part of his total religious perspective, just as with the Brethren.

Suffering is an inevitable concomitant of Christianity, made so by the very nature of the gospel and of the world: "What

[11] Mack Junior, a poem concerning suicide, in Heckman, *op.cit.*, stanzas 30-32, pp. 152-55 [I have amended the translation—V.E.]. Cf. the poem by Sauer Junior in Brumbaugh, *op.cit.*, pp. 434ff.

[12] See, for example, *Stages on Life's Way*, pp. 415ff., and *Postscript*, pp. 390ff.

is the Christianity of the New Testament? It is the suffering truth. In this mediocre, miserable, sinful, evil, ungodly world (this is the Christian doctrine) the truth must suffer, Christianity is the suffering truth because it is the truth and is in the world."[13] At times S.K. did direct his attention to how the Christian should meet suffering in general, but primarily he was concerned to preserve *Christian* suffering as a distinct— and indeed, unique—category:

"The decisive mark of Christian suffering is the fact that it is voluntary, and that it is *the possibility of offense for the sufferer*."[14]

"To suffer in likeness with Christ does not mean to encounter the unavoidable with patience, but it means to suffer ill at the hands of men because as a Christian or by being a Christian one desires and strives after the Good, so that one could avoid the suffering by ceasing to will the Good."[15]

And thus S.K. was particularly incensed against the sort of preaching that is quick to credit the patient endurance of every affliction and inconvenience as being *Christian* suffering.

Although the point has not been well heeded by his critics, S.K. was at some pains to make it clear that his doctrine of suffering did not imply melancholy (S.K.'s own melancholy was a personal accident which he strove to overcome, not a theological conviction he strove to defend). He was ready— with the Brethren—to follow the biblical injunctions to "Count it all joy . . ." (James 1:2) and "Rejoice and be exceeding glad . . ." (Matthew 5:12). As the melancholy Kierkegaard himself said: "After all, Christianity is not a melancholy thing, on the contrary it is so glad a thing that it is glad tidings to all melancholy men; only the frivolous and the defiant can make it gloomy."[16]

---

[13] *Attack upon "Christendom,"* p. 268.

[14] *Training in Christianity* (Pt. II), p. 111.

[15] "Lifted Up On High" (Pt. III, Reflection 3) in *ibid.*, p. 173.

[16] "I Have Heartily Desired . . ." (Pt. IV, Discourse 1) in *Christian Discourses*, p. 262.

How these seemingly contrary propositions regarding Christianity as suffering and as joy are to be reconciled, S.K. answered with a very effective figure of speech:

"In reality the star is situated high in the heavens, and it is no less high for the fact that seen in the ocean it seems to be below the earth. Likewise, to be a true Christian is the highest exaltation, although as reflected in this world it must appear the deepest humiliation. Humiliation is therefore in a certain sense exaltation. As soon as you eliminate the world, the turbid element which confuses the reflection, that is, as soon as the Christian dies, he is exalted on high, where he already was before, though it could not be perceived here on earth."[17]

In emphasizing suffering to the extent he did, it was inevitable that S.K. would run a great risk, namely the temptation to value suffering in and of itself, for its own sake. Although often accused of doing just this, the charge is not justified—except, as we shall see, during the very last, "black cloud" period of his life. Actually, S.K. himself saw the danger and took pains to avoid it:

"One must never desire suffering. No, you have only to remain in the condition of praying for happiness on earth. . . . You must certainly dare, for to dare (for the truth, etc.) is Christianity. . . . But if suffering cannot be, humanly speaking and understood, avoided, and you nevertheless understand yourself before God in being obliged and willing to dare: yet suffering itself must never be the *telos*, you must not dare in order to suffer, for that is presumptuous, and is to tempt God. To expose yourself to suffering for the sake of suffering is a presumptuous personal impertinence and forwardness towards God, as though you were challenging God to a contest. But when it is for the cause—even though you see that suffering is humanly speaking unavoidable, just go on and dare.

[17] "Lifted Up On High" (Pt. III, Reflection 4) in *Training in Christianity*, p. 196. Cf. "The Joyfulness of Following Christ" (Discourse I) in *The Gospel of Suffering*, p. 6.

Do not dare for the sake of suffering, but you dare in order not to betray the cause."[18]

This journal entry is dated 1852, which is quite late in S.K.'s career, following the close of the authorship proper and antedating only *Attack upon "Christendom."* And it would seem to be the case that anything S.K. said about suffering up until this time—no matter how strongly he may have insisted upon its inevitability in the Christian life, its propriety in the Christian life, and even its value as an indicator that one's actions are indeed Christian—anything he said could yet be reconciled with the above statement. However, after this time, within a period hardly longer than a year preceding his death, along with the hints of misanthropy which we have already noted there is evidence (although only *scattered* evidence) that S.K. was succumbing to the very temptation he had countered so effectively as late as 1852. We quote but one frightening instance:

"When one is able to endure the isolation involved in being a single individual, without the mitigation of any intermediate terms, without the alleviation of any illusion, alone in the endless world and the endless world of men—out of a million men 999,999 will lose their senses before they attain this isolation—alone before the face of God—then the fact of loving God and being loved by God will appear to him so blessed that for sheer happiness he must say: O, my God, now I have but one wish, one prayer, one desire, one passion, that I may experience suffering, become hated, persecuted, mocked, spit upon, put to death."[19]

"Now cracks a noble heart!" What agony of soul S.K. must have been enduring at this writing and what was its portent regarding the progress of his life and thought, we know not. The statement is not at all typical, even of his last years, and is completely contradictory to the Kierkegaard we have seen

[18] *Dru Journals*, 1270 (1852).
[19] *Dru Journals*, 1336 (1854). Cf. *Rohde Journals*, 238 (July 1855).

heretofore. Here he perverted *den Enkelte* into a solitary atom, denied the equality of all men before God (if it be that only one in a million can endure the relationship), and actually prayed for suffering. It is, of course, not this Kierkegaard who was sectarian; that, rather, was the one who held Christian suffering in dialectical balance with "the joy that was set before him."

D. RESTITUTION OF THE EARLY CHURCH

> *Christianity was an imposing figure when it stepped vigorously forth into the world and spoke its opinion, but from the moment it tried to set bounds through the pope or wanted to throw the Bible, or later the creed, at the people's head, it became like an old man who thinks that he has lived long enough in the world and wants to retire.*[1]

Most studies of sectarianism (particularly those of Reformation Anabaptism) tend to read the ideal of restoring the early church as being a central if not *the* central motif of the sectarian perspective. There is a great deal of truth in this analysis but also a suggestion that is somewhat misleading. At least in S.K. and the Brethren, there was no tendency to idealize, value, or emulate the early church *for its own sake*, just because it was the *early* church and thus entitled to some sort of special authority. Rather, with both S.K. and the Brethren, the primary foci were, as we have seen, obedience, *Nachfolge*, and, as we shall see, adherence to the New Testament. However, because the early church *was* obedient to God, *did* follow Christ, and *did* adhere to the New Testament (which last is hardly surprising inasmuch as it also *formulated* the New

---

[1] *Dru Journals*, 31 (1835). Most of S. K.'s statements in this vein come from the "post-authorship" attacker of Christendom; this one comes from the "pre-authorship" university student.

Testament)—but because the early church did these things and was as it was, it is only right and proper that it be looked to as something of an ideal.

Thus, in point of fact, the concept of restitution is *derived* from these other emphases rather than being an independent (let alone "*the* central") principle in and of itself. In order to keep this relationship clear, we have chosen to treat restitution as an appendage of *Nachfolge*.

Neither S.K. nor the Brethren spoke at any length regarding restitution per se; in passing, they did make a great number of references to the faith and life of the early Christians, which by implication make it quite clear that restitution would be an accurate description of what they desired for modern Christianity.

By all odds the most significant statement on the subject from Brethren literature is by Mack Senior. One of the queries put to him by his Radical Pietist opponents was: "On which point, then, can the undoubted divinity of your new church be recognized before all others in the whole world?" To which Mack replied:

"We have neither a new church nor any new laws. We only want to remain in simplicity and true faith in the original church which Jesus founded through His blood. We wish to obey the commandment which was in the beginning. We do not demand that undoubted divinity be recognized in our church fellowship. Rather, we would wish that undoubted divinity might indeed be recognized in Christ himself, and then in the church at Jerusalem. If this and its divinity in teaching, words, and commandments were to be acknowledged, then it could be determined whether a church has this divine teaching in it or not. If this is realized, then we think that it would be sufficient to recognize a church before all other churches in the whole world, if she is subject, as a true wife to her husband Christ, to His commands, yes, if it still strives to be even more submissive. Whoever has not known

Christ in the divinity of His commandments will hardly recognize His church even if the twelve apostles were serving as its bishops and teachers."[2]

Ultimately there is but one source and test of any church's authority, legitimacy, or value. This, of course, has nothing to do with its size, worldly power, or reputation. But neither has it to do with the antiquity of its tradition, the continuity of its government with the apostles, the "orthodoxy" of its dogma, or anything of the sort. Indeed, the ground of a church's validity is such that even having the apostles as its bishops and teachers would carry no weight; and certainly it follows that the honor and respect given the early church is not occasioned by *who* its leaders may have been. There is one test of a church: whether "she is subject as a true wife to her husband Christ" and is striving "to be even more submissive." Mack certainly implied—if not specifically granted—that the early church came closer to meeting that test than has any other church. However, the Brethren ideal should not be stated simply as a desire to restore the early church but as the desire to restore the sort of Christian obedience to which the early church gave demonstration. In short, the early church is not itself the goal but the prime example pointing toward the goal.

S.K. did not use such terms as "restitution" (nor did the Brethren). However, he did say enough to alert Hermann Diem to the possibility that some readers might *think* that S.K. advocated something of the sort. Diem himself, however, resists such an interpretation: Diem quotes S.K.: "This 1800 years of Christian history must be swept aside!" and then comments:

"But we must carefully consider in what sense Kierkegaard means this. He does not wish to put the clock back in Christian history, and hence his demand has nothing to do with all

---

[2] Mack Senior, *Basic Questions*, in Durnbaugh, *Origins*, Question 38 and its answer, pp. 341-42. Cf. Mack Junior as quoted above, p. 74.

those attempts to go back to an earlier stage of Christian development, primitive Christianity for example, in order to set over against modern Christianity as an ideal or critical criterion a type of Christianity which has not yet become involved in the complications of history and has developed no dogmatic positions. Kierkegaard is by no means such an unhistorical thinker. His concern is not to replace a later stage of history by an earlier one, but to insist on the presuppositions underlying the situation of contemporaneity with Christ, in which these historical differences—that cannot and ought not to be removed—lose their relevance for faith."[3]

But Diem's explanation will not do. He has taken a partial truth, which actually is a caricature of true sectarianism, and by disassociating S.K. from it, feels that he has satisfied the question of restitution altogether.

It is true, of course, that S.K. did not propose simply "to put the clock back in Christian history" or "to replace a later stage of history by an earlier one." Certainly not S.K., but none of the leading classical sectaries either, were such "unhistorical thinkers," such naive and unrealistic thinkers as to believe that restitution could be accomplished simply by closing one's eyes to the present and living solely in the past. Not this easily can S.K. be divorced from "all those attempts to go back"; and rather than having "nothing to do" with them, S.K.'s demand has everything to do with them. For the sophisticated interpretation given in Diem's concluding sentence simply is not adequate as exegesis of a radical demand like: "Oh, that there were someone (like the heathen who burnt the libraries of Alexandria) able to get these eighteen centuries out of the way—if no one can do that, then Christianity is abolished."[4]

But the actual distance between S.K. and Diem's interpreta-

[3] Diem, *Dialectic*, pp. 106-07.

[4] *Training in Christianity* (Pt. II), p. 144. Cf. *Rohde Journals*, 173 (1848). Cf. *Smith Journals*, XI¹ A 15, XI¹ A 22, XI² A 234, and XI² A 371 (all 1854).

tion of him becomes apparent when we realize that the factors out of church history which Diem is sure S.K. would have insisted on *preserving* (thus making it impossible that he *truly* desired the elimination of the 1800 years) are precisely those that S.K. wanted to *eliminate* by cancelling out the 1800 years. Diem names it as a defect of primitive Christianity that it had not yet "become involved in the complications of history." But that all depends upon how one understands "the complications of history." S.K. read the matter thus:

"*Witnesses for the truth* [i.e. the early Christians] . . . did not live on the doctrine, along with a family [as do modern clerics], but lived and died for the doctrine. Thereby Christianity became a power, the power which mastered and transformed the world. Thus it was served for wellnigh three hundred years; thereby Christianity became 'the power' in the world. . . . Alas, by this time there had already begun the retrogression, the illusion; instead of transforming the world, they began to transform Christianity. Worldly shrewdness hit upon the idea of turning the life of these witnesses, their sufferings, their blood, of turning it into money, or into honor and prestige."[5]

The period of the church which Diem accuses of not being involved in history S.K. understood as the period when the church actually was a power transforming the world. S.K. saw true involvement to be the church's standing out against the world, transforming it by acting as a fixed point against which the turbinations of history could be broken up. Apparently, what Diem understands as involvement in history is the church's getting into the worldly power struggle as one institution among others—precisely that which S.K. characterized as the world in process of transforming Christianity. Rather plainly, Diem and S.K. are talking past one another, and there is here no grounds for denying S.K. a doctrine of restitution.

[5] "To Become Sober" (Discourse I) in *Judge for Yourselves!*, p. 144.

The second defect Diem identifies in the early church is that it had "developed no dogmatic positions." But S.K. said:

"And verily the eighteen centuries, which have not contributed an iota to prove the truth of Christianity [and if the purpose of dogma is not absolutely to "prove," it is certainly to "explain" or "make rationally comprehensible" the truth of Christianity], have on the contrary contributed with steadily increasing power to do away with Christianity. It is by no means true, as one might consistently suppose when one acclaims the proof of the eighteen centuries, that now in the nineteenth century people are far more thoroughly convinced of the truth of Christianity than they were in the first and second generations—it is rather true (though it certainly sounds rather like a satire on the worshippers and adorers of this proof) that just in proportion as the proof supposedly has increased in cogency . . . fewer and fewer persons are convinced."[6]

Diem, plainly enough, wants nothing to do with a restitutionist ideal, but he has not made the case that S.K. was of the same mind.

There is good evidence that S.K. died in 1855 and stopped writing about the same time, but when one reads statements like the following he has cause to wonder.

"Once New Testament Christianity was reduced to the simply historical, and men imagined next that Christianity was perfectible, it was a quite straightforward discovery that there were various epochs. The epoch of the Son was New Testament Christianity, and now the epoch of the Spirit is at hand. No, no: Christianity in the New Testament *is* Christianity. And Christianity is life's examination. . . . In Christian terms there is absolutely no meaning in speaking of progress from

---

[6] *Training in Christianity* (Pt. II), pp. 143-44. Cf. S.K.'s words quoted above, pp. 318 and 332.

generation to generation. Every generation begins at the beginning, the examination is the same."[7]

"We laugh when we see a man looking for his spectacles when they are on his nose.

"But the striving of 'Christendom' is in its way even more ridiculous.

"The truth about the Christian ideal is that it has existed, Christ has lived, the Model has been given. And this ideal is related to the single person [*den Enkelte*]. Only as a single person can there be any talk of striving for it. And if the single person is to strive for it he must as a matter of course turn in the direction of the existence of the ideal, he must turn back to it, if he really is to strive for it. Christendom has turned the matter thus: the ideal for being a Christian is a goal lying infinitely distant in the future, and this is what we must strive for. So Christendom turns its back on the true ideal, which has existed, and (in the name of striving for it) strives away from it."[8]

It is possible that S.K. did not have in mind Thomas Altizer and William Hamilton of the death-of-God school or even Harvey Cox, J. A. T. Robinson, and such conservatives among the "new theologians," but if he did, his words would not need to be changed in the slightest. For S.K. has spotted what is the basic presupposition of all our "radical theology" so-called, namely, that the course of the world (which, unfortunately, S.K. was so ill-advised as to characterize as "the constant advance of nonsense"[9]) has in our day produced a man come of age who, in turn, requires a new, twentieth century Christianity (or at least a new essence of Christianity).

For the sake of honesty it should be kept very plain that, even though S.K. shows a critical temper, an iconoclasm, a religionlessness, that sounds quite similar to what we are hear-

[7] *Smith Journals,* XI[2] A 38 (1854).
[8] *Smith Journals,* XI[3] B 197 (1854).
[9] See above, p. 347.

ing today, nevertheless the entire course and movement of his religious thought is oriented in a direction diametrically opposed to that of our present-day radicals. No matter how much they choose to quote him, they have some obligation to recognize this fact.

And strictly speaking, if the word "radical" is to retain any connection with its etymological derivation, then it is S.K.'s theology that deserves the adjective and not this other. "Radical" means "to drive toward the *root*, to go back to *origins*." This precisely is the principle delineated by S.K. in the statements above and precisely the opposite of a theology that is avant-garde, "far out," and driving toward the periphery.

It should be noted that S.K.'s insistence that only *den Enkelte* can make this radical effort does in no way preclude the idea of a *Gemeinde*; obviously a caravan can move only by its members making their individual movements. But S.K.'s point is that this caravan, these individuals, move according to the daily instructions they receive from the headquarters located in the first-century revelation and not by taking a vote as to where the company thinks they might like to go next.

S.K.'s statements make it rather apparent that he did in fact desire a situation which with accuracy could be typified as restitution, the ideal of a church ready to "go it alone" with just the New Testament and without the "help" of 1800 years of creed, dogma, tradition, and theology. There would seem to be no convincing reason why we should not read S.K.'s "elimination of the 1800 years," his references to "the Christianity of the New Testament and the primitive age"[10] and to testing modern Christianity "by the measure of primitive Christianity,"[11] as meaning essentially what classic Protestant sectarianism has meant by "restitution of the early church."

[10] *Attack upon "Christendom,"* p. 183.
[11] *Ibid.*

CHAPTER XIII

THE CHRISTIAN'S BOOK

Was I not in the right,
and am I not, in saying
that first and foremost everything
must be done to make it perfectly
definite what is required in the
New Testament for being a Christian?[1]

To be alone with the Holy Scriptures!
I dare not! When I turn up a passage in it,
whatever comes to hand—it catches me instantly,
it questions me
(indeed it is as if it were God Himself that questioned me),
"Hast thou done what thou readest there?"[2]

A point on which Kierkegaard and the Brethren show as much affinity as anywhere is their view and use of the Bible. An accurate and very useful study regarding S.K.'s position already has been made—this as the preface to the Minear-Morimoto Index, *Kierkegaard and the Bible*.[3] Rather than attempting to duplicate this work of one who is recognized both as a Bible scholar and an authority on S.K., we will confine

[1] *Attack upon "Christendom,"* p. 25.
[2] ". . . The Mirror of the Word" (Discourse I) in *For Self-Examination*, p. 56.
[3] Minear and Morimoto, *op.cit.*, pp. 3-13. We are assuming that Minear was the one primarily responsible for the preface itself.

ourselves to the comparison with sectarianism. However, much of what Minear has to say is germane to our topic. He establishes the central role that Scripture played in S.K.'s life and thought, saying: "It is safe to assert that the Scriptures exerted a more continuous, a more creative, a more profound constraint upon his nimble thoughts, than did any other book or any comparable group of books. . . . In short, no area of S.K.'s life or work was exempt from the repeated impact of that Scripture through which God had chosen to speak to him."[4] Indeed, Niels Thulstrup—who may well qualify as the foremost Kierkegaard authority of our time—has pushed this emphasis so far as to maintain that the orientation of S.K.'s thought toward the New Testament was so complete that his writings can be understood, analyzed, and criticized only against the biblical background—rather than according to the customary norms of philosophical or theological methodology.[5]

The truth of Thulstrup's assertion does not make itself evident upon the first reading of S.K. For one thing, he was not given to the citation of proof texts or to constant appeals to scriptural authority. For another, the pseudonymous literature vastly complicates the picture, for here the biblical bases of S.K.'s thought were deliberately suppressed; material written by non-Christian pseudonyms for the benefit of "non-Christian Christians" could hardly afford to show its true colors. Nevertheless, as a great deal of our previous discussion has indicated, even the pseudonymous ideas (such as *den Enkelte,* the leap of faith, subjectivity, etc.), when traced through to their denouement, become quite recognizable as New Testament concepts—which undoubtedly is where S.K. originally got them and what he had in mind all along. And by far the

---

[4] *Ibid.*, p. 6.

[5] Niels Thulstrup, "The Complex of Problems Called 'Kierkegaard,'" in *Critique*, p. 295. Cf. John Wild, "The Rebirth of the Divine," in *Christianity and Existentialism*, pp. 159, 165.

greater part of his religious works—all of the discourses and such—are expositions of scripture texts. To be sure, they do not represent critical, scientific *exegesis*, but they are *expositions* of scripture for all that. Indeed, a review of the topics we have lifted up in this study, done with the New Testament (and particularly the Gospels) in mind, would make the orientation of Kierkegaardian thought quite evident.

Further, Minear makes a rather surprising judgment regarding the quality of S.K.'s use of the Bible:

"He was a particularly gifted interpreter of the Bible. In fact, we do not hesitate to predict that coming generations will increasingly reckon with him not so much as a philosopher, as a poet, as a theologian, or as a rebel against Christendom, but as an expositor of Scripture."[6]

"Neither Fundamentalists nor scientific historicists are likely to make much sense of Kierkegaard's methods of exposition. No longer, however, are these two schools of historiography the dominant ones. Everywhere one may detect signs of a spreading revolt, not only against Protestant bibliolatry but also against the idolatries implicit in rationalism and historicism. And wherever this revolt is found, there will also be found the hermeneutical influence of this Danish layman."[7]

Minear maintains that S.K. has an important contribution to make regarding biblical studies; we will maintain that this contribution is essentially that of sectarianism.

In the first place, S.K. was very insistent that the New Testament constitutes the norm and definition of Christianity. Not the creeds, catechisms, or symbols; not the tradition of the church; not the theological formulations of either the past or the present; not personal experience or one's own understanding of existence; not the demands of the age; but the New Testament is *the* norm and definition. In the *Attack,* the phrase S.K. used as a technical term to denote the ideal and goal for which he strove was "the Christianity *of the New*

---

[6] Minear and Morimoto, *op.cit.,* pp. 7-8.   [7] *Ibid.,* p. 11.

Testament." In the very first item of that *Attack* he suggested putting "the New Testament alongside Mynster's sermons";[8] and his programmatic statement appealed to the same norm.[9] Elsewhere he said, "Christianity (that is, the Christianity of the New Testament—and everything else is not Christianity, least of all by calling itself such) . . ."[10] He spoke of his "unaltered conviction that the Christianity of the New Testament is Christianity, the other [i.e. the modern version] being a knavish trick."[11] And, very bluntly: "The New Testament indeed settles what Christianity is, leaving it to eternity to pass judgment upon us. In fact the priest is bound by an oath upon the New Testament—so it is not possible to regard that as Christianity which men like best and prefer to call Christianity."[12]

Indeed, S.K. held this thought so passionately that he could describe the nature and course of his own authorship as a case in which the "poet suddenly transformed himself, threw away the guitar, if I may speak thus, [and] brought out a book which is called *The New Testament of Our Lord and Savior Jesus Christ*."[13] It would not be inaccurate to epitomize S.K.'s entire career as an attempt to apply the New Testament norm to the Christianity of his day.

At first blush this might seem to be simply a restatement of the Reformation principle of the return to scripture. It is that, but it is more than that; it is—as all sectarianism is—a Reformation principle somewhat more radically interpreted and applied than the churchly tradition would do. Thus, on the pages that follow, as we discover *how* S.K. approached the Bible and *what* he understood it to be, it will become clear that his return to scripture was not simply that of Protestantism but even more specifically it was that of Protestant sectarianism.

---

[8] *Attack upon "Christendom,"* p. 5.
[9] See it quoted above, pp. 23-24.
[10] *Attack upon "Christendom,"* p. 29.
[11] *Ibid.*, p. 162.
[12] *Ibid.*, p. 32. Cf. S.K. as quoted above, p. 32.
[13] *Ibid.*, p. 118.

At the outset it should be noted that S.K. consistently spoke of "the New Testament," not "the Bible." The distinction is significant. S.K., of course, made use of both Testaments; witness, for example, his preoccupation with the figures of Abraham and Job. But there was a difference. The Old Testament provided material for contemplation and edification, but S.K. did not credit it with the binding and definitive *authority* that he did the New. He never derived commandments or norms from the Old, although he found them in abundance in the New. At one point early in his career S.K. gave voice to the distinction; his practice would indicate that he held this opinion throughout: "That's the difficulty of it, that one has both the Old and the New Testament; for the Old Testament has entirely different categories. For what would the New Testament say to a faith which thinks it should get things quite to its liking in the world, in the temporal, instead of letting this go and grasping the eternal? Hence the inconstancy of the clerical address, according as the Old or the New Testament is transparent in it."[14]

The Brethren position coincided with that of S.K. both as regards the *normativeness* of the New Testament and the fact that it is the *New* Testament that is normative. Indeed, Brethren adherence to the idea was conspicuous enough that the colonial historian Robert Proud was led to mention it: "[The Brethren] have a great esteem for the New Testament, valuing it higher than the other books; and when they are asked about the articles of their faith, they say they know of no others but what are contained in this book; and therefore can give none."[15]

With the Brethren, as with S.K., reference was customarily made to "the New Testament" rather than to "the Bible"— although also, as with S.K., the early Brethren did in no way

[14] *Papirer*, IV A 143 (1843), quoted in the translator's introduction to *Repetition*, p. xli.
[15] Robert Proud, *op.cit.*, quoted in Brumbaugh, *op.cit.*, p. 524.

reject or neglect the Old Testament as a help toward under-standing the New. The anonymous Brethren tract *Ein Geringer Schein* became quite specific. In explaining (for the benefit of benighted Quakers who had challenged Brethren practice) why the command of baptism is binding while that of circumcision is not, the text about the law and the prophets being until John is quoted, and it is prescribed that, since the coming of Christ, only his commands have normative status.[16] Later, in a rather lengthy passage, the point is strongly emphasized that "if anyone receives a spirit which inwardly persuades him of being the Spirit of God," and if this spirit "does not remind him of all that which Jesus of Nazareth taught to his disciples 1700 years before," it is manifestly a lying spirit. Indeed, by the single test of obedience to the New Testament teachings of Christ one can determine whether he truly believes and truly possesses the Spirit of God.[17]

A further principle has here become evident: it is not simply the New Testament that is normative, but within the New Testament, the teachings of Jesus become the ultimate authority for the Christian life. Mack Senior stated this unequivocally in one of the earliest Brethren documents, his letter to Count Charles August, dated 1711:

"The sinner shall repent and believe in the Lord Jesus and should be baptized in water upon his confession of faith. He should then seek to carry out everything Jesus has commanded and publicly bequeathed in His Testament. If we are doing wrong herein, against the revealed word of the Holy Scriptures, be it in teaching, way of life, or conduct, we would gladly receive instruction. If, however, no one can prove this on the basis of Holy Scriptures, and yet persecute us despite this, we would gladly suffer and bear it for the sake of the teachings of Jesus Christ."[18]

[16] *Ein Geringer Schein*, pp. 18-19.
[17] *Ibid.*, pp. 27-28 [my trans.—V.E.].
[18] Mack Senior, a letter to Count Charles August (1711), in Durn-

No one has made a tally of the biblical references in early Brethren literature, but the impression certainly is that Brethren usage conformed to Brethren theory, i.e. there was a tendency to focus on the Gospels, on the teachings of Jesus, and even more pointedly, on the Sermon on the Mount. Indeed, one present-day Brethren historian avows that the "clearest" characteristic of primitive Brethrenism is its emphasis on the Sermon;[19] but whether "clearest" or not, it is plain that the Brethren reading of scripture was of this order.

A tally *has* been made of the scriptures exposited and cited by S.K., and even a cursory scanning of the Minear-Morimoto Index is most revealing. Clearly, S.K. valued and used the Gospels more than the Epistles;[20] the Synoptics seem to get more attention than John; among the Synoptics it is quite evident that Matthew (the "teaching" Gospel) is strongly favored; and most unmistakable of all is the fact that the Sermon on the Mount attracted S.K.'s attention and comments more than any other comparable passage of scripture—with

baugh, *Origins*, p. 163. The letter is an apology and plea for tolerance addressed to the Count, who had expelled Mack and the other Brethren from his territory.

[19] Mallott, *op.cit.*, p. 15.

[20] S.K.'s appeal to the Gospels, on the face of it, might seem to coincide with the general movement of nineteenth century theology, with its Quest of the Historical Jesus and all. However, there was a decided difference in orientation which makes any correlation very problematical. Most certainly, S.K. did not use the New Testament as a source book for dogmatic definitions (in any case, this interest inevitably centers in the Pauline materials rather than the Gospels). But just as certainly, S.K. did not use the New Testament as source material for a scientific-critical study designed to explain the origin and rise of Christianity as a historical phenomenon which consequently had evolved into a nineteenth century religion. S.K. showed no interest at all in this "objective" problem of New Testament research nor in the scientific methods of exegesis it employed. The pages that follow will make it clear that S.K. did not read the Gospels in order to formulate Søren Kierkegaard's opinion of Jesus of Nazareth but to discover Jesus' opinion of Søren Kierkegaard. This personalized, devotional, life-centered approach is essentially sectarian-pietistic rather than nineteenth century historical-critical.

the possible exception of what S.K. once called his favorite passage, the first chapter of James.[21]

This coincidence between S.K. and the Brethren is, of course, more than just "coincidence"; it is the natural consequence of their emphasis on contemporaneousness and *Nachfolge*, on religion as life rather than doctrine. S.K., at least, was well aware that he read scripture from a somewhat different angle than did traditional churchly Protestantism; he commented on the fact a number of times:

"Luther's doctrine is not merely a reversion to primitive Christianity but a modification of Christianity. He drags St. Paul one-sidedly to the fore and uses the Gospels less. He himself supplies the best refutation of his own biblical theory; he rejects the Epistle of St. James, and why? because it does not belong to the Canon? No, he does not deny that; but on dogmatic grounds, and consequently his starting point is above the Bible."[22]

"It is easy to see that Luther's preaching of Christianity distorts the Christian standpoint. He concerned himself one-sidedly with the Apostle Paul and then goes so far (and this often happens) as to use the Apostle retrospectively as the norm for testing the Gospels; if he does not find Paul's doctrine in the Gospels then he concludes, '*Ergo* this is no Gospel.' Luther seems to have been completely blind to the fact that the true situation is that the Apostle has already degenerated by comparison with the Gospel. And this misguided attitude which Luther adopted then continued in Protestantism, which made of Luther the absolute criterion."[23]

---

[21] *Dru Journals*, 1225 (1851).

[22] *Dru Journals*, 1008 (1849). Luther could have spared himself at least some of S.K.'s wrath if he had picked any book other than James to call "straw"; but seriously, the completely different evaluation that Luther and S.K. put upon that epistle stands as a very accurate symbol of the difference between churchly and sectarian Protestantism.

[23] *Papirer*, XI¹ A 572 (1854), quoted in Diem, *Dialectic*, p. 177. Cf. *Rohde Journals*, 213, and *Attack upon "Christendom,"* pp. 282-83, note.

Whether S.K. knew that the Pauline epistles were written *before* the Gospels is not clear; doubtlessly the Brethren did not know this. But nevertheless, the knowledge would not have changed the case, because the intent of S.K. and the Brethren was not primarily the scholarly one of getting back to the most primitive sources but the doctrinal one of re-establishing the historical Jesus both as the Savior who is the ground of faith and as the Pattern who is the ground of *Nachfolge.*

And a point which we have made time and again needs to be reiterated here. This appeal from Paul to Jesus sounds suspiciously like the Liberalism of the Old-Quest period; however, with both the Brethren and S.K., the context, motivation, and results of the move were entirely different. It is not with the sectaries as with the Liberals an attempt to escape, or even to de-emphasize, the deity of Christ, his unique role in atonement for and redemption from sin. Both S.K. and the Brethren understood what post-Liberal scholarship has demonstrated, that the Gospels are every bit as kerygmatically oriented as are the writings of Paul. The distinction is, then, that Liberalism wanted to flee the Pauline kerygma by having recourse to a merely historical Jesus of the Gospels (as though the Gospels knew anything of a *merely historical* Jesus); S.K. and sectarianism, on the other hand, wanted to keep the kerygma firmly grounded in the historical Jesus who was not only the source and object of the proclamation but the pattern of the Christian life as well.

In fact, even though S.K. spoke of the Apostle's "degeneration," his quarrel was not so much with Paul as with what the church has tended to make of Paul:

"In particular, the purely natural historical truth of things is overlooked. Thus it is forgotten that the Apostle is a person engaged in existence, who with flashes of insight flings out a few words of comfort in order to keep a Christian community going. At first people transformed the Apostle's hastily-written letters into something fantastic, God knows what. Now they are distorted in a doctrinal sense. In reality they are impulsive. When everything is at stake, and when each day it is a question of winning new converts or of maintaining the faith of those who are already won, there is no time for fantastic speculations or doctrinal applications. People forget Paul the man over the shreds of manuscript which he dashed off and which are now treated in a most un-Pauline way."[24]

At this point, S.K.'s opinion of *which* scriptures are most important leads directly into his hermeneutical theory on *how* scripture is to be read. S.K.'s main thrust—in which the Brethren concurred completely—was that the Bible is not intended to be read objectively (impersonally) as a sourcebook either of dogma or of history but subjectively (personally) as God's guidance and instruction for *den Enkelte*. It is this aspect of his thought which S.K. presented so clearly and compactly in one discourse, "How to Derive True Benediction from Beholding Oneself in the Mirror of the Word,"[25] and which Paul Minear so well discusses. We need indicate only the main outline of the view.

S.K. was passionately concerned to resist the tendency to "make God's Word something impersonal, objective, a doctrine—whereas instead it is as God's voice thou shouldst hear it."[26] Or as he elsewhere so bitingly put it: "People treat the Scriptures so scientifically that they might quite as well be anonymous writings [rather than *God's* word to *them*]."[27] The alternative, then, is this: "The divine authority of the Gospel speaks not to one man about another man, not to you, the reader, about me, or to me about you—no, when the Gos-

---

[24] *Papirer*, X² A 548 (1850), quoted in Diem, *Dialectic*, pp. 174-75. Our study has come full circle. We used Deissmann's statement about Paul to introduce a thesis concerning S.K. The compliment is here returned as S.K. supports Deissmann's thesis.

[25] This is Discourse I in *For Self-Examination*, pp. 33ff.

[26] *Ibid.*, p. 64.

[27] *The Book on Adler*, p. 27.

pel speaks it speaks to the single individual. It does not speak *about* us men, you and me, but it speaks *to* us men, you and me."[28]

In his core discourse, S.K. brought this entire line of thought to its climax in a most impressive figure of speech, likening the scriptures to a love letter from God.[29] He pursued the analogy at some length, noting a number of implications, such as how the lover will want to be alone with the letter rather than calling in others to help interpret it and how he will focus not simply upon the text of the communication but upon the one whom it communicates. However, one of S.K.'s points merits our particular attention. He assumed that in the letter the beloved had made a request or expressed a desire. In such case, S.K. pointed out, a true lover will not be inclined to ponder and puzzle and worry over the wording, uncertain as to whether he completely understands, afraid that he might do more than the beloved had in mind. Rather, the impulse of his love will be to strive for an immediate, uninhibited obedience that is much more afraid of showing reluctance than inaccuracy. As S.K. put it: "When thou readest God's Word, it is not the obscure passages which impose a duty upon thee [to investigate and consult until they be deciphered], but that which thou understandest; and with that thou must instantly comply."[30]

S.K.'s view has much in common with that of modern existentialist, kerygma theology (which is in large part derived from him), but there are also significant differences. The emphasis on the Word as a living communication directed to me, concerning my existence, to be appropriated by me—this is similar. However, modern theology understands that Word almost exclusively as a word *about* Christ (the kerygma) which I need only *accept*; lacking is the Kierkegaardian em-

[28] *Works of Love*, p. 31; cf. pp. 103-04.
[29] ". . . The Mirror of the Word" (Discourse I) in *For Self-Examination*, pp. 51ff.
[30] *Ibid.*, p. 54.

phasis on the word *of* Christ which I am called upon to *obey*.

The Brethren view, on the other hand, was so completely in agreement with S.K.'s that if the two were exchanged the deception would be difficult to detect. Mack Senior, for example, said: "A faithful child of God looks only to his heavenly Father, and believes and follows Him in His revealed Word, because he is certain of and believes that God and His spoken Word are completely one."[31] And Michael Frantz observed that, for Christians, the word is "cherished as a seed from God planted in their hearts."[32]

The most impressive Brethren statement, however, we quote at length—precisely because the parallel with S.K. is so striking. The section of the anonymous *Ein Geringer Schein* which deals with scripture opens thus:

"Holy Scripture is a letter from God which he, through the working of his eternal Spirit, has caused to be written to the human race.

"That which stands written in the New Testament is directed particularly to all those who have hope of becoming inheritors of the good which in the New Testament is bequeathed to the children of the new-testamental covenant. Now whoever is such a one, he has grounds for seeing the New Testament as a letter from the eternal God written to him; and all other books, writings, letters, and opinions—and particularly his own ideas—draw him further and further away from God's letter. And as is the case among us, that a person's testament becomes fixed through the death of him who made it—so that we know that this is the whole of his last will and that afterwards nothing more can be added to it (Heb. 9:17)—thus Christ also, through his death, has fixed and sealed the New Testament.

"Therefore it is urgently required of Christendom that all

[31] Mack Senior, *Rights and Ordinances*, in Durnbaugh, *Origins*, p. 383.
[32] Michael Frantz, *op.cit.*, p. 36.

the words of Christ and his Spirit come to be so read, considered, and believed that they be carried with groanings in prayer to God; that they be received and appropriated in true contrition of heart; that the whole New Testament be written by the finger of God on the heart of the reader until his entire life becomes a living letter from God in which all men can read the commands of Christ (2 Cor. 3:3). It is not enough for a person to see the New Testament as a book where, indeed, the truth stands written, yet, nevertheless, one which does not greatly apply to us or does not commit us to the practice of the commands of Christ."[33]

Whoever wrote *Ein Geringer Schein* might well be identified as Kierkegaard *redivivus* (or more accurately, *predivivus*).

If the Bible is primarily a personal communication in which God instructs *den Enkelte*, then the use to which *den Enkelte* must put scripture is as a test, or measure, of his own life. S.K. was insistent on this score and centered on the idea by using the mirror analogy from James 1:22-25:

"If thou dost assume an impersonal (objective) relationship to God's Word, there can be no question of beholding thyself in a mirror; for to look in a mirror surely implies a personality, an ego; a wall can be seen in a mirror but cannot see itself or behold itself in the mirror. No, in reading God's Word thou must continually say to thyself, 'It is to me this is addressed, it is about me it speaks.' "[34]

"It is only too easy to understand the requirements contained in God's Word—'give all thy goods to the poor,' 'when a man smites thee upon the right cheek, turn to him also the left,' 'when a man takes away thy coat, let him have thy cloak also,' 'rejoice always,' 'count it all joy when ye fall into divers temptations,' etc. . . . No poor wretch of the most limited intelligence can truly say that he is unable to understand the require-

[33] *Ein Geringer Schein*, pp. 1-2 [my trans.—V.E.].
[34] ". . . The Mirror of the Word" (Discourse I) in *For Self-Examination*, p. 68.

ment—but flesh and blood are reluctant to understand and be obliged to do accordingly."[35]

The Brethren affirmed this view as strongly as did S.K. In this case it was Michael Frantz who anticipated Kierkegaard even to using the mirror analogy:

> A mirror is thy word so beautiful
>   Wherein I truly can see myself—
> Whether I proceed according to Jesus—
>   Which cannot be seen in the same
>   way in things of the world.
>
> Thy word, Lord Jesus, is a scales
>   With which I truly weigh myself
> As to whether I am disposed toward thee
>   To do thy will in all things.[36]

And elsewhere he suggested that "in the mirror of what Christ has taught one sees whether he is a new man or old."[37]

A final observation is in place regarding the Brethren-Kierkegaardian approach to scripture. Both the Dunkers and the Dane were inclined to be quite uncritical (in a scholarly sense) in their reading of the Bible. For the Brethren—as simple, unlettered believers living in the eighteenth century—there was, of course, no alternative; the science of biblical criticism had not yet developed. With S.K., however, it had to be deliberate; he lived late enough and knew enough that we would expect him to show much more critical sophistication than he does.

However, even though both S.K. and the Brethren accorded scripture the highest sort of authority, and even though both read it uncritically, yet their position was very far from being

---

[35] *Ibid.*, p. 59. S.K.'s examples of Christian requirements are as revealing as the point to which he was speaking.

[36] Michael Frantz, *op.cit.*, stanzas 65-66 [my trans.—V.E.].

[37] *Ibid.*, stanza 321.

literalistic, legalistic bibliolatry. Indeed, the Brethren may well have had a somewhat freer and more "liberal" view of scripture than did most of their eighteenth century churchly compeers. For one thing, the very fact that both S.K. and the Brethren could and would grant a higher degree of authority to the New Testament than to the Old; and within the New Testament, to the Gospels; and within the Gospels, to the commands of Jesus—this is demonstration enough that they were not fettered to a "dead-level" concept of inspiration that sees every letter of the Bible as equally and infallibly God's word.

Also, their antipathy to impersonal, objective theologizing as much as outlaws fundamentalistic, or even scholarly, "proof-texting" (which is about as highly objectivizing a procedure as one could devise).[38]

Then, too, by positing the reading of scripture as being personal communion with God and thus opening up a vital role for the guiding and enlightening work of the Spirit, both S.K. and the Brethren again far transcended a narrow literalism. For the Brethren, these implications became most apparent in Mack Junior's open letter on feetwashing, where he developed a total view that eventuated in statements such as:

"Scripture must be understood and looked upon with a spiritual eye of love and calmness. . . . True wisdom and her lovers must be minded as James teaches and says, 'But the wisdom from above is in the first place pure; and then peace-loving, considerate, and open to reason.' . . . Therefore the Scriptures call for spiritual eyes, mind, and understanding. Otherwise, through literalistic interpretation, if a person without true illumination were to try to hold fast to the letter in one place, he would have to disregard and act contrary to it in another place, and thus we would have nothing but trouble and division. Therefore, dear brethren, let us watch and be

---

[38] In this regard, see S.K.'s statement quoted above, pp. 330-31.

careful. And above all, preserve *love*, for then we will preserve *light*. . . . Then our good God, who is love purely and impartially, can and will add by degrees whatever may be lacking in this or that knowledge of the truth."[39]

[39] See the full text above, pp. 83ff.

Part Three
The Opening Conclusion

CHAPTER XIV

WHAT SHALL WE DO WITH S.K.?

The central nerve of my work as an author
really lies in the fact
that I was essentially religious
when I wrote Either/Or.[1]

Whatever of true Christianity
is to be found in the course of the centuries
must be found in the sects and their like.[2]

The central and omnipresent orientation of Søren Kierkegaard's life-work was religious existence; he was not essentially a philosopher, a psychologist, a theologian, a social critic, or a literatus, but a teacher of Christianity (actually, a *pastor*, or shepherd of souls). And the perspective from which Søren Kierkegaard viewed Christianity was a radical discipleship essentially one with the concept of classic Protestant sectarianism. This has been our thesis, and we have endeavored to give it demonstration.

But more: the anomaly of the situation is that after the historical period of classic Protestant sectarianism was as good as completed, there then appeared on the scene its greatest ex-

---

[1] *Dru Journals*, 795 (1848).   [2] *Papirer*, XI[2] A 435 (1855).

ponent, its shrewdest analyst, its most able apologist, its best presenter. None of the recognized leaders of the sectarian tradition even begin to match S.K.'s profundity or breadth of understanding regarding the basic nature and dynamic of Protestant sectarianism. By rights, S.K. should have lived along with Luther and Calvin, at the beginning of his tradition and not at its conclusion.

But the role of being one "untimely born," one for whom "the times are out of joint," was ever Kierkegaard's. In an early letter written to his boyhood friend Emil Boesen at the time when S.K. was breaking through into an intimate and personal commitment to the Christian faith, he said, "The more I think about our motto: '*A church stands in the distance*,' the more I too feel the truth of what you once noted, that it has come considerably closer—but more than an *auditor* I cannot become just yet."[3]

In truth, this motto—dating no one knows how early from S.K.'s student days—is the story of his life and work. *A church stands in the distance.* A symbol of Christianity dominated his horizon; even when S.K. seemed to be looking at aesthetics, at philosophy, at the world—still the shadow of that spire fell across everything within his field of vision, for a *church* stands in the distance. But a church stands *in the distance*. Although the journey of his life, the course of his authorship, was that of "coming considerably closer," nevertheless, more than an "auditor" he could not become just yet. And S.K.'s "just yet" never came in this life. Ever approaching, never arriving—a church stands in the distance.

There never lived a more fervent Protestant than Søren Kierkegaard; yet, precisely because of his fervency, because he was a Protestant's Protestant, he could never be happy in Protestantism; in fact, he felt impelled, in the name of Christianity, to mount an attack upon Christendom. But likewise,

---

[3] S.K. to Emil Boesen (July 17, 1838), in *Breve og Aktstykker*, p. 42 [my trans.—V.E.].

as a sectary born after the age of sectarianism, and as a melancholy genius, one of mankind's ugly ducklings, where was he to find the *Gemeinde* which he described but never knew? Where, in the nineteenth century, was the sort of church he sought? A church stands in the distance, but it has no door for Søren Kierkegaard.

A church stands in the distance, and S.K.'s very name reflects the symbol, for, in Danish, the word *Kirkegaard* means "churchyard," the complex of parsonage, cemetery, etc., that surrounds the church proper. S.K.'s ancestors had adopted this surname because, as poverty-stricken peasants, they were living in the manse of a church parish which was too small and weak to merit a resident minister.[4] And traditionally, this is about where S.K. and sectarianism belong—in the churchyard. Too authentically Christian to be absolutely excluded, too radical to be comfortably included, churchly Protestantism has tended to relegate its sectarian brethren (including S.K.) to the churchyard—whether to the cemetery where the dead are put away, or to the parsonage where the leadership of the church lives, we will not venture to say. But a man named "churchyard," before whom a church stands, yet always with him on the outside—this is S.K. the Sectary.

But if this be Kierkegaard, what shall we do with him? What is the ultimate significance of this study? What, if anything, does it portend for Kierkegaard studies and for the uses to which Kierkegaardian ideas and influences are put? In short, what difference does it make whether S.K. was a sectary or not?

For one thing, to achieve a more accurate identification of his religious perspective cannot but lead to more accurate interpretations of his thought. For example, getting him into the correct context immediately clears up some problems which have plagued Kierkegaard studies: how it could be that

[4] Walter Lowrie, *Kierkegaard* [first published 1938], (New York: Harper Torchbooks, 1962), Vol. I, p. 20.

he was neither a typical Protestant nor a typical Catholic and yet not some sort of ungainly hybrid; and how his attack upon Christendom could be understood as honestly and sincerely radical and yet not ultimately intended for the destruction of the church.

But if our thesis is correct, its implications reach far beyond "Kierkegaard studies." If he was as we have described him, if the central motifs of his thought were as we have described them, then it is clear that, no matter how influential in how many fields S.K. has been for modern thought (and, in our judgment, by far the greater part of that influence has been for the good), nevertheless S.K. has not yet been recognized in the witness he personally was most concerned to make. S.K. knew that his work was for the future, saying, "Should it prove that the present age will not understand me—very well then, I belong to history, knowing assuredly that I shall find a place there and what place it will be."[5]

But if our thesis is correct, that time and place are not yet. Certainly there can be no complaint about the *extent* of honor and attention he has received in our day, but whether the world actually has heard what he was intent to say is another matter. If our thesis is correct—then look again at the Contents with its list of the themes and motifs that identify S.K.'s understanding of radical discipleship. Few of these are ideas with which the name Kierkegaard is associated today, few are ideas that figure strongly in Christian thought today. What the world has yet heard is only the prelude of the Kierkegaardian witness.

If our thesis is correct, and if S.K. were allowed to speak his own piece in his own way, the result would be what we might call "Neo-Sectarianism," or "Kierkegaardian Sectarianism." If it was appropriate for the Reformation of the sixteenth century to have a radical, sectarian wing, perhaps Neo-Reformation thought of the twentieth century could do with the same

[5] *Point of View*, p. 98.

sort of adjunct. S.K. would be the man to give it leadership.

What form a Neo-Sectarian movement might take would be hard to say. Clearly, it would consist of a new emphasis upon the major insights of classic sectarianism, mediated through the writings of Kierkegaard, and applied to the contemporary scene. It definitely would *not* result in theological systems to compete with those of Neo-Reformation thought. Just as classic sectarianism accepted and assumed the major premises of Protestant doctrine and constructed upon this base not simply a different variety of theological elaboration but the radical definition of a way of life, so could Neo-Sectarianism start with the basic insights of Neo-Reformation thought and proceed in its own unique direction. Not the creedal system of a Barth nor the philosophic-theological system of a Tillich, but the free and unstructured approach of a Kierkegaard is the only method appropriate to radical discipleship.

In this day of ecumenical freedom and dialogue, Neo-Sectarianism probably would not be forced into founding new denominations, as earlier was the case. Today the churches are much more open to inner renewal and change than they were in the time of Menno Simons, Alexander Mack, or even Søren Kierkegaard. Those churches that are descended from the classic sects would have a contribution to make, but there is no reason why a Kierkegaardian Sectarianism would have to center in them. There is, indeed, some cause to believe that these churches might not be adequate for such a role; their new-found "acceptance" within the ecumenical order has had the psychological effect of making them eager to merit this trust by proving that they can be "churches" along with the best of them. In many respects their present drift is toward the evading of their heritage and not the recovery of it.

Neo-Sectarianism, if true to its Kierkegaardian as well as its Radical-Reformation heritage, would have to be a very broadly based, multi-voiced and multi-centered, grass-roots movement of the infiltrating and leaven-working sort. Organization, formalism, and institutionalism, of course, would be completely antithetical to its genius.

There are some indications that modern Christendom may be ready for a move toward radical discipleship; there are some situations opening the way for such a witness; there is current among us some thinking to which such a witness could relate. For one thing, Kierkegaard scholarship itself seems to be tending toward a more sectarian-like interpretation of S.K. And the name Kierkegaard now enjoys sufficient authority and prestige that his "sponsorship" would provide entrée for Neo-Sectarian emphases. S.K. would be listened to where Menno Simons and Alexander Mack would not.

In the second place, sectarian studies (particularly those of the Radical Reformation) have progressed to the point that there are now available the materials and analyses which make possible a much better understanding, a much fairer and more accurate picture of the true nature of sectarianism, than ever has been the case before.

Further, the modern ecumenical movement with its atmosphere of mutuality, of being willing to listen and learn from all traditions that make up the body of Christ—this affords many new opportunities for sectarian ideas to get a hearing. Neo-Sectarianism could speak from within the councils of the church in a way that was completely forbidden to the classic sects.

As the Reformation provided the only proper theological seed-bed in which classic Protestant sectarianism could germinate and grow, so might Neo-Reformation thought provide a ground for Neo-Sectarianism in a way that no other modern theology could. The relationship would be more than coincidental, for through his influences in the formulation of Neo-Reformation thought, S.K. already has been preparing the soil for his sectarian planting. Enough hints have been given earlier to indicate our judgment that the theology of Emil Brunner (already impregnated with Kierkegaard) is best suited to the purpose, but many of the current theological emphases are to the point.

Closely related, of course, is the rather new and growing interest in Bible study which is penetrating even to the lay level. A faith as strongly Bible-centered as sectarianism craves precisely such an atmosphere; and Paul Minear's prediction about S.K. coming to the fore as a Bible teacher simply underlines the possibilities for Neo-Sectarianism. In this regard, we commented earlier upon how the New Quest of the Historical Jesus seems to be putting scholarly support under the Kierkegaard-sectarian Christology, thus preparing the way for new emphases upon contemporaneousness and *Nachfolge*. Neo-Sectarianism could help to direct and apply these developments.

Clearly, one of the major movements in the church today is the search for a new role for the laity. An emphasis upon radical discipleship, with a Kierkegaardian doctrine of the equality of all men before God and a sectarian doctrine of Christians who are neither clergy nor lay, could help ensure that this trend eventuates in something more than a few rather meaningless concessions on the part of the clergy.

Psychology is singing the praises of the therapeutic value of small-, in-group experience. Churches are experimenting with the techniques. Neo-Sectarianism could make a great contribution by elucidating the nature and practice of *religious Gemeinschaft*.

It may be that in this moment when man has it in his power to create a push-button Armageddon and in his will to risk such—it may be that the time has come when a sectarian doctrine of gyration-braking nonresistance (and not simply a political doctrine of direct nonviolent action) would be heard and understood. At least, Neo-Sectarianism could make the effort.

Then, too, some ideas are appearing in the forefront of theological discussion which would seem to point rather directly toward a Kierkegaardian view of radical discipleship. These concepts are being built up from suggestions—bare suggestions—which emanated from the prison cell of Dietrich Bonhoeffer. Although not presenting nearly as consistent a picture as S.K., Bonhoeffer also showed some rather striking sectarian tendencies. Neo-Sectarianism could have a voice in the follow-through. The original German title of Bonhoeffer's *The Cost of Discipleship* was simply *Nachfolge*, a book which John Macquarrie rightly calls "reminiscent of Kierkegaard."[6] This is not the Bonhoefferian theme which currently is drawing theological interest; perhaps it should be.

But the Bonhoefferian "hints" now getting all the attention are two. One is that the world is entering a "post-Christian era." If this means (as it seems to have meant for Bonhoeffer) that the church and the world have decided to make their relationship honest, that both the church and the world are beginning to recognize what always has been the case, that the state is not Christian in any real sense of the term, that culture forms no real support for Christianity, that the world actually does not need the sanction of the church in playing its role nor does the church need the support of the state to play its—if this is what a "post-Christian era" means, a world declaring itself free from Christian presuppositions, then Neo-Sectarianism is made to order for the situation. Sectarianism never has operated on any other premise, never desired any other premise, but that the era is post-Christian, or rather, that it never has been Christian. Sectarianism is precisely that version of Christianity designed to work and witness in the context of an indifferent and even inimical culture. Perhaps it could be of help now.

Bonhoeffer's second hint deals with "secular, or religionless Christianity." If this suggests a brand of Christianity that centers not in a churchly institution, not in rites and rituals con-

[6] John Macquarrie, *Twentieth Century Religious Thought* (New York: Harper, 1963), p. 331.

fined within churchly walls, not in Sabbath days and holy days set aside for religion, but rather a Christianity that centers in life, in a person's everyday mode of existence, in the way one treats his neighbors and associates, in the livingroom where (S.K. said) the battle must be fought—if this is "secular Christianity," then, again, Neo-Sectarianism might make a valuable contribution. If, on the other hand, "secular Christianity" suggests what some people are taking it to suggest, namely the obliteration of the distinction between Christianity and worldliness, the writing of clever theologies that are "God-less" yet somehow "Christian," the preaching of slick sermons based on sick novels, the presentation of a faith so sophisticated as to be invisible—if this is what "secular Christianity" suggests, well then, perhaps Neo-Sectarianism is needed to save Dietrich Bonhoeffer from his followers. In more ways than one, the world may be ripe for Kierkegaard's view of radical discipleship.

A church stands in the distance. Kierkegaard never arrived there in his lifetime; his day did not come. He did not really expect it to, although within himself he was confident that sometime it would. With God's help, ours could be that day.

INDEX OF NAMES

Haecker, Theodor, 28n
Hamilton, Kenneth, 135n
Hamilton, William, 406
Heckman, Samuel B., 83n
Hegel, G.W.F., 144, 381
Hegler, Alfred, 11
Heidegger, Martin, 107n
Heinecken, Martin, 25n
Henderson, Ian, 314f
Hochmann, E. C., 57, 70ff, 72n, 74
Höffding, Harald, 22n
Holmer, Paul, 6
Hong, Howard and Edna, 16n, 19n, 205
Hummer, Catharine, 340f

Jaspers, Karl, 22n

Kaufmann, Walter, 22n, 34
Keller, Ludwig, 11
Kierkegaard, Michael (S.K.'s father), 207
Kierkegaard, Peter (S.K.'s brother), 24f
Knox, Ronald, 11ff
Kolderup-Rosenvige, J.L.A., 277f

Lamennais, Felicite, 39
Latourette, K. S., 288f
Lefever, Ernest, 44n
Le Fevre, Perry, 6, 178n
Ligouri, Alphonsus, 39
Littell, Franklin, 47n
Longenecker, Christian, 89f, 136f, 171n
Lowrie, Walter, 22n, 26n, 177, 218, 220, 258, 310f
Lund, Henriette (S.K.'s cousin), 38n
Luther, Martin, 7f, 12f, 23, 102f, 172f, 301ff, 387f, 415, 428

MacGregor, Geddes, 218n, 220
Mack, Alexander Senior, 68ff,
72n, 74f, 77ff, 140f, 147, 157, 160, 163, 165, 169ff, 188f, 214, 233, 244f, 285f, 314, 321, 381f, 393, 401, 413, 419, 431f
Mack, Alexander Junior, 72, 74f, 83ff, 92, 126ff, 140n, 141f, 155, 157, 161, 167, 171n, 189ff, 214, 216f, 232, 244, 253f, 382, 395, 402n, 422f
Macquarrie, John, 434
Mallott, Floyd, 67n, 177n, 340n, 414n
Martin, H. V., 25n
Menno Simons, 72n, 74, 431f
Minear, Paul, 160, 408ff, 417, 433
Mynster, J. P., 289

Naas, John, 80, 285
Niebuhr, H. Richard, 43ff, 63, 228f
Niebuhr, Reinhold, 7, 185, 390
Nygren, Anders, 260, 270

Ockham, William, 8
Olsen, Regina, 109n, 203, 207ff, 236, 241

Pascal, Blaise, 9, 203, 325
Paul, the Apostle, 3f, 8, 10, 241, 247, 415ff
Peterson, E., 35
Pope, Liston, 43, 46
Price, John (1702-24), 82f, 214f
Price, John (1772), 155
Proud, Robert, 320, 412
Przywara, E., 218

Ragaz, Leonhard, 9ff, 11
Reitz, 85
Renkewitz, Heinz, 70n
Ritschl, Albrecht, 11
Robinson, J.A.T., 406
Roos, Heinrich, 29n
Ruysbrock, Jan van, 39

INDEX OF SUBJECTS

INDEX OF THE WORKS
OF KIERKEGAARD

AS QUOTED AND/OR CITED HEREIN

The works are listed in chronological order. The dates are of the original publication or, in some cases, the composition of the work.

PUBLISHED WORKS